Edward Hicks

Edward Hicks

His *Peaceable Kingdoms* and Other Paintings

Text by Eleanore Price Mather
Catalogue by Dorothy Canning Miller
and Eleanore Price Mather

AN AMERICAN ART JOURNAL/KENNEDY GALLERIES BOOK

Newark: University of Delaware Press
New York, London, and Toronto: Cornwall Books

Associated University Presses, Inc.
Cornwall Books
4 Cornwall Drive
East Brunswick, NJ 08816

Cornwall Books
25 Sicilian Avenue
London WC1A 2QH, England

Cornwall Books
2133 Royal Windsor Drive
Unit 1
Mississauga, Ontario
Canada L5J 1K5

Library of Congress Cataloging in Publication Data

Mather, Eleanore Price, 1910–
   Edward Hicks, his peaceable kingdoms and other
paintings.

   (An American art journal/Kennedy Galleries book)
   Bibliography: p.
   Includes index.
   1. Hicks, Edward, 1780–1849.   I. Hicks, Edward,
1780–1849.   II. Miller, Dorothy Canning, 1904–
III. Title.   IV. Series.
ND37.H58M29   1983   759.13   81-71405
ISBN 0-87413-208-8 (UDP)
ISBN 0-8453-4760-8 (Cornwall)

Printed in the United States of America

CONTENTS

FOREWORD

THE ROOTS OF THIS BOOK REACH BACK TO THE LATE 1930s. IT WAS AT THAT PERIOD THAT Dorothy Miller, after a decade of pioneering in the folk art movement with her husband, Holger Cahill, began systematically to collect data on the works of Edward Hicks in preparation for compiling a catalogue raisonné. But at the time she was in the midst of a busy career as curator of painting and sculpture at the Museum of Modern Art, which left scant leisure for independent writing.

As for me, I did not encounter Hicks till the 1960s—and then not as an art student but in pursuit of family genealogy and Quaker history, the artist/preacher's *Memoirs* having been recommended as an interesting example of the traditional Quaker journal. Once I discovered him I could not leave him alone. I wrote a number of articles, but was always frustrated because so large a percentage of each had to be spent repeating basic facts. If I only had the space, I thought, to pursue the lesser-known facets of the painter's background and character: the Quaker aesthetic, symbols of signcraft, his relation to William Blake, the pastoral syndrome of his late years, above all the intriguing paradox of his natural pugnacity and constant quest for peace—in short, if I could only write a book!

It was not till 1975, when Dorothy Miller and I first met at the exhibition "Edward Hicks: A Gentle Spirit" at the Andrew Crispo Gallery in New York, that the publications of which we had individually been dreaming began to merge into one. The result is the present volume, in which a catalogue raisonné is accompanied by a text covering areas that hitherto have been little explored. I should add that this project could not have been accomplished without the practical assistance and supportive enthusiasm of my husband, Robert W. Mather.

ELEANORE PRICE MATHER

ACKNOWLEDGMENTS

SUCH A WORK AS THIS INVOLVES MANY SOURCES. FOREMOST AMONG THOSE TO WHOM WE are indebted is Alice Ford, whose classic biography *Edward Hicks: Painter of the Peaceable Kingdom* is referred to many times in the following pages. We also wish to express appreciation to Mrs. Mark T. Swartz, Jr., great-great-granddaughter of the artist, for her generosity in sharing family relics and providing insights that could come only from close personal association with family tradition.

Among institutions the two libraries of Swarthmore College have been of unique importance: the Thomas McCabe Memorial Library with its art books and journals, and the Friends Historical Library with its wealth of Hicksite Quaker material. To the director of the latter, Dr. J. William Frost, and to members of the staff—Jane Rittenhouse Smiley, Albert W. Fowler, Nancy Speers, Jane Thorson, and Patricia Neiley—our text owes much. Their assistance made it possible to reconstruct from the Swarthmore Collections the artist's relationship to the Hicksite-Orthodox controversy. We are likewise in debt to the Haverford College Library, to its director, Dr. Edwin B. Bronner, and to Barbara Curtis and Shirley Stowe, bibliographers, for Orthodox references pertaining to that unhappy conflict.

Supplementing these resources were those of nearby Philadelphia, as represented by the American Philosophical Society, the Historical Society of Pennsylvania, the Library Company of Philadelphia, and the Free Library of Philadelphia, while Carol A. Wojtowicz, curator of the Mutual Assurance and Contributionship Companies, and Debra J. Force, curator/director at the Insurance Company of North America, graciously provided access to their respective historical collections. All made available prints and engravings reflecting the aesthetic climate of Hicks's own time.

For the recapture of everyday life in the early nineteenth century, the Mercer Museum of the Bucks County Historical Society at Doylestown, Pennsylvania, under the care of James R. Blackaby, offered its remarkable collection of artifacts, and thanks to the files of its Spruance Library and Terry A. McNealy's courteous staff—with special thanks to Judith Hohmann—the provenances of several of Hicks's works have been recovered. Other helpful agencies in Bucks County were the Newtown Historic Association and Historic Fallsington, whose curator, Ann Bobo, made possible the examination of a Hicks tavern board. A similar courtesy was extended by Edna Sweely, curator of the Delaware County Historical Society at Chester, Pennsylvania.

Two prominent institutions in the art world deserve particular mention. One is the Abby Aldrich Rockefeller Folk Art Center at Williamsburg, Virginia, with its superb collection of Hicks's paintings and a store of valuable information on his life and work. We feel much gratitude to its director, Beatrix T. Rumford, and to her predecessor, Thomas N. Armstrong, III, for their active support of art scholarship, and wish also to thank Barbara R. Luck, associate curator, and Ann Barton Brown, former research associate, for their knowledgeable aid.

The other institution referred to is the Frick Art Reference Library of New York City and its former librarian Mildred Steinbach, from whom we acquired photographs that maintain the Frick standard of excellence, and a body of information on individual pictures that, together with Dorothy Miller's records, formed a groundwork for our catalogue raisonné.

It goes without saying that we are deeply grateful to the museums and private collectors who supplied data on their paintings and have given permission for their reproduction. Without their cooperation such a catalogue as ours could not exist. They are credited in our listings, but we would like to note certain museum personnel who have provided unusually detailed or extensive information:

> Herdis Bull Teilman, curator, Department of Fine Arts, Carnegie Institute, Pittsburgh, Pennsylvania.
> Katherine S. Howe, associate curator, the Museum of Fine Arts, Houston, Bayou Bend Collection, Houston, Texas.
> Sallie A. Muir, assistant; Margaret Lawson, secretary; John K. Howat, curator; Amy L. Welsh, assistant; Kathleen Luhrs, editor, all of American paintings and sculpture, the Metropolitan Museum of Art, New York, New York.
> Linda L. Ayres, assistant curator, American art, and research assistant, Laurie Weitzenkorn, National Gallery of Art, Washington, D.C.
> Fearn C. Thurlow, curator of painting and sculpture, the Newark Museum, Newark, New Jersey.
> Karol A. Schmiegel, registrar, and E. McSherry Fowble, associate curator, the Henry Francis du Pont Winterthur Museum, Winterthur, Delaware.
> Helen Cooper, curator of American painting, and Sarah Cohen, assistant to the curator, Yale University Art Gallery, New Haven, Connecticut.

Additional information of value has been provided by historically minded dealers. We thank Robert Carlen of Philadelphia, a pioneer in the preservation of Hicks data; Norman Hirschl, Stuart P. Feld, and Joyce Rambo Durning of Hirschl & Adler Galleries, New York City; Ann Somerville Weigert and Nancy C. Little of M. Knoedler & Co., New York City; and F. Frederick Bernaski of Kennedy Galleries, New York City.

Other individuals who have been of assistance are Anita Schorsch of the Pennsylvania Historical and Museum Commission; Richard Walton, former president of the Newtown Historic Association; Edward R. Barnsley, noted archivist and former president of the Bucks County Historical Society, and his son-in-law, Robert H. Bartels, president of the Newtown Library Company; Arthur Smith of Wycombe, Bucks County historian; Marion Conrad and the late Marian Conrad Beans, Newtown art dealers; and Dr. David Tatham of Syracuse University, Syracuse, New York, authority on the painter's cousin and apprentice, Thomas Hicks.

Last we wish to thank John I. H. Baur, director emeritus of the Whitney Museum of American Art, for his wise and experienced editing of our material.

ELEANORE PRICE MATHER
DOROTHY CANNING MILLER

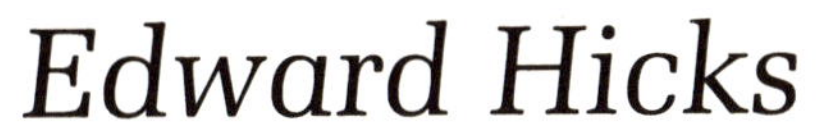

Edward Hicks

PART 1

THE CHILD AND THE BRANCH

1

THE FORBIDDEN TREE

EDWARD HICKS IS THE MOST POPULAR OF AMERICAN FOLK PAINTERS, AND HIS PICTURES
command prices far beyond those of other primitive artists. Why does this
early-nineteenth-century coach and sign painter—known better during his
lifetime as a Quaker preacher—find such a response in the secular modern
world? The answer lies in the psychological content of his work. Most of his
mature canvases reflect a single theme: the nature of man and his relation to the
Divine. In illustration of this, his *Peaceable Kingdoms*, his serene farmscapes,
and his many vistas into the tranquil domain of William Penn breathe a spirit of
peace. Yet beneath their serenity lurks a tension that speaks more to the present
time than it did to the nineteenth century.

To the Quaker farmers who were his contemporaries, the *Peaceable Kingdoms* of Edward Hicks must have appeared either as pious biblical statements
or the vagaries of a disordered mind. To the more sophisticated twentieth-
century viewer, the great lions and leopards with their anguished eyes are
symbols that present a drama of inner conflict. For the painter this conflict was
a highly personal one. In the unfolding sequence of his *Kingdoms* are portraits
of the artist's inner self, torn between what he was and what he wanted to be. It
was a division that plagued him all his life. His desire was to be steadfast,
patient, and loving. Nature had made him fitful, hot-tempered, and fiercely
proud. And his journey through life was the search for a power that would
redeem and unite his own divided spirit.

It was probably this yearning for inward peace that led Hicks to join the
Society of Friends. His parents, Isaac and Catharine Hicks, were Anglicans, as
was his grandfather, Gilbert, who was chief justice of Bucks County, Pennsylvania, under the British Crown. Born in his grandfather's mansion at Langhorne
on April 4, 1780, the future painter should by rights have grown up in luxury.

But the Revolutionary War brought ruin and sent the Tory judge and his son into hiding. On the day of the British surrender at Yorktown, Catharine died, leaving her eighteen-month-old son, practically speaking, an orphan. His fate would have been an unhappy one had it not been for Elizabeth Twining, a kindly matron and close friend of his mother, who took him into her home and raised him side-by-side with her own daughters. The memory of her sheltered household clung to him all his life, and in his later years he pictorialized it in his four versions of *The Residence of David Twining*, where we see Elizabeth, wearing the traditional cap and kerchief of the Quaker woman, reading the Bible to small Edward.

This religious instruction, received at her knee, survived the restless years of Hicks's adolescence in the face of some difficulties, because at the age of thirteen he was apprenticed to the coachmakers William and Henry Tomlinson of Langhorne. The coach shop was a far hail from the sheltered atmosphere of the Twining farm. Holidays were enlivened with apple and spinning frolics, "raffling matches" (dicing), and convivial trips to city taverns. "Thus the garden of my heart was too soon overrun with those noxious weeds— licentiousness, intemperance, angry passions, and devilishness," wrote the painter in his *Memoirs*.[1] Near the end of his seven-year apprenticeship he was stricken by severe illness while on a holiday spree in Philadelphia. Providentially restored to health, Hicks was overwhelmed with repentance. "Yet," he tells us, "notwithstanding all my promises to live a better way of life, such was my strong passion for music, dancing, and singing, that I was participating in all these amusements before I was able to leave the city and ride home."[2]

The case for such a backslider might seem hopeless. But three years later, after an interlude that involved much inner searching, he became a member of the Society of Friends.

What sort of religion was it that turned this tavern-haunting reveller into a plain-coated Quaker? We have suggested that he was in search of inward peace. He may also have been seeking the immediate experience of God's presence, which lay at the heart of Quakerism, because his fellow meeting-goers, gathering in bare-walled rooms without altar, pulpit, or lectern, were not led by any ordained minister, nor did they listen to a previously prepared sermon. Instead, they waited upon the Lord in silence, out of which might break a spontaneous message from any man, woman, or child who felt the direct call of the Holy Spirit.

Their term for the Holy Spirit was the Light Within, and though all might share in the Light and give it utterance, it was acknowledged that some possessed a greater measure than others. When, in the autumn of 1812, Middletown Meeting recorded Edward as a minister, his fellow members were recognizing in him a very special gift.[3]

This religious commitment was the most important fact in the life of Edward Hicks. He cherished it above all else, and it affected his life and art profoundly. But it also raised a practical problem: Quaker ministers received no pay.

The relationship of a Friends minister to his meeting was not that of a pastor to his church. A local meeting might have several such ministers, or, conceivably, none. In any case there were no sermons to prepare, nor outward sacraments to administer, and the usual parish tasks were shared by the general membership as organized in a monthly meeting for business. But it was expected that the inner voice would bid him travel, carrying the word of Truth to other gatherings.

Accordingly, in the spring of 1813 and during the following winter Edward preached in and around Philadelphia. These journeys soon resulted in a financial predicament, since they took him away from the work that supported his family. Even before undertaking his travels in the ministry he was in arrears. In 1803 he had married his Quaker sweetheart, Sarah Worstall, and set up shop as a coach painter in Milford, borrowing money to build their house. Eight years later they moved to Newtown, and by the time Edward became a minister he had a family of four young children. While still in Milford he had expanded his painting trade to include household objects and signboards. Now, to meet his debts and growing expenses, he increased the production of trade and tavern signs. These, with their figures and emphasis on decoration, led him ever nearer to "ornamental painting," as his Quaker friends called it, and one suspects that they deeply engaged his interest. They also paid well. By 1813 his shop ledger notes a tavern sign for James Corson for $25.00—good money for the times.[4]

But his conscience was uneasy, and because such elaborate works seemed inappropriate to the plainness of a Friends minister he gave up painting and became a farmer.[5] This proved a disaster. From sad experience he later wrote, "I quit the only business I understood, and for which I had a capacity, viz. painting, for the business of a farmer, which I did not understand and for which I had no qualification whatever."[6] And his burdens were increased by the arrival of a fifth child, Sarah, late in 1816.

His position was even worse than might appear, because at this time in Quaker history business failure—involving the loss of other people's money—frequently resulted in loss of membership. In this crisis Hicks had many well-wishers, but it was his friend John Comly who did something about it. Himself a minister and much-esteemed schoolmaster, he had been instrumental in converting Edward to Quakerism. Now he was concerned not only about his friend's personal distress, but also about the loss to the Society of Friends should he be driven to bankruptcy.

Appealing to the painter's wealthy Long Island relative, Isaac Hicks,[7] he explained that to pay his debts the young minister had resorted to "the forbidden tree"—that is, easel painting—much against his own scruples in regard to Christian simplicity. Comly continues:

> Thou wilt wonder to think that with such impressions and such views, *any consideration* relative to this world should induce such a man as Edward to return again with eagerness and such application as often keeps him up till near twelve o'clock at night painting pictures—and to make the thing more glaring, has advertised in the Bucks County papers "to execute Coach, Sign, and Ornamental Painting, *of all descriptions,* in the neatest and handsomest manner"—with his name annexed. . . . His plans are to pursue this very lucrative branch of his business for a time, hoping to clear $1200 a year by it—a delusive dream!! and then when his debts are paid, quit it.[8]

Estimating the deficit as between two and three thousand dollars, Comly continues, "But what would it be for Isaac & Samuel Hicks to loan their cousin Edward such a sum, without interest, as would relieve him, set him at liberty to run on his Master's errands unshackled, help him out of the deep mire of the paint, and set his feet, through the blessing of Heaven, on firm ground?"

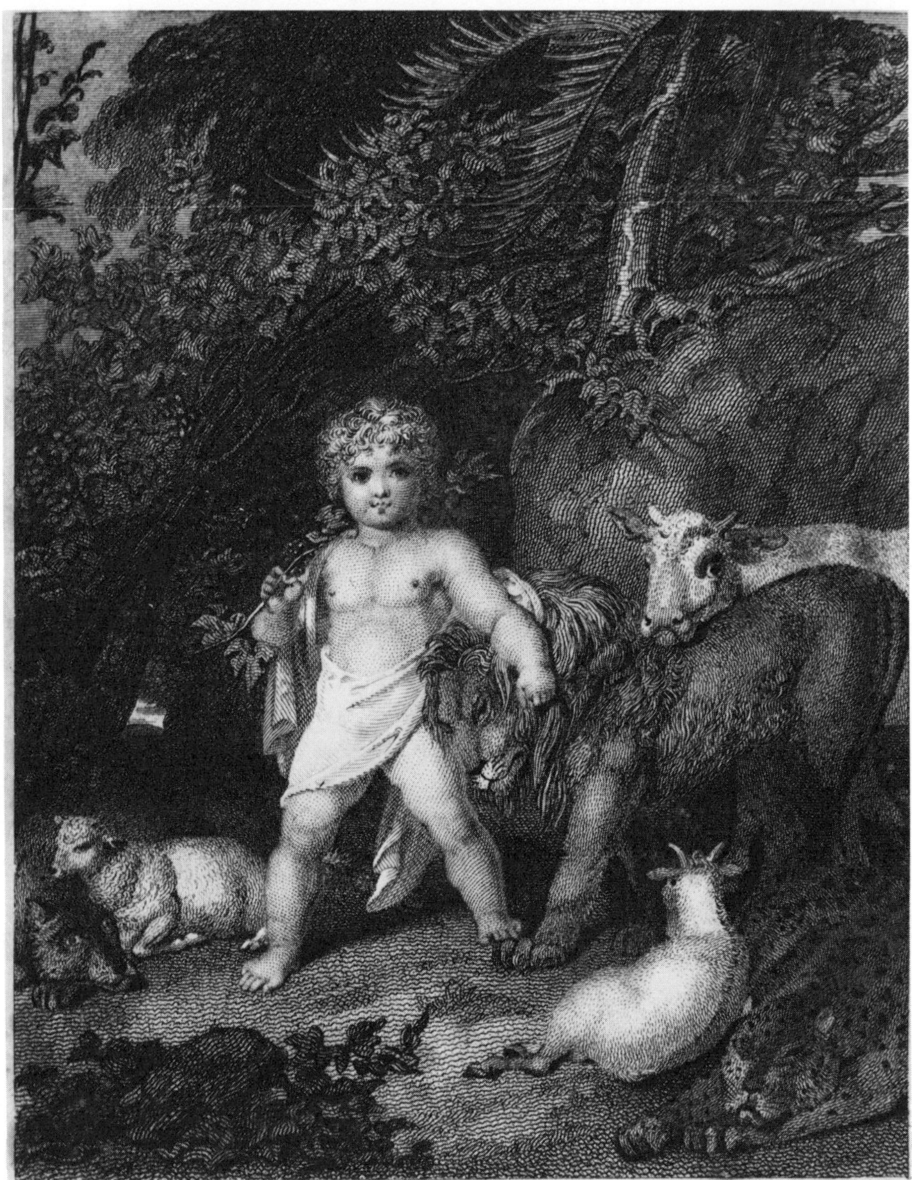

The Peaceable Kingdom of the Branch by Richard Westall, R.A. (1765–1836), was the source of Hicks's favorite theme. Engraving by Charles Heath in The Holy Bible (3 vols.; London: White, Cochrane and Co., 1815). (Rare Book Department of the Free Library of Philadelphia.)

This letter makes clear Comly's good will. It also makes clear his views on art. Like other Friends of his time he had no objection to the painting of coaches, signs, or other useful pieces. But art for its own sake he looked on with disapproval. It would never have occurred to him that a work of art might be a reflection of truth. Note, however, that he does not disparage his friend's talent. He calls it "a genius and a taste for imitation, which, if the Divine law had not prohibited, might have rivalled Peale or West."

Thanks to the generosity of Comly, cousins Isaac and Samuel, and other good friends, the debts—which, it was later discovered, amounted to $5,000[9]—were paid in full.

Edward was saved from ruin. But it is ironic that in the wake of these efforts to preserve his gift in the ministry an event occurred that made him known to posterity, not as a Quaker preacher but as a Quaker artist. For around 1820 he solved his own moral dilemma by discovering the *Peaceable Kingdom*. As Alice Ford has pointed out in her biography, he borrowed the composition from a Bible engraving after Richard Westall, R.A.[10] In it is a child caressing a lion, surrounded by the other animals that appear in the sixth verse of the eleventh chapter of Isaiah: "The wolf also shall dwell with the lamb, and the leopard shall lie down with the kid; and the calf and the young lion and the fatling together: and a little child shall lead them."

To the modern humanist this passage celebrates a world in which human warfare has happily ceased. But to the Old Testament prophet, peace on earth was only a by-product of his essential message: the redemption of his people by a Messiah, later identified by Christianity with Jesus Christ. Because Isaiah appeared to foretell the coming of Christ he became the prophetic link between the Old and New Testaments, inspiring in the Christian a reverence beyond that accorded to any other Hebrew prophet—which is why, in scenes of the Annunciation, one sees not only the lily of purity and dove of the Holy Spirit, but also, on a lectern beside the Virgin Mary, the Book of Isaiah, which declared, "Behold a virgin shall conceive and bear a son, and shall call his name Immanuel" (7:14).

The redemption of man is the great theme of orthodox Christianity, and Western art has dealt richly with it in terms of the birth and death of Christ. But it has done little with his peaceable kingdom on earth.[11] Paradise regained has never been as popular as paradise lost, possibly because a Prince of Peace, ruling a landscape in which all conflict has ceased, lacks the heroic tension that the Western world demands from the adult male, whether divine or human.

For this problem Westall's own era provided a solution, because late-eighteenth-century Romanticism had discovered the child, and nineteenth-century sentimentalism made the most of it.[12] Responsive to the mood of his age, the British illustrator embodied the reign of the Messiah, when even savage beasts forsake their fury, in the person of the little child who shall lead them.

In all of Hicks's early *Kingdoms* this child is the dominant figure. Is it the Christ Child? Not as a literal representation. But because the viewer senses a special charisma in the figure, we will call it the Divine Child to distinguish it from the other infants that later find their way into the landscape.

Though Hicks, who knew the Bible well, had long been thoroughly familiar with Isaiah's prophecy, it was apparently not until he saw Westall's illustration that he was prompted to portray this theme. He may have been drawn to it for several reasons: his fondness for children, interest in animals, genuine love of the Scriptures. Or it may have been a matter of the psychological moment, when he correctly perceived in the biblical engraving a sermon on salvation that would justify the pictorial work he inwardly craved.

NOTES

1. *Memoirs of the Life and Religious Labors of Edward Hicks. Late of Newtown, Bucks County, Pa.* (Philadelphia: Merrihew & Thompson, 1851), p. 35. Includes also a diary and two previously published essays, "A Little Present for Friends and Friendly People" [Goose Creek Sermon] and " A Word of Exhortation to Young Friends."

2. Ibid., p. 37.

3. Minutes of Middletown Monthly Meeting, 10 mo. 8, 1812, Friends Historical Library, Swarthmore College, Swarthmore, Pa., hereafter abbreviated to FHL.

4. Alice Ford, *Edward Hicks: Painter of the Peaceable Kingdom* (Philadelphia: University of Pennsylvania Press, 1952), p. 28. Reprint 1973 by Kraus Reprint Co., Millwood, N.Y., with additional material. This pioneer study of Hicks's life and works is indispensable to all students of the subject.

5. Hicks purchased eighteen acres and eighty-six perches from Thomas Ross for $1,357.62, with $339.42 downpayment. Recorded July 6, 1814, in Deed Bk. 43, p. 337. See "Edward Hicks Land Transactions" in back of Ford reprint (n.p.).

6. *Memoirs*, p. 71.

7. See Robert A. Davison, *Isaac Hicks: New York Merchant and Quaker 1767–1820* (Cambridge, Mass.: Harvard University Press, 1964).

8. John Comly to Isaac Hicks, Westbury, L.I., June 15, 1817, FHL.

9. Revised to $5,000 in a letter from Comly to Isaac Hicks, 12 August 1817. The negotiations went on for several years, but were finally settled in August 1818.

10. The engraving appears in "The Holy Bible, containing the Old and New Testaments and the Apocrypha embellished with engravings by Charles Heath from Designs by Richard Westall, R.A.," 3 vols. (London: White, Cochrane and Co., 1815), n.p. This Heath engraving had already been issued two years earlier by the same publisher. For other engravings of the Westall composition see Ford, Edward Hicks, p. 42.

11. Julius Held has pointed out some interesting exceptions in "Edward Hicks and the Tradition," *Art Quarterly* 14 (1951): 121–136.

12. J. William Frost, director of the Friends Historical Library at Swarthmore College, cites the ready Quaker acceptance of this romantic approach in *The Quaker Family in Colonial America,* (New York: St. Martin's Press, 1973), p. 87.

2

EXPERIMENTS ON THE EASEL

DURING THE THIRTY REMAINING YEARS OF HIS LIFE EDWARD HICKS PAINTED MANY *Peaceable Kingdoms*, at least sixty of which survive. Alice Ford divided these into early, middle, and late periods, corresponding approximately to the decades of the 1820s, the 1830s, and the 1840s. But because of their great number they are here reduced to more explicit categories.

The earliest category that can properly be called such is *The Peaceable Kingdom of the Branch*. This was the full title of Westall's engraving, and in the Hicks version that most closely resembles it—a fireboard given to the Yale University Art Gallery by the artist's great-grandson, Robert W. Carle—the words appear on the upper portion of the frame.

Evident also in this Yale work is that the Divine Child, like that in the engraving, carries over his right shoulder a leafy bough bearing grapes. What does this branch represent and why is it emphasized? The answer lies in the opening verse of Isaiah's eleventh chapter: "And there shall come forth a rod out of the stem of Jesse, and a Branch shall grow out of his root." In other words, Isaiah's branch is a vivid Hebrew metaphor indicating that the Messiah will come from the royal house of David, son of Jesse. Students of art history may recall "Jesse trees," portrayed on the walls and in the window glass of medieval churches, which trace the descent of Jesus from this remote ancestor.

But the branch as a grapevine was Westall's contribution. It put the imprint of Christian orthodoxy on his work, symbolizing both the redemptive blood of the cross and the wine of Holy Communion. Before the cross became the established icon of Christianity, the grape was much used as an emblem of salvation and has served as such throughout the centuries ever since. In Cirlot's *Dictionary of Symbols* a woodcut of 1512 shows Christ crucified on a tree that bears both apples and grapes, thus combining the fruit of man's fall with the fruit of his redemption.[1]

The grape branch, however, was a curious choice for Hicks the Quaker minister, since Friends did not observe the outward sacraments. Yet in this early work he does not hesitate to commit himself to this sacramental symbol, which appears not only on the branch held by the Divine Child but also in the tangle of vines in the background.

Though Hicks followed his model closely he made some innovations of his own. Indeed, the whole Kingdom series gives evidence of continuous ex-

21

perimentation. In the Yale fireboard he has clothed Westall's cherub in strangely exotic garments, while in a lesser-known but very endearing version in the Rockefeller Collection at Williamsburg, Virginia, the Divine Child is clad in a simple pantaloon suit such as any Quaker boy of the period might have worn. A similar outfit, with the addition of long sleeves and a hat, is worn by an 1831 doll on exhibit at Arch Street Meeting House in Philadelphia.[2]

The painter introduced into both these *Peaceable Kingdoms* a small scene of Penn's treaty with the Indians, for he considered the Quaker settlement of Pennsylvania a practical demonstration of the Old Testament prophecy. And with complete indifference to geography he placed this detail within the arch of the Natural Bridge of Virginia, which towers above it like a stage backdrop.

Artists of the early nineteenth century, whether formal academicians or primitives, had few scruples about borrowing. The Treaty group was lifted from Benjamin West's famous *William Penn's Treaty with the Indians*—or more

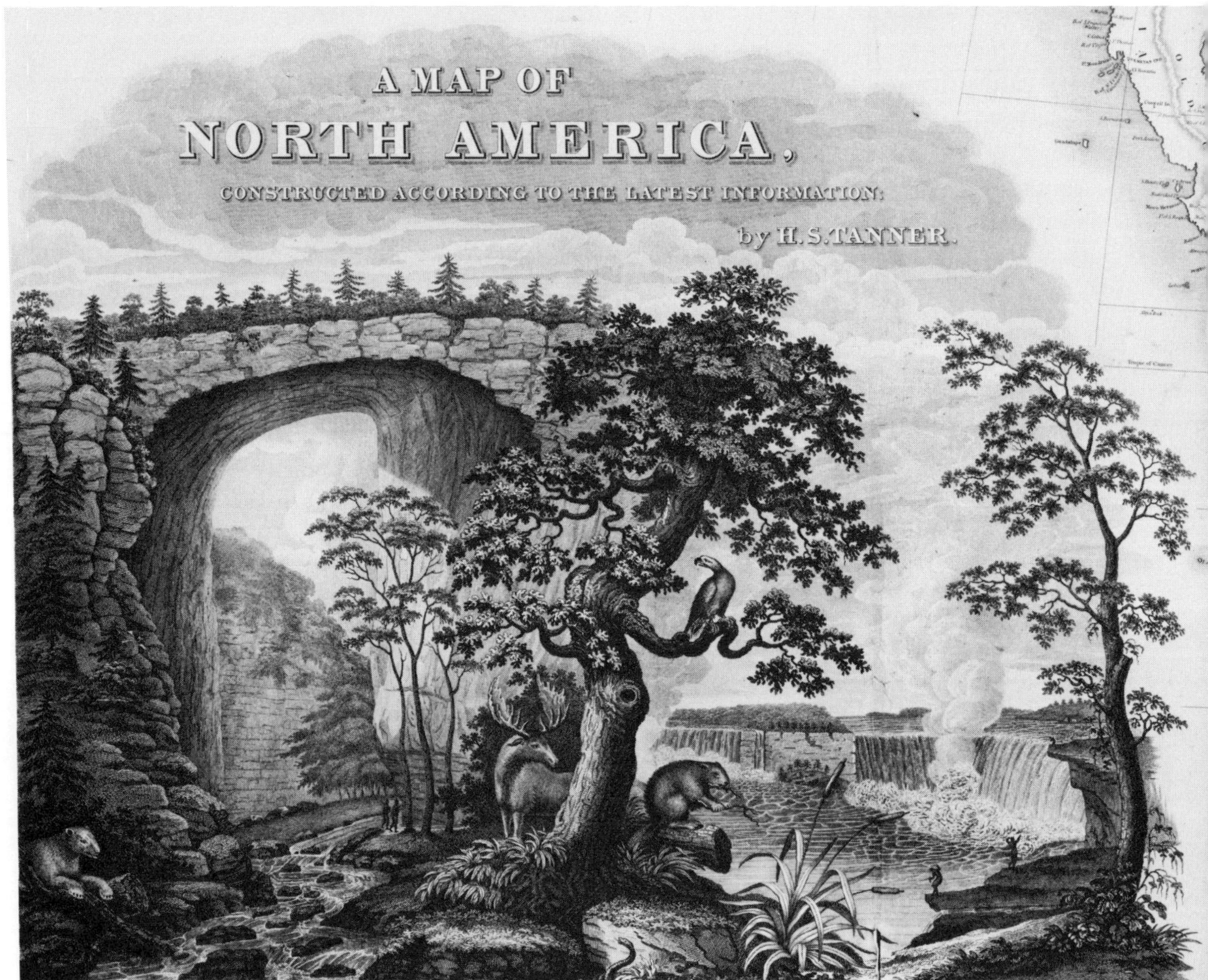

Vignette from A Map of North America *by Henry S. Tanner (1786–1858), Philadelphia, 1822, whi[ch] provided Hicks with the Natural Bridge of Virginia in certain Peaceable Kingdoms and with t[he] composition for his two landscapes of Niagara Falls. (Library of Congress, Washington, D.C., Geogr[a]phy and Map Division.)*

probably from some simplified print taken from it—and the Bridge came from a map of North America engraved by Henry S. Tanner, where a single extraordinary vignette combines the Natural Bridge and Niagara Falls, the two wonders of nature separated only by a large oak tree.[3]

All of these elements appear on Hicks's canvases. The artist's interest in the falls had already been roused by a ministerial journey to the area in 1819–20, when he was accompanied by two friends: Isaac Parry, a Quaker elder of Horsham, and Mathias Hutchinson, a young Friend of Newtown.[4]

The result of this journey was two Niagara landscapes on which the painter thriftily incorporated the falls, the oak tree, and four distinctively American animals—eagle, moose, beaver, and rattlesnake—all gleaned from Tanner's engraving. One of these landscapes, the gift of Colonel and Mrs. Garbisch to the Metropolitan Museum of Art, bears in its decorative border the date 1825.[5] The other is an undated wooden fireboard given to the painter's friend Dr. Joseph Parrish, who attended the Hicks family in the mid-1830s. It has been estimated as of 1835, but may be earlier. The date of this work poses an intriguing problem. We know that Tanner's map was issued in 1822, which means that Hicks could not have painted the Niagara fireboard before that date. How soon afterward he did so remains the question.

It is tempting to speculate that this Niagara fireboard and the Yale fireboard—which we now know was also a Parrish possession—were both part of a creative explosion occurring shortly after the issue of the map in 1822. This is pure speculation, but not too unlikely, since the map was printed in nearby Philadelphia, and so marked was its impact on the artist that one might assume his response to be immediate.

It was indeed a critical period in his life. In 1821 he sold his Court Street house in Newtown to his friend Comly and built a stone house a few blocks away on Penn Street on a lot adjoining the grounds of Newtown Meeting, which he had been instrumental in founding in 1815 and where he sat in the Ministers' Gallery for the rest of his days.

The latter part of the year probably found him involved in moving into his new dwelling. One hopes so, as otherwise poor Sarah must have borne a heavy burden. Fortunately the four older children—Mary, Susan, Isaac, and even ten-year-old Elizabeth—were now of an age to be useful, and their grandparents, the Worstalls, lived close by on Court Street. But as the wife of a Quaker minister, Sarah must have been used to burdens by this time, and probably accepted her husband's frequent absences from home philosophically.

By the end of the year Hicks was preaching in Philadelphia with a new impressiveness. Early in 1822 a city Friend, Townsend Sharpless, describes him as spiritually "favored beyond former occasions," and remarks on his natural eloquence and the crowds that attended him:

> He was here some weeks since, and not having relieved his mind, returned to discharge his unfinished concern. After his first visit he received an Epistle from Caleb Pierce on the subject of his sermon which he replied to, and afterward had an interview with our Elders, the result of which appears to have been satisfactory to Edward; whether so to other party I cannot say.[6]

This interview with Caleb and the Philadelphia elders is intriguing. One suspects they were challenging the Bucks County minister on some point of

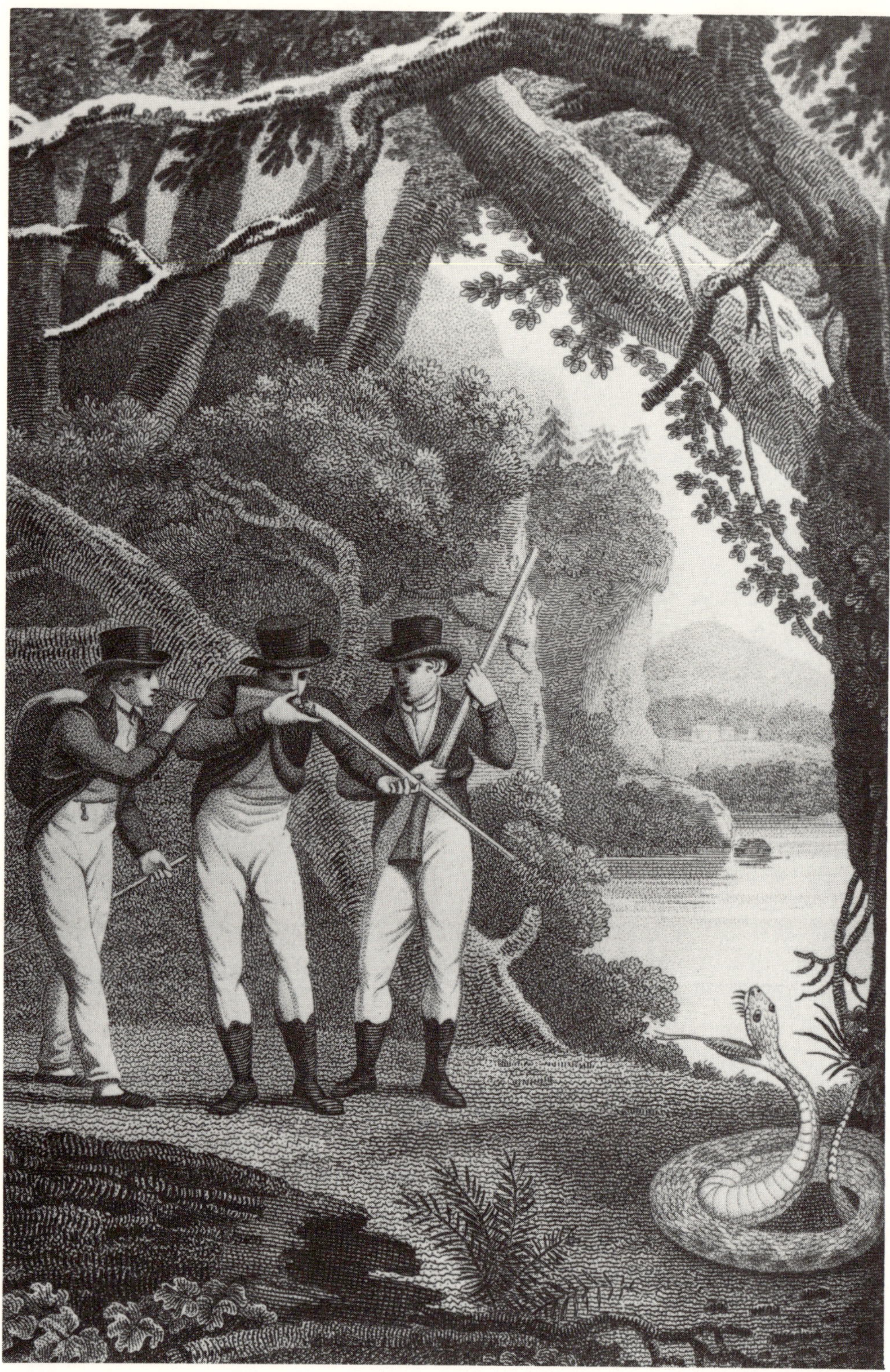

Scene on the Susquehannah, illustration from "The Foresters," a long poem in which Alexander Wilson (1766–1813), father of American ornithology, described his journey to Niagara Falls with two companions—a pattern followed by Hicks. Drawn by Wilson and engraved by George Cook of London, this first appeared in a Philadelphia literary magazine, The Port Folio, August, 1809. (Library Company of Philadelphia.)

doctrine. Though Quakerism made many demands on its members in the area of conduct, it had not hitherto required doctrinal conformity. But a new preoccupation with theology was in the air and its effect was divisive.

Nor could the interview have been improved by Hicks's own hot temper and troubled spirit, because he was in a period of great inward stress. Sharpless refers to the minister's emotional state: "He was much broken in the course of his preaching, and appeared in a very affectionate and humble frame of mind," and he concludes, "His farewell, he said, was final, and he several times alluded to the probability of not being continued long among us."

This premonition of death was a false alarm, but it came close to being prophetic. In February, while Hicks was making religious visits among the families of the recently established Makefield Monthly Meeting, his shop burned down, and along with it all the tools of his trade. A few weeks later he was seized with chills and fever and went through six or eight days of delirium. During the course of this delirium he was given up for lost by his despairing family, with the exception of his daughter Elizabeth who, as she sat reading her Bible, was inwardly and steadfastly convinced that he would recover.

And so it proved. His recuperation was miraculous. Stricken sometime in March, he was on the road again in May, this time to New York Yearly Meeting.

NOTES

1. J. E. Cirlot, *Dictionary of Symbols*, trans. Jack Sage (New York: Philosophical Library, 1962), p. 99. For grapes and vine see also George Ferguson's useful *Signs and Symbols in Christian Art* (New York: Oxford University Press, 1954, pp. 31–32 and 39–40, and André Grabar, *Christian Iconography: A Study of Its Origins*, Bollingen Series 25 vol. 10 (Princeton, N.J.: Princeton University Press, 1968). For a more exhaustive study see Gertrud Schiller, *Iconography of Christian Art*, trans. Janet Seligman, 2 vols. (Greenwich, Conn.: New York Graphic Society, 1971), I: 22 and fig. 42.

2. One of two dolls representing Richard Cadbury and his sister, Mary Ann. They were sent to the children's grandmother in England to show her what her Philadelphia grandchildren were wearing.

3. Henry S. Tanner [1786–1856], *A Map of North America, Constructed according to the Latest Information* (Philadelphia, 1822). Engraving 46½ by 60½ inches. See James Ayres, "Edward Hicks and His Sources," *The Magazine Antiques* 109 (1976): 366–68. Alice Ford, in her biography of the artist written before the discovery of the map, believed Hicks took his composition from a J. Merigot engraving of

one of John Vanderlyn's views of the falls. It is entirely possible that the Merigot print was Tanner's source, in combination with an F. C. Lewis engraving of another Vanderlyn *Niagara*, as viewed from Table Rock. Both prints are of 1804 and can be found in the fine Vanderlyn collection at the Senate House-Museum, Kingston, N.Y. See Kenneth C. Lindsay, catalogue for 1970 exhibition at the State University of New York, Binghamton, *The Works of John Vanderlyn, From Tammany to the Capitol* (Binghamton, N.Y.: University Art Gallery, 1970), figs. 40 and 43.

4. See "Mathias Hutchinson's Notes of a Journey (1819–20)," ed. Pat M. Ryan, *Quaker History* 68 (1979): 92–102, and 69 (1980): 36–57.

5. Borders on both landscapes are formed of couplets from Alexander Wilson's "The Foresters," first published in *The Port Folio*, a Philadelphia literary magazine (3 [1809–10]: 183), issued as a separate publication by S. Siegfried and J. Wilson (Newtown, Pa., 1818).

6. Townsend Sharpless to Mary Jones of Charlestown, Chester County, Pa., January 17, Sharpless MSS (FHL).

3
COUSIN ELIAS

In New York the painter encountered the subtle alignment of two Quaker factions: one favoring the trend toward orthodoxy, the other resisting it. Here he also encountered his cousin Elias Hicks, in whom the forces opposing orthodoxy found a center and a symbol.

Elias Hicks of Jericho, Long Island, was the most controversial figure in Quaker history. His gift in the ministry was extraordinary. As a boy, Walt Whitman heard him and never got over it. The setting was a Brooklyn ballroom, and the poet retained all his life the image of that strange scene: the lights, the colors, the uniforms of the officers from the Navy Yard, the elegant dresses of the women—all in contrast with the tall, straight figure in drab on the platform with its great expanse of forehead and large and clear black eyes.[1]

Sixty years later Whitman wrote as though the scene were still before him: "I cannot follow the discourse, it presently becomes very fervid and in the midst of its fervor, he takes the broadbrim hat from his head and almost dashing it down with violence on the seat behind, continues with uninterrupted earnestness . . . a pleading, tender, nearly agonizing conviction and magnetic stream of natural eloquence, before which all minds and natures, all emotions, high or low, gentle or simple yielded entirely, without exception.[2]"

Partly because of his unorthodox beliefs, and partly because of his passionate and consistent opposition to slavery, the Long Island patriarch has been called a liberal. But the term is misleading, for in its modern sense it hardly applies to a man who disapproved of voting, public schools, and most kinds of mechanical transportation.

Elias's opposition to usury, luxury, higher education, and the "hireling priesthood" had a profound effect on Edward. After the painter visited his cousin in 1820, a New York Friend complained:

> It is very humiliating to observe there are ministers among us who so much admire Elias Hicks as to imitate and copy after him, at least in the unchristian and violent manner in which he abuses the clergy. . . . Edward Hicks[3] at a public meeting on Long Island, at a place where no Friends reside, and in company with his cousin, Elias, in the course of a long communication, disclaimed in a most severe manner against the clergy, their Common Prayer Book, and many of the religious observances of the Church of England (one of their ministers was present).[4]

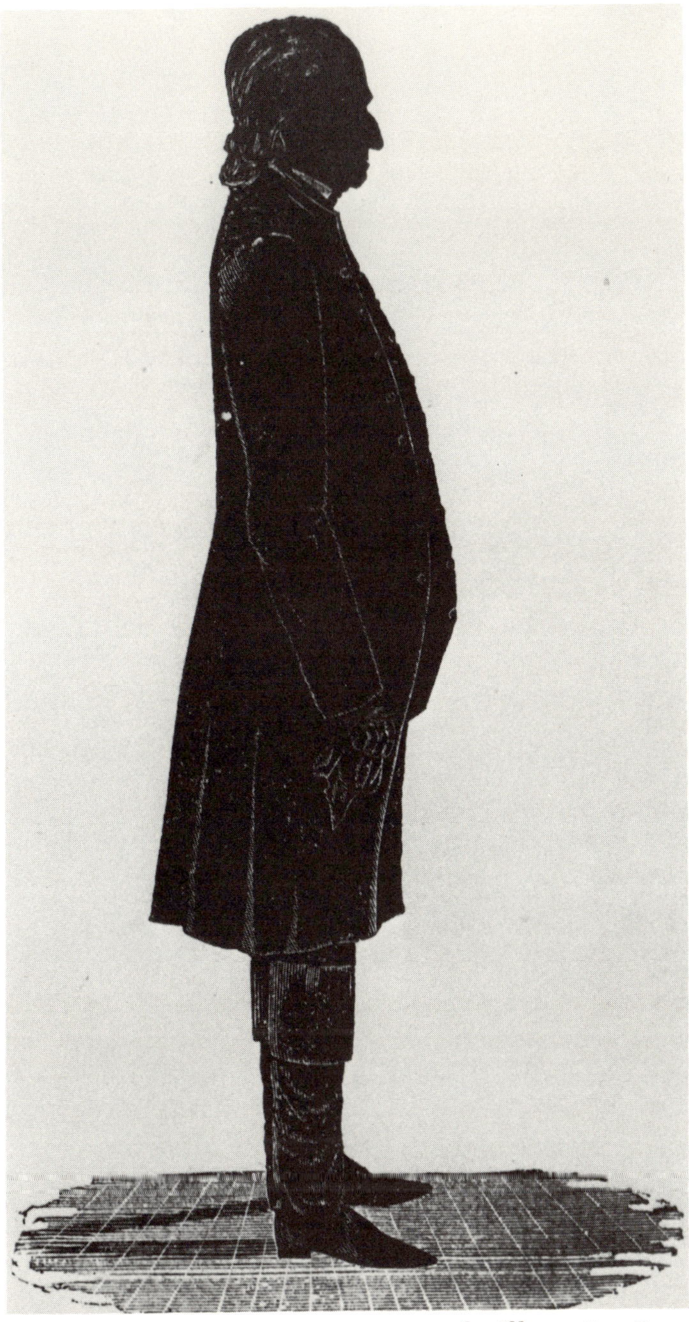

Elias Hicks (1748–1830), engraved silhouette, 6 × 9¾ inches, published by John Hopper, New York, 1830. Famous preacher and cousin of the painter, Elias was the central figure in the Hicksite/Orthodox controversy that divided American Quakerism in 1827 and that profoundly affected the Peaceable Kingdoms of Edward Hicks.

Elias himself reacted to the incident very differently. He wrote to Edward, "We had a very good meeting at Rockaway when thou hadst to make an experiment by putting the hireling priests and Soldiers and Sailors in a bag and shaking them, to see which would first come out."[5] From this comment it is easy to see why Elias appealed more to Walt Whitman than to certain sedate members of his own Society of Friends.

His stand on slavery suggests the social activist. He was that, but he was also—and essentially—a mystic, stressing inward experience rather than doctrine.[6] In placing an exclusive emphasis on the saving power of the Inner Light he believed that he was following in the path of primitive Quakerism. So did most of his hearers. But a strong minority felt that his lack of reference to the Scriptures and to Jesus as Christ ignored a necessary element of the Quaker message.

Because the Hicksite schism irreversibly altered the course of the *Peaceable Kingdoms*, it is necessary to explain its development.

When George Fox founded Quakerism in the seventeenth century he, too, had stressed the Light Within. But he had not rejected the Scriptures nor the miraculous life and death of Christ. And for the next 150 years Friends maintained a balance between the inward or experiential aspect of their faith, and the outward or doctrinal.

But with the latter eighteenth century new winds began to blow. The Methodist Revival had already established a popular fusion of orthodox belief and moral purpose and was now reinforced by a reaction against rationalism and the excesses of the French Revolution. City Friends, through non-Quaker neighbors and business associates, were more influenced by the trend toward orthodoxy than their country cousins, whose self-contained farm and village life tended to preserve the traditional Quaker emphasis on the Inner Light. This increased the unhappy division that had long existed between town and country.[7]

Most of the supporters of Elias Hicks were countrymen, and the painter was among them. But though devoted, Edward was not uncritical. He wrote cautiously, "It is among the possible circumstances that dear Elias was led to an extreme in the Unitarian speculation, while opposing the Trinitarian. . . . But I have no recollection of ever hearing him in public testimony, and I have heard him much, when his speculative views or manner of speaking destroyed the savor of life that attended his ministry."[8]

The savor of life: that was what Elias had, and that was what thousands flocked to hear. It was probably his enormous popularity as much as his doctrines that provoked resentment. When he arrived in Philadelphia late in 1822 the elders sought to curtail his preaching, as earlier in the year they had apparently sought to curtail Edward's. But here they overreached themselves, since as a member of New York Yearly Meeting, Elias was not under their jurisdiction.

He agreed to their demand for a confrontation, but invited some of his local supporters to accompany him. Among these was Edward, who refused, fearing his presence would only incite hostility in the elders—and in himself. He knew the Philadelphia elders only too well, and he warned his kinsman to be "wise as serpents and harmless as doves" in dealing with them.[9] Possibly due to this advice the interview never took place, because the ten elders wished to appear in force while restricting the Long Island preacher to a single companion— terms that Elias rejected firmly.

In a further move to counter his influence they produced a document titled the *Extracts,* a collection of early Quaker writings so edited that they sounded like a confession of faith.[10] Approved by what was then called the "Meeting for Sufferings" (the executive body of Philadelphia Yearly Meeting), the statement was read on the opening day of the annual asembly the following April, 1823. It met with a stunned silence, broken at length by John Comfort of Falls, a representative from Bucks: "As regards this creed, or declaration of faith, who hath required this at your hands?"[11] Creed was a fighting word, and on the following day Edward served as a voice for many when he protested, "The Meeting for Sufferings cannot and dare not urge or saddle this creed upon our Society."[12]

Presiding over this session was Samuel Bettle, then clerk of the Yearly Meeting. He later complained that he saw faces that day that he had never seen before. It is possible that the Hicksite opposition had packed the house, and they were unquestionably a noisy lot. But people are apt to speak loudly when they are not being heard, and there is evidence that the Philadelphia establishment was making a point of not hearing them.[12]

The Quaker method of procedure made this possible. In business meetings no votes were taken; the "sense of the meeting" determined the decision, not a majority. "Weight" outbalanced numbers. How this weight was determined depended on the fairness and sensitivity of the presiding clerk. Some years later Bettle was examined in a court case involving meeting property. In regard to those who had opposed the *Extracts* in 1823 he was asked, "Did you consider that such persons were entitled to equal weight and influence in your meetings?" To which he replied, "I never considered them entitled to any weight at all."[13]

It was an honest answer, but not a conciliatory one.

NOTES

1. Henry Bryan Binns, *A Life of Walt Whitman* (London: Methuen & Co., 1905), p. 16, quoted by Henry W. Wilbur, *The Life and Labors of Elias Hicks* (Philadelphia: The Friends General Conference Committee, 1910), p. 218.

2. *The Complete Writings of Walt Whitman*, ed. O. L. Triggs, 10 vols. (New York: G. P. Putnam's Sons, 1902), 3:258, quoted by Wilbur, *Elias Hicks*, p. 219.

3. Printed "Elias" but corrected to "Edward" in John Comly's personal copy (FHL). The painter describes the episode in *Memoirs*, p. 89. His position in relation to the "hireling ministry" was somewhat ironic in view of the fact that he was a nephew-by-marriage to Samuel Seabury, first suffragen bishop of New York. For the relationship between the painter and his cousin see David Tatham, "Edward Hicks, Elias Hicks, and John Comly: Perspectives for the Peaceable Kingdom Theme," *The American Art Journal* 13 (1981): 37–50.

4. Thomas Eddy of New York to John Warner of Philadelphia, reprinted in anonymous pamphlet, *The Cabinet, or Works of Darkness Brought to Light* (Philadelphia: Privately printed, 1824), p. 17.

5. Letter of 12 Mo. 28th, 1821 (FHL), quoted in *Memoirs*, p. 91.

6. Bliss Forbush, *Elias Hicks: Quaker Liberal* (New York: Columbia University Press, 1956), p. 194. For quietism in relation to Elias Hicks see Howard Brinton, *Friends for 300 Years* (New York: Harper & Bros., 1952), pp. 66–67.

7. Robert W. Doherty, *The Hicksite Separation: a Sociological Analysis of Religious Schism in the Early Nineteenth Century* (New Brunswick, N.J.: Rutgers University Press, 1967), p. 86.

8. *Memoirs*, p. 92.

9. An undated letter to David Seaman, traveling companion to Elias, seems to be Edward's answer (FHL).

10. *Extracts from the Writings of Primitive Friends Concerning the Divinity of Our Lord and Saviour Jesus Christ.* (New York: Solomon W. Conrad for Philadelphia Yearly Meeting, 1823).

11. William Bacon Evans, *Jonathan Evans and His Time, 1759–1839* (Boston: Christopher Publishing House, 1959), p. 69. Based largely on a remarkable manuscript by Thomas Evans, son of Jonathan, which is now in the Quaker Collection, Haverford College Library, this gives a vivid description of Yearly Meeting in 1827.

12. Ibid., p. 70.

13. Jeremiah J. Foster, *An Authentic Report: Thomas L. Shotwell vs. Joseph Hendrickson and Stacy Decow*, 2 vols. (Philadelphia: J. Harding, Printer, 1831), 1:82.

4

IN THE LAND OF PENN

FROM THIS TIME ON THE FRICTION WAS CONTINUOUS, INCREASED BY A SPATE OF publications, including a satirical pamphlet entitled *A Chapter of Modern Chronicles, In Which Certain Events Which Lately Took Place in the City of Gotham Are Truly Set Forth*. This referred to New York Yearly Meeting in May, 1826, and after citing the first names of well-known representatives from Philadelphia, it adds, "Edward also came from the land of Penn but he fled, and the people wist not what had become of him."[1]

What, indeed, had become of him? Edward's *Memoirs* make no mention of a flight from New York. Was he afraid of his own anger, or of provoking anger in his opponents, as when he refused to accompany Elias Hicks into the presence of the Philadelphia elders in 1822? Or had his conscience as husband and provider sent him home to work?

In spite of his own avowed disapproval, the fruit of the "forbidden tree," as John Comly had called it, was frequently on his easel. Alice Ford cites two *Kingdoms* delivered to Friends in New York this spring of 1826, one to Silas Hicks and another to Dr. John Cheesman, a prominent but not too plain Friend.[2]

The former was acknowledged by a letter from Cousin Silas, thanking the artist for the gift of his picture, enclosing a check for a hundred dollars, and concluding on the urgent note: "I hope thee will not fail to be at our Yearly Meeting, as we shall be most gratified to have thy company, and shall probably need thy help, for the Orthodox continue to dispute every inch of ground with us."[3]

In all probability the painting concerned is one bearing an inscription to "Dear Cousin Sarah"—the name of Silas's wife—and dated "4 mo. 1st, 1826." Prior to the discovery of this work, the first firm date for a *Kingdom* was August 26, 1826, on a canvas given to the artist's friend Harrison Streeter of Fallsington and presently at the Philadelphia Museum of Art.

In both of these exactly dated works, painted within a few months of each other, the Penn scene has been expanded and placed on the bank of the Delaware River, where it now shows a recognizable resemblance to the treaty as portrayed by Benjamin West. But the angle of vision is different. Instead of looking inland, one sees the Jersey shore across the river from Bucks County—

30

much as it must have appeared to Penn himself as he returned upriver in his barge after a burdensome session in the city.

The world associates Penn with Philadelphia, but Bucks County looked on him as her own because he made his beautiful manor of Pennsbury, near the falls of the Delaware, his headquarters in the New World.[4] There is no doubt

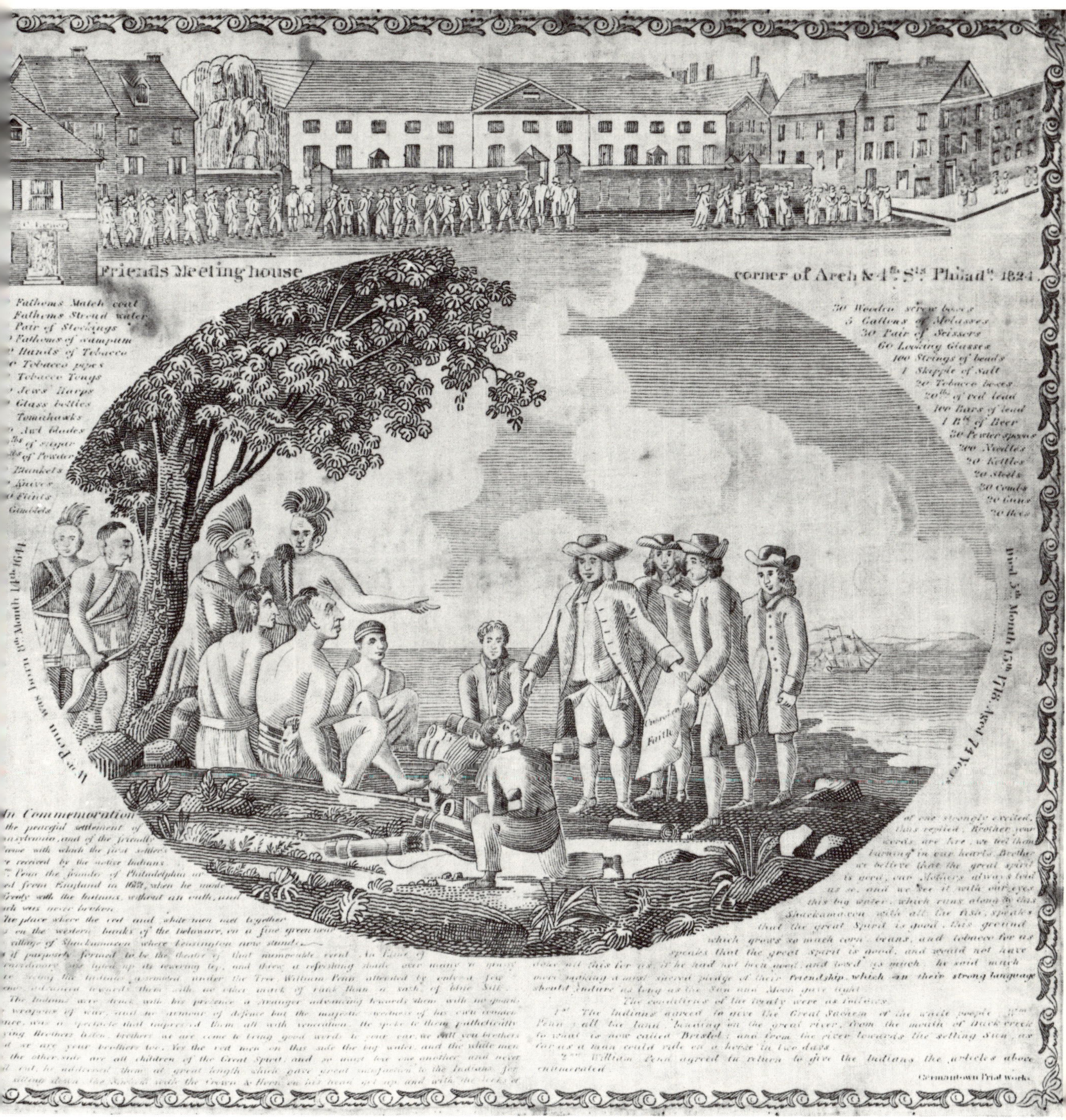

Printed linen handkerchief, 14¼ × 14½, manufactured by the Germantown Print Works, 1824. A simplified version of West's *William Penn's Treaty With the Indians after John Hall's* engraving, this may have been the model for the small Penn Treaty insets in Hicks's early *Peaceable Kingdoms. Above the treaty oval is Arch Street Meeting House, Philadelphia, center of Delaware Valley Quakerism. (Swarthmore College Peace Collection.)

that he was emotionally attached to Bucks County. He named it for Buckinghamshire, the native county of his young wife, Guglielma, whom he had left
behind with their children in England. He wrote of her, "She was good, wise,

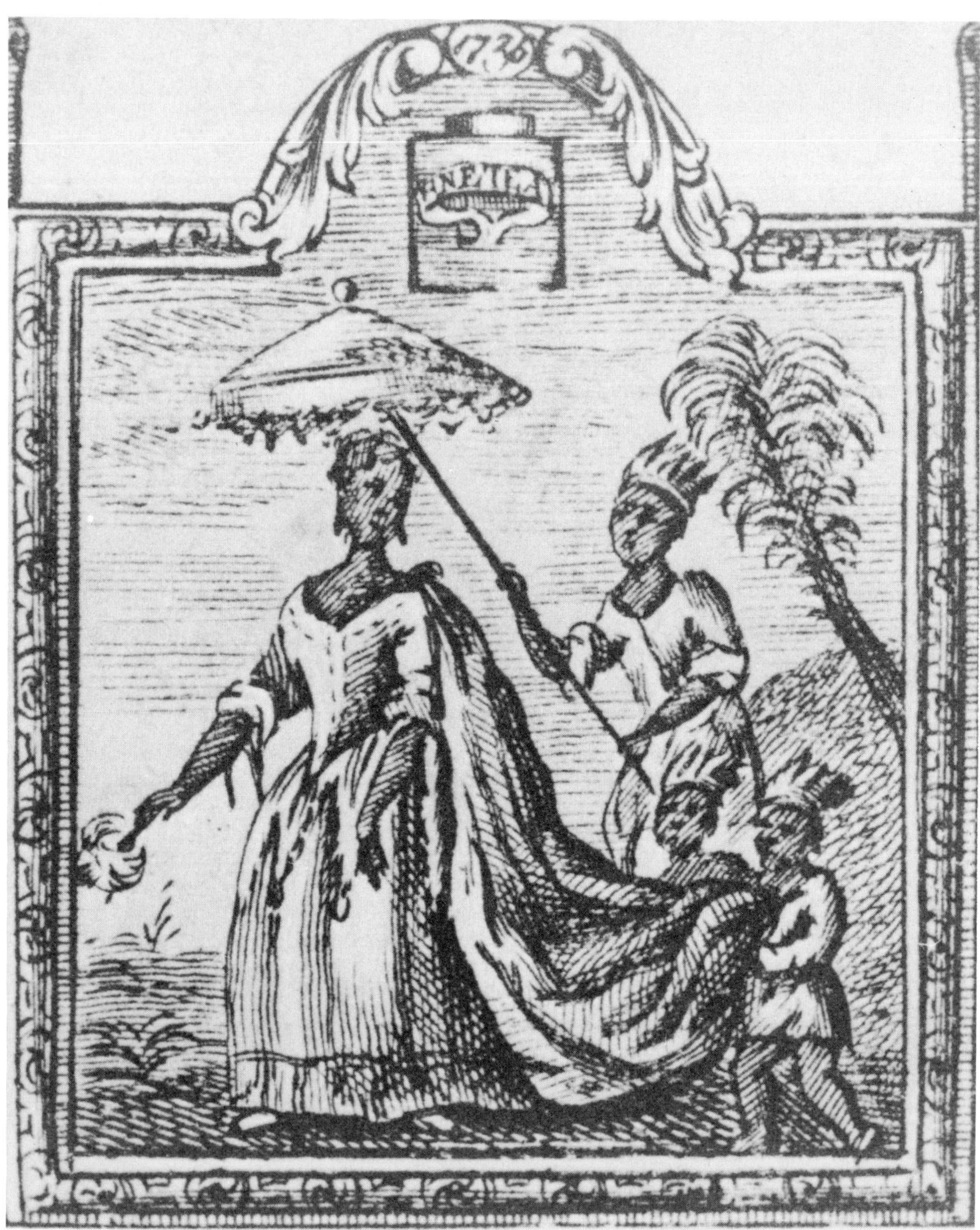

The Indian Queen emblem was inherited from signcraft, not only decorating many
tavern boards, but also advertising dealers in silk, tea, and playing cards. (1) An
eighteenth-century trade sign shows the queen with one attendant holding an umbrella while two others carry her train. (From Ambrose Heal's Signboards of Old
London Shops (London, 1947), p. 51. (2) Detail from a Peaceable Kingdom With
Rhymed Borders demonstrates Hicks's adaptation: the larger attendant, her umbrella
discarded, now holds the queen's train, leaving the other two free to support a bolt of
cloth. (Philadelphia Museum of Art.)

chaste, humble, plain, modest, industrious, constant, and undaunted."[5] She was also very charming, and her memory lingers in the story of this great but not always happy man.

On the Harrison Streeter canvas Penn wears a blue sash, which is unique in the *Peaceable Kingdoms*. It is traditionally correct, though it does not appear in West's original. Hicks may have discovered it in Thomas Clarkson's biography of Penn, which described the Founder's appearance at the treaty: "William Penn appeared in his usual clothes. He had no crown, sceptre, mace, or sword, halbert, or any insignia of eminence. He was distinguished only by wearing a sky blue sash round his waist, which was made of silk network, and which was of no larger apparent dimensions than an officer's military sash, and much like it except in color."[6] The original sash, by tradition knitted by Guglielma, still survives at the Historical Society of Pennsylvania in Philadelphia.[7]

Another interesting touch in this particular *Kingdom* is the seductive female, plumed and clad in leopard skin, who presides over the negotiations.[8] She is exactly what she looks like: an Indian queen who must be a carry-over from his sign-painting trade. Not only was "Indian Queen" a popular name for taverns,

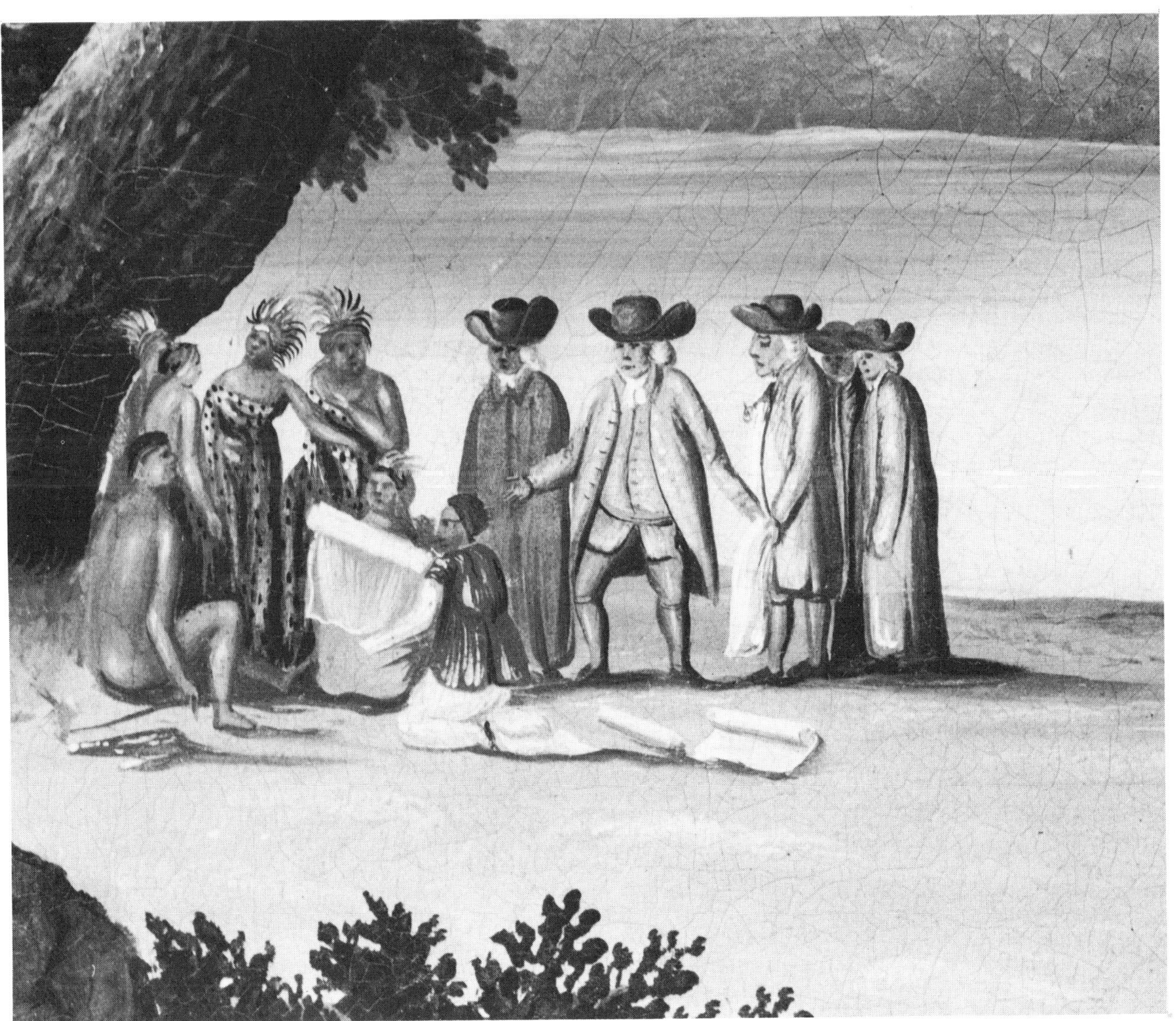

but it served as a trade emblem for mercers and linen drapers, presumably because of the sumptuous fabrics imported from the East Indies. To the colony-conscious Britisher, an Indian was an Indian, regardless of hemisphere. The stereotype for these signs in England—and no doubt likewise in America as a former colony—shows the queen accompanied by attendants who carry her train and hold over her an umbrella. Here there is no umbrella; instead, the tall attendant holds the train, while the two smaller ones kneel to support a roll of fabric. In view of the Indian queen's connection with the mercers' trade, it is appropriate that she stands with hand graciously extended, endorsing Penn's yard goods.[9]

A trace of signcraft also appears in the decorative inscription that frames the composition. This gives the category the name *Kingdom With Rhymed Borders* and presents Hicks's own paraphrase of Isaiah's prophecy, in which he relates the peaceable kingdom to Penn's establishment of Pennsylvania:

> The wolf did with the lambkin dwell in peace
> His grim carnivorous nature there did cease
>
> The leopard with the harmless kid laid down
> And not one savage beast was seen to frown
>
> The lion with the fatling on did move
> A little child was leading them in love;
>
> When the great PENN his famous treaty made
> With Indian chiefs beneath the Elm-tree's shade.

Note the reference to the "Elm-tree's shade." As a country boy Hicks was thoroughly aware of what an elm looked like. Yet the tree on his canvas, obviously borrowed from Tanner's 1822 map engraving, appears to be a handsome oak.

This typically primitive touch recalls Holger Cahill's term *innocence of vision*, as applied to folk artists who "set down not so much what they saw as what they knew and what they felt."[10] *Innocence of vision* bears a similarity to, though it is not the same as, the inward eye of the mystic. When Edward introduced the Niagara tree into his *Kingdom*, his outward eye readily discerned that it was not the elm tree of nature. But his inward eye told him it was the tree he wanted, and so he used it. Remote as the Quaker mystic seems from the image-making sign painter, both shared a dimension beyond the limitations of naturalism, and both were fused in the person of Edward Hicks.

Meanwhile, the controversy that was tearing apart his beloved Society of Friends continued. The tension increased with each Monthly and Quarterly Meeting, gatherings attended not only by the Meeting's members but by many visitors, some sorrowful and concerned, some curious and sensation-seeking, but all intoxicated with the terrible and heady wine of conflict. The missionary efforts of visiting English ministers only made matters worse. They were welcomed by the Orthodox because, as Robert Doherty has pointed out, they "offered acceptable doctrine without distasteful forms of worship."[11] That is, they combined a stress on the atonement and scripture authority with characteristic Quaker practices: plain dress and speech, lack of outward sacraments, spontaneous ministry, and the traditional meeting structure. But they roused Edward's already anti-British prejudice to a peak of fury, and even among those more moderately disposed their effect was divisive.

Even so, the ultimate schism might have been avoided had Elias kept away from Philadelphia. But such was not to be. Toward the close of 1826 the Long Island preacher, returning from Baltimore, attended Pine Street Meeting, the very nadir of orthodoxy and home meeting of Jonathan Evans, most powerful of Philadelphia elders. Elias and Jonathan had been warm friends early in the century, but today each took issue with the other in the course of his ministry, and at the close of the service Evans refused his old friend's proffered hand.

After this there was no turning back. Nearly two years earlier Elias had written, "Surely, when will the Philadelphians learn wisdom, and be willing to submit to right order? May it not be right for some plain, simple countrymen, under right direction, to step in and lend them a hand?"[12]

This was precisely what some plain, simple countrymen were now preparing to do. At Bucks Quarterly Meeting in February of 1827 it was proposed to enlarge their representation to the coming Yearly Meeting and to take other measures that might strengthen the rank and file in their struggle against the city hierarchy, propositions endorsed by Edward with an ardor that, as he tells us, "offended the orthodox and alarmed my dear friend John Comly."[13]

But by this time even Comly considered the situation intolerable. He spent that night at Newtown with Edward, conferring with Friends as to what move they should next take.

NOTES

1. Anonymous, p. 2. Copy at the Free Library of Philadelphia.

2. An 1840 silhouette shows a Cheesman reception with musical instruments. Owned by the New-York Historical Society, this silhouette is illustrated in *The American Heritage History of Notable American Houses,* ed. Marshall P. Davidson and Margot P. Brill (New York: American Heritage Publishing Co, 1971), p. 190. A letter of 4th mo. 20th, 1826, to Hicks, acknowledging receipt of a painting, is given in Ford, *Edward Hicks,* p. 49.

3. Letter of 5 mo. 1st, 1826 (Ford, *Edward Hicks,* p. 49.

4. The manor complex had been built between Penn's first visit to his colony (1682–84) and his second (1699–1701). John F. Watson in *Annals of Philadelphia and Pennsylvania* (Philadelphia: E. L. Cary & A. Hart, 1830), rev. ed. 1857, tells of a "plot of Philadelphia, signed by Phineas Pemberton, Surveyor General, that fully appeared to have been in Pennsbury Manor." (1:56), implying that Penn had once considered the area as a site for Philadelphia.

5. *Newtown 275th Anniversary* (Newtown, Pa.: Newtown Anniversary Committee, 1959), p. 5.

6. Thomas Clarkson, *Memoirs of the Public and Private Life of William Penn,* 2 vols. (London: Longmans, Hurst, Rees, Orme and Brown, 1813), 1:339–40.

7. M. Atherton Leach, "Guglielma Maria Springett, First Wife of William Penn," *Pennsylvania Magazine of History and Biography* 57 (1933): 111–13.

8. She appears in only one other *Kingdom,* a similar composition in the Rockefeller Collection at Williamsburg.

9. For samples of the Indian queen trade sign see Sir Ambrose Heal, *The Signboards of Old London Shops* (London: Batsford, 1947).

10. Holger Cahill, *American Folk Art* (New York: Museum of Modern Art, 1932), pp. 15 and 28.

11. Robert Doherty, "The Growth of Orthodoxy," *Quaker History* 54 (1965): 25. Between 1818 and 1828 the following Friends ministers came from England to America: William Forster, George Withy, Anna Braithwaite, Elizabeth Robson, George and Ann Jones, and Thomas Shillitoe, some making several journeys. See Rufus M. Jones, *Later Periods of Quakerism,* 2 vols. (London: Macmillan, 1921), 1:459–60.

12. Elias Hicks to Samuel Comfort, July 19, 1825, in *Letters of Elias Hicks* (New York: Isaac T. Hopper, 1834), p. 187.

13. *Memoirs,* p. 108.

5

QUAKERS BEARING BANNERS

TWO MONTHS LATER THE FOLLOWERS OF ELIAS HICKS CAME TO A PARTING OF THE WAYS with their Orthodox brethren. Led by John Comly, they withdrew from Philadelphia Yearly Meeting on the closing day of proceedings, April 21, 1827.

The Orthodox claimed that the schism was a theological dispute, in which they had defended Quakerism against heresy. The Hicksites maintained that it was not a doctrinal matter, but a struggle for religious liberty.[1] Both sides saw themselves as the spiritual and legal heirs of the primitive founders. This led to a round of disputes over properties. The city meeting houses, except for Green Street, long a refuge for Hicks's supporters, went to the Orthodox.

One bizarre episode involved the Friends' burial ground in Philadelphia, traditionally shared by all five city meetings. After 1827 it was closed by the Orthodox trustees, who refused to give the key to Green Street. To make an interment, members of that meeting knocked down a portion of the west wall and built a gate. This resulted in several arrests, considerable litigation, and a satirical pamphlet entitled *The Hole in the Wall, or a Peep at the Creed Worshippers.*[2] It included an illustration showing Samuel Bettle testing the "weight of the meeting" on a huge pair of scales, whereon one Orthodox "Rabbi" outweighs the entire Hicksite leadership, portrayed as a pyramid of Quaker faces headed by Comly.

Who was the artist? Though anonymous, the title page states, "Embellished with Cuts by the Author," thus restricting authorship to one who could both write and draw. One thinks immediately of Edward himself.[3] But the drawing is too precise and mechanical. A more likely possibility is his friend Benjamin Ferris who, as a surveyor, was skilled in drafting and already versed in polemic writing through a theological debate known as "The Letters of Paul and Amicus."[4]

One wonders if this caricature with its pyramid of Hicksites is reflected on Hicks's canvases. For he now begins to paint *Peaceable Kingdoms* in which a mountain of Quakers replaces Penn's Treaty. This mountain is topped by thirteen rays of light, from which descends a banner supported by the drab-coated Friends and inscribed "Behold I bring glad tidings of great Joy. Peace on earth and good will to men" (Luke 2:10–14). Hence the cumbersome but descriptive title, *Kingdoms with Quakers Bearing Banners.*

36

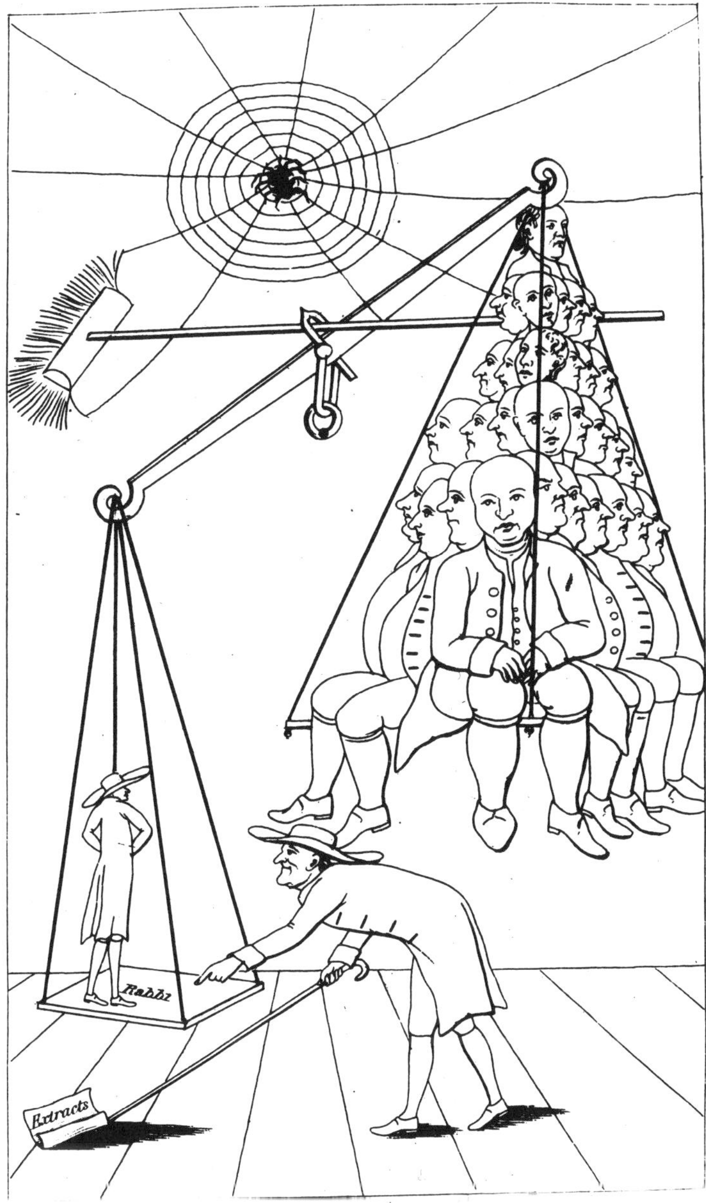

Weight of Members, a Hicksite caricature satirizing Orthodox authority. It presents Samuel Bettle, presiding officer of Philadelphia Yearly Meeting, assessing the judgment of his fellow Quakers. From anonymous pamphlet, The Hole in the Wall *(1828), plate 3 (Quaker Collection, Haverford College Library; photograph by Theodore B. Hetzel.)*

Alice Ford recognized that the thirteen rays of light represented Christ and the Apostles.[5] It was clear that these canvases had something to do with Christianity and Quakerism, but there seemed to be a further element that eluded explanation. This element was discovered when Mary C. Black, then curator of the Abby Aldrich Rockefeller Collection at Williamsburg, perceived their source in the so-called Separation of 1827.[6]

Once pointed out, this was obvious. Not only was conflict evident in the faces of the animals and in the harsh erosions of the landscape, as Mary Black noted, but it was also suggested by the divided composition, the arid back-

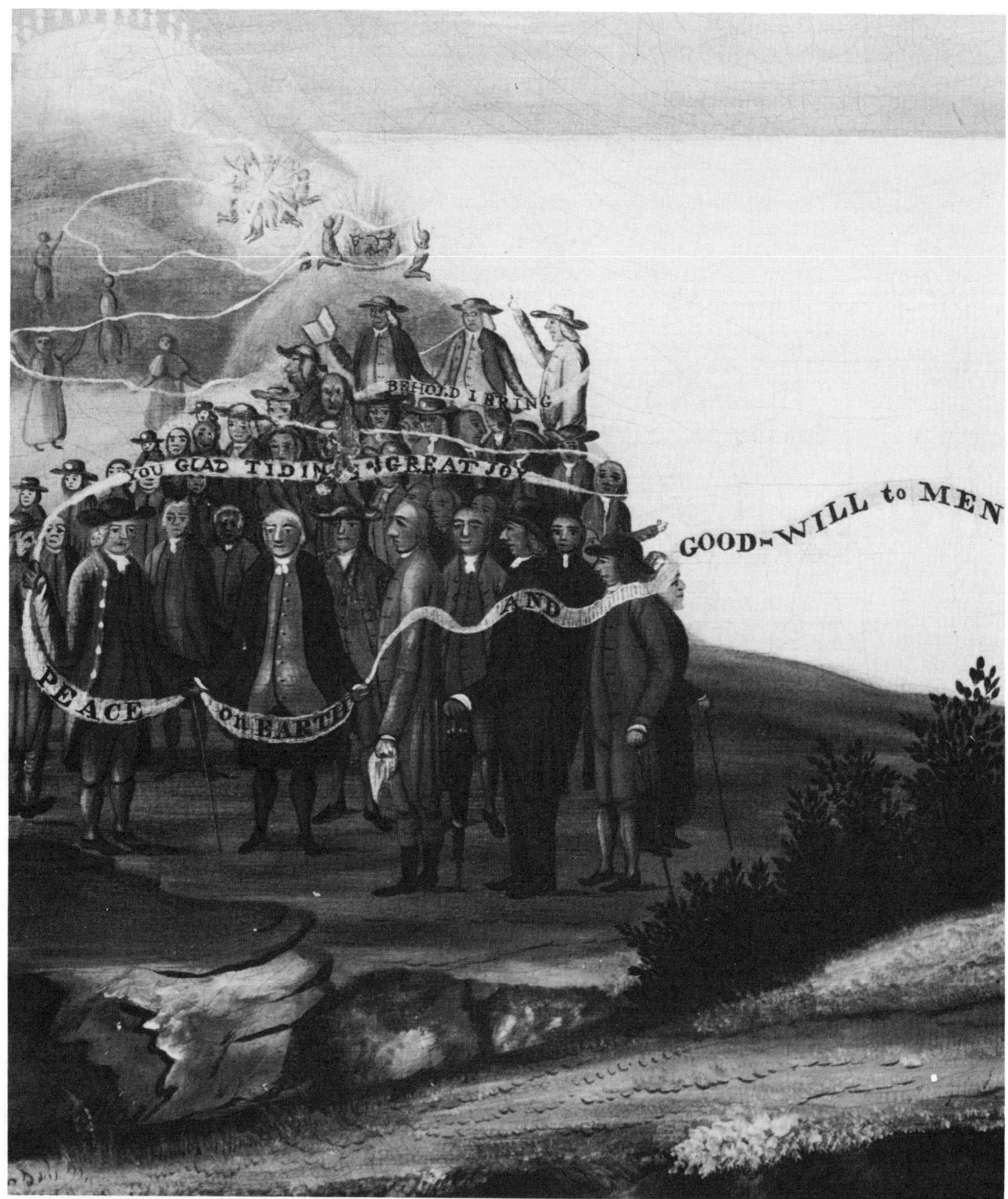

*In Peaceable Kingdoms With Quakers Bearing Banners, the Penn Treaty scene is
replaced with a pyramid of plainly clad Friends, while the mountain above is
crowned with thirteen rays of light representing Christ and the Apostles. From the
central ray descends a banner, indicative of the progress of religious liberty, which
entwines the Protestant Reformers before reaching the seventeenth-century founders
of Quakerism: (from right to left) George Fox, William Penn, and Robert Barclay.
(Detail, Yale University Art Gallery.)*

ground, and the cleft tree of the Swarthmore version, where one half is a
ghostly gray, the other a warm brown extending into a living branch. In the
Cahill and Winterthur variants the symbolism is handled a little differently: the

whole tree trunk is a dead stump, but a live shoot rising from it indicates the spiritual vitality of the Hicksite movement.

In general terms the Quaker controversy was certainly the motivation for these *Banner Kingdoms*. But Frederick B. Tolles, head of the Friends Historical Library at Swarthmore College, found a more specific source in a long poem entitled, "To Edward Hicks on his proposition for painting an Historical piece commemorative of the progress of religious liberty."[7] The author was Samuel Johnson of Buckingham, who urged his friend the painter to illustrate the troubled course of religious freedom from the birth of Christ to truth's culminating victory in the Separation. From Johnson's lines we learn that beneath the Apostles is the flaming pyre of Michael Servetus, Spanish heretic. Then come the Protestant Reformers, somewhat shapeless in outline—probably because Hicks had only a hazy idea of what a Protestant Reformer looked like.[8]

If the *Hole in the Wall* cartoon left its mark on these compositions, it was only in the pyramidal form of the Quaker group, not in the individuals concerned. The Quakers in the *Banners Kingdoms,* as in Johnson's poem, are placed chronologically, at their apex three men in drab: George Fox, founder of Quakerism, preaching with hand upraised; William Penn with arms characteristically outstretched in welcome; and Robert Barclay, theological defender of the movement, proffering his book, the *Apology.* These were the three great pathfinders of Quakerism, and their identity is unmistakable.[9]

Below them extend a nameless host until the bottom row, where Tolles has suggested Washington as the central figure. This suggestion is not entirely satisfactory, but there seems no likely alternative. Johnson had specifically warned the artist *not* to include this military figure, but Edward, who did not share all of Johnson's opinions, was an intense admirer of the general, and his enthusiasm for this vanquisher of the British was probably heightened by his resentment against visiting English ministers. Furthermore, the Father of his Country would seem to be the only personage big enough to take the center spot from Elias Hicks, who stands beside him.

There is no question that this is Elias, the pose lifted from a silhouette published shortly after the preacher's death in February, 1830.[10] He is hatless and wears the riding boots of a traveling Friends' minister. A limp handkerchief in his left hand testifies to hour-long sermons that frequently left him soaked with perspiration. Johnson writes:

> The Apostle *Hicks's* venerable face
> On the foreground should fill conspicuous place.

Also mentioned are certain of his followers: Comly, the Comforts, and Thomas Wetherald. Which is which is purely conjectural, but one can make some speculations. Comly always wore the plain dress, which at this period would involve knee breeches. This might place him as the second figure from the left with cane in hand. The *Hole in the Wall* caricature and a photograph at Friends Historical Library showing him seated with hands crossed over the head of his cane offer comparisons; a resemblance, though not marked, is possible. As for the Comforts, all were countrymen and probably dressed plainly. Two faces in the second row look rather similar, so one might dub them Stephen and Samuel, both close friends of the painter. As for their brother

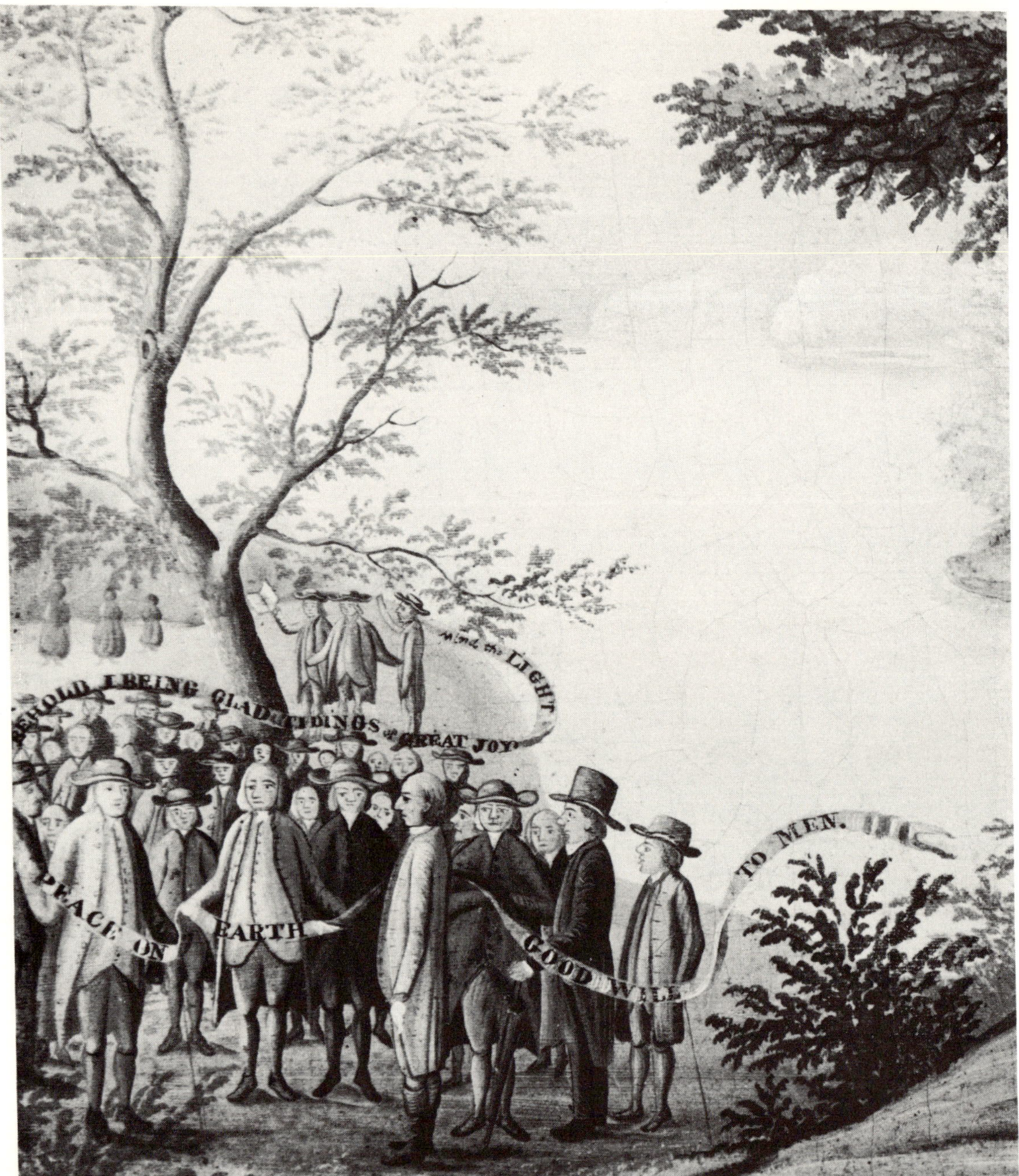

This Peaceable Kingdom With Quakers Bearing Banners emphasizes the presence of Elias Hicks, who stands in the foreground, in riding boots and with handkerchief in hand, easily recognizable from his silhouette. (Detail, Henry Francis du Pont Winterthur Museum.)

John, the doughty challenger of the "Creed," he may be the figure to the extreme right whose cane projects behind him. His pose sets him a little apart from the rest, as one who can stand alone.[11]

Who is the man with the umbrella? He wears long trousers and what—in the Winterthur version—looks perilously like a top hat. Judging by costume and by process of elimination one is left with Wetherald, the last on Johnson's list of Quaker worthies:

And Wetherald, greatly good, should have a place
Beside the foremost in the Christian race;

"Beside the foremost"—that is, beside Elias, behind whom the man with the umbrella apears in most of these works. The lack of plain dress may relate to a statement in one of Wetherald's sermons: "It is not the cut of a coat, nor shape of a bonnet—it is not any of these things which some of us have any concern about, and we have not been ashamed to admit it. . . . And I verily believe there is much less pride in some of those who wear fashionable apparel, than in those who have adopted a particular system of religion, and have come under the influence of systematical and Pharisaical self-righteousness."[12]

Though Johnson cites no females as aiding the progress of religious liberty, his friend Edward, who was partial to women, included several, but who they are we do not know. Most of the women prominent in the controversy were English ministers whom the painter would on no account admit to his mountain of the elect. However, the Hicksites had one heroine, Priscilla Hunt, a minister from Ohio. It is possible that the skirted figure at the extreme right of the Swarthmore *Banners Kingdom* is she. Or it may be Rebecca Jones (1739–1818), the leading woman minister of Philadelphia Yearly Meeting during the late eighteenth and early nineteenth centuries. This well-known Quaker died before the Separation. One suspects that if she had lived she would have gone with the Orthodox. But her spiritual gifts were unchallenged, and Edward would have respected them.[13]

The phrase *Mind the Light* appears on the Winterthur and two other examples. In all cases the words are inscribed on a portion of the banner close to Fox, since the admonition, as Hicks points out, was "the favorite advice of George Fox."[14]

This Winterthur version is unique among the *Banners Kingdoms*. Out of its sober group of Quakers rises a tree, a moving and fascinating sign of growth that finds an echo in the misty shoreline returning to the middle distance. The work was a turning point in the sequence of the *Kingdoms*, for the tide of creative evolution was carrying the artist/preacher into the realm of a new symbol and a new hero.

NOTES

1. James Cockburn, *A Review of the General and Particular Causes Which Have Produced the Late Disorders and Divisions in the Yearly Meeting of Friends, Held in Philadelphia: with Introductory Remarks on the State of the Primitive Churches, their Gradual Declension, and Subsequent Advancement in Reformation, to the Rise of the Society of Friends* (Philadelphia: Philip Price, 1829), p. 278.

2. Philadelphia, 1828.

3. In his *Memoirs* Hicks refers to Ezekiel's vision (18:7–12), the obvious source of the pamphlet's title: "I now saw, I thought, through something like a hole in the wall, what the ancients of Israel were doing in the dark, notwithstanding the thick black cloud that seemed to rest upon them" (p. 99). But here he is referring to an earlier phase of the conflict, c. 1821.

4. Benjamin Ferris, "The Letters of Paul and Amicus" (Wilmington, Del.: R. Porter, 1823). Lewis P. Bush speaks of Ferris's "nice capacity for drawing and sketching with playful illustrations" in "Memoir of Benjamin Ferris," *Papers of the Historical Society of Delaware*, vol. 37 (Wilmington, 1903), p. 30. The *Hole in the Wall* caricatures would certainly quality as "playful illustrations."

5. Alice Ford, *Edward Hicks: Painter of the Peaceable Kingdom* (Philadelphia: University of Pennsylvania Press, 1952).

6. Mary C. Black, "& a Little Child Shall

Lead Them," *Arts in Virginia*, 1 (Autumn, 1960).

7. Frederick B. Tolles, "The Primitive Painter as Poet with an Attempted Solution of an Iconographical Puzzle in Certain of Edward Hicks's *Peaceable Kingdoms*," *Bulletin of the Friends Historical Association* 50 (1961):12–30. Johnson wrote two poems to Edward Hicks, one undated. The other was dated October 3, 1839, and was answered promptly by Hicks with a long poem of his own on October 8. Tolles assumed the undated poem followed Hicks's reply, which would mean that *Quakers Bearing Banners* could not have evolved until the closing months of 1839, which Mary Black saw was too late in the context of the painter's other work. Since the publication of Tolles's article, the Friends Historical Library has acquired a rare copy of Johnson's *Poems on Various Subjects* (Philadelphia: W. P. Gibbons, 1835), which contains the undated poem, indicating that it was written no later than 1835, which is consistent with Black's reasonable estimate of 1827–35 for these *Kingdoms*. We should add that the identifiable figures in the paintings relate to this undated version.

8. Four figures usually appear as Reformers. Johnson specifies Calvin and Luther. Hicks adds Wycliff and Huss in his *Memoirs*, p. 29. These references were prompted by Johan Lorenz Mosheim's *An Ecclesiastical History* (London: A. Millar, 1765), a work that strongly influenced Elias Hicks and his followers. Surrounding the Protestant Reformers on certain *Kingdoms* is a blurred multitude, presumably the persecuted Huguenots, as in Johnson's line:

See the poor Huguenots by thousands slain.

9. Hicks refers to this trio many times in his *Memoirs*, pp. 251, 258, 277, 359, and 360. On late versions of the painting, four or more figures appear instead of three. Nothing in Johnson's poem indicates who they may be. In these Fox does not have his arm upraised.

10. Tolles, "The Primitive Painter as Poet," n. 45.

11. Our only likeness of any of the Comfort brothers is a late photograph of Samuel in a plain coat with his second wife (FHL).

12. *Sermons by Thomas Wetherald*, transcribed by Marcus T. C. Gould (Baltimore, Md.: J. Young, 1864), pp. 217–18. Born in England, Wetherald (1791–1832) was a powerful preacher, second only to Elias Hicks—with the possible exception of Edward himself. His letters to his wife (FHL) tell of journeys from one frontier settlement to another, of riding his horse belly-deep across swollen creeks, of clothes that never got dry, of strained lungs after one- and two-hour sermons. No wonder he died of tuberculosis at the age of 41. The figure with the umbrella is that of a relatively young man.

13. See the silhouette of Rebecca Jones in Anna Cox Brinton, *Quaker Profiles, 1750–1850* (Wallingford, Pa.: Pendle Hill, 1964), p. 20.

14. *Memoirs*, p. 355.

6

THE SEATED LION

THE PERIOD FOLLOWING THE SEPARATION WAS A SEASON OF PREACHING FOR EDWARD HICKS. Later in life he wrote harshly of his extensive travels in the ministry, condemning himself for leaving his poor wife to struggle with domestic problems while he went "a travelling as a preacher, to be waited upon, flattered, and fed upon the best my friends could provide for me, thus squandering other people's money, and idling away that time, that, in one sense, properly belonged to my creditors."[1]

Nonetheless, off he went—touring the areas of Philadelphia, New York, and Baltimore Yearly Meetings. On these journeys his ministry was, as always, spontaneous. He never wrote or memorized a sermon, though certain ones were recorded in shorthand by others. Sometimes he did not speak at all—as we learn from Mary Pennock of Chester County, who wrote in a letter of 1829, "This has been our Quarterly Meeting today. We had the company of Edward Hicks in silence."[2]

In December of 1829 he went to Ohio, then known to the Eastern seaboard as the "Western country." On this trip his companion was an amiable Chester County elder, Benjamin Price. It was customary, though not obligatory, for a minister to be accompanied by an elder, whose ripe years and sober judgment might counteract any undue exuberance on the part of the preacher. As a matter of fact, Benjamin was a rather unusual elder, considerably younger than Edward and of a lively turn of mind.

He later occasioned the painter's displeasure by establishing a boarding school. Edward was always critical of ventures in secondary education, probably feeling defensive because his own formal schooling did not go beyond the elementary grades. But in spite of his disapproval he wrote of Benjamin, "Of all the companions in travel I have ever had, take him in the whole, I have never had the equal of dear B.P."[3]

Apparently none of his sermons on this western journey were recorded, but one can safely assume that their message was the saving power of the Inner

Light. During this period Hicks's ministry must have carried a very special burden—to justify the Hicksite withdrawal from the official body of Philadelphia Quakerism—and this necessarily involved a defense of the religious principles that motivated it.

Soon these beliefs were reflected on the painter's canvases. One of the most fascinating aspects of the *Kingdoms* is their growth from a borrowed composition to one that is completely Hicks's own. Though all of his early versions bore the imprint of Westall's engraving, they moved gradually away from this source. In the early 1830s the artist made the final break, and after several

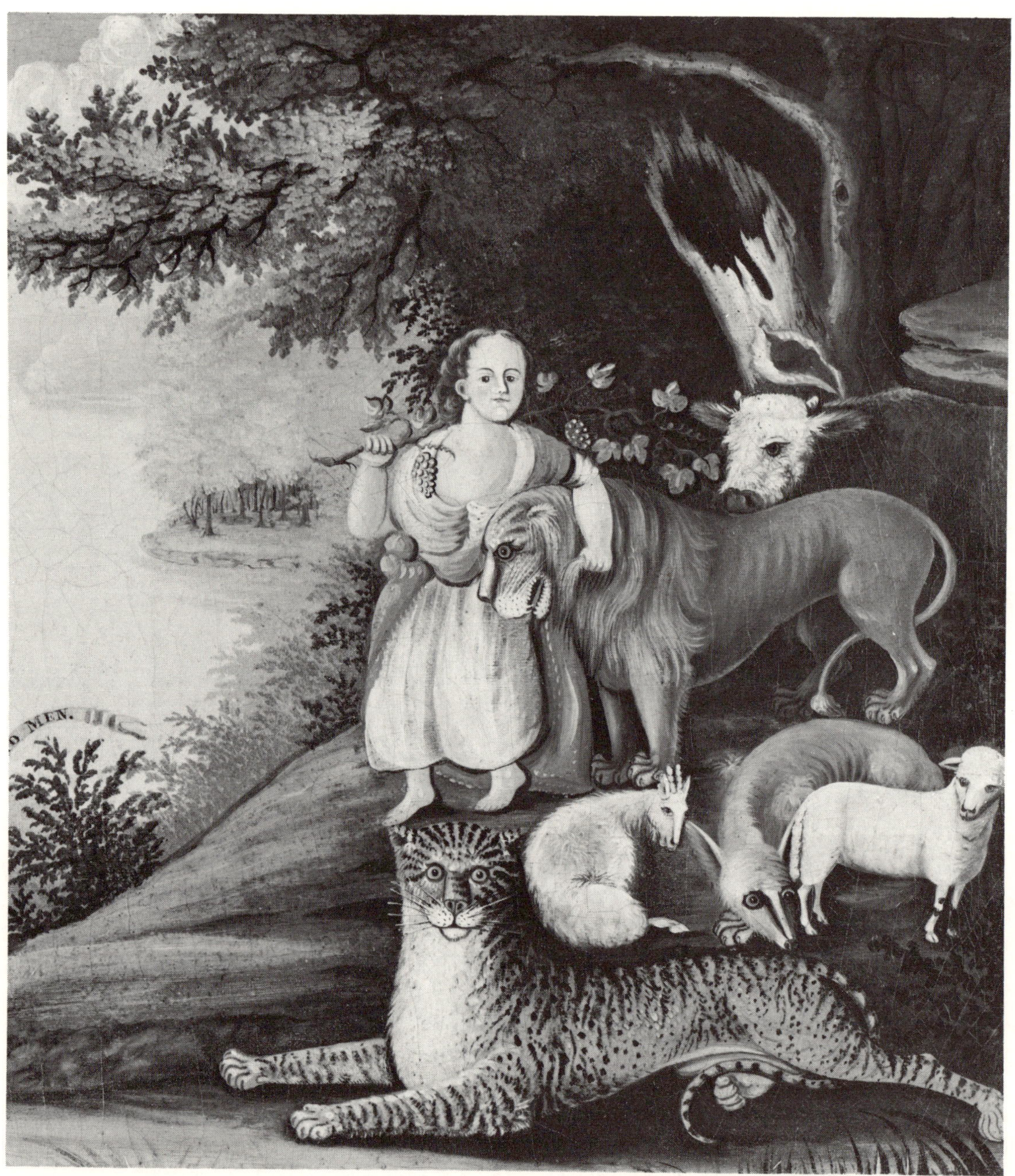

The iconography of all early Kingdoms centers in the grape branch held by the Divine Child. Borrowed from Westall's original work, the grapes symbolize the redemptive blood of Christ as the source of salvation, a basic concept of orthodox Christianity. (Detail, Peaceable Kingdom With Quakers Bearing Banners, courtesy of The Henry Francis du Pont Winterthur Museum.)

tentative and transitional efforts he achieved a totally new composition. It is that popular variant, the *Seated Lion.*

The differences between this composition and the preceding *Banners King-doms* are immediately evident. First, Penn's Treaty has returned, bigger and better than ever with more Indians, more Quakers, and more color. Second, the scene is crowded with a host of new figures, including a fourth pair of animals—a bear and a cow—and two extra children, the "sucking child" and the "weaned child." Here the painter uses *all* the creatures in Isaiah's prophecy; Westall had used only those in verse 6.[4]

Third and most important, the Divine Child is no longer the principal figure. The artist has found a new hero, the seated lion. He dominates the canvas, creating a unity of effect in spite of the additional animals and children. As for

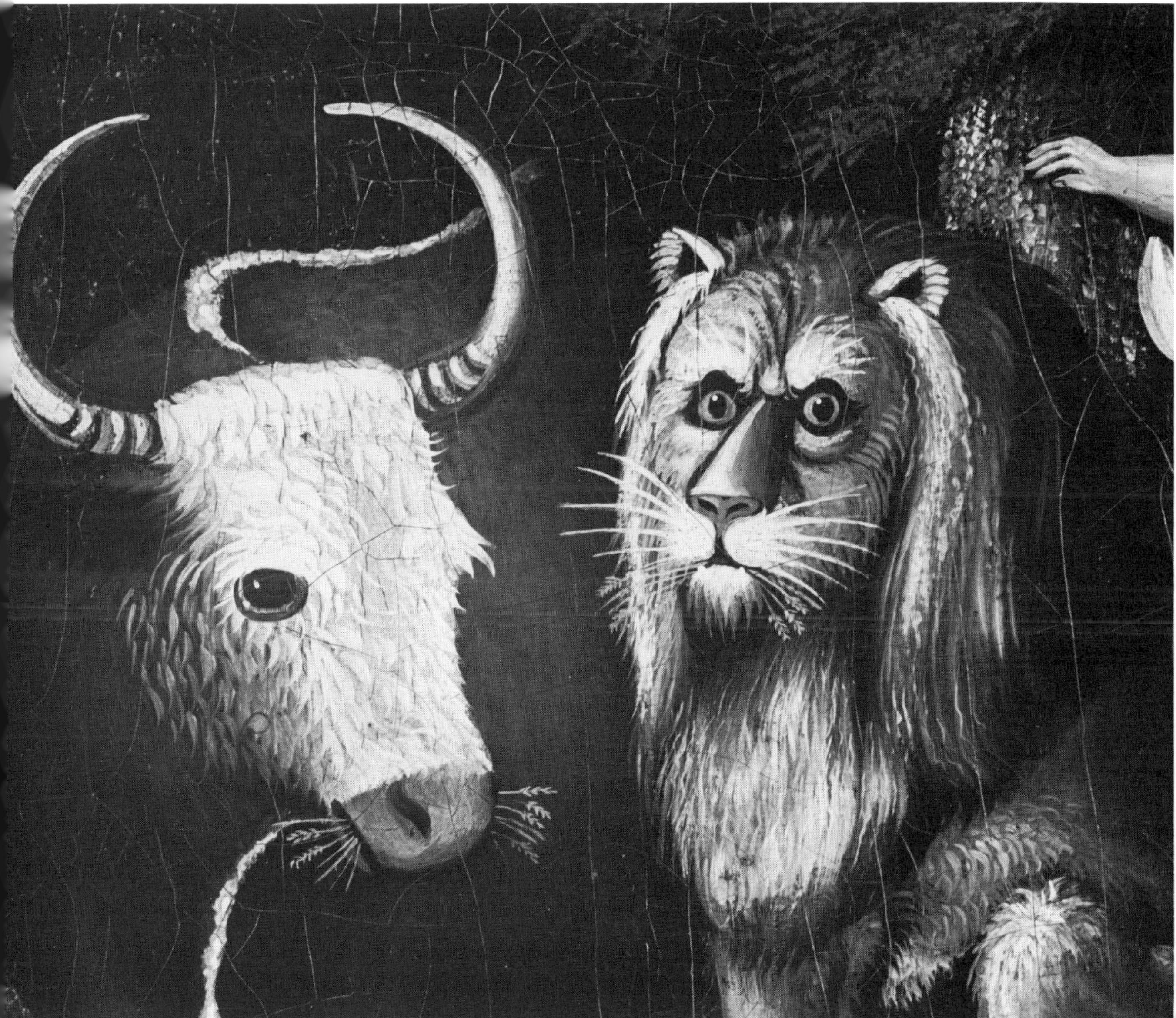

h the emergence of the Peaceable Kingdom with Seated Lion *a new icon appears: the lion eating straw* 1 the ox, *a symbol of the lion's submission to the Divine Will, the goal of Quaker quietism. Note the* ld's *empty hand at upper right, bereft of the Branch. (Detail, courtesy of Worcester Art Museum,* rcester, Massachusetts.)

the Divine Child, the little girl of the *Banners Kingdom* has been replaced by a small boy.[5] Much reduced in size and marginal to the action, he continues to embrace the lion of verse 6, which has now become young and maneless. But his extended right hand is empty, for the grape branch has vanished.

This rejection of the grape is the clue to the iconography of the new *Kingdom*. All of Hicks's early versions, whether *Branch*, *Border*, or *Banners*, shared one element in common: the child and the grape branch, a symbol of Christ's death on the cross inherited from Westall. The artist/preacher has removed the grape because he wishes instead to proclaim salvation by the Light Within.

Earlier we noted the words *Mind the Light* on the Winterthur and certain other *Kingdoms*. Now Hicks translates this into a pictorial symbol—the seated lion and his companion the ox, who side-by-side command the center of the new composition.

But what, a viewer might reasonably ask, has a seated lion to do with the Inner Light? Though obscure, the connection is there, but it takes some knowledge of Quaker quietism to recognize it. Look closely at the king of beasts. Here is no ordinary lion, for in his mouth—somewhat camouflaged by whiskers—are ears of grain. The figure comes from verse 7 of Isaiah's peaceable prophecy, and Hicks has paraphrased it in the lines:

> . . . the old lion, thwarting nature's law
> Shall eat beside the ox the barley straw.[6]

Salvation does not come without a price. In sacrificing his natural craving for meat and accepting the vegetarian diet of the ox the lion has yielded self-will to the Divine Will. In short, he has become a Quaker quietist.

Where the Hebrew prophet found a metaphor for salvation in the Branch of Jesse, and Westall in the eucharistic grape, Hicks uses a straw-eating lion to illustrate the transforming power of the indwelling light.

The realization of this symbol must have been something of a shock to the artist. Obviously it is for the lion, whose staring eyes fix us with alarm. And at first sight the concept is ludicrous. But on sober reflection there is in it a certain appropriateness. In the Western world the lion's great nimbus of a mane has long connoted the rays of the sun, and the color of his coat, like the grain in his mouth, is golden. Furthermore, the barley grain—an original touch by the artist, since Isaiah had mentioned only straw—is a form of seed, and in early Quaker writings *seed* was a metaphor for spiritual rebirth, as was *sun* a metaphor for God, whose light nurtured the reborn spirit.[7]

It may well be objected that grain is as eucharistic as grapes, since the bread and wine together form Holy Communion, sometimes represented in Flemish art by clusters of grapes and grain.[8] Why substitute one eucharistic symbol for another?

There is a reasonable answer to this question. Hicks's use of the grain suggests that his objection to the grape was probably more partisan than theological.[9] He may have adopted Westall's grapes without much thought about their doctrinal implication. But as the Orthodox/Hicksite controversy progressed, certain words and phrases took on a partisan flavor. As Quaker historian Elbert Russell writes: "The Inner Light came to be regarded by the Orthodox as a Hicksite expression, the phrase, 'the blood of Christ,' became a badge of orthodoxy."[10]

But striking as is the revolution in composition and symbolism, even more significant are the psychological contents of this new *Kingdom*. Up to this time the lion had been only an animal—an angry and disturbed one in the *Banners Kingdoms*, but still an animal. Now, in these initial canvases of Hicks's middle period, a human element enters the lion's staring eyes, never to leave them during the remaining course of the *Kingdoms*.

No sensitive viewer acquainted with the artist's life and his battles with his fellow Quakers during the controversial years of the 1820s can fail to be shocked by coming face to face with the Brooklyn lion and seeing in his fixed eyes a very human soul, riven by the guilt and fear that came in the wake of the Separation. And with it, curiously, one catches something of the flair of the born performer. Here is a clown among lions, aghast at himself yet, withal, amused.

With the new and inward *Kingdom* Hicks leaves behind the composition he borrowed from Richard Westall with its balance of Divine Child and beast, and presents instead the soul of man in animal garb—the lion and his other self, the ox—caught between the divine and bestial. This was man,

> Distinguish'd link is being's endless chain!
> Midway from nothing to the Deity.[11]

NOTES

1. *Memoirs*, p. 63.

2. Mary Pennock to Mary Jones, near Meeting House, Uwchlan, 2nd mo. 16, 1829 (FHL).

3. *Memoirs*, p. 184.

4. Verses 7 and 8 read: "And the cow and the bear shall feed; their young ones shall lie down together: and the lion shall eat straw like the ox. And the sucking child shall play on the hole of the asp, and the weaned child shall put his hand on the cockatrice's den." This increased regard for biblical accuracy may have been, at least partially, in answer to the Orthodox charge that the Hicksites undervalued the Scriptures. The scriptural source of the reference is emphasized by the inscription on three transitional canvases: "Isaiah 11 Chap. 6, 7, 8." See catalogue nos., 26, 27, and 28. For the gradual transition from the *Banners* to the *Seated Lion*, see Eleanore Price Mather, "A Quaker Icon," *Art Quarterly* (1973), reprinted with revisions in *Edward Hicks: A Gentle Spirit*, catalogue of the exhibition of the Andrew Crispo Gallery, New York, N.Y., Spring, 1975, and idem, "The Inward Kingdom of Edward Hicks," *Quaker History, Bulletin of the Friends Historical Association*, 62 (1973).

5. Borrowed from a print after Hyacinthe Rigaud that hung in the painter's bedroom [Alice Ford, p. 43]. (Or John Francis Rigaud, R.A.?)

6. Hicks sometimes presented a rhymed paraphrase of Isaiah's prophecy along with the gift of a *Peaceable Kingdom*. See Arthur Edwin Bye, "Edward Hicks, 1780–1849," *Bulletin of the Friends Historical Association*, 32 (1943): 60.

7. See J. William Frost, *The Quaker Family in Colonial America* (New York: St. Martin's Press, 1973), p. 15. The phrase *bread of life*, a figure related to the symbolic grain, was a favorite with Hicks. The lion's eating of the grain suggests a greater degree of participation than the mere carrying of the Branch, since it implies a degree of personal sacrifice. One of the Hicksites' objections to the doctrine of the atonement was its vicarious aspect. Quakerism stressed the experiential, though in a spiritual rather than physical sense. At this point it is closer in theory to Roman Catholicism than to Protestantism, which emphasizes faith in Christ's sacrifice rather than participation in it.

8. George Ferguson, *Signs and Symbols in Christian Art* (New York: Oxford University Press, 1954), p. 31.

9. Unlike certain other Hicksites Edward was not a Unitarian but an eighteenth-century type of Quaker mystic. He had gone through a highly orthodox phase shortly after his marriage in 1803 (*Memoirs*, pp. 51–52); even as late as 1834, in a sermon on the Light Within delivered at Green Street Meeting House on April 18 he acknowledges Jesus Christ as the outward saviour (*A Sermon by Edward Hicks* [Darby, Pa.: Printed by Y. S. Walter, 1834], p. 8).

10. Elbert Russell, *The Separation After a Century* (Philadelphia, The Friends Intelligencer, 1928), p. 51.

11. Edward Young, "Night I," lines 74–75 in *Night Thoughts* (London, 1742) quoted by Edward Hicks in his Carpenters' Hall sermon on August 19, 1827, in *The Quaker, Being a Series of Sermons by Members of the Society of Friends*, taken in shorthand by Marcus T. C. Gould (Philadelphia, 1827), 2:194. A decade later he repeated the quotation in his famous Goose Creek Sermon, 1837, on the meaning of the peaceable kingdom.

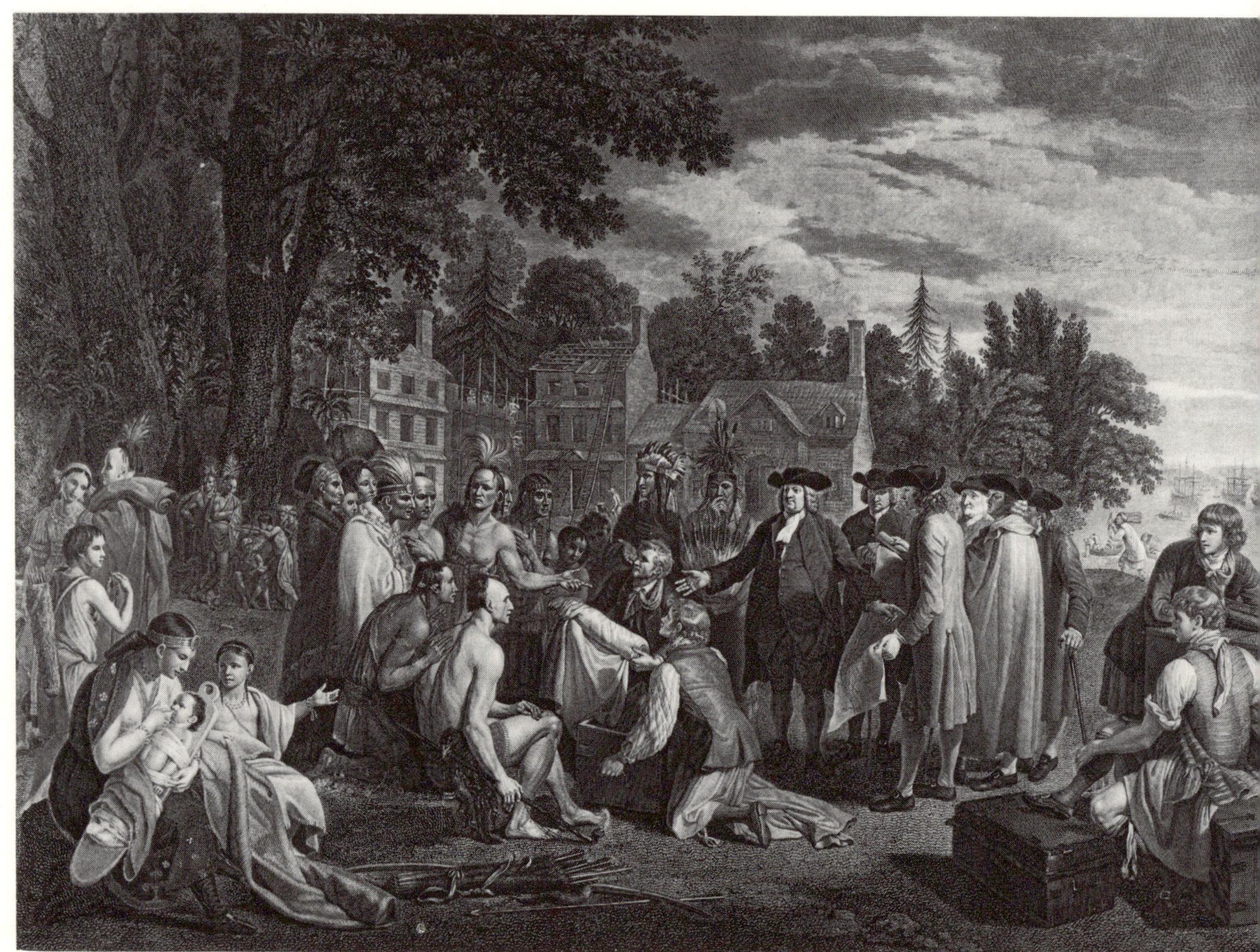

Engraving of Benjamin West's William Penn's Treaty with the Indians *by John Hall, published by John Boydell, London, 1775 (19⅜ × 24¹⁄₁₆ inches). This print made West's painting famous in England and America. As in Hicks's derivatives, the composition is reversed from that of the original, the tree appearing at the left. (Historical Society of Pennsylvania, Philadelphia.)*

7

THE QUAKER AESTHETIC

THE TRIALS OF THE SEPARATION, WHICH HICKS SAW AS A STRUGGLE FOR RELIGIOUS LIBERTY, made the painter particularly appreciative of Penn the Founding Father, whose liberal theology and provisions for civil and religious freedoms in his colony were so congenial to Hicksite Quakerism. Probably at about the same time that the artist was developing a new and expanded treaty scene as a vignette for his *Seated Lions,* he was also devoting whole canvases to the subject. These works were set in cherry-veneered frames similar to those surrounding the *Banners Kingdoms,* and bear the title *Penn's Treaty* on the lower border.[1]

The treaty scene, with its English and Welsh immigrants who were the ancestors of many of Hicks's own Bucks County contemporaries, was an embodiment of the Quaker community that Penn established on the banks of the Delaware in 1682. Here, to a greater extent than perhaps in any other secular community in the Western world, the peaceable kingdom was briefly realized in fact.

But a price was paid for this blessing. As in all small worlds the social pressures were intense, and these pressures included a prejudice against the arts. Here one must proceed with caution, however, for as Holger Cahill astutely observed, "It is true that the Puritans, and the Quakers as well, were not a gay people, and that pleasing the eye was not a dominant interest with them. Yet it is a fact to be remarked that the earliest development of American art took place in the Puritan and Quaker sections."[2]

The question of Quakerism and the arts is complex. One reason for its complexity is that the attitude varied with the particular art; another is that Quaker prohibitions were never formally codified, consisting as they did of individual decisions by various meetings. But in Thomas Clarkson's *Portraiture of Quakerism* is a fairly clearcut summary of the Quaker position.

From it one gathers that the performing arts—music, dancing, and above all the theater—were taboo, in just about the order named. This included singing, a point at which Friends differed from other Protestant denominations, however austere. These activities were forbidden because they were considered so exciting to the senses that they distracted from obedience to the Inner Light. "For how," wrote Clarkson, "can a man whose earthly passions are uppermost be in a fit state to receive . . . the spiritual admonitions of this influence?"[3]

This is pure Quaker quietism, and if one accepts the premise, the above prohibitions follow logically.

In regard to pictorial art, however, the case becomes clouded. Clarkson does

49

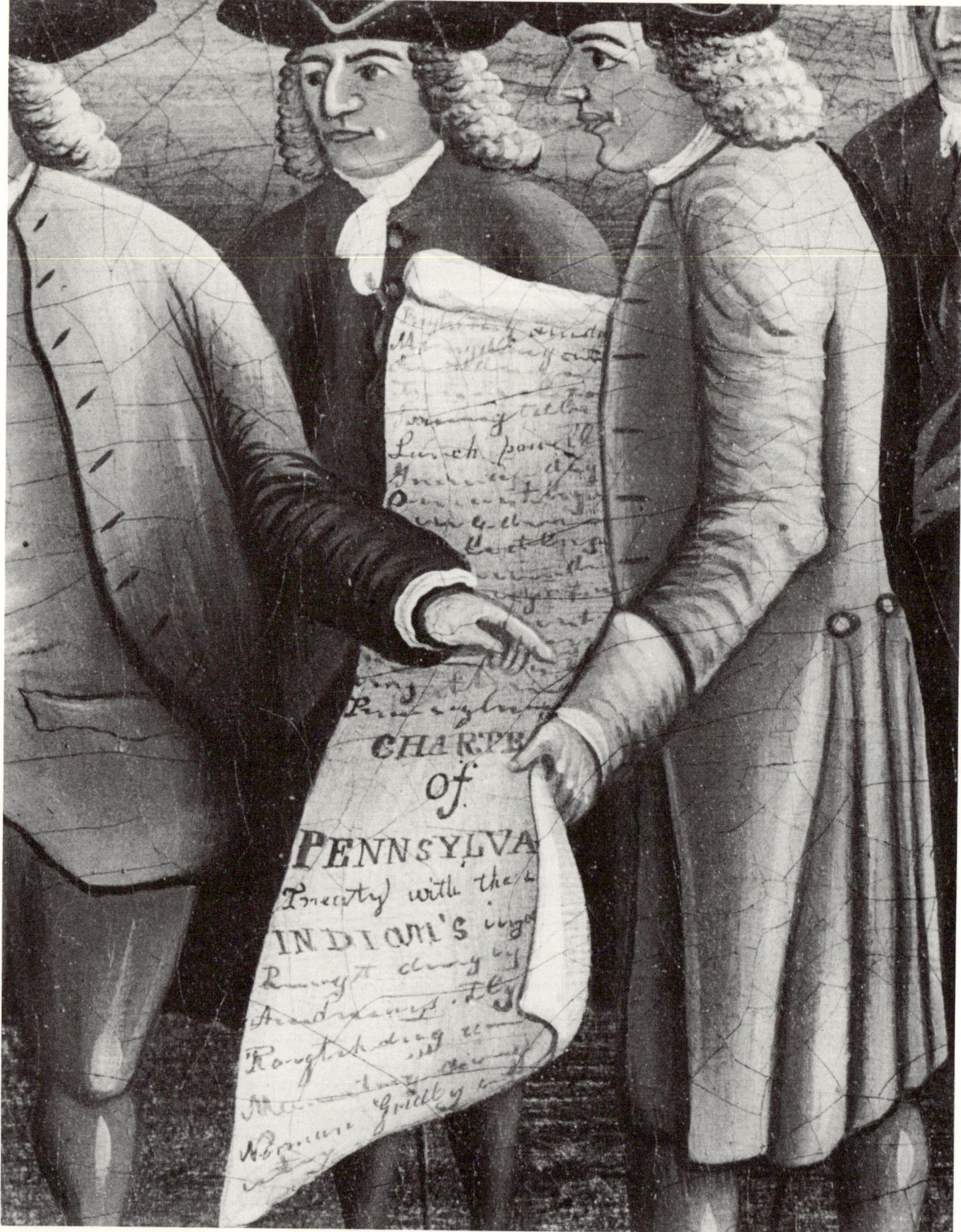

Detail from a Hicks Penn's Treaty: the scroll shows "make believe" writing that appears legible till the reader attempts to decipher it. (Museum of Fine Arts, Houston, Tex., Bayou Bend Collection; gift of Alice Simkins.)

not mention the Quaker artist. Penn, who makes some sharp comments on Friends' behavior, says nothing against painting and even encouraged the Swedish artist Gustavus Hesselius (1682–1755) to visit his colony, providing him with a letter of commendation.[4] Benjamin West, brought up in the Quaker tradition, was somewhat reluctantly permitted to pursue his art, but the fact remains that he did pursue it. And a search yields no specific fiat against the graphic arts mentioned in J. William Frost's *The Quaker Family in Colonial America*, though this valuable work is replete with prohibitions of other activities.

One suspects that here the Quaker attitude was much like that of other nonconformists. Shortly after the Pennsylvania Academy of the Fine Arts was organized in 1805, Charles Willson Peale wrote to Robert Fulton of steamboat fame—less well known as a portraitist—"I long very much to hear what will be said by the *friends* and other denominations of Xans [Christians]," evidently anticipating disapproval from both groups.[5]

It is important to remember that the English tradition favored neither art nor the artist, due not to religious scruple so much as to the stigma of low income and the "trickery" of presenting what appeared to be real but was not.[6] When Chester Harding (1792–1866) returned from Kentucky in the 1820s, after a stint of portraiture that included Daniel Boone among his sitters, he was taken to task severely by his New York State grandfather, who wrote, "Chester, I want to speak to you about your present mode of life. I think it very little better than swindling to charge forty dollars for one of those effigies. Now I want you to give up this course of living and settle down on a farm and become a respectable man"[7]—exactly the course Hicks pursued with such lamentable results. The attitude it reflects was not peculiarly Quaker.

This is not to say that Quakerism provided a congenial climate for the graphic arts. There is an interesting letter in the Quaker Collection at Haverford College written in 1830 by John Linnell to Bernard Barton, poet and member of the Society of Friends.[8] Linnell is best known as a friend of William Blake's later years, and he has bequeathed to us a valuable likeness of that prophetic genius. He asks Barton, to whom Blake had apparently introduced him, whether there is a chance for an artist to become a Quaker. Unfortunately we do not have Barton's answer, but Linnell's own comment is significant: "What I foresee as the greatest difficulty or impediment is that I should require more liberty than would be allowed me, and I infer this from the great uniformity of dress and mode of expression, etc. adopted by all members of the Society and though I entirely agree as to the Spirit of those things yet I do not like its being compulsatory to follow them exactly."[9]

This "compulsatory" atmosphere is what Hicks had to endure for approximately thirty-five years—that is, from the time he began ornamental painting till his death in 1849. The strain of the situation was increased, of course, by the fact that he was not only a Friend but a recorded minister. This tension produced a marked dichotomy between word and deed. Though he deplored art verbally, he went right on painting—and nobody stopped him. Arthur Edwin Bye, art historian and Bucks County antiquarian, writes that the painter once preached a vehement defense of art, and in consequence was visited by a committee of protest.[10] But there is no record of any formal action against him in the minutes of either Newtown Preparative or Makefield Monthly Meeting.

Out of this ambiguous situation emerge two somewhat contradictory facts: one, that Quakers did not approve of pictorial art; two, that they did not forbid it. This ambiguity was not extended to the other arts. Had Hicks chosen to become a fiddler or dancing master he would not long have retained his seat in the ministers' gallery of his own or other meetings.

Why was a certain amount of tolerance accorded to the pictorial arts? There is no single answer, but several circumstances may have united to produce this result. Consider first of all the nature of the art itself. Painting and graphics are not among the performing arts, so did not involve the element of public display and social excitement so threatening to Quaker quietism. More important, painting lay in a twilight zone between art and craft. Probably early Friends had no concept of "art." They would have called painting a trade, requiring, like any other trade, the sober and diligent attention of a mechanic. And it was, indeed, by this route that Edward Hicks slipped into the realm of art. Long before he was either preacher or artist he had set up shop as a painter of coaches and useful household objects.

Under the cover of utility, members of Penn's colony enjoyed a beauty of which they were not fully conscious: the luster of walnut and mahogany against bare walls, the sheen of silver on a polished tea table, the exquisite samplers made by young Quaker girls ostensibly to learn their stitches, but resulting in colorful embroideries that we now call folk art. These objects were justified by their use. Likewise draftsmanship was useful—in fact, absolutely indispensable to the surveyor of property in a young country where there was still much land to measure. Benjamin Ferris of Wilmington, the Quaker controversialist, was a surveyor by profession and made many sketches of buildings. These were accepted as records of history and property, both of which were highly regarded by Friends of the period. During his apprenticeship in Philadelphia in the 1790s, Ferris wrote home unabashedly for his paint box. Nor was he alone in making use of it.[11] Alexander Wilson, the ornithologist whose poem *The Foresters* inspired Hicks's Niagara pictures, was taught drawing by the Quaker botanist William Bartram and his niece Ann. "I have murdered your rose," wrote Wilson in 1803, after copying one of Bartram's sketches: "I traced the outline with great patience but in coloring and shading I got perfectly bewildered."[12] Since the natural sciences were looked on with favor by Quakerism as studies of God's creation, illustrations of birds, beasts, and plants were approved. In short, so long as art served function or fact it was acceptable.

One element that increased its acceptability was the respect accorded by Quakers to the craft system. George Fox had urged a trade for every boy, with the usual seven-year apprenticeship, a practice reinforced by the prejudice among early Friends against higher education. Throughout the eighteenth century Philadelphia was full of skilled craftsmen: potters, pewterers, silversmiths, glassmakers, and above all, cabinetmakers. Savery and Affleck, Randolph and Gostelowe, Evans[13] and Letchworth, like the Townsends and Goddards of Newport, were all Quakers or of Quaker families, and the tradition lasted well into Hicks's own lifetime. Their religious discipline stressed simplicity, but said nothing against fine materials and harmonious proportion. The result varied from endearing simplicity to austere elegance. Perceiving the phenomenon, Frederick Tolles has called it the "Quaker esthetic." He even saw in the limitations imposed by the Quaker ethic a source of salutary restraint.[14]

And how does Edward Hicks relate to this tradition? Only negatively. He is an exception to the Quaker aesthetic rather than an example. The restrained elegance of the Quaker craftsmen was foreign to him. He was a primitive, while Savery and Affleck, like the Federalist cabinetmakers of his own time, could not conceivably be called such. And their craft, by its very nature, lacked the emotional and spiritual content of Hicks's work.

But the area where the painter differs most with the tradition is color. Ask anyone the color of Quakerism, and he or she will answer, "Gray." This is not quite accurate. "Drab" is more exact, a word derived from the woolen fabric woven from the fibers of both white and black sheep, and much worn by plain Friends in the eighteenth and early nineteenth centuries.[15] The combination resulted in a yellowish gray, as shown correctly by Hicks in his pyramid of Quakers in the *Banners Kingdoms*. It is a difficult shade to define—a sort of noncolor, in comparison with which white, black, or even clear gray seems relatively aggressive.

Whether called gray or drab, it is the characteristic hue of Quaker quietism. And reasonably so, for color is the most exciting of visual elements. Shun it to maintain the quiet mind and stick to drab, which evokes a minimal emotional response.

Historically, this neutral shade did not always dominate the Quaker spectrum. In the seventeenth century there were no color prohibitions. Fox, Penn, and Barclay, who stand at the top of Hicks's pyramid in uniform drab, would not have appeared thus in their own time. There was nothing uniform about early Quakerism, and not much that was drab. Pioneers of the first two generations stripped from their clothes the "superfluities," as they called them, but did not alter basic line or color.[16] One finds George Fox buying "a piece of crimson cloth for a mantle" for his wife, Margaret Fell Fox, and neither Margaret nor her daughters ever gave up colors in dress, according to the household account book.[17]

But with the eighteenth century came a more restrictive spirit. In 1738 John Reynell, a wealthy Philadelphia merchant whose prestige was equally high in both meeting house and counting house, ordered from London "2 Japan'd Black Corner Cupboards, with 2 Doors to Each, no Red in 'em, of the best Sort but Plain."[18]

"No red in 'em." Quakerism was getting uneasy about red, the color of passion. Frederick J. Nicholson, in his *Quakers and the Arts*, has called this rejection "the Quaker fear of color."[19] Why fear? Is it the quietist's fear of being seduced by sensuous delight? In general terms, yes. But the key to a more specific source of this fear may lie in Reynell's directive, "of the best Sort, but Plain." As wealth increased in the Society of Friends, clothing and house furnishings became richer. Whereas elegant fabrics had formerly been taboo,[20] silks and satins now appeared on the women. Perhaps the Quaker woman felt that she could not, morally speaking, have it both ways. So she opted for fine fabric and paid for it by renouncing color and withdrawing to a world of beautifully muted silks. This muting of color also prevailed in housewares such as china, draperies, and, as Reynell indicates, furniture. An absence of vivid color had become central to the Quaker aesthetic.

Edward Hicks, on the other hand, reveled in brightness and richness of tone. Though he was a quietist in religious belief and wore the plain coat, the pigments on his palette were not limited to the Quaker spectrum. However much his fellow meeting-goers rejected red, the painter embraced it, introducing into his *Penn Treaties* a scarlet cloak where West showed none and adorning the children of his *Peaceable Kingdoms* with scarves and sashes of the same intense hue.

One should note, however, that in his farmscapes the figures are costumed in realistically subdued tones. The clothing of the family in *Leedom Farm* is a foil to the bright red roofs of the house and farm buildings. Here Hicks has made use of what was evidently a Quaker convention of the period. Like all codes, the proscription of color had exceptions. It was permissible to show buildings as bright red. This is seen in the delightful frontispiece of *Westtown Through the Years*, a history of the famous old Quaker school in Chester County, Pennsylvania, founded in 1799.[21] Thomas Clark, who entered the school as a student in 1805, portrays the building with vermilion walls, Prussian blue shutters, and yellow trim. Helen G. Hole, author of the book, discovered that in the early days of the school the use of strong color was limited to two areas: the girls' samplers and the boys' maps and drawings of buildings. The school's Treasure Room preserves a beautiful collection of this student handiwork.

Did some such concept, referring to the historical or biblical nature of Hicks's works, free him from the restriction of color? Or did the homespun character of his product, combined with his chronic poverty, relieve the painter from the self-imposed penance of denying color? We do not know. Certain it is that he was an extraordinary phenomenon, the Quaker preacher applying vivid pigment to his canvases without a recorded word of rebuke from his Monthly Meeting.

It is possible that the element of Quaker realism enters here. Makefield Monthly Meeting was well aware that this gifted member of their flock had come near the brink of financial ruin, which would have meant for them the loss of a valuable preacher. Scruples against a paid ministry prevented them from subsidizing him financially. Perhaps they decided to settle for the feasible. If Edward could support his family by painting, "it being the only business he was able to follow," as they described it apologetically in their Memorial to him after his death, so be it.[22] They simply could not do without him. Ironically, the very ministry that was so in conflict with his painting may have protected his career as an artist.

NOTES

1. Like the vignettes in the *Kingdoms*, these were after West's *William Penn's Treaty with the Indians* (now at the Pennsylvania Academy of the Fine Arts, Philadelphia) through the medium of the Boydell/Hall engraving. See Ellen Starr Brinton, "Benjamin West's Painting of Penn's Treaty with the Indians," *Bulletin of the Friends Historical Association*, 30 (1941): 99–189. These separate treaty canvases also show the influence of two engravings by T. H. Mumford in Watson's well-known *Annals of Philadelphia*, vol. 1, facing p. 127. These illustrate Penn's arrival both at Chester and Philadelphia.

2. Holger Cahill, *American Folk Art* (New York: Museum of Modern Art, 1932), p. 3.

3. Thomas Clarkson, *Portraiture of Quakerism*, 3 vols. (London: Longmans, Hurst, Reed, Orme and Brown, 1806), 1:33.

4. Virgil Barker, *American Painting: History and Interpretation* (New York: Macmillan Co., 1950), p. 97.

5. "Extracts from the Correspondence of Charles Wilson Peale Relative to the Establishment of the Academy of the Fine Arts," *Pennsylvania Magazine of History and Biography* 9 (1885): 129.

6. Neil Harris, *The Artist in American Society: The Formative Years 1790–1860* (New York: G. Braziller, 1966), p. 60. For Protestant objection to religious art see Barker, *American Painting*, pp. 8–10.

7. William Salisbury, "American Old Masters," *The Antiquarian*, 11 (1929): 42.

8. For Barton see Mary Hoxie Jones, *Quaker Poets Past and Present* (Wallingford, Pa.: Pendle Hill, 1975), pp. 16–17.

9. John Linnell to Bernard Barton, from Portchester Terrace, Bayswater, May 10, 1830,

Quaker Collection, Haverford College, Haverford, Pa.

10. Arthur Edwin Bye, "Edward Hicks, 1780–1849," *Bulletin of the Friends Historical Association* 32 (1943): 58.

11. See Jonathan L. Fairbanks, *Benjamin L. Ferris: A Friend of Many Talents*, Catalogue of the Delaware Antiques Show (Wilmington, Del., December 1–3, 1966), pp. 77–81.

12. Quoted by Ernest Earnest, *John and William Bartram: Botanists and Explorers* (Philadelphia: University of Pennsylvania Press,1940), p. 167.

13. Uncle of Jonathan Evans, the Orthodox leader.

14. Frederick Tolles, "Of the Best Sort but Plain: The Quaker Esthetic," *American Quarterly*, 11 (1959): 484–502.

15. Clarkson, *Portraiture of Quakerism*, 1:263.

16. Amelia Mott Gummere, *The Quaker: A Study in Costume* (1901; reprint ed., New York: Benjamin Blom, 1968), pp. 16–17.

17. Elizabeth Braithwaite Emmott, *The Story of Quakerism* (London: Friends Book Centre, 1929), p. 132, and Isabel Ross, *Margaret Fell: Mother of Quakerism* (London: Longmans, Green and Co., 1949), p. 378.

18. Quoted by Tolles, "Of the Best Sort but Plain," p. 499.

19. Frederick J. Nicholson, *Quakers and the Arts* (London: Friends Home Service Commission, London Yearly Meeting, 1968), p. 57.

20. Ross, *Margaret Fell*, p. 378, and Gummere, *The Quaker*, p. 134.

21. Helen G. Hole, *Westtown through the Years*, (Westtown, Pa.: Westtown Alumni Association, 1942).

22. "A Testimony of Makefield Monthly Meeting, concerning our beloved Friend, Edward Hicks, deceased." Signed at Newtown, 10th of Fourth Month, 1851 by Joseph Flowers and Sarah P. Flowers, clerks of the men's and women's meetings. Published in *Memoirs*, pp. 1–10.

8
SIGNCRAFT AND SYMBOLISM

IN 1932 THE MUSEUM OF MODERN ART IN NEW YORK CITY HELD AN EXHIBITION ENTITLED "American Folk Art/the Art of the Common Man in America 1750–1900." It was an epoch-making event in the cultural life of the United States, and for its catalogue Holger Cahill, director of the exhibition, wrote an introduction that has become a classic.

After stressing the survival character of the objects in the show he said of those who created them, "The work of these men is folk art because it is the expression of the common people, made by them and intended for their use and enjoyment. It is not the expression of professional artists made for a small cultured class, and it has little to do with the fashionable art of its period. It does not come out of an academic tradition passed on by the schools but out of the craft tradition plus the personal quality of the rare craftsman who is an artist."[1]

Most of this comment would apply to Hicks. But was he really a folk artist? Cahill thought so; Arthur Edwin Bye disagreed. A native of Bucks County and brought up in its traditions, Bye knew that Hicks did not reflect those traditions in the same way that the Pennsylvania German artisans expressed the culture of Lancaster and Berks counties. "While it is true," Bye conceded, that "his farm scenes picture Quaker life, and his allegories illustrate a phase of Quaker thought, he stood alone and apart as a Quaker artist, as a man gifted with vision and imagination."[2]

To some extent this is a legitimate argument. Though Hicks was well integrated socially and religiously in the Society of Friends, his work does not illustrate the Quaker aesthetic, as we have pointed out. Nor can one very well call him a "common man," in spite of his references to himself as a "poor illiterate mechanic," pursuing the path of "humble industry."[3] Born in a mansion and dining off ancestral mahogany and silver, as Alice Ford has noted, he scarcely seems to qualify for the homespun reputation that has been attributed to him.[4] And entirely aside from his outward circumstances, the evolving ideas and increasing sophistication of technique that we trace in the *Kingdoms* are certainly not typical of the folk artist. Indeed, he was too extreme an individualist to be typical of anything.

But he does share certain elements with other American primitives that justify assigning his work to the realm of folk art. These were the elements to which Cahill referred when he wrote of Hicks's innocence of vision, simplicity,

56

and freshness of expression, and most of all his thorough grounding in the European craft tradition.

This tradition represented the growth of many centuries, since British signcraft, from which American sign painting was derived, had roots in the pictorial conventions of northern Europe. Dominated by the Flemish, its techniques evolved from the art of manuscript illumination. From this source, with its limitations and opportunities, came the use of oils, vibrant color, linear style, and love of detail characteristic of the late medieval period. It is not surprising, considering its derivation from the lettered page, that such art had no scruple against combining the verbal with the pictorial. Painters of the fifteenth century decorated their compositions with lettered streamers and other inscriptions, a technique that survives in Hicks's *Rhymed Border* and *Banner Kingdoms.*

When the more sophisticated artists yielded to Italian influence, the medieval flavor native to Northern Europe still lingered on shop and tavern boards. This flavor was reinforced by another inheritance from the Middle Ages, the phenomenon of heraldry with its menagerie of stylized beasts, factual and mythical. The taverns of England were frequently run by retired servants of noble households who borrowed the coats of arms of their former masters, or, if tradesmen, proclaimed the patronage of a former employer by flaunting his lion, or boar, or other heraldic symbol.

The city of London was blazoned with such insignia well into the eighteenth century, so that Joseph Addison complained, "Our streets are filled with blue boars, black swans, and red lions; not to mention flying pigs, and hogs in armor, with many other creatures more extraordinary than any in the deserts of Africa."[5] Similar colorful figures also decorated colonial cities such as Philadelphia, which "excelled in the quantity and quality of her signboards."[6] Names like the Golden Lion, Saint George and the Dragon, Noah's Ark, the Durham Ox, Sign of the Black Bear, Bacchus and the Leopard, and Bird in Hand reflect not only the contributions of heraldry but of the Bible, late classical tradition, and folklore.

The American Revolution brought changes, to be sure; the George and the Dragon became the George Washington, and the Golden Lion became the Yellow Cat. But in spite of these alterations Hicks as a sign painter fell heir to a rich treasury that compensated in color, symbolism, and the common touch for the lack of these features in Quakerism.

From this reservoir of design must have come his seated lion. In choosing the lion as the dominant figure of his *Middle Kingdoms* Hicks had fixed upon the most popular animal of the Western world. Its history as a symbol is ancient, reaching back many millennia. But of concern here is the lion of medieval heraldry, which appeared in various poses. In the warrior culture of feudalism the *lion rampant* was the favorite. It is not surprising that one never sees him thus in the *Peaceable Kingdoms.* But Hicks incorporated other poses in his *Middle* and *Late Kingdoms:* the *sejant* (seated), *passant* (walking, with one foot lifted), and *statant* (standing, with all four feet on the ground).[7] Many have their heads turned toward the viewer, an attitude called *guardant* in heraldic terms. That is, the familiar Brooklyn lion is a *lion sejant guardant.* Since Hicks was no antiquarian we assume that he took this medieval relic from a sign board.

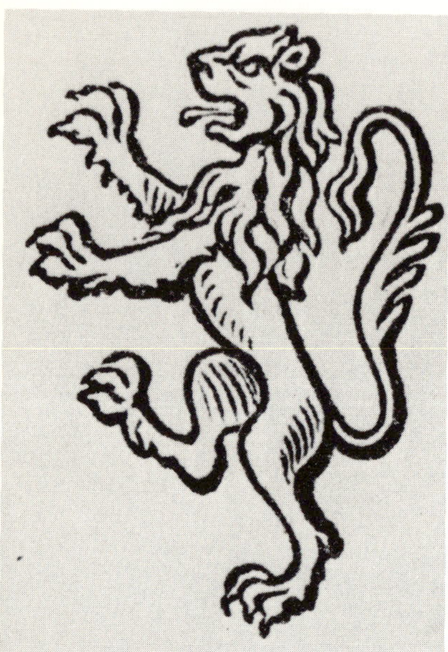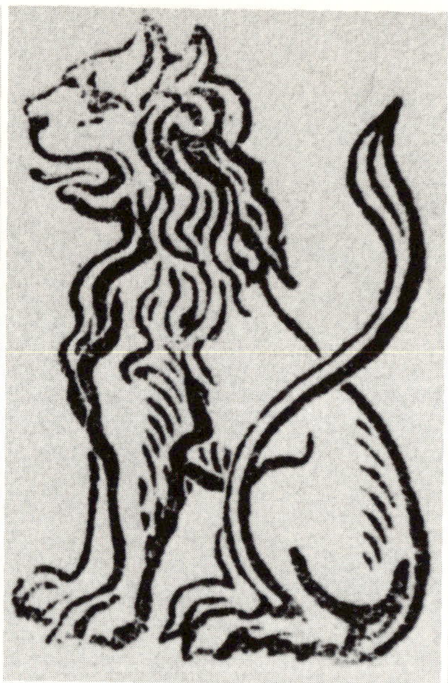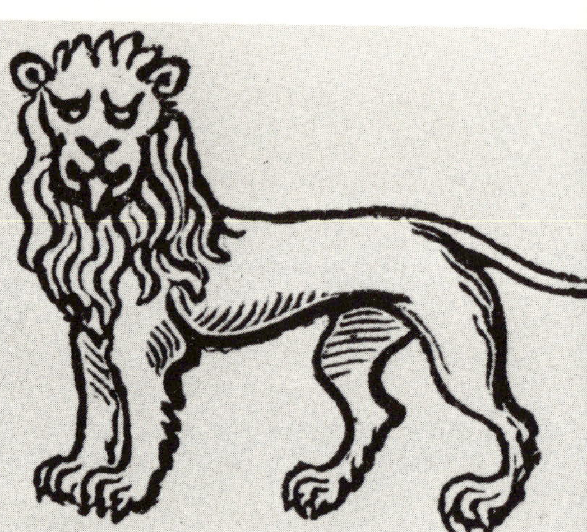

Heraldic Lions: A Medieval Legacy. Sign painters of later centuries inherited the following poses: (1) Rampant, the most popular stance of the middle ages, but never used by Hicks (2) Sejant (sitting), seen in his Peaceable Kingdoms of the early 1830s (3) Statant guardant, favored by him later in the decade. (Wood engravings by R. B. Utting from Charles Boutell, English Heraldry, rev. ed. (London, 1907), p. 85.)

Signcraft also provided him with the dove of peace. If the lion's history is a long one, so is the dove's. In fact, the bird seems indestructible. An attribute of the great mother goddess of the Mediterranean, she became the bird of Aphrodite and her Roman counterpart, Venus. Christianity transformed her into a symbol of the Holy Spirit, and with wings outspread she descends upon the Virgin in numerous pictures of the Annunciation.

But sign painter's symbology assigns her to the Old Testament as the bird of Noah, in her beak the olive branch that she carries back to the Ark in proof of the receding waters of the Flood.[8] There was a Dove and Rainbow Inn in colonial Philadelphia, as in many British towns. Silk dyers also sported the device because the varied hues of the rainbow symbolized their craft, and the London guild presented *The Deluge* as their annual mystery play at Whitsuntide.[9]

The dyers' emblem showed a bird in flight framed by a rainbow, with a bit of landscape beneath.[10] The total effect is not unlike the dove and lamb motif of certain *Rhymed Border Kingdoms*, where the dove, with olive branch, hovers above a recumbent lamb.[11]

But the British version differs from Hicks's in that the bird flies upward instead of downward. Conceivably the painter's version may have been influenced by a "moon ark" engraved by William Blake.[12] Here the dove descends toward a crescent moon that floats upon the sea much as Hicks's lamb rests upon its cushion of clouds.

So far we have dealt with what Hicks borrowed from the traditions of European signcraft. But elsewhere he reversed this process and transposed into signs the compositions of his contemporaries, most of them patriotic in subject. The earliest extant is an 1825 sign for the Newtown Library Company, painted after David Martin's "thumb portrait" of Franklin.[13] In 1834 he executed two

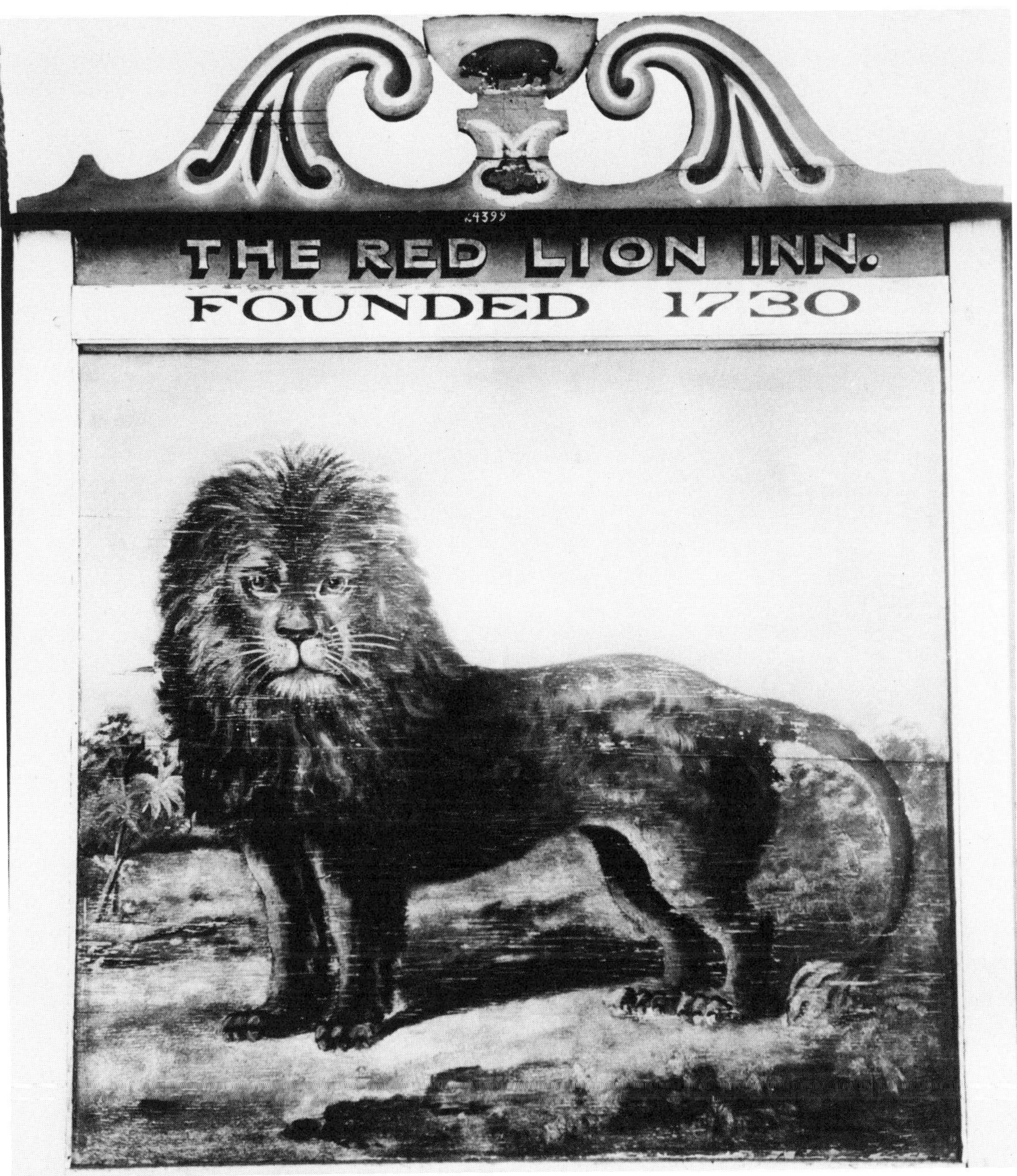

The Red Lion Inn, *Bensalem, Bucks County. Anonymous. This signboard displays a lion statant guardant that Hicks must often have seen on his journeys to Philadelphia. At the top of the board are the pig and whistle (wassail) informing travelers that food and drink are served within. (Mercer Museum of the Bucks County Historical Society, Doylestown, Pa.)*

boards after Thomas Sully's *Washington at the Passage of the Delaware,* which were placed at either end of a bridge across the river, one at Taylorsville, Pennsylvania—known in Revolutionary times as McConkey's Ferry and presently as Washington's Crossing—the other on the Jersey side. Nearly identical, they commemorate that storm-ridden night when Washington ferried his ragged army across the Delaware to make a surprise attack on the British at Trenton.

The sign from the Pennsylvania end of the bridge lay for many years in the

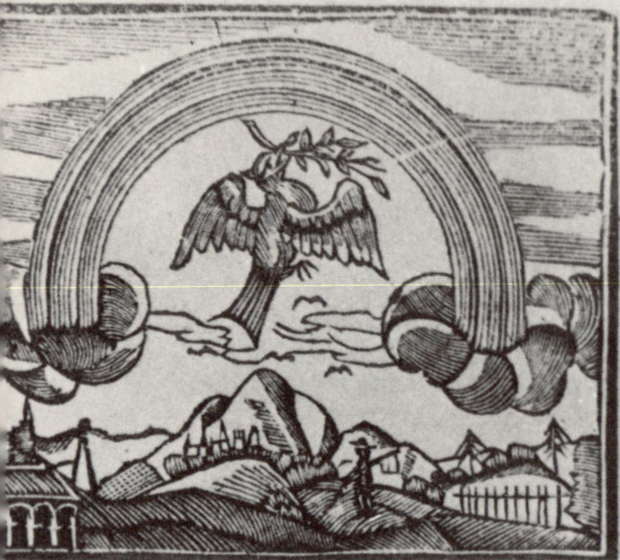

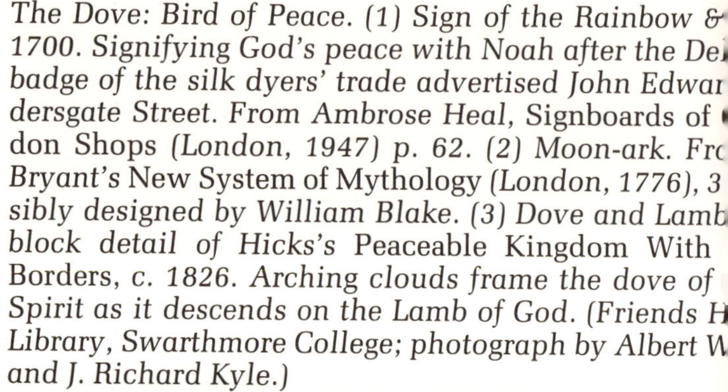

The Dove: Bird of Peace. (1) *Sign of the Rainbow &* 1700. *Signifying God's peace with Noah after the De[luge], badge of the silk dyers' trade advertised John Edwar[d] dersgate Street. From Ambrose Heal,* Signboards of [Lon]don Shops *(London, 1947) p. 62. (2) Moon-ark. Fr[om] Bryant's* New System of Mythology *(London, 1776), 3[,] sibly designed by William Blake. (3) Dove and Lamb block detail of Hicks's* Peaceable Kingdom With [Letters] Borders, *c. 1826. Arching clouds frame the dove of [Holy] Spirit as it descends on the Lamb of God. (Friends H[istorical] Library, Swarthmore College; photograph by Albert W[eber] and J. Richard Kyle.)*

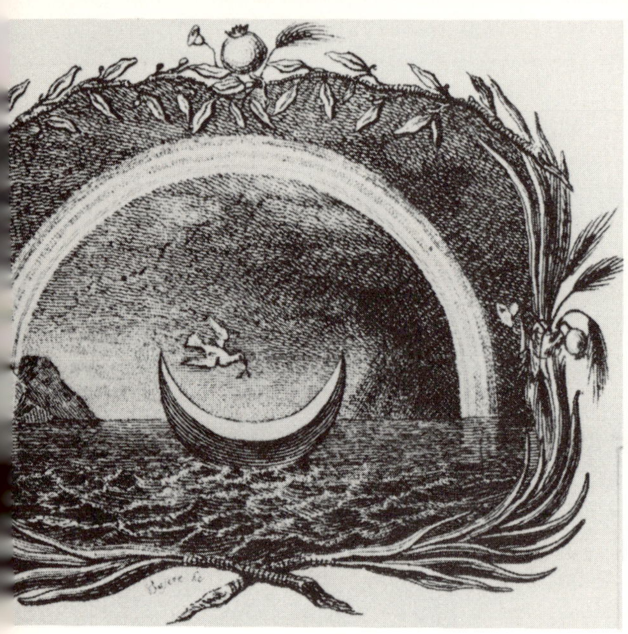

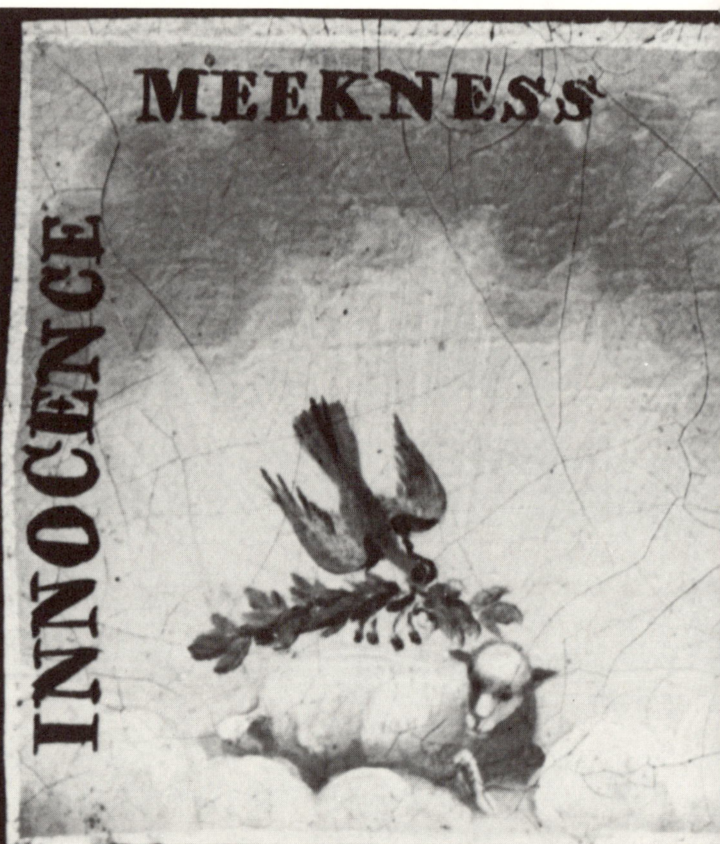

attic of Mahlon Taylor's store before a subsequent owner presented it to Henry Chapman Mercer, who placed it in the museum at Doylestown that bears his name. This occurred in 1889, forty years after the death of Edward Hicks. Mercer may rightly be called the first collector of Hicks's works—not as art objects but as local antiquities. Archaeologist and curator of the Bucks County Historical Society, he was also the great grandson of Abraham Chapman from whom the painter bought his first house in Newtown, and as a child had heard tales of the artist/preacher and seen his paintings on family walls.

Tradition tells of another signboard at the Ferry Inn, Taylorsville, presenting on one side a Noah's Ark, on the other a fleet of the sturdy Durham boats that conveyed Washington's soldiers across the river.[14] But a better known memorial of that fateful night was the Washington sign, no longer existing, that adorned Joseph Archambault's Brick Hotel, the former Red Lion in Newtown. Mounted on top of a pole, this work bore on its reverse *The Declaration of*

Independence, after Trumbull, probably taken from the frontispiece for Goodrich's *Lives of the Signers to the Declaration of Independence*, a copy of which the artist owned.[15] And traceable on a wall in the handsome foyer of the hotel—which still welcomes patrons under its current name of the Oppert Arms—is a mural design reputedly by Hicks: an eagle, facing left, accompanied by an American flag and other banners.

In an upper room of this inn Lafayette is said to have entertained Hessian officers after their capture at Trenton. Newtown, indeed, served as the base for Washington's successful exploit, a fact unfortunately overlooked by most historians. It is small wonder that the memory of this dramatic event lingered long in the mind of the artist and his neighbors, who in their youth must have hung upon the stories of participants and eyewitnesses.

A little-known facet of the famous attack is the contribution of Robert Morris, financier of the Revolution, as reflected in a sign at the Mercer Museum of the Bucks County Historical Society. One side is a portrait of Morris; the reverse depicts him accepting from a plainly dressed man a bag of money marked "10,000." The scene is explained by an anecdote in Goodrich. Seeking funds to pay for military intelligence necessary for the capture of Trenton, Morris met by chance an old Quaker who lent the required sum with no security but his word.[16] "Thy word is thy bond," reads the inscription.

The attribution to Hicks has been questioned because "Pictorial Sign Company of Philadelphia" is stamped in the lower right corner of the reverse. But this may well have been the imprint of a firm to which the sign was sent for repair. A newspaper reference of 1875 has recently been discovered that assigns the work to Hicks.[17] Most significantly, the illustrated episode would be extremely appealing to the Quaker limner who, as an ardent patriot, was probably embarrassed by the neutral attitude of the Society of Friends during the Revolution. And the use of the plain language in the inscription likewise suggests his hand.

Hicks also painted a signboard for the Bird-in-Hand, the oldest building in Newtown.[18] The name of this former tavern is believed to have been taken from the Franklin adage "A bird in the hand is worth two in the bush." But both the proverb and its application to a public house were ancient long before Franklin's era,[19] there being at one time 174 houses of this name in England. The Newtown building has been attractively renovated by Edward R. Barnsley, local historian and antiquarian, who, around 1939, designed the sign that now hangs in front of the old tavern. Patterned after an eighteenth-century engraving by Hogarth, it was painted by Barnsley's friend and fellow townsman Thomas Bayard Beatty, and shows a human hand closing on a bird.[20] But what Hicks's original sign was like we do not know.

NOTES

1. Holger Cahill, *American Folk Art* (New York: Museum of Modern Art, 1932), p. 6. In 1932–33 Cahill was acting director of the Museum of Modern Art. See Alice Winchester, *The Flowering of American Folk Art*, exhibition catalogue (New York: Viking Press and Whitney Museum of American Art, 1974), pp. 12–13 (introduction).

2. Arthur Edwin Bye, "Edward Hicks, 1780–1849," *Bulletin of the Friends Historical Association* 32 (1943): 59–60.

3. The title of Hicks's famous sermon on the peaceable kingdom at Goose Creek was "A Little Present for Friends and Friendly People in the Form of a Miscellaneous Discourse by a Poor Illiterate Mechanic." He made many

references to "humble industry" in his *Memoirs*.

4. Alice Ford, *Edward Hicks: Painter of the Peaceable Kingdoms* (Philadelphia: University of Pennsylvania Press, 1952), p. 27, and n. 2, p. 122.

5. From the *Spectator* (1710), quoted by Alice Morse Earle, *Stagecoach and Tavern Days* (New York: Macmillan Co., 1900, p. 140.

6. Alice Morse Earle, *Home Life in Colonial Days* (New York: Macmillan Co., 1898), p. 359.

7. Charles Boutell, *English Heraldry* (London: Reeves & Turner, 1907), pp. 84, 87.

8. George Ferguson, *Signs and Symbols in Christian Art* (New York: Oxford University Press, 1954), pp. 15–16.

9. Jacob Larwood and John Camden Hotten, *The History of Signboards from the Earliest Times to the Present Day* (London: John Camden Hotten, 1866), p. 259.

10. Sir Ambrose Heal, *Signboards of Old London Shops*, (London: B. T. Batsford, 1947) p. 62.

11. The combination of the dove of Noah and the lamb, representing Christ, unite the Old and New Testaments. This union evidently appealed to the painter, who, in a sermon at Rose Street Meeting, May 15, 1825, said, "How descriptive is the dove of the state of youth and innocence. It takes to itself the wings of the morning, light and active, and flies to the uttermost parts of the earth. But are there not some of you who find no rest for the sole of your foot? . . . Come you away to Christ, of whom Noah was the antetype, and here find rest for your souls." *Sermons Delivered by Elias Hicks and Edward Hicks / in Friends Meetings*, taken in shorthand by L. H. Clarke and Marcus T. C. Gould (New York, 1825), pp. 67–68. Of course, it is also possible to interpret both dove and lamb in New Testament terms; see Catalogue No. 13.

12. The work is signed by Basire, the engraver to whom Blake was apprenticed in 1774–76, but Ruthven Todd, a Blake authority, believes it to be the product of Basire's gifted pupil, since Blake did several moon arks in his subsequent *Jerusalem* (1804–18). The vignette served as a tail piece for vol. 3 of Jacob Bryant's *A New System or An Analysis of Ancient Mythology*, 3 vols. (London: For T. Payne, P. Elsmsley, *et al*, 1774–76). See Kathleen Raine, *William Blake* (New York: Praeger, 1971), p. 14.

13. Edna Pullinger, *Newtown's First Library Building*, vol. 1, Bicenntenial publication of the Newtown Library Company (Newtown, Pa., 1976), p. 6.

14. Letter from Henry Chapman Mercer to the *Doylestown Intelligencer*, April 10, 1889, Fonthill MSS., series 22, fol. 4, p. 28, courtesy of Cleota Reed, who is researching the life and work of Mercer.

15. Ford, *Edward Hicks*, p. 66.

16. Charles A. Goodrich, *The Lives of the Signers to the Declaration of Independence* (New York: William Reed & Co., 1829), pp. 236–37.

17. Discovered by Terry A. McNealy, director of the Spruance Library, Bucks County Historical Society, in the *Doylestown Democrat*, June 8, 1875, BCHS files.

18. Pullinger, *Newtown's First Library Building*, p. 6.

19. In Roman times Plutarch (46–120 A.D.) wrote, "He is a fool who lets slip a bird in the hand for a bird in the bush," trans. John Dryden, ed. Arthur Clough Hough in John Bartlett, *Familiar Quotations*, eds. Christopher Morley and Louella D. Everett (Boston: Little and Co., 1951), p. 1120.

20. Information from Edward R. Barnsley, courtesy of his son-in-law, Robert H. Bartels of Newtown.

9
LIONS IN PROFILE

One aspect of Hicks's charm is his naiveté. Like a child, he does not cover his tracks. In the large 1834 *Seated Lion*[1] now in the National Gallery the painter is uncertain as to which of two leopard poses to choose. He settles the problem by giving both, the full face and staring eyes of one projecting like a paper cutout above the crouching form of the other, whose nose one of the children leans over to pat—an endearing touch unique in the *Kingdoms*.

This double exposure prefigures a new category: *Lions in Profile*. Here is a lion *statant*, or standing, a heraldic pose often seen on signboards. The Bucks County Historical Society has among its fine collection one such board. It was not made by Hicks but must often have been seen by him. Topped with a "pig and whistle" (pig and wassail, indicating both food and drink), it attracted wayfarers to a popular tavern on the route to Philadelphia. John Adams, one of its patrons, wrote, "A good dinner, a cold glass of milk and excellent company the traveller always finds at the Red Lion."[2] The old sign stood just within the Bucks County line at Bensalem, and the artist, as he rode up the Bristol Turnpike on his return from the city and its hostilities, must have seen it as a friendly beacon welcoming him to home territory.

Hicks's *Profile* lion does not stand alone. Like all the carnivorous beasts of the Kingdom he has as a companion the animal who is his natural prey. This is not the lamb, as many otherwise well-informed viewers assume. Though the lion may lie down with the lamb elsewhere,[3] in the *Peaceable Kingdoms* he never lies down with anyone. And if he did, it would not be with the lamb, who is opposite to the wolf in the Old Testament prophecy. Hicks was too scrupulous biblically to place the lamb otherwise than as Isaiah directed, and Isaiah was too much of a realist to pair the lion with an animal so small that he would be a mere snack. The Hebrew prophet lived closer to the wilderness than we do and knew that the great cat's natural prey was the antelope, or, among domestic beasts, the ox.

The pairing of lion and bovine has haunted the Mediterranean world since ancient times, one symbolizing the sun, the other the moon.[4] It is inconceivable that Hicks was consciously aware of this sun/moon contrast. But in a fine example of a *Profile Kingdom* at the Everson Museum in Syracuse, New York, the golden splendor of the lion's mane and the twin silver crescents of the ox's

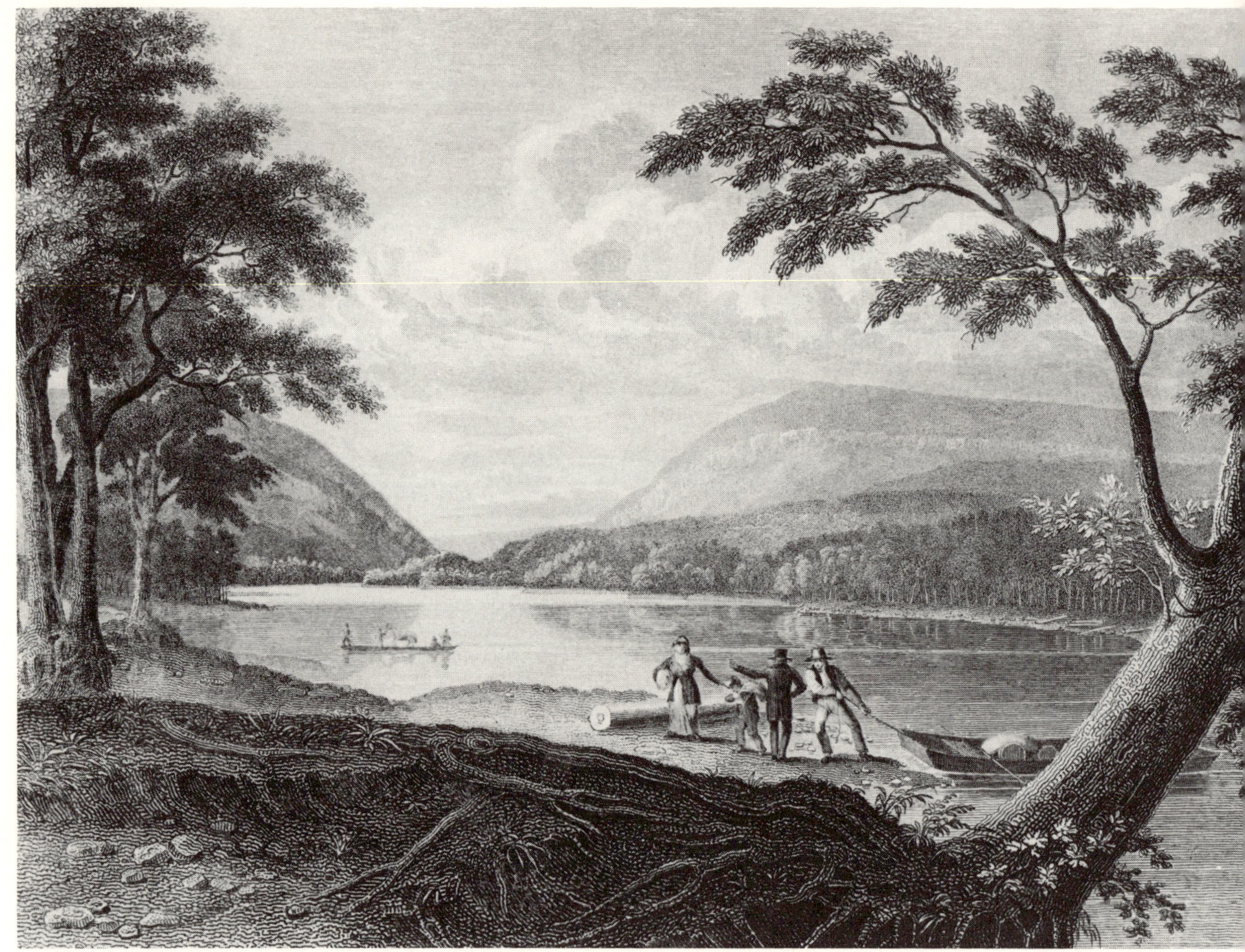

View on the Delaware, *drawn and engraved by Asher B. Durand (1796–1886), portrayed the Delaware Water Gap in the first and only number of* The American Landscape, *New York, 1830. (Historical Society of Pennsylvania, Philadelphia.)*

horns reveal an innate grasp of symbol that goes far beyond the stereotypes of
traditional signcraft.

In the background of this canvas, and in all subsequent *Kingdoms*, is the
Delaware Water Gap, probably taken from an 1830 engraving by Asher B.
Durand.

One wonders how the painter came in contact with this work. Was he seated
in the parlor of some affluent New York Friend—either before or after an excellent dinner—leafing through a portfolio of Durand's well-known *American
Landscape* series, and was his eye suddenly and irretrievably caught by "View
on the Delaware"? Or did his daughter Susan send him a newspaper clipping
from the *New-York Mirror*, which reproduced the engraving over the title
"Delaware Water-Gap"?[5] In 1832 Susan had married John Carle, a prosperous
New York apothecary, and thenceforth there was a steady interchange between
the metropolis and Newtown.

One is apt to think of Hicks as living in a small and isolated world surviving
from an earlier age, as reflected in his nostalgic scene of Twining Farm. In point
of fact, he did inhabit such a world, but he was no recluse. His preaching made

him known to Friends and non-Friends alike far beyond the areas where he appeared in person. His nephew and namesake, Edward Hicks Kennedy, reporting from Saint Louis on a local dispute, quoted an old lady as protesting, "What would Mr. Hicks say to such manoevres?" "What Mr. Hicks?" asked young Kennedy. "Why the famous Quaker preacher in Pennsylvania" was the prompt answer.[6]

Likewise, his art, though shaped by a tradition centuries old before he was born, was also open to contemporary influences. We have noted his borrowings from Westall, Tanner, Sully, and Trumbull, to which we now add Durand, leading exponent of the Hudson River school.

By the mid-1830s the painter was incorporating in his *Kingdoms* the kneeling figure of a girl in white, a dove on her upraised right hand, and an eagle drinking from a goblet at her left knee. The dove was probably Hicks's own contribution,[7] but the constellation of girl, cup, and eagle was a popular one in neoclassical art. Louis C. Jones has traced its source to William Hamilton's *Hebe* (1791), where the goddess, as cupbearer of the Olympians, proffers refreshment to the eagle of Zeus; he cites various derivations therefrom, including Edward Savage's *Liberty as the Goddess of Youth*.[8]

In consequence, Savage's engraving has been referred to as a Hicks source. But Savage's pose is completely different from Hicks's, though the same symbolic elements are present. The two would appear to be parallel developments from Hamilton's work, rather than a derivation one from the other. Of course, Hicks may have taken his design from a source other than a print, such as the side panels of a city fire engine. These panels, decorated with mermaids, water nymphs, and scantily clad goddesses, represented the "cheesecake" of their day. When the alarm rang the treasured panels were left in the safety of the firehouse, but they appeared in their full glory in the city parades, accompanied by elaborately hatted and caped firemen. The Hibernia Company, one of Philadelphia's many volunteer fire companies, sported Hebe and the eagle, painted, presumably, by the popular commercial artist John A. Woodside. The pose is not identical with Hicks's, but it is closer to it than is the Savage engraving. Some day the exact source may turn up. If it does, we will probably find that the object in Hebe's upraised hand is a jug of wine, which Hicks, a peace-loving temperance man, replaced with a dove.

Symbols have a tenacious life of their own. The image survives, though the meaning changes. An example is the eagle, which is to birds what the lion is to animals. Representing power from the earliest times, it adorned the royal escutcheons of Hapsburgs, Hohenzollerns, and Romanoffs, only to be transformed into the bird of liberty at the close of the eighteenth century. This national emblem comes from the naturalistic eagle of republican Rome, after which the young American nation patterned itself.

It was probably as a patriotic symbol that Hicks introduced the Hebe vignette into his canvases. But in doing so he added another pair of opposites to his *Kingdom*: the eagle and the dove. Isaiah does not mention them, but Hicks's Yankee contemporary, the Reverend Jonathan Fisher of Blue Hill, Maine, writes in his poetic version of the Peaceable Kingdom:

> Why does a God of boundless power,
> And of unmeasured skill,

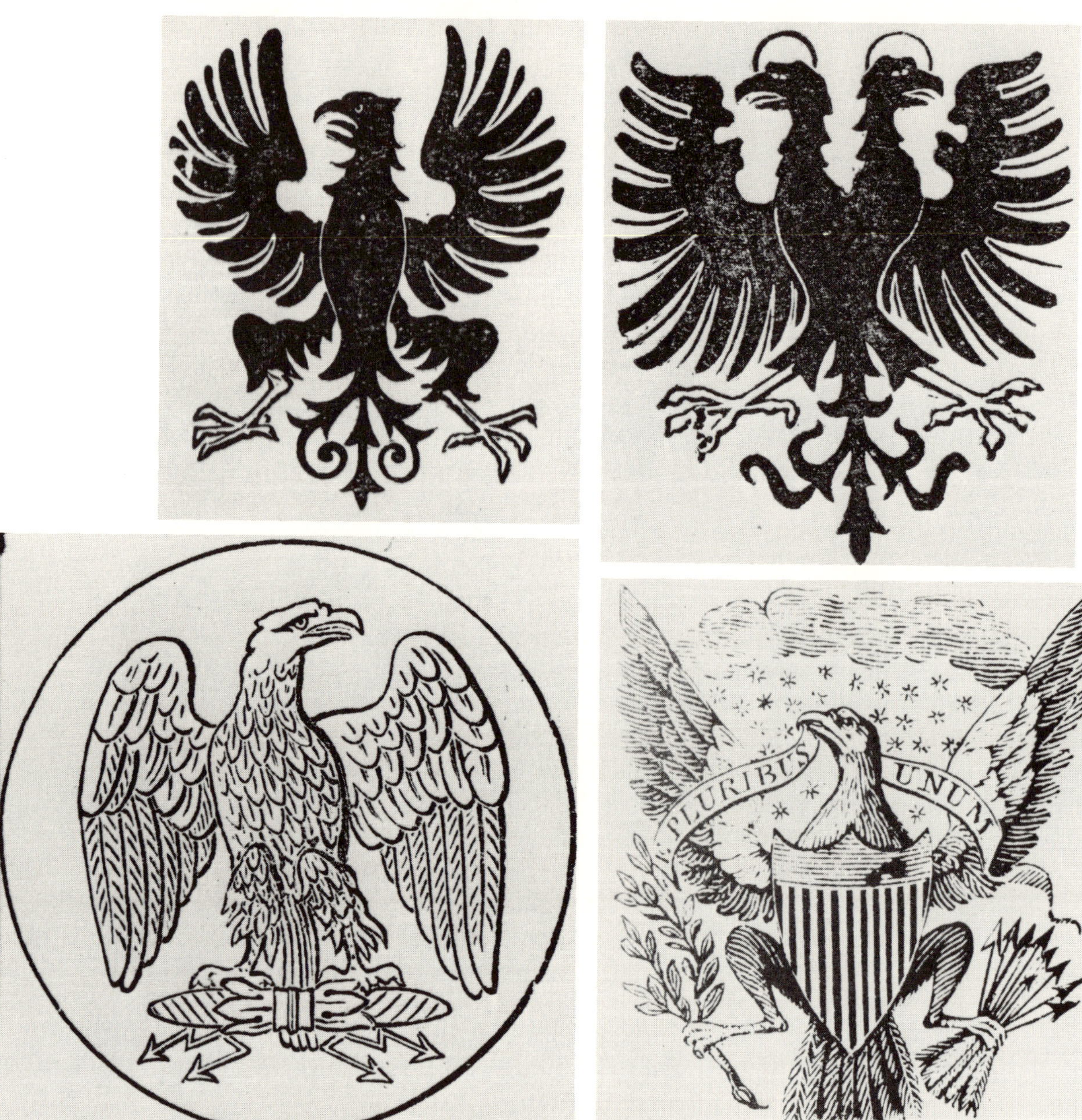

The Eagle: A Symbol of Power. Known in classical times as the bird of Zeus and Jupiter, the eagle has since varied in form: (1) Heraldic eagle of medieval Europe, with wings displayed. (2) Double-headed eagle of the Austrian, German, and Russian empires. (3) Napolean's imperial eagle, holding in its claws the thunderbolt of Jupiter. (4) The American eagle, naturalistic in detail but here, as in Hicks's Wm. Wood's Tavern Sign, heraldic in pose. (Engravings 1, 2, and 3 by R. B. Utting, Charles Boutell's English Heraldry (London, 1907), p. 99.

> Permit one creature to devour
>   Another at his will?
>
> The wolf devours the harmless lamb,
>   The eagle tears the dove;
> How shall we vindicate the name
>   Of him who reigns above?[10]

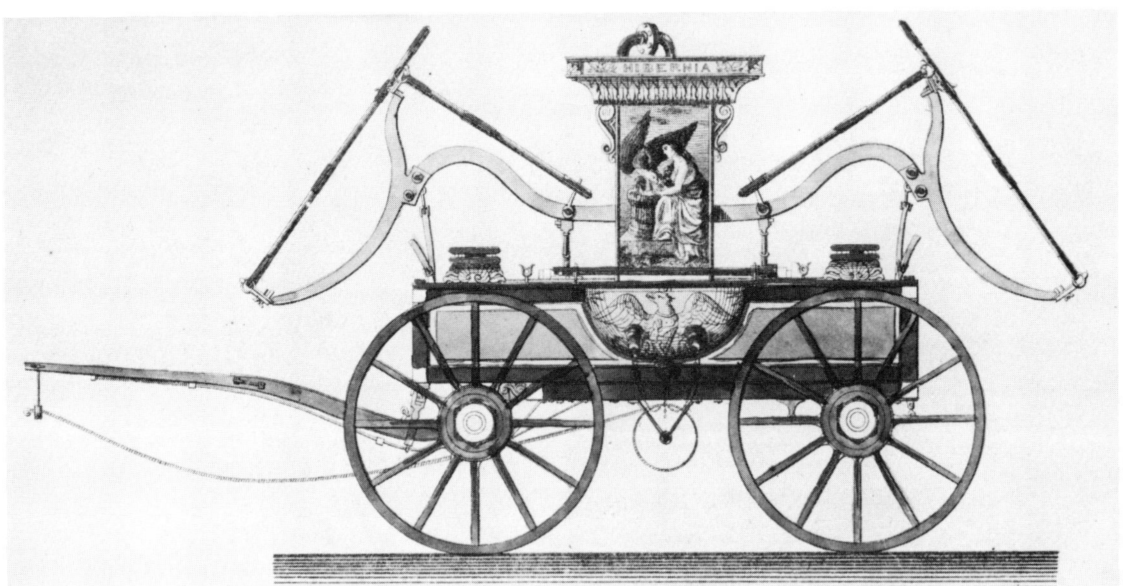

Hicks saw the eagle as a symbol of liberty, and painted it in many works, including *Liberty, Meekness, and Innocence*. This title evidently reconciled the artist/preacher to the un-Quakerly figures of the goddess Hebe and the eagle of Zeus, a combination then popular in many media, from needlework to the decoration of fire engines: (1) Hibernia Engine Comp. No. 1, Philadelphia, 1828, engraving by J. Kohn. Decorative panels attributed to John A. Woodside. (Courtesy of the Philadelphia Contributionship for the Insurance of Houses.) (2) *Hebe Feeding Zeus in the Form of an Eagle*, panel from Aetna No. 16 Fire Engine Company, New York, c, 1832. Oil on wood, 28 × 17¼ inches. (INA Corporation Museum, Philadelphia).

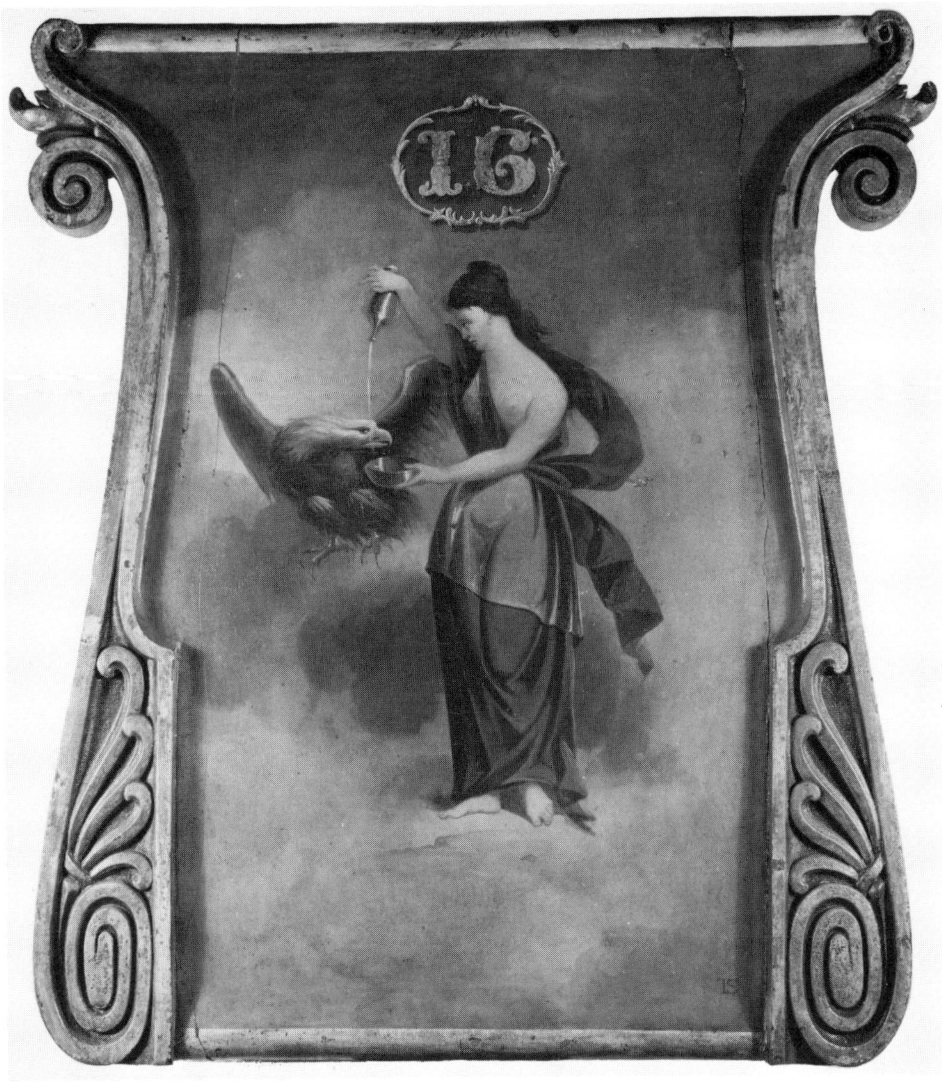

This was a question that Hicks probably never asked. Certainly by the time he reached the *Middle Kingdoms* he was not concerned with animals as such, but with the human qualities they represent.

In February of 1837 he visited Goose Creek Meeting in Loudon County, Virginia. There he preached a sermon on the nature of man and his relation to the divine in terms of the Kingdom animals.[11] These he identified with the medieval humors: the melancholy wolf, the sanguine leopard, the phlegmatic bear, and the choleric lion. All human beings are ruled by one of these four temperaments. If they remain in their natural state they will destroy one another. But if they yield self-will to the Divine Will they may be reborn into the gentle spirit of the lamb, the kid, the cow, or the ox.

He makes some specific comments that are worth noting. There are many Quaker wolves, he tells us. Sober, industrious, and frugal, they are prone to hypocrisy. But if they will submit their wolfish nature to the light of Christ Within, they may become as innocent as lambs, and he cites George Fox and John Woolman as examples of this spiritual rebirth.

Though Quakerism has many wolves, it has few leopards. These symbols of sensation and rapture do not find quietism congenial. However, they are "quite disposed to be religious, provided they can have it on their own terms; but it must be spotted, like the beautiful animal that rules in them, and full of excitement and activity,"[12] such as that provided by the popular revival meetings of the period. As for bears, they are able, matter-of-fact characters, indifferent to the sufferings of their fellow creatures until transformed into the generous cow, and he recalls a kindly Quaker merchant who helped him when he was on the brink of financial disaster.[13]

It is interesting to compare what Hicks says with what he paints. However dominant the wolf and bear may be in the Quaker community, they are not prominent on his canvases. They evidently do not engage the painter's interest because he does not identify himself with either of them. He knows that he can never become a pious wolf, much less a practical bear. But a volatile leopard, yes, and most certainly a hot-tempered lion.

In the majestic lion the artist/preacher saw willful, contentious leaders like himself who, through excess of zeal, had brought upon the Society of Friends the tragedy of the Hicksite-Orthodox Separation. For he was desperately aware that the lion's sins were his own: his quick temper, his wayward tongue, his barbed wit, and that elation in his gift for the ministry that he tried constantly to repress.

This was the way Hicks looked to himself. How did he appear to others? Fortunately at about this period his apprentice cousin, Thomas Hicks, painted a portrait of him. Tom Hicks was not more than fifteen when he produced this work, but he had already developed a gift for significant details such as the pugnacious nose, the kindly eyes, the tell-tale flecks of scarlet pigment on the palette and sombre coat. Edward sits in his Windsor chair with brush in hand, spectacles pushed back on his forehead, as if pausing for a moment of rest. Beside him lies an open Bible, and on his easel is a *Peaceable Kingdom* like the beautiful and familiar version from the late 1830s in the Cahill Collection.

On this canvas the lion stands to the extreme right. His woeful eyes reveal the anguish of guilt. Above him towers the ox, his lyre-shaped horns emphasizing his height and growing presence. He has become a sort of superego, embodying

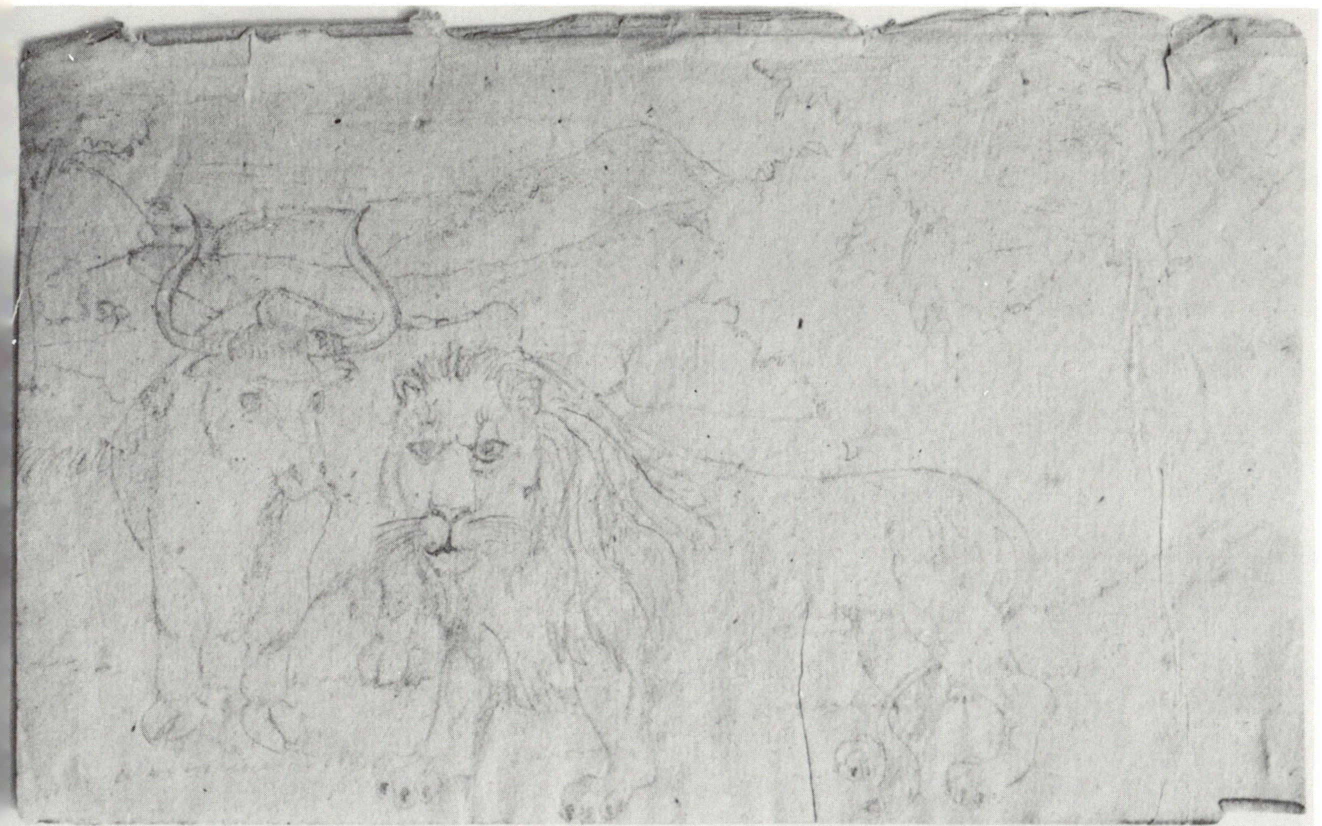

Study of Lion and Ox, 1835–40. Pencil, 5 × 8⅛ inches. Drawn on the *flyleaf of an old book, this anonymous sketch indicates a clear understanding of the Peaceable Kingdoms of the late 1830s, for it selects the most significant pair of animals in relation to Hicks's message at this period, and sets them against the appropriate Kingdom background. (Kenneth C. Lindsey and Ann McCoy Weymouth, Antiques [Gallery], Chadds Ford, Pa.; photograph by Peter Ralston.)*

a moral excellence that the poor lion feels he can never attain. This contrast between those who are good and those who are not so good is not the reconciliation of opposites that Isaiah prophesied.

But it is what Hicks was preaching at the time. He was telling human lions, like himself, that their only hope lay in acquiring the patient docility of the ox. This was the counsel of the Quaker quietist. It would have been rejected stoutly by William Blake, who maintained that "One Law for the Lion and the Ox is Oppression."[14] For in *The Marriage of Heaven and Hell* he, too, struggled with the tension of the opposites.

Hicks and Blake had much in common: their self-education and craft training, their love of children and animals, their inward vision and symbolism, most of all their preoccupation with the Bible and search for a new Jerusalem.

There are also similarities between the Goose Creek Sermon and Blake's early work *The Gates of Paradise* (1793). Its frontispiece bore the inscription "What is man?" beneath a caterpillar chrysalis with the face of a human child,[15] suggesting, as did Hicks, a rebirth of spirit. The work also includes figures symbolizing water, earth, air, and fire,[16] the elements that the Quaker preacher, early in his sermon, identified with the fourfold nature of humanity and its various humors. Where Hicks acquired these fragments of late classical and medieval lore we do not know. But they had been with him for a decade. In 1827 he said in a sermon, "The outward man, being of the earth, earthy, is composed of the four principal elements."[17]

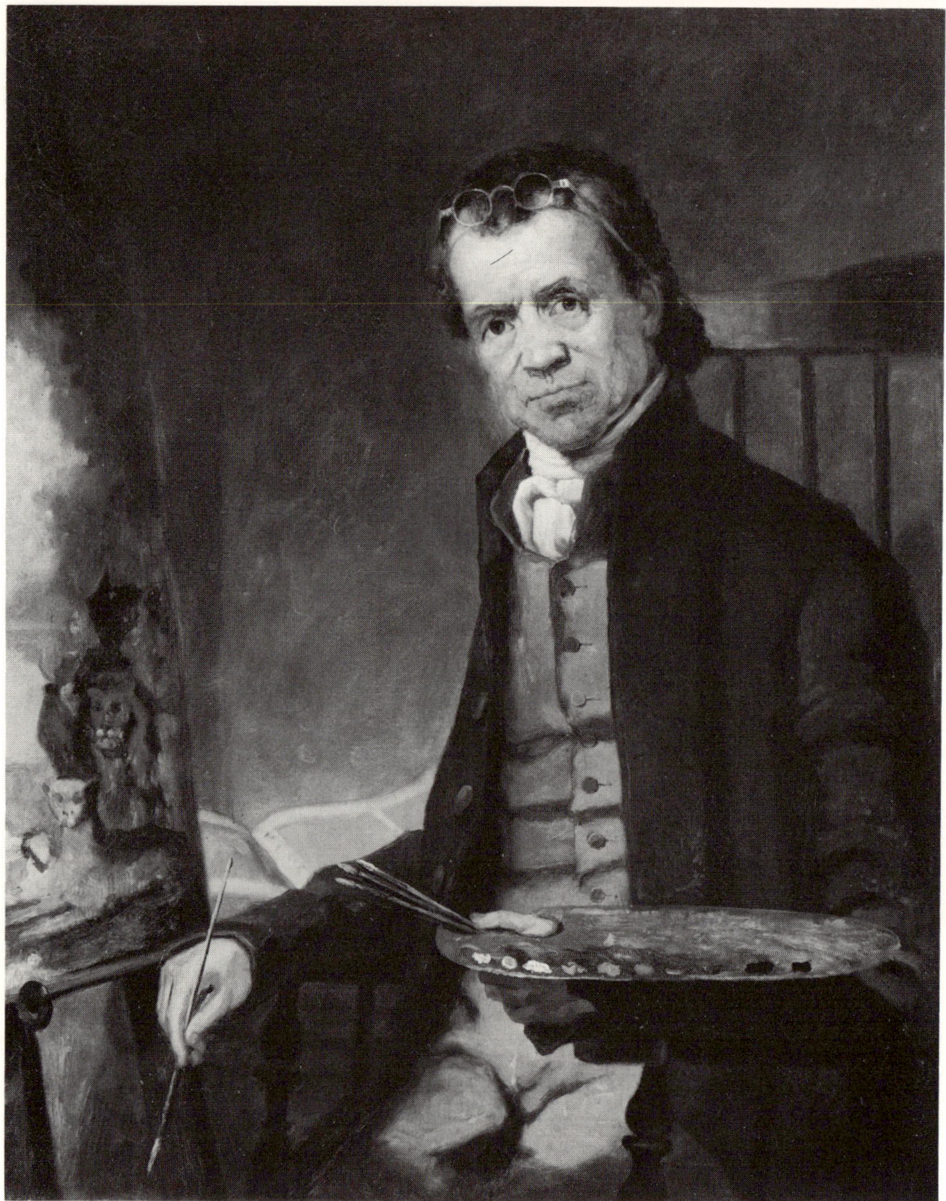

Portrait of Edward Hicks, *ca. 1838, painted by his cousin Thomas Hicks (1823–90), his apprentice for several years and later a noted portraitist. The work was exhibited at the National Academy of Design, New York, in 1838 and 1842. (Abby Aldrich Rockefeller Folk Art Center, Williamsburg, Virginia.)*

Both Hicks and Blake considered the destiny of man their province. Both saw salvation in a spiritual rebirth. But rebirth into what? Hicks recommended the patient ox. Blake proffered Orc, a sort of Divine Child flaming with energy and impulse.[18]

In the course of time each modified his concept. For Hicks this did not come for some years. Throughout the 1830s he was oppressed by the tyranny of opposites inherent in the moral dualism of quietism, made acute by the impact of the Separation. But with the closing of the decade a shifting of attitudes came with changing outward circumstances.

The fledgling Hicksite Yearly Meeting of Philadelphia had survived the ordeal of its sudden and premature birth and had adjusted to new responsibilities. It far outnumbered the Orthodox in certain areas. And in 1839 Jonathan Evans died—Evans, who had nodded approval of Edward when as a young minister he had first preached in the Lions' Den of Pine Street Meeting, Evans the friend, and later the bitter opponent of Elias Hicks.[19]

In 1840 Edward wrote his old friend Hugh Balderston, who had sided with the Orthodox, "I can not help thinking of the man we met with ten years ago travelling in the Western country [Ohio]. He was a very respectable looking man, and he addressed my companion with this language, 'Have you Quakers done quarrelling yet? I think you ought to be ashamed of yourselves.' Oh, dear Hugh, I think so too."[20]

NOTES

1. See No. 34 in Catalogue.

2. Terry A. McNealy, "The Red Lion Inn," *Bucks County Historical Society Journal* 1 (1974): 6. See also William J. Buck, "The Red Lion Inn, Bensalem Township," *Bucks County Historical Society Papers* (Easton, Pa., 1885), 1:485–488.

3. J. E. Cirlot, *A Dictionary of Symbols* (New York: Philosophical Library, 1962), p. 168.

4. Ibid., p. 181; for *ox* see p. 236. See also Joseph Campbell, *Occidental Mythology* (New York: Viking Press, 1964), pp. 57–58.

5. Bound opposite title page of vol. 11; June 7, 1834; under print is "Drawn and engraved by A. B. Durand" and "Printed by Illman and Pilbrow." Information courtesy of A. K. Baragwanath, senior curator, Museum of the City of New York. See also John Durand, *The Life and Times of A. B. Durand* (1894, reprint ed., New York: Kennedy Graphics, 1970), pp. 72–73.

6. Alice Ford, *Edward Hicks: Painter of the Peaceable Kingdom* (Philadelphia: University of Pennsylvania, 1952), p. 68.

7. Sometime in the mid-1830s Hicks painted a small canvas (14 × 9¾″) entitled *Liberty, Meekness, and Innocence*, showing eagle, dove, and white-robed girl with a lamb at her right. See Catalogue No. 79.

8. Louis C. Jones, "Liberty and Considerable License," *The Magazine Antiques*, July 1958, pp. 40–43.

9. Engraving by J. Kohn of Hibernia Engine in "Circular" soliciting contributions, dated October 6, 1828. Courtesy of Carol Wojtowicz, curator, Mutual Assurance Company Museum, Philadelphia.

10. Jonathan Fisher, *Scripture Animals*, fwd. Mary Ellen Chase (1834; reprint ed., Princeton, N.J.: Pyne Press, 1972), p. 191.

11. Published under the title *A Little Present for Friends and Friendly People, in the Form of a Miscellaneous Discourse, by a poor Illiterate Mechanic* (Philadelphia, 1846). Reprinted in *Memoirs*, pp. 267–331.

12. Ibid., p. 291.

13. Ibid., pp. 314–15.

14. June K. Singer, *The Unholy Bible: A Psychological Interpretation of William Blake* (New York: Harper & Row, 1970), p. 170.

15. Kathleen Raine, *William Blake* (Praeger, 1971), p. 37.

16. Ibid., pp. 64–65.

17. "Sermon at Carpenters' Hall, Philadelphia, Afternoon of August 19, 1827," *The Quaker* 2 (1827):193.

18. Singer, *The Unholy Bible*, pp. 201–7.

19. Hicks later wrote of Evans, "I believe what I said of him was true; that he was a choleric man, and too much like myself, malignant and bitter toward his enemies, which he supposed we were, and called us Hicksites, separatists, infidels, etc. But I cannot help considering him as honest as Saul of Tarsus, and when Jesus Christ was revealed in him, and established his kingdom, the lion ate straw like the ox" (*Memoirs*, p. 138).

20. January 25, 1840 (FHL). Balderston had been presiding clerk of Baltimore Yearly Meeting.

PART 3
A DECADE OF RECONCILIATION

10

ARCHING LEOPARDS

IF THE TENSION OF THE *MIDDLE KINGDOMS* REFLECTS THE GUILT THAT CAME IN THE WAKE OF the Separation, the more tranquil mood of Hicks's last period is due to the artist's sense of approaching death and his need to make peace with himself and others.

On his sixty-third birthday—April 4, 1843—he began the preparation of his *Memoirs*, in which he summed up his life and his relation to the Quakerism of which he had so long been a part. In so doing he was following the pattern set by many Friends' ministers. But his *Memoirs* was not at all a typical Quaker journal. Though he dwelt at length on the inward and religious aspects of life, he also made a good many crisp comments about his fellow Quakers. These are interesting to read but proved embarrassing to his friends when faced with the problem of publishing them, as Alice Ford has indicated.[1]

A month after the painter undertook this enterprise his youngest daughter, Sarah, married Isaac G. Parry, son of the kindly Abington elder who journeyed with him to Niagara Falls. The birth of Phoebe Ann Carle a decade earlier had made him a grandfather, and with June of 1844 came a grandson and namesake, Edward Hicks Carle, referred to by the artist as "dear little Ned."[2]

But there were other changes going on in the greater life around him. It was a different world from that in which he had pursued his fearful way to Pine Street Meeting House on his first ministerial journey to Philadelphia. Then the city streets had echoed to martial music, since the War of 1812 was in progress. Now peaceful and thriving trade had replaced conflict with the British. The American eagle was pushing westward, and in the area of public transportation the shrill horn of the stagecoach had yielded to the steam whistle of the iron horse.

Even as conservative a realm as Bucks County Quakerdom felt the impact of change. By mid-1844 Joseph Watson, a prosperous Friend of Middletown

72

Township, had built for his growing family a house on the Bristol to Newtown Road, filling it with a wealth of curly maple furniture and commissioning a *Peaceable Kingdom* from Edward Hicks.

Unfortunately there is no picture of the Watson interior. But a direct descendant, Jane Brey, has given a detailed description of its furnishings.[3] There is also a silhouette by August Edouart of another Quaker household of the period: the Underhills in their summer home on the Eastern Shore of Maryland.[4] This attractive period piece shows the sort of people who bought Hicks's pictures and how they lived. From it one sees that country life has altered greatly since the painter's boyhood days on Twining Farm. Kitchen and barnyard are no longer the prime centers of social activity. Here, in this sedate nineteenth-century parlor, ladies have time to fix flowers and gentlemen in high collars have time to talk to ladies.

For Joseph Watson's new mansion on the Bristol Road, Hicks's *Peaceable Kingdom* was the crowning touch and occupied the place of honor above a large marble-topped curly maple pier table.[5] A superb canvas—now at Williamsburg, Virginia,—it must have shown like a jewel among the quiet colors of that Quaker home.

But to the thoughtful observer it is a puzzling picture. Here are two leopards, one recumbent, the other arching and snarling above it either in anger or ecstasy.[6] Neither would seem appropriate to a *Peaceable Kingdom*. Indeed, this arching leopard exhibits qualities that the quietist preacher specifically advised his listeners to shun.

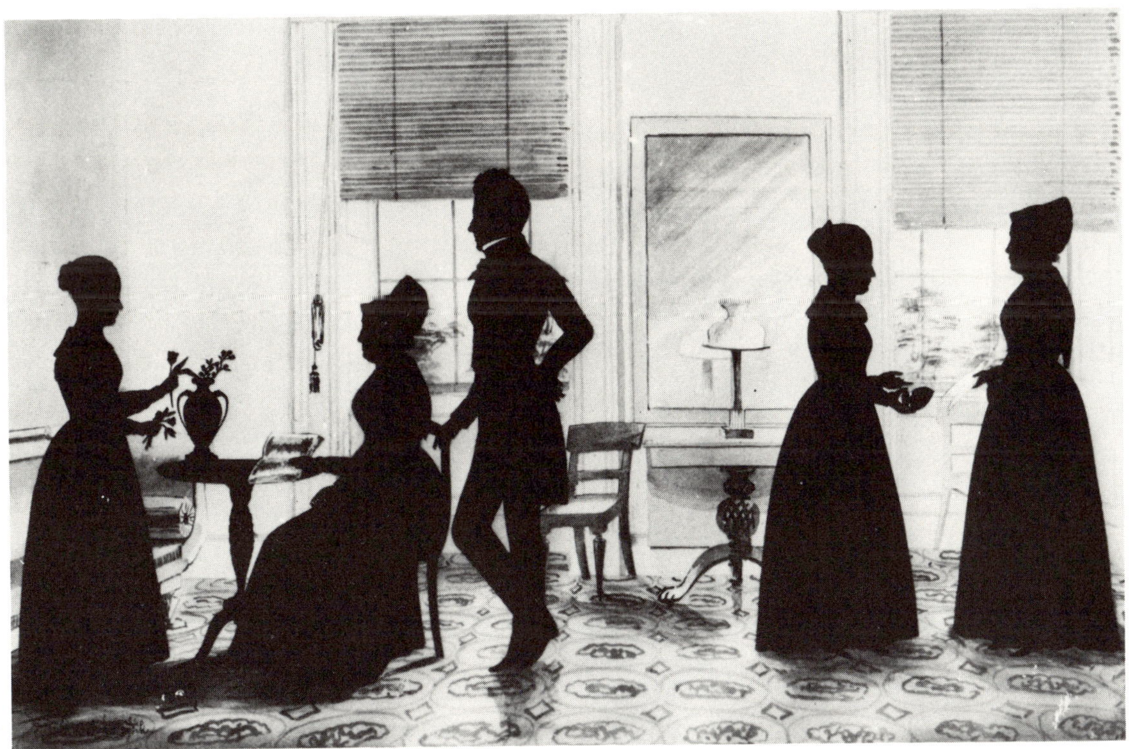

The Underhill Family, 1844, *silhouette by August Edouart (1789–1861). The summer home, on the Eastern Shore of Maryland, belonging to Abraham Underhill of New York—the sort of room in which the friends and relatives of Edward Hicks hung his pictures. From Anna Cox Brinton's* Quaker Profiles *(Wallingford, Pa.: Pendle Hill, 1964).*

But however perplexing, there is no question that Hicks knew what he was painting. For the Goose Creek sermon makes it clear that the artist thoroughly understood the nature of the leopard. This was the beast of the vine god, Dionysus, known as Bacchus to the Romans. Lustful and capricious, savage and seductive, the animal and its mottled pelt celebrated the divinity on Greek vases and in the mosaic of Roman pavements. With Christianity his glory waned. No longer an embodiment of divine energy, he became a mere symbol of incontinence, a creature of the Antichrist.

Not till the late Renaissance did he regain some measure of his former luster in Titian's *Bacchus and Ariadne* and Rubens' *Leopards*, where three gorgeous specimens share the fruit of the vine with a satyr, a nymph, and two cherubs. In a fascinating study of this work Julius Held cites an engraving of it by Wenceslas Hollar that resembles the *Peaceable Kingdoms*.[7] He could have gone further and noted correspondence between Rubens' original and Hicks in the sylvan landscape, in the harmony between child and beast, and in the fact of supernatural presence—the satyr representing Dionysus much as the Divine Child represents Christ. But the message could not be more different. Rubens created a paean to sensuality, Hicks a sermon on Quaker quietism.

In spite of its dionysiac symbol, the Watson *Kingdom* is just such a sermon. Careful examination reveals elements that balance and counter the leopard's frenzy. The lion is no longer distraught; his eyes reflect a gentle bewilderment rather than fear. And he has risen from his former lowly position so that he now stands nose-to-nose with the ox. As for that great bovine, he is a monument of tranquility. If in the lion is the bemused soul of the artist/preacher, in the ox is some substantial elder like Isaac Parry or Joseph Briggs or James Walton, all close personal friends who accompanied the Quaker minister on his religious travels. Of just such an elder Hicks wrote, "The most valuable father in the church of Christ I ever knew, was a man of choleric complexion, and in his first nature like a lion; but when I knew him he was as patient, submissive and powerful as an ox."[8]

The leopard's counterpart, the kid, offers no such balance as the ox accords the lion. In Westall's original engraving this animal was a full-sized goat, nearly as large as the leopard. By the time he reaches the late *Kingdoms* he is insignificant. This failure to develop a substantial opposite suggests Hicks's secret sympathy with the leopard and his works. Conceivably it is the protest of Hicks the artist against the moralism of Hicks the preacher and his fellow meeting-goers. Is the unchallenged splendor of the leopard a defense of his art as a gift to be cherished rather than to be subdued by Quaker quietism?

If this was his purpose it must have been a fleeting one, because the same canvas bears a further evidence of quietism in a new symbol, the yoke. And the Divine Child has returned to a meaningful function. Having regained a central position in the last phase of *Lions in Profile*—where the artist, seeming not to know what else to do with him, put an olive branch of peace in his upraised hand—he now settles down to a real job: the yoking of the young lion, the calf, and the fatling together. The infant works quietly and unobtrusively at his task, his small form almost lost among the great beasts. Though the metaphor "Take my yoke upon you" comes from the New Testament (Matt. 11:29), the equipment involved is strictly Hicks's own idea. It is nothing more nor less than the tasseled cord of a nineteenth-century venetian blind, as illustrated in the

Underhill silhouette. Its use would have been as surprising to the prophet Isaiah as would the Indian corn that the artist provides the cow and bear. In the Watson canvas the Child has already secured the calf and is at work on the lion cub. And in this case the animal really looks like a cub and not, as so frequently happens, a domestic kitten.

The yoking process, like the lion's eating of straw, represents the conquest of self-will, the goal of Quaker quietism. One recalls a phrase from an 1822 letter of Cousin Elias at the time of the painter's nearly fatal illness: "God keeps the reins in his own hands."[9] But the cord not only controls; here it also unites, thus bringing the content of this work closer to Isaiah's original concept of universal reconciliation than were earlier *Kingdoms*.

Watching the Child struggle with his cord and tassel, one wonders if the model was Silas Carle, the painter's grandson.[10] On the other hand, Jane Brey notes that according to family tradition the children are Joseph Watson's, because Hicks made it a practice to include the patron's children in his paintings; she points out that here they are "more slight in form than usual."[11] In any case, it is entirely probable that Hicks pictured specific children, for his love of young people is obvious.

NOTES

1. Alice Ford, "The Publication of Edward Hicks's Memoirs," *Bulletin of the Friends Historical Association* 50 (1961): 4–11.

2. Alice Ford, *Edward Hicks: Painter of the Peaceable Kingdom* (Philadelphia: University of Pennsylvania Press, 1952), p. 97. Three of the painter's nephews were also named for him: Edward Hicks Kennedy, Edward Hicks Worstall, and Edward Hicks Phipps, to the last-named of whom he gave a *Banners Kingdom*. His friend James Walton also named a son for him.

3. Jane Brey, *A Quaker Saga* (Philadelphia: Dorrance & Co., 1967), p. 479. Invaluable for the genealogy and Quaker culture of Bucks County.

4. Anna Cox Brinton, *Quaker Profiles: Pictorial and Biographical 1750–1850* (Wallingford, Pa.: Pendle Hill, 1964), frontispiece and p. 37.

5. Brey, *A Quaker Saga*, pp. 479 and 480.

The canvas was delivered by the artist's son Isaac, on September 23, 1844, with a note referring to it as "one of the best paintings I ever done." The price was $21.75 in cash.

6. There are four of these *Arching Leopard Kingdoms*. One formerly owned by Leonardo Beans also shows the yoking process, which does not appear on the remaining two. Of these, the Dallas Museum version shows the Divine Child with an olive branch; that of a private collector includes a later appearance of the kneeling "Innocence" with dove and eagle.

7. Julius Held, *P. P. Rubens: The Leopards* (Privately printed, 1970).

8. *Memoirs*, p. 325.

9. Dated Jericho (L.I.), 9th of 4th mo., 1822 (FHL).

10. His portrait was painted c. 1843 by Thomas Hicks.

11. Brey, *A Quaker Saga*, p. 482.

11
THE LEOPARD OF SERENITY

THE ARCHING LEOPARD HERALDS ANOTHER AND VERY DIFFERENT MEMBER OF THE SPECIES: A serene creature extending across the composition as though basking in a spotlight on a stage. This is the typical leopard of Hicks's last years, to which Arthur Edwin Bye referred when he wrote of the artist, "He loved the spotted leopard best, and often put him spread out on the foreground like a magnificent rug."[1]

The pose is not new. It first appeared in the *Banners Kingdoms,* where a rigidly heraldic beast frowns severely at the viewer. Now, touched with grace, it radiates a curiously pervasive and inescapable luster.

He—or she, for the animal transcends the limitations of sex—is seen against the rich and somber shadows of an 1845 *Kingdom* once owned by the artist's great-grandson Robert Carle and bequeathed by him to the Yale University Art Gallery. This dramatic canvas is marked by a return of the bridge. But it is not the Natural Bridge left behind in the early 1830s. If one looks closely, one sees the patterned stonework and the three slim trees that entered the *Kingdoms* by way of Tanner's engraving, but the power of the scene is such that one forgets these details and feels only the magic of a door opening from this world to the next.

Julius Held has pointed out the relation of the Orpheus myth to the peaceable kingdom in pictorial tradition. "There is . . . little doubt possible that the representations of Orpheus amidst the animals formulated in antiquity are the real fountainheads for all later renderings of a peaceful assembly of animals in biblical or mythological themes," he writes, and cites a Renaissance figure of Orpheus at the mouth of the underworld as "a curious anticipation of Hicks's use of the 'Natural Bridge.'"[2]

Orpheus was that divine-human hero who went down to Hades to bring back his wife, Eurydice, only to lose her at the last gate—himself able, as an immortal, to return from the land of the dead, but suffering as a mortal from what he must leave behind. A figure of transformation, he is a missing link between paganism and Christianity, and, with his magic lyre that attracts and subdues all animals, a precursor of the Divine Child who reconciles the beasts on Hicks's canvases. Reflecting on these late bridge *Kingdoms*—for another is at the Denver Museum of Art—one senses the Orphic mood and is tempted to wonder if Edward Hicks, too, was not a master of animals, taming them with his brush as Orpheus did with his music.

Certainly he has wrought a miracle with the leopard. In his Goose Creek sermon he defined the animal as fitful and restless. Yet these works of the 1840s, where the leopard is so prominent, are essentially serene. To have discovered tranquility in this spotted beast represents a fusion of opposites that reveals the painter's inward longing for reconciliation.

In 1845, the same year that produced the Yale *Kingdom*, he published *A Word of Exhortation to Young Friends*,[3] an attempt to heal the wounds of the Orthodox/Hicksite controversy. Unhappily, it did not do that. Most of it is a condemnation of usury and the hireling priesthood. Only occasionally does his sincere desire for peace with his fellow Quakers break through a wearisome round of complaint, as in the appealing outburst "Under the influence of this blessed spirit, my soul feels a sweet union and communion with all God's children in their devotional exercise, whether it is performed in a Protestant meeting house, a Roman cathedral, a Jewish synagogue, an Hindoo temple, an Indian wigwam, or by the wild Arab of the great desert with his face turned toward Mecca."[4]

In the late *Kingdoms* the supremacy of the leopard is challenged by a dynamic lion who plunges forward, his tail upraised, a pose probably lifted from one of the many representations of "Daniel in the Lions' Den" to be found in contemporary Bibles. Its foreshortening shows a more sophisticated technique than the painter's earlier borrowings. "The type of this lion," wrote Dr. Held of one at the Albright-Knox Art Gallery in Buffalo, "can actually be traced to Flemish artists under the influence of Rubens,"[5] and he points out the linear counterplay between the diagonal lion and the horizontal leopard.

Sometimes it is hard to decide which is the dominant animal. Both are commanding in different ways. In the above example the gorgeous leopard with serpentine tail reigns supreme,[6] while in that at the Phillips Collection, Washington, D.C., a charming vignette of a lioness and her cubs emphasizes the lion motif.

The Phillips canvas was completed before Hicks's sixty-sixth birthday. Knowing the exact date would disclose whether the brooding expression on the old lion's face was prophetic or revealed a grief already experienced, because this was to be the saddest year of the artist's life. It was also the year about which we know most. Sensing that his own time was drawing close, Edward began a diary on February 12, 1846—later incorporated in his *Memoirs*—whose first entries cite the recent deaths of contemporaries.

Two weeks later came word of the illness of his beloved granddaughter, Phoebe Ann Carle. Good news alternated with bad. At nine o'clock on the morning of First Day (Sunday), March 8, he attended the funeral of a friend's daughter, and at sight of the slim corpse was overcome with a premonition of Phoebe Ann's departure. Such manifestations were not new to him: he had sensed the deaths of his sister Violetta and Cousin Samuel at the moment of their happening. The next entry reads, "This day received a letter from New York containing the heartrending intelligence of the death of our precious little Phoebe Ann. She died a little after nine o'clock on first day morning."[7]

It was the great tragedy of his life, and he never got over it. In his diary he confided, "I have never known what such sorrow was before."[8]

His family rallied round, and his daughter Sarah Parry, newly a mother, drove eleven miles in stormy weather to console him. During the following

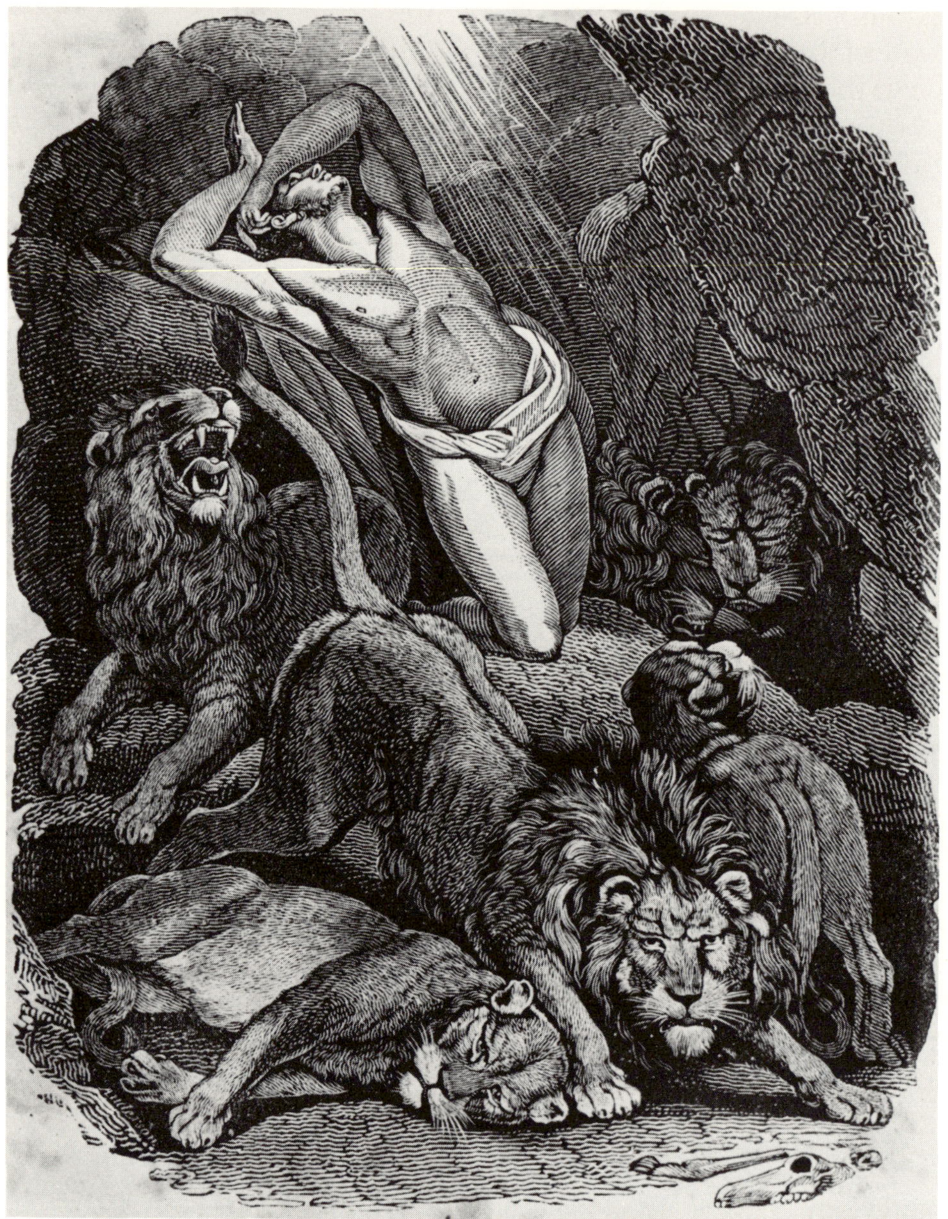

Daniel in the Lions' Den, *wood engraving, Alexander Anderson (1775–1870) in a German Bible, Biblia. Die Ganze Heilige Schrift . . . (Philadelphia: Kimber and Sharpless, 1834). A possible source for Hicks's dynamic lions of the 1840s. (The Rare Book Department of the Free Library of Philadelphia.)*

weeks he fluctuated between resignation and despair, sustained largely by his own religious faith. Asked to the funeral of an aged friend, he was "almost determined to go another way on business; but felt so uneasy that in my great strait I opened the Bible that lay before me, and was solemnly admonished. . . . I gave up immediately to what I thought a heavenly vision, and went to the funeral, and to me it was a memorable opportunity, for which my poor soul overflowed with gratitude."[9]

But within a week he wrote of his own oncoming death: "Oh, how awful the consideration; I have nothing to depend upon but the mercy and forgiveness of God, for I have no works of righteousness of my own; I am nothing but a poor old worthless insignificant painter."[10]

This was a strange statement considering that he had just finished his *Noah's Ark,* one of the truly superb works of American folk art—and all the more strange in the light of his daughter Sarah's comment. For having dropped in on the family at Newtown that same day she wrote her sister Elizabeth, who was then in New York, "Before I left Father came in. He looks quite well again and is in good spirits. He is so interested in his new painting. He says he thinks he is a much smarter workman than Noah, he has completed his ark in so much shorter time."[11]

Nothing illustrates more clearly his sincere but mercurial feelings. This is the volatile temperament that he attributed to the leopard in his Goose Creek sermon and that he freely acknowledged in himself.[12] It is the stuff of which many brilliant performers are made, including those gifted in the ministry. And the artist/preacher was acutely aware of the hazard this presented to a Quaker quietist. He knew that when he was asked to funerals it was in the hope that he would speak, but as a conscientious Friends minister he must wait for the prompting of the Holy Spirit.[13]

In spite of his cough—for he was a consumptive for many years—and his deafness, which now kept him from visiting the sick, he still remained a vehicle for the inward voice, which could touch him without warning. Of one funeral he wrote, "I felt so poor in spirit when I took my seat by the house that I could not get at one crumb of heavenly bread or one drop of living water, but I soon felt the necessity of standing forth in the midst, when to my astonishment, my dry withered soul was quickened into life."[14]

NOTES

1. Arthur Edwin Bye, "Edward Hicks, 1780–1849," *Bulletin of the Friends Historical Association* 32 (1943): 61.

2. Julius Held, "Edward Hicks and the Tradition," *Art Quarterly* 14 (1951): 121–36, esp. 129 and 134, n. 3.

3. Edward Hicks, *A Word of Exhortation to Young Friends, Presented to Them Without Money and Without Price by a Poor Illiterate Minister* (Philadelphia: J. Richards, 1845). Later included in *Memoirs,* pp. 337–65.

4. Ibid., p. 349.

5. Held, "Edward Hicks and the Tradition," p. 126.

6. For Hicks's lack of emphasis on the serpent as symbol see Eleanore P. Mather, *Edward Hicks, Primitive Quaker* (Wallingford, Pa.: Pendle Hill, 1970), p. 29.

7. *Memoirs,* pp. 141–42. Entry March 9, 1846.

8. Ibid., p. 142. Entry March 11, 1846.

9. Ibid., p. 148. Entry April 13, 1846.

10. Ibid., p. 149. Entry April 18, 1846.

11. Alice Ford, *Edward Hicks: Painter of the Peaceable Kingdom* (Philadelphia: University of Pennsylvania Press, 1952), p. 102.

12. The whole concept of the leopard is puzzling, representing as it does "men and women in whose animal economy the element of air predominates, producing that constitutional character called sanguine" (*Memoirs,* p. 287). One can see why the militant lion is called choleric, and why his flamelike mane suggests the element of fire. But what has the leopard to do with air? Is it the changeful motion of the animal, subtle and unseizable as rising smoke or shifting breeze? To the primitive mind there is a magic in the wind attributable to deity. "God is the wind," writes Carl Jung, "stronger and mightier than man, an invisible breath-spirit" (*The Portable Jung,* ed. Joseph Campbell, trans. R. F. C. Hull (New York: Viking, 1971), p. 80). Archaic also is the belief that the wind can impregnate new life, or express the voice of divinity, as in the whispering leaves of Dodona.

But granting the relevance of the leopard to air, why associate it with the "sanguine" temperament, a term implying blood? The connection was not invented by Hicks, but was apparently an accepted belief of earlier times. "To air corresponds the red constituent of blood," writes a modern scholar, Titus Burckhardt, in *Alchemy* (trans. William Stoddart [Middlesex: Penguin, 1971], p. 129, n. 6). One recalls in religious art the vermilion tongues of flame on the heads of the Apostles touched by the Holy Spirit at Pentecost, and the use of scarlet in church ritual on the commemoration of that day. To a primitive psychology, both breath and blood signified spirit because both represented the essence of life.

13. Hicks had a good deal to say about ministers of the gospel. It is no accident that it is in the leopard section of his Goose Creek sermon that he describes the descent of the Holy Spirit at Pentecost as "the rushing of a mighty wind" (Acts: 2.2), and saw a similar phenomenon in early Quakerism, where frequently "the whole body shakes, sometimes to a degree bordering on convulsions and too often, for want of getting into a child-like state of resignation, ends in fanatical derangement" (*Memoirs*, pp. 296–97). This type of experience often occurred with seventeenth-century Friends, causing them to be called "Quakers," or, in French, "Trembleurs," but has been generally assumed to be obsolete by the nineteenth century.

14. *Memoirs*, pp. 204–5.

12

THE PASTORAL COMPLEX

SOMETIME DURING THE LATTER 1840s HICKS PAINTED A *PEACEABLE KINGDOM,* INHERITED BY the Abendroth family, which is remarkable for having five extra sheep—five, that is, in addition to the lamb that dwells with the wolf throughout the series. Their presence gives a pastoral quality also observable in his *Noah's Ark* of April, 1846, suggesting the *Kingdom* to have been painted around the same time. In both works wild and domesticated beasts are side by side. But during these last years of his life he did other canvases where all the animals were domesticated, as in his pastorals, farmscapes, and the several versions of *The Grave of William Penn.*

This pastoral element is related to the mood of reconciliation prevalent throughout the late *Kingdoms,* at the same time illustrating the subduing of the self that was basic to Quaker quietism. Domesticated animals, as the preacher pointed out in his Goose Creek sermon, symbolize the redeemed souls that have yielded to the yoke of the Holy Spirit.[1]

For want of a better term we will call this phenomenon the *pastoral complex.* One aspect of it is a trend toward the familial. In the *Kingdoms,* understandably, there is scant reference to male and female as such, except subtly as in the cow or the full-maned lion. But in farm life differences in sex are essential to survival and constitute in themselves a union of opposites. A white mare marches proudly by her dark mate in the procession to the Ark. Among the many sheep of the Abendroth canvas are a ram and a ewe with sucking lamb, which are unique in the *Kingdoms,* though much used by the artist in his other pastoral subjects. And the later *Penn Treaties* include a squaw nursing her papoose, as in West's picture, which the artist omitted in his earlier versions.[2]

Throughout his life Hicks reveals a wistful yearning for maternal tenderness. Orphaned from his mother at eighteen months, he clung to every detail he could learn about her, and when he died her letters to his father were in his pocket. As for his foster mother, Elizabeth Twining, who rescued him as a homeless waif, his devotion reached its most poignant expression pictorially in *The Residence of David Twining,* one of the treasures of the Rockefeller Collection at Williamsburg.[3] Here is seven-year-old Edward with his foster parents: David the patriarch in broad-brimmed hat and plain coat, Elizabeth in cap and kerchief, with her Bible on her lap. "How often," wrote the painter, "have I

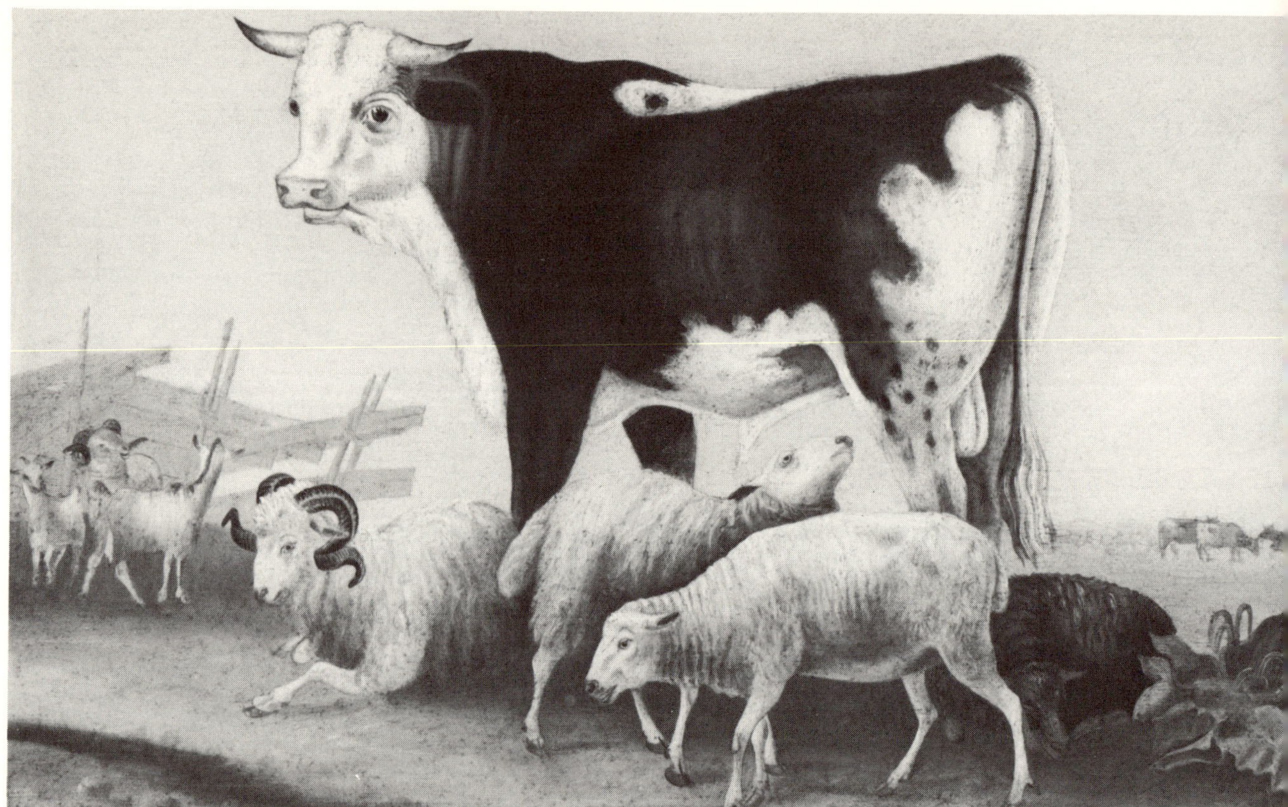

James Cornell's Prize Bull, 1846 (Abby Aldrich Rockefeller Folk Art Center, (Williamsburg, Virgin[ia]).
Hicks derived this pastoral from a series of lithographs by Gustavus Canton: (1) the bull, a stereoty[pe]
of Dutch landscape painters; (2) curly-horned ram, also from the Dutch School; (3) three ewes t[hat]
Hicks presents in reverse, omitting the lamb.

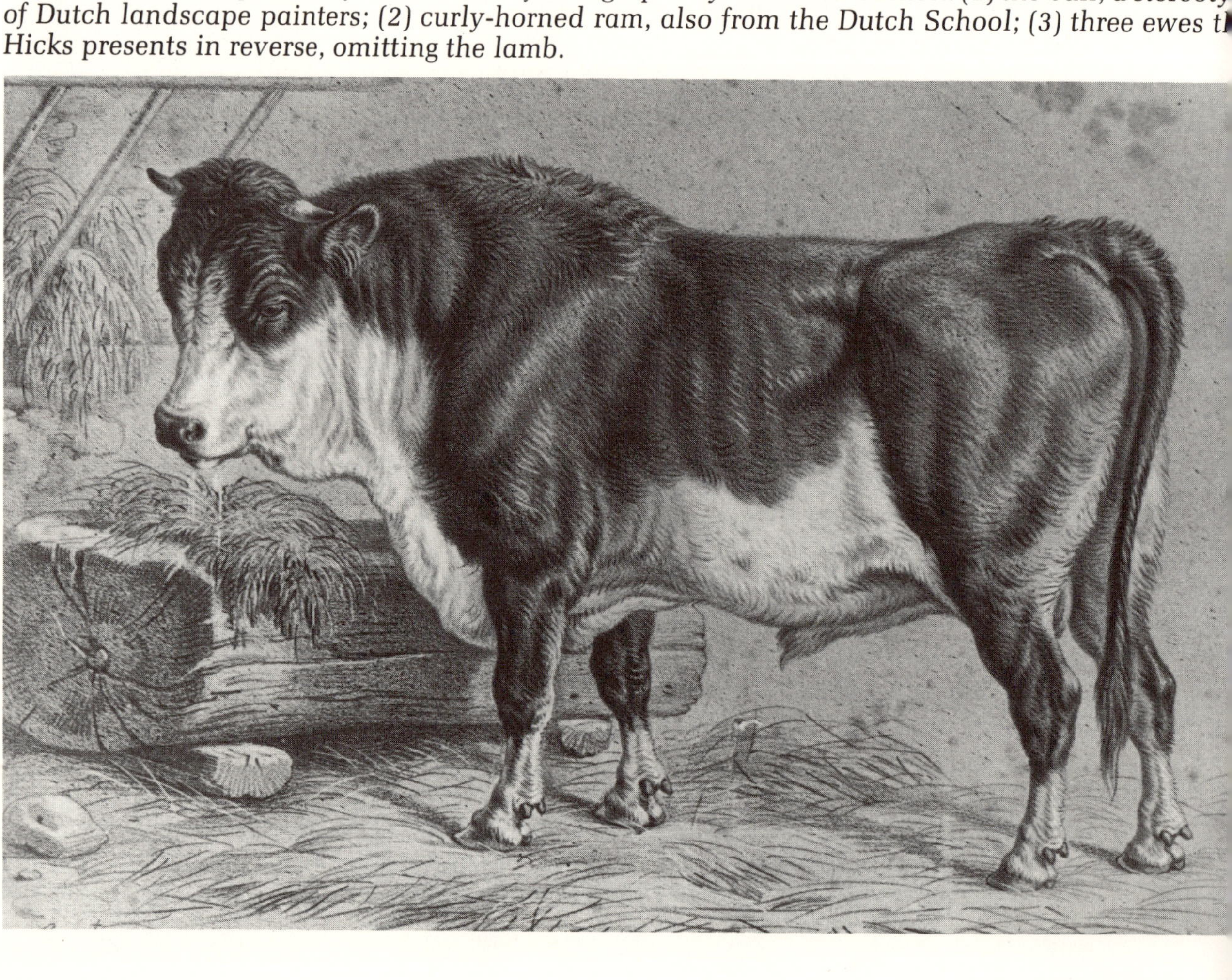

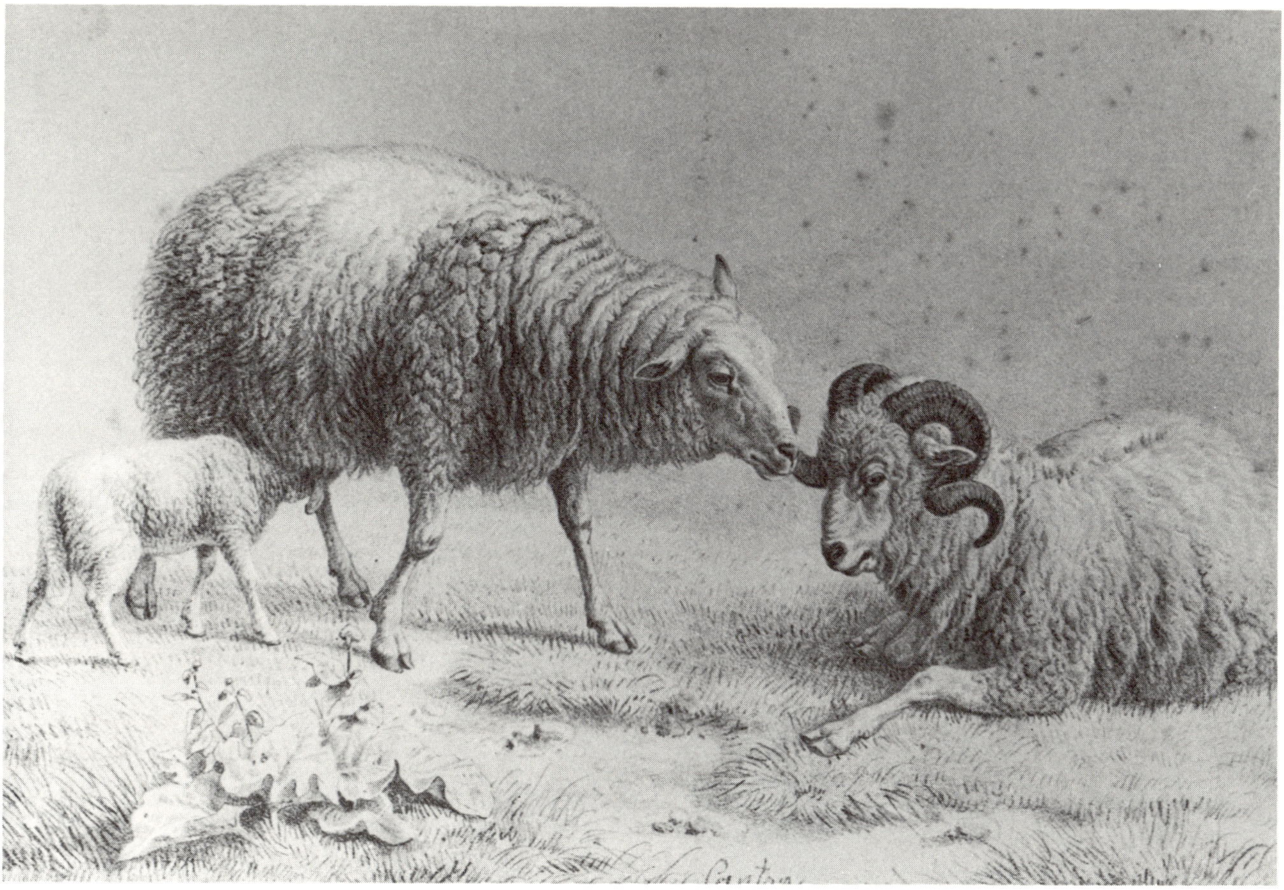

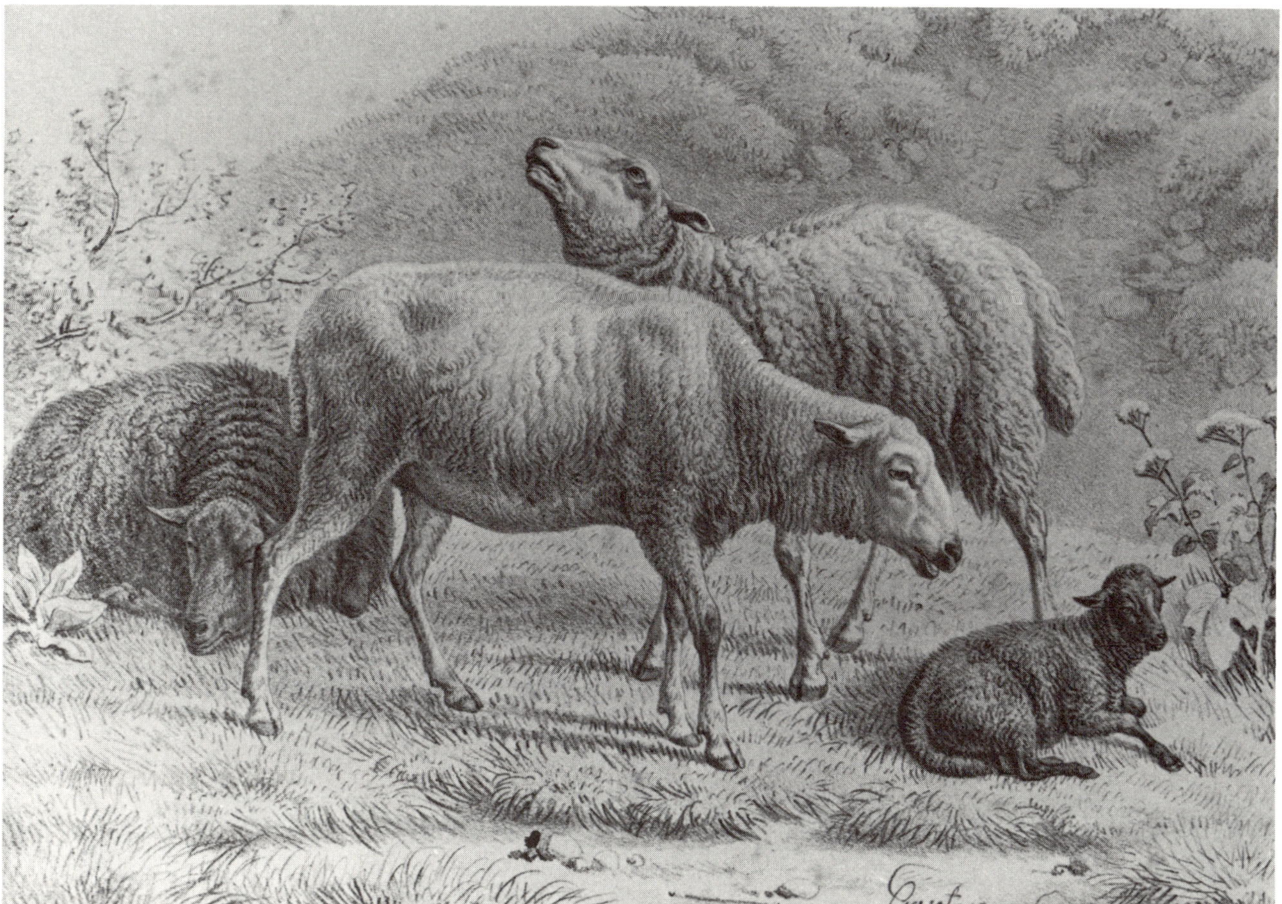

Canton

Canton

stood or sat by her, before I could read myself, and heard her read, particularly the 26th chapter of Matthew."[4]

The figures exist in a dream light, without sun or shadow. Above them spreads a tree whose foliage might have been lifted from a fifteenth-century tapestry, such as Hicks never saw. Elsewhere on the canvas, mare and foal, cow and calf, ewe and lamb stress the maternal theme. In the doorway of the stone farmhouse stands the artist's foster sister and staunch friend, Beulah Twining,[5] and closer to hand her sister Mary, seated on a vigorous mount, waits for her young husband, Jesse Leedom, to swing into his saddle. All are part of the peaceable kingdom of the artist's long-lost childhood.

Of the Twinings's four daughters, "Mary and Beulah," wrote Edward, "being younger, were more like my sisters, and indeed they seemed to have adopted me as their brother in my infancy."[6]

Mary was his favorite. Later, in *Leedom Farm,* she stands in old age by the fence and looks at the livestock of her son, David—named, we assume, for his grandsire, David Twining. She is only a tiny gray shadow of a figure, but without her this farm world, so rich in man and beast, would not have been. Hicks called her "the best friend I have in the world not of my own family. She was more like her mother than any of her sisters."[7]

Hicks's relationships with women—with some spectacular exceptions due to controversial issues—were good ones:

> On woman's mercy the whole man depends,
> The first, the last, the best of earthly friends[8]

he wrote to his poet correspondent Samuel Johnson.

Though he had many devoted friends of both sexes, his deepest relationships were with women. We are not speaking here of his partiality for the opposite sex, which he would have been the first to acknowledge, but of a kinship of spirit, as with Elizabeth Twining and little Phoebe Ann Carle, and most particularly with his daughter Elizabeth, whom Isaac Parry referred to as "his Beloved Elizabeth, who knew almost his secret thoughts."[9] A vivid picture of this appealing young woman is drawn in Alice Ford's biography, and of her special rapport with her father. She spent much time with her married sister Susan in New York, and excerpts from the painter's letters pleading with her to come home to Newtown suggest an almost childlike dependency. At his funeral her anguish broke forth in a "short but most pathetic supplication."[10] It would have been greatly comforting to Hicks to know that two years later the Makefield Monthly Meeting would record her as a minister.[11]

Elizabeth was attractive to young men, but she did not marry until after her father's death, and then chose a Baltimore widower, Richard Plummer, who was considerably older than herself.[12] She was separated intermittently from her husband by bouts of mental illness, when she would withdraw to Newtown.

The feminine and maternal in Hicks's pastoral compositions is countered by a masculine note in the rams and bulls. There were no bulls in the *Peaceable Kingdoms.* The bovine specified by Isaiah was the ox. But in 1846 the artist painted *James Cornell's Prize Bull,*[13] and on the right margin of *Noah's Ark* is the head of another male of the species, whose dappled flank also appears in a pastoral and among the Twining livestock. He becomes gigantic and serene in *Cornell Farm*, where his spots have nearly vanished. In *Leedom Farm* he is pure white, supremely solid and yet dreamlike against the greenness of the pasture. He dominates the farm scene as the serene leopard dominates the *Kingdoms*, and with the same meaning: energy transmuted into spirit.

Hicks's loyalty to his small agrarian world pervades his farmscapes. William Blake sang of the New Jerusalem in England's green and pleasant land as a wistful city dweller who seldom saw the greenness he celebrated. But the Quaker preacher spent a lifetime in the green and pleasant land of Bucks County, and out of that experience grew his Hillborn, Twining, Cornell, and Leedom farmscapes. Critics remark on the ethereal beauty of their skies. This is partially due to the artist's increasing skill and the relative serenity of his later years. But something must also be credited to the simple assets of nature, because to a considerable extent Bucks County *was* the Peaceable Kingdom.

In these farmscapes Virgil Barker and Alice Ford both see a possible reflection of Woodside. That Hicks was aware of this Philadelphia contemporary seems entirely likely. John A. Woodside (1781–1852)[14] was the great sign painter of his day, and his tavern boards, fire engine panels, and railroad carriage decoration must have been as generally well known in his own time as were the engaging *Saturday Evening Post* covers of Norman Rockwell a century later. Hicks could scarcely have missed them. But Miss Ford questions whether the Quaker artist, who did not go to exhibitions, would have seen an easel picture such as Woodside's *Country Fair*. Though it is harder to make a case for this, it is still not impossible. And there are marked resemblances between this work and *Cornell Farm*; as for example in the arklike barn, the central emphasis on the pigs, the black-hatted men with their lively gestures, and most of all the end-to-end placement of animals in the foreground and their curiously lateral extension across the canvas, a pattern that is evident in the last two farmscapes.

This lateral movement, as of flocks and herds on the march, recalls a story from the Gospel of Pseudo Matthew, an apocryphal work that combines Isaiah's peaceable prophecy with the Flight into Egypt to escape the wrath of Herod. It is frankly fabulous, but like many fables, illustrates a truth·

> Now at first when Mary saw the lions and panthers, and various kinds of wild beasts, coming about them, she was much afraid. And the infant Jesus looked into her face with a joyful countenance, and said, "Be not afraid, mother, for they come not to do thee harm, but they make haste to serve both thee and me." With these words He drove all fear from her heart. . . . They walked among wolves and feared nothing; and no one of them was hurt by another. Then was fulfilled that which was spoken by the prophet: Wolves shall feed with lambs; the lion and the ox shall eat straw together. There were together two oxen drawing a wagon with provision for the journey, and the lions directed them in their path."[15]

NOTES

1. This concept was not unique with Hicks, for André Grabar, writing of the Judaic belief in the Peace to come with the reign of the Messiah, comments, "The motifs of animals expelled as hostile to man after the original sin, but assured of return domesticated at the time of the Peace, is a part of this theme" (*Christian Iconography: A Study of Origins*, Bollingen Series, vol. 10 [Princeton, N.J.: Princeton University Press, 1968], p. 54).

2. Such *Treaty* canvases are in the Mercer Museum, Shelburne Museum, National Gal-

lery, Dietrich Brothers, and a private collection.

3. Other versions of *Twining Farm* belong to Carnegie Institute and to two private collectors.

4. *Memoirs*, p. 24. This chapter from Matthew deals with the betrayal of Christ and Peter's denial of his Master, a passage which struck close to Hicks's heart, for he identified himself with Peter, the variable "leopard" among the Apostles. The painter wrote of himself in his youth, "Poor sanguine young man. Peter like, I was a swearer and a liar, but I was not yet ready, like Peter, to weep bitterly for sin" (*Memoirs*, p. 36). For Peter as a leopard, see pp. 304 and 306.

5. For Beulah Twining's career, see *Memoirs*, pp. 22–23. Edna Pullinger gives an interesting account of her literary tastes, which were not always Quakerly, in *Newtown's First Library Building* (Newtown, Pa.: Newtown Library Company, 1976), pp. 14–15.

6. *Memoirs*, p. 22.

7. *Ibid.* For Mary Leedom (1768–1843) and her daughters, Hicks painted *Peaceable Kingdom no. 13.*

8. Dated October 8, 1839, these verses were published (Philadelphia, 1845) along with the second of Johnson's two poems inscribed to Hicks *(Letter from Samuel Johnson, to Edward Hicks; with His Reply).* Hicks's metrical answer is quoted in full with commentary by Frederick Tolles in "The Primitive Painter as Poet," *Bulletin of the Friends Historical Association* 50 (1961):15–20.

9. Parry to Benjamin Ferris, November 6, 1849 (FHL).

10. Amos Willets to Benjamin Ferris, New York, N.Y., August 30, 1849 (FHL). Quoted by Alice Ford, *Edward Hicks: Painter of the Peaceable Kingdom* (Philadelphia: University of Pennsylvania Press, 1952), p. 122.

11. Minutes of November 6, 1851.

12. For data on Elizabeth after her father's death see chap. 8, n. 1, of the revised edition of Ford's biography, *Edward Hicks* (Millwood, N.Y.: Kraus Reprint Co., 1973), n.p.

13. 1846. Now at Williamsburg, Virginia.

14. Virgil Barker, *American Painting* (New York: Macmillan Co., 1950), p. 530, and Ford's biography, *Edward Hicks*, p. 97. For Woodside and his career see Joseph Jackson, "John A. Woodside, Philadelphia's Glorified Sign Painter," *Pennsylvania Magazine of History and Biography* 57 (1933): 58–65. A good list of Woodside references is given by George C. Groce and David H. Wallace in *The New York Historical Society's Dictionary of Artists in America, 1564–1860* (New Haven, Conn.: Yale University Press, 1957), p. 701.

15. *The Flight into Egypt*, ill. Gus Ullman, printed by Mildred and Walter Kahoe (Moylan, Pa.: The Rose Valley Press, 1972). The material for this, arranged by Walter Kahoe, comes from chaps. 17, 18, and 19 of Pseudo Matthew.

13
KINGDOMS OF DEPARTURE

IN 1847 HICKS DEVELOPED A SPECIAL PHASE OF HIS PASTORAL THEME IN *The Grave of William Penn*, a composition borrowed from a Dutch artist, H. F. de Cort.[1] Here are the only meeting houses Edward Hicks ever painted. A group of figures in plain garb cluster around the graves of the Penn family, and in certain versions an inscription reads, "Grave of Wm. Penn at Jordans in England, with the old Meeting House & Burial ground and J. J. Gurney & Friends looking at the Grave."

This reference to Gurney was a strange error, since the principal figure at the graveside in de Cort's original was not the evangelical Gurney but the free-thinking French philosopher Montesquieu, presumably paying homage to the liberal ideals of Penn.[2] The mistake is all the more curious because, though Gurney had many admirers, Hicks was not one of them. He wrote of this handsome and gifted British contemporary, "I could say much about the inconsistency of the wealthy and learned Joseph John Gurney in continuing his connection with the Society of Friends, and at the same time going hand in glove with hireling priests."[3]

A tranquil preoccupation with oncoming death dominates these landscapes, wherein a great bull leads a gentle herd of beasts slowly but steadily toward the burial enclosure. In at least two cases the animal is black, which combines with the thunderous sky to create a mood that is awesome but not fearful.[4]

One last preaching journey took the artist from Newtown in July of 1847. This time he went to Westbury, Long Island, and one wonders if the fact that Phoebe Ann was buried there had some part in drawing him to the spot.

Hicks had long had a speaking acquaintance with death. Ill with tuberculosis in 1819, he survived by a miracle for the better part of three decades. Now that he was approaching his three score years and ten, the increasing nearness of his own end made him pause and consider the day-to-day happenings of life more closely. He notes in his diary, "My dear Sarah was very unwell last night, a high fever and pain in the breast. Ah! we must part even if she gets better this time. She has been an excellent and faithful wife to me for more than forty years."[5]

Not much is known about Sarah Hicks. Her name does not often appear in the minutes of Makefield Monthly or Newtown Preparative Meeting. In the Quaker world of her time such meeting activity provided the recognized outlet for those women whose interests went beyond their own households. The records do refer frequently to Edward's foster sisters Mary Leedom and Beulah Twining. Indeed, the latter, disowned for her marriage "out of meeting" to a Dr. Torbert, after her subsequent divorce made an acknowledgment to Wrightstown Meeting and was readmitted to become the clerk of its Women's Meeting, as she was later to become the women's clerk at Makefield.[6] She was a very capable woman who managed her father's estate in his last years and became his principal heir.

But it is hard to catch any glimpse of Sarah outside her own family—or even in it, except for mention of her in letters from the Hicks Collection quoted in Alice Ford's biography, references treasured all the more for their scarcity. No doubt her very self-effacement and dedication to the home made her a perfect companion for Edward. It is clear that she got along with him for a lifetime (d. December 30, 1855), and this was no mean accomplishment.

For Hicks remained contentious to the last. Much as he longed for peace, he was doomed not to find it till after further dissension. The Hicksites, who had stood together so staunchly in the face of Orthodox oppression, were now divided: some, like himself, retained the old quietism; others pursued the cause of antislavery and temperance so strenuously that they seemed to him to be forsaking the mystical heart of Quakerism and espousing the Unitarianism of many of their fellow abolitionists.

His bitterness over this division was even more painful than his resentment toward Gurney and the Orthodox, since it separated him from his former allies. Late in 1839 Samuel Johnson, whose poem "To Edward Hicks on his proposition for painting an Historical piece commemorative of the progress of religious Liberty" had inspired the *Banners Kingdoms*, wrote another poem to his friend.[7] In it he urged the painter to become a leader in the cause of abolition. Hicks responded with a long poem that acknowledged the evils of slavery, but saw the answer to them in Christian faith as interpreted by Quakerism. And he went on to extol Benjamin Lay, Anthony Benezet, and John Woolman, whose peaceful but tireless persuasion had led the Friends of the Philadelphia Yearly Meeting to free their slaves in 1774.[8]

Hicks's point of view, though disputed by Johnson, was shared by many of his other friends, including Comly. As Lucretia Mott, the eloquent and popular antislavery leader, noted, "John Comly continues to preach against the reformatory movements of the day, and so does Edward Hicks sometimes."[9]

Of course, neither Hicks nor Comly were defending slavery, an institution they both abhorred. But they saw the abolition movement drawing Quaker leaders out of the Society of Friends and causing them to become impatient with their fellow members.

Hicks particularly resented Lucretia Mott. Though most of his relationships with women were good, his antipathy to this greatly admired figure was almost pathological. They had been on the same side in the Hicksite/Orthodox controversy. But as this issue faded, their basic incompatibility became evident. Lucretia was essentially practical, handling the affairs of her own and other people's lives with great competence. Edward's vagaries and failures in such matters must have been incomprehensible to her. Both of these very different characters were recorded ministers. But while the woman preacher's religious impulse realized itself in social activism, the artist's turned increasingly to the inward life, as is evident in his late *Peaceable Kingdoms*. One also suspects that she did not set much value on "the painter's eye with noble light inspired," as the more appreciative Johnson had phrased it.[10]

Though her residence was many miles from Newtown, Hicks felt that her influence was invading the Makefield Monthly Meeting. He wrote, "I do not know but what Lucretia Mott, that talented creature in Philadelphia, has done more toward destroying the unity of our Monthly Meeting than Jonathan Evans with all his influence as a meeting elder could do twenty years ago, for he only got two silent satellites, while she appeared to have two of our most chattering members."[11]

One of these was a young man named Oliver Schofield, who several months earlier in a meeting for worship had made faces and stamped his feet while Edward was preaching.[12] And, complained Edward, "He will keep talking in meeting for business, and that, too, while sitting in his seat. I reproved him openly according to the advice of the Apostle and he retorted. I felt uncharitably towards him, but I was silent; of course I did not manifest my feelings."[13]

The last statement is a little hard to believe. But one must credit the painter with insight on his own shortcomings, for the next day he confessed in his diary, "I awakened this morning with a renewed conviction and confirmation of the dreadful consequences of an Orthodox spirit. It was unnecessary for me to hunt up some of my poor Orthodox Friends to try to fit the spirit as a coat upon their backs, for I could find nobody that it would fit better than myself."[14]

Hicks had a gift for peering into the human soul, and into none did he peer more unsparingly than his own. Sometime in 1847 he painted a plunging lion with an anguished face. This great *Kingdom*, long ago discovered by Robert Carlen, is the one more than any other where the artist identifies himself with the king of beasts. The face is obviously human and appears sorrowful, but whether from memories of Phoebe Ann or concern over the Society of Friends or fear for his own soul, we do not know. It is a veritable King Lear of a lion, and as a psychological study it is a masterpiece.

From this poignant character study, and from the harshly self-belittling comments in his *Memoirs*, one might reasonably conclude that the painter was held in low esteem during the last years of his life. But this was not really the case. In his struggle over abolition he was backed by his Monthly Meeting, most members resenting the discourtesy shown to an aged and honored minister whose point of view they shared. Friends had been in the forefront of the antislavery movement, but as midcentury approached, the cause became more militant, and many Friends now perceived that any politically achieved abolition would endanger that other Quaker testimony, peace—though few could have foreseen that in little more than a dozen years North and South would be at war.[15]

Late in 1848 Makefield united with Newtown Preparative Meeting in condemnation of Oliver Schofield for disorderly conduct, a decision sustained by Bucks Quarter. Ultimately an appeal to the Yearly Meeting resulted in a reversal, but this reversal did not come till many months after the painter's death.[16]

In spite of his meeting's support Hicks knew that he had violated that peace for which his heart was searching, and in June of 1849 he wrote an acknowledgment expressing regret that he had occasioned disunity in the Makefield Monthly Meeting and asking Friends to continue him "an object of their care, their sympathy and prayers."[17]

It is no coincidence that in the beautiful Galerie St. Etienne *Kingdom* the Divine Child has returned to the foreground with a triumphant smile. At last he has looped his tasseled cord around the neck of the young lion. Nor is it accidental that some weeks later Hicks concluded his diary with the words "But I am writing too much and saying too little, and had better mind my own business, which, if I am not mistaken, is to bear a simple, child-like testimony to the goodness and mercy of my blessed saviour."[18]

The day before his death he was working in his shop when a letter was delivered. It announced a visit from his cousin Henry Hicks on the following Saturday to discuss the publication of the *Memoirs*. The painter was pleased, but said that his work was now done, that he had no anxieties, and that he felt love and peace for everyone. Henry, he added, would not arrive in time to see him, but would be able to attend the funeral.[19]

Then he turned back to his easel. On it was a *Kingdom* intended for his beloved Elizabeth. So convinced was he that this was to be his last that we must look on it as his final testament. It is a dreamlike landscape. The mountains part and float in a pearly mist. The old lion chews the straw of redemption, the young lion obediently follows the Divine Child, while between them extends the tranquil leopard whose eyes already contemplate another world.

NOTES

1. Alice Ford, *Edward Hicks: Painter of the Peaceable Kingdom* (Philadelphia: University of Pennsylvania Press, 1952), p. xv. For Hendrik Frans de Cort see Ellwood Parry, "Edward Hicks and a Quaker Iconography," *Arts Magazine* 49 (1975): 92–94.

2. Ford, *Edward Hicks*, pp. 105–6.

3. *Memoirs*, p. 253.

4. See Nos. 98 and 99 in the Catalogue.

5. Entry of April 26, 1846, *Memoirs*, p. 150.

6. Edna Pullinger, *Newtown's First Library Building* (Newtown, Pa.: Newtown Library Company, 1976) pp. 2, 5–6, and 10.

7. Dated October 3, 1839. See Frederick Tolles, "The Primitive Painter as Poet," *Bulletin of the Friends Historical Association* 50 (1961): 13–15.

8. Thomas E. Drake, *Quakers and Slavery in America* (New Haven, Conn.: Yale University Press, 1950), p. 71.

9. Mott to Nathaniel Barney of Nantucket, Mass., Philadelphia, October 8, 1842, in *James and Lucretia Mott: Life and Letters*, ed. Anna Davis Hallowell (Boston: Houghton, Mifflin & Co., 1884). See Margaret Hope Bacon, *Valiant Friend: The Life of Lucretia Mott* (New York: Walker, 1980).

10. From Johnson's undated poem "To Edward Hicks on his proposition for painting an Historical piece commemorative of the progress of religious Liberty," line 3. See chap. 5 of this volume, "Quakers Bearing Banners", n. 7.

11. *Memoirs*, p. 175, June 4, 1846.

12. *Memoirs*, pp. 153–54, May 7, 1846. Oliver's daughter, Martha, did valuable work in black education in South Carolina after the Civil War. See Mary S. Patterson, *Martha Schofield: Servant of the Lord*, 1839–1916 (Wallingford, Pa.: Privately printed, 1944).

13. *Memoirs*, p. 221, December 3, 1846.

14. Ibid.

15. Drake, *Quakers and Slavery*, chaps. 8 and 9. Thaddeus Kenderdine, writing of the resistance to the antislavery and temperance movements in Bucks County, points out, ". . . there was a conservative element in our society, presided over by the 'weight' that would not tolerate any extreme measures toward the eradication of the evils, so that an abolition or temperance lecturer dare not occupy a Friends meeting house to express his views. . . . But politics had much to do with this. Outside of the extreme abolitionists among them, Friends in our section were strong Whigs and extremely sensitive to any attempts to break into their party's lines, particularly in the times of the Clay (1844) and Taylor (1848) presidential campaigns. Hence the intolerance toward the Abolition and Free Soil Parties" (Centennial of Newtown Friends Meeting, 1815–1915. [Newtown, Pa.: Printed by the Newtown Enterprise, 1915], p. 22). The minutes of Makefield Monthly Meeting reveal that an antislavery address from Sadsbury Monthly Meeting, Lancaster County, Pa., was

not read on July 6, 1848, because of "insufficient unity."

16. Minutes of Makefield Monthly Meeting, September 6, 1849, and June 6, 1850.

17. Ferdinand J. Dreer Collection, Historical Society of Pennsylvania. See Ford, *Edward Hicks,* p. 110.

18. *Memoirs,* p. 261, July 13, 1849.

19. Amos Willets to Benjamin Ferris, New York, N.Y. August 30, 1849 (FHL). Quoted in Ford, *Edward Hicks,* p. 122.

CATALOGUE OF WORKS

NOTE: Information for the exhibitions listed in this catalogue is given in full the first time the exhibit appears. Thereafter, the longer citations are abbreviated. For example, Abby Aldrich Rockefeller Folk Art Center becomes AARFAC, and the Carnegie Institute Museum of Art and the Corcoran Gallery of Art becomes Carnegie/Corcoran. (Full citations for these exhibits are under number 1.) All references to "New York" indicate the city of that name.

PEACEABLE KINGDOMS

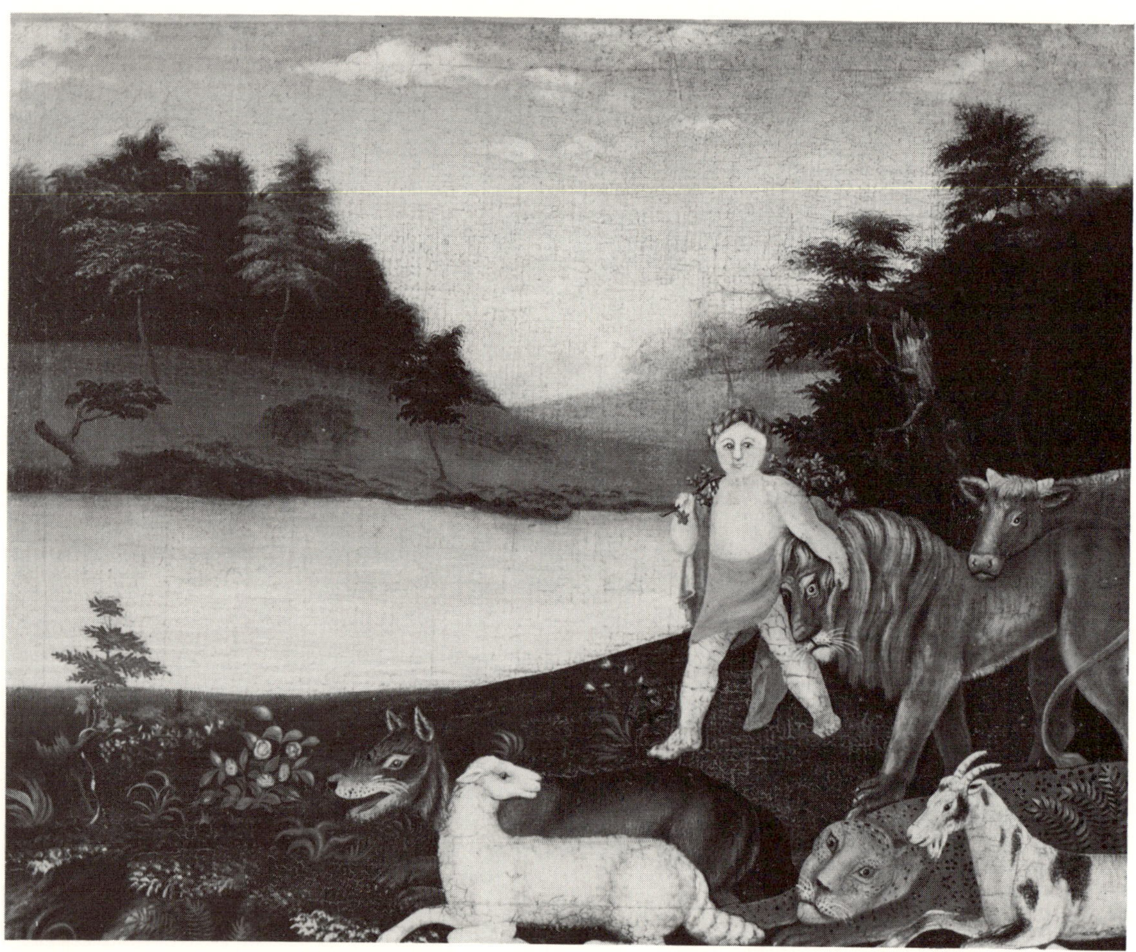

No. 1

EARLIEST KNOWN PEACEABLE KINGDOM, ca. 1820. Oil on canvas, 18¾ × 23½ inches. Frame probably original, 2½ inch birch veneer. The Cleveland Museum of Art; gift of Hanna Fund.

COMMENT: Hicks borrowed his composition from a Bible engraving by Richard Westall, R.A., a fact first discovered by Alice Ford (*Edward Hicks: Painter of the Peaceable Kingdom* (Philadelphia: University of Pennsylvania, 1952), pp. 41–43). The arrangement consists of a child and six animals: wolf and lamb, leopard and kid, lion and fatling (young steer). All come from Isaiah 11:6, "The wolf also shall dwell with the lamb, and the leopard shall lie down with the kid, and the young lion and the calf and the fatling together, and a little child shall lead them." Westall omitted the calf, presumably from a sense of aesthetic economy. To the background Hicks has added a pond or small lake.

The authorship of this canvas has been questioned, but its provenance in the Hayhurst family tends to confirm authenticity. A minute of sojourn for one of the artist-preacher's ministerial journeys was signed on June 7, 1820, by Benajah Hayhurst, clerk of Wrightstown Meeting (information courtesy of Arthur Smith, Wycombe, Pa., Bucks County historian).

COLLECTIONS: Hayhurst family, Lambert-ville, N.J.; Lewis's Antique Shop (Lewis Steinberg and David Y. Ellinger), Hatboro, Pa.; John E. Abbott, New York; Downtown Gallery (Edith Gregor Halpert), New York; Valentine Galleries, New York; the Cleveland Museum of Art, Cleveland, Ohio.

EXHIBITIONS: Akron Art Institute (Akron, Ohio, November, 1945), no. 6, ill.; Abby Aldrich Rockefeller Folk Art Collection, "Edward Hicks, 1780–1849: A Special Exhibition Devoted to His Life and Work" (Williamsburg, Va., September 30–October 30, 1960), cat. Mary C. Black and Alice Ford, no. 5, ill. p. 10;

Carnegie Institute Museum of Art, Pittsburgh, Pa., and Corcoran Gallery of Art, Washington, D.C., "Three Self-Taught Pennsylvania Artists: Hicks, Kane, Pippin" (Pittsburgh, October 21–December 4, 1966/Washington, D.C., January 6–February 19, 1967), cat. Leon Anthony Arkus, p. 1; University Art Museum, Berkeley, Calif., "The Hand and the Spirit: Religious Art in America 1700–1900" (Berkeley, Washington, D.C., Dallas, Tex., Indianapolis, Ind., June 28, 1972–April 15, 1973), cat. Jane Dillenberger and Joshua C. Taylor, no. 37, p. 88 (not ill.).

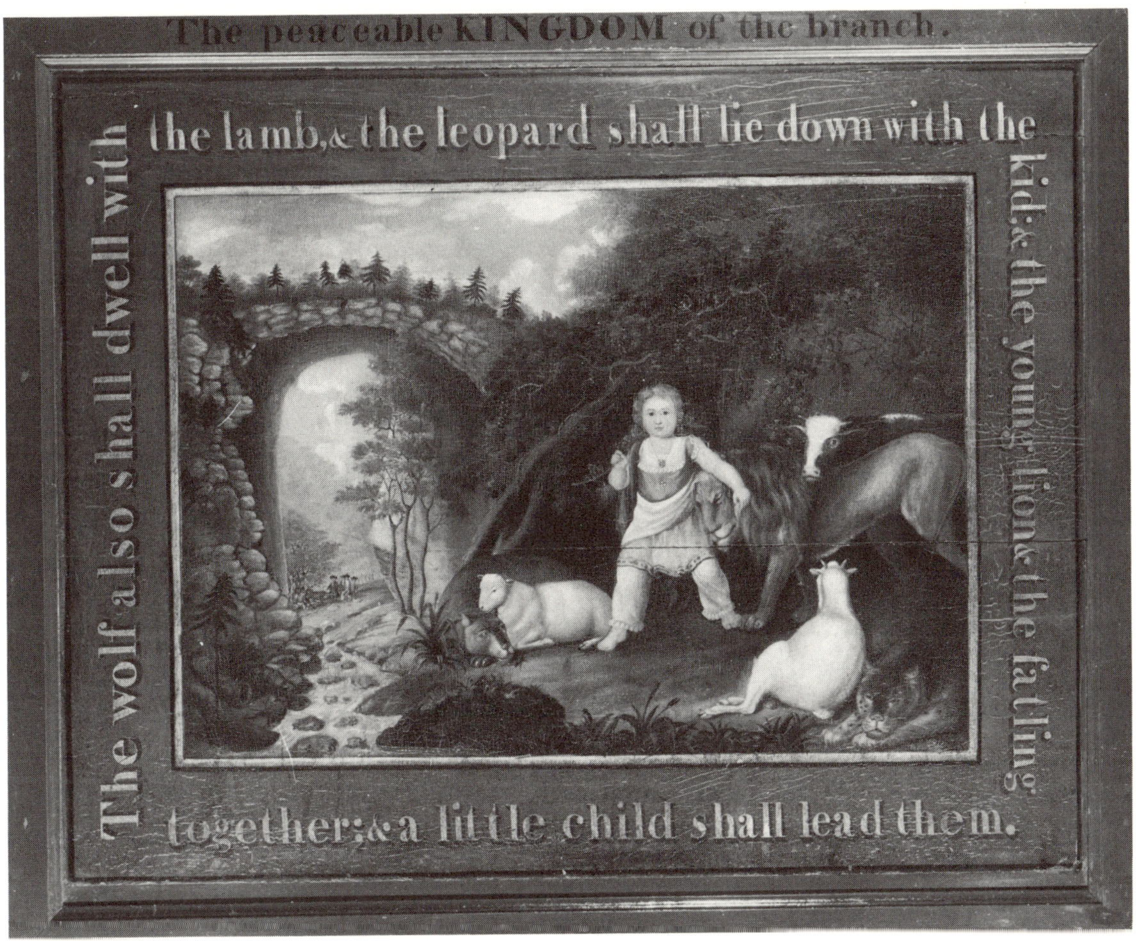

No. 2

PEACEABLE KINGDOM OF THE BRANCH, 1822–25. Oil on wood fireboard, 36¼ × 44⅞ inches. Inscribed on upper member of frame: "The peaceable KINGDOM of the branch." Composition surrounded by inscription in gold: "The wolf also shall dwell with/ the lamb, & the leopard shall lie down with the/ kid; & the young lion & the fatling/ together; & a little child shall lead them" (Isaiah 11:6, omitting the calf). Yale University Art Gallery; gift of Robert W. Carle.

COMMENT: The grape branch over the child's shoulder, like the thicket of vines behind him, symbolizes the redemptive blood of Christ and is derived from Westall. But Hicks adds to Westall's design a Natural Bridge of Virginia from Henry Tanner's 1822 map (James Ayres, "Edward Hicks and His Sources," *Antiques* 109 [1976]: 366–68) and a very small and simplified vignette of *William Penn's Treaty With the Indians* after Benjamin West (1738–1820).

COLLECTIONS: Apparently painted for Dr. Joseph Parrish, Philadelphia, the artist's good friend and personal physician; by descent to Miss Helen Parrish, Philadelphia; purchased 1933 by Dr. Arthur Edwin Bye, Holicong, Pa.; acquired by Edward R. Barnsley, Newtown, Pa.; sold to the painter's great-grandson, Robert W. Carle, New York, who gave it to the Yale University Art Gallery, New Haven, Conn.

EXHIBITIONS: U.S. Section of the International Commission on Folk Arts, "Exhibition of Folk Art" (New York, March–May, 1935); Museum of Modern Art and the Grenoble Museum, France, "Masters of Popular Painting: Modern Primitives of Europe and America" (New York, April 27–July 24, 1938), cat. Holger Cahill, Maximilien Gauthier, Jean Carson, Dorothy C. Miller, et al., no. 1265; AARFAC, "Edward Hicks" (1960), no. 10, ill. p. 11.

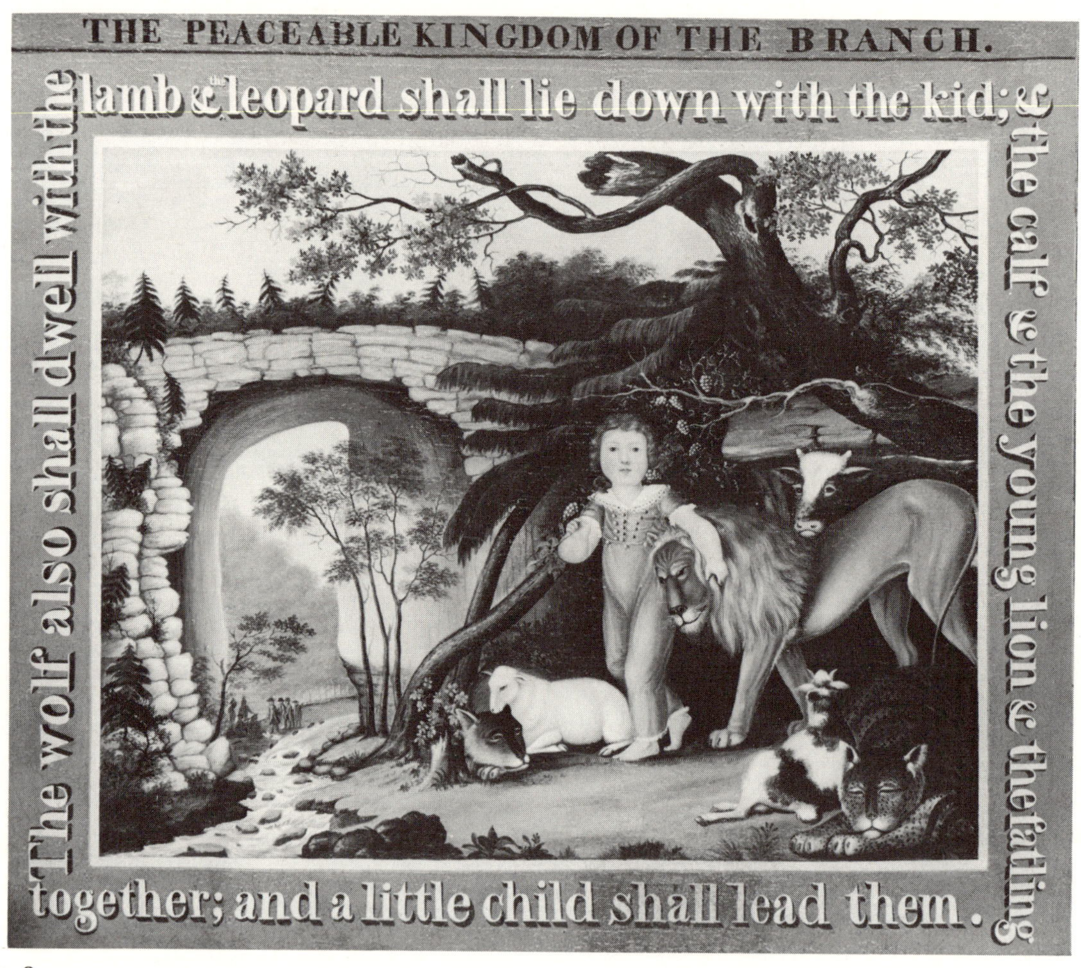

No. 3

PEACEABLE KINGDOM OF THE BRANCH, ca. 1825–30. Oil on canvas, 32¼ × 37¾ inches. Across top of canvas in black: "THE PEACEABLE KINGDOM OF THE BRANCH." Inscription in gold surrounding the picture: "The wolf also shall dwell with the/ lamb & the leopard shall lie down with the kid; &/ the calf & the young lion & the fatling/ together; and a little child shall lead them." Abby Aldrich Rockefeller Folk Art Center.

COMMENT: The biblical inscription in the border quotes Isaiah exactly, including the calf—which, however, does not appear pictorially. Note the contemporary pantaloon suit of simple style: this is the only *Kingdom* in which the child is clothed naturalistically. We do not believe that Hicks intends to portray the infant Jesus, for such a representation would have been as foreign to Quaker quietism as to Puritanism. But to distinguish this figure from the other children who later enter the *Peaceable Kingdoms*, we will call this the Divine Child.

COLLECTIONS: Provenance unknown, lying discarded for years in a midwestern attic. From an unknown dealer to Chester R. Smith, Indianapolis, Ind.; Abby Aldrich Rockefeller Folk Art Center, Williamsburg, Va.

EXHIBITIONS: Abby Aldrich Rockefeller Folk Art Collection, "Then and Now" (Williamsburg, Va., April 20–July 15, 1970).

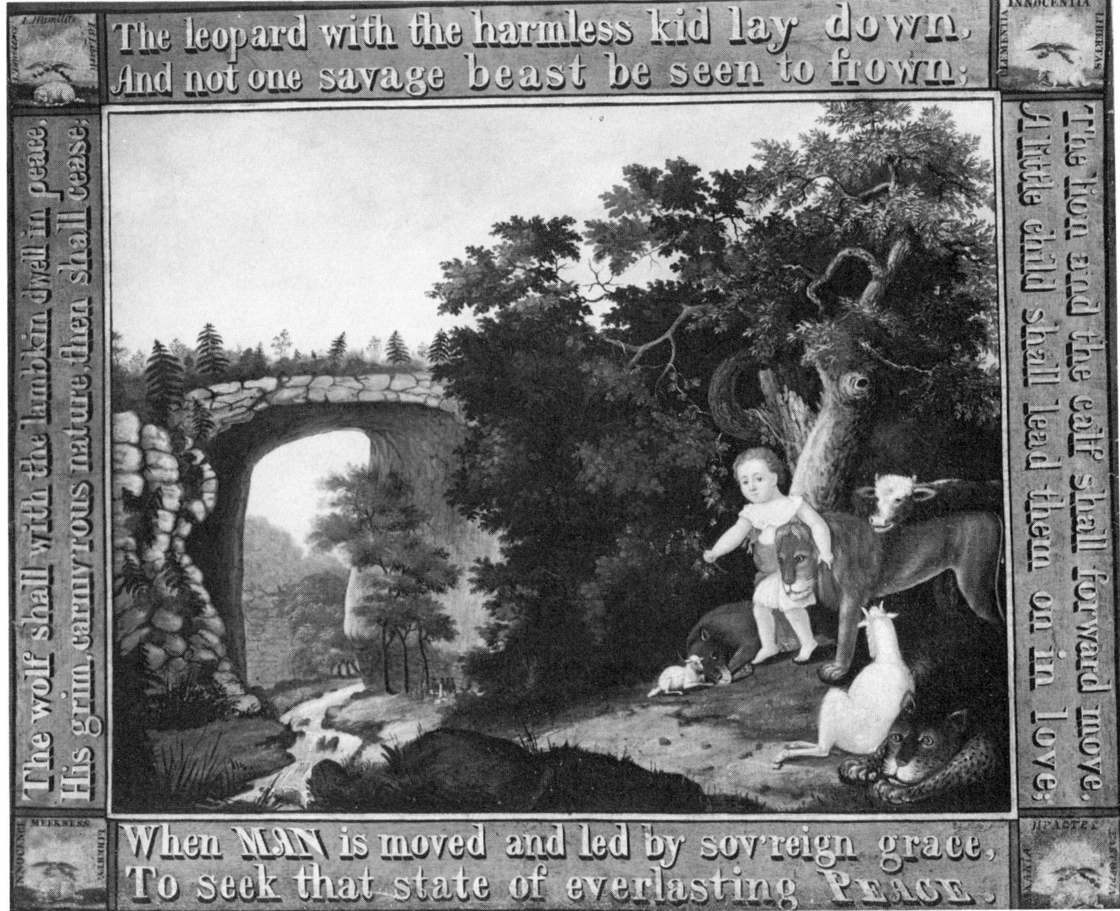

No. 4

PEACEABLE KINGDOM OF THE BRANCH, 1825–26. Oil on canvas, 29 × 35½ inches. Signed on border at lower right, "Edw Hicks Pinx[t]." Couplets surrounding composition read:

The wolf shall with the lambkin dwell in
  peace,
His grim, carniv'rous nature, then shall cease;
The leopard with the harmless kid lay down,
And not one savage beast be seen to frown;
The lion and the calf shall forward move,
A little child shall lead them on in love;
When *MAN* is moved and led by sov'reign
  grace,
To seek that state of everlasting *PEACE*.

Mead Art Museum, Amherst College; gift of Stephen C. Clark.

COMMENT: Natural Bridge scene is surrounded with couplets by artist who decorates corner blocks with a dove, a lamb, and the words *Liberty*, *Meekness*, and *Innocence* in French, Latin, English, and Greek—doubtless with the aid of some erudite friend, since Hicks knew no foreign languages.

COLLECTIONS: Dr. Joseph Parrish*; Arthur Edwin Bye, Holicong, Pa.; Julius Weitzner, New York; Garvan Collection, Yale University Art Gallery, New Haven, Conn.; Richard Loeb, Hampton, N.J. (1942); Maxim Karolik, Boston (1943); Macbeth Gallery, New York; Knoedler & Co., New York; to Macbeth Gallery, New York (1946); to Knoedler & Co., New York (1948); to Macbeth Gallery, New York (1948); to Stephen C. Clark, New York, who presented it to Amherst College, Amherst, Mass.

EXHIBITIONS: University of Kansas Museum of Art, "Masterworks from University and College Art Collections: Thirtieth Anniversary Exhibition" (Lawrence, Kan., 1958); University of Massachusetts (Amherst, Mass., 1958);

---

*This, like several other works by Hicks, was evidently painted for Dr. Joseph Parrish. Arthur Edwin Bye, in an unsigned manuscript at the Bucks County Historical Society, Doylestown, Pa., refers to a *Peaceable Kingdom*, 29 × 35 in., with both a Natural Bridge of Virginia in the background and rhymed borders, which he purchased from Miss Helen Parrish in 1933. She said it had always been in the family.

Hirschl & Adler Galleries, "The Amherst Sesquicentennial Exhibition" (New York, 1972), no. 8; Andrew Crispo Gallery, "Edward Hicks: A Gentle Spirit" (New York, (1st ref.) May 16–July 27, 1975), cat. Eleanore Price Mather, no. 1 (col.).

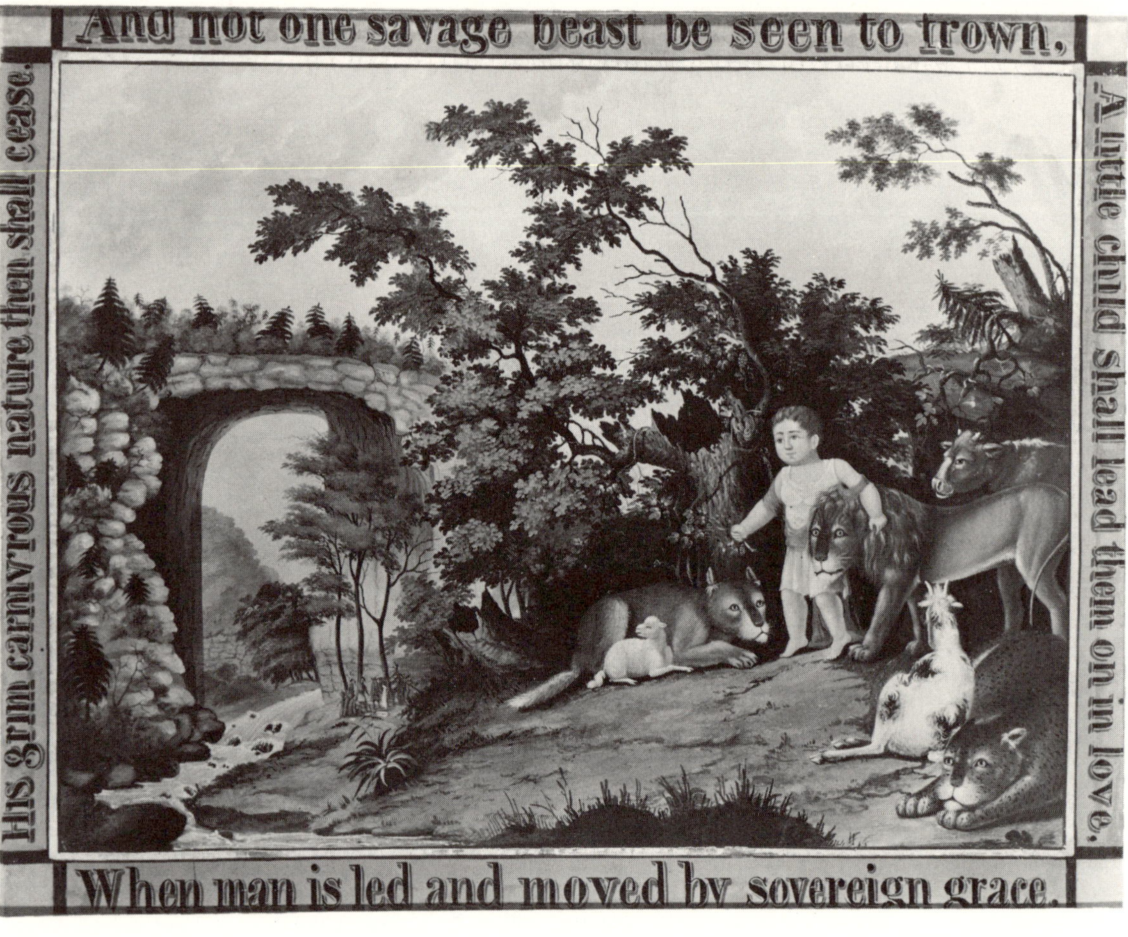

No. 5

PEACEABLE KINGDOM OF THE BRANCH, ca. 1826. Oil on canvas, 24⅜ × 31⅝ inches. Border inscriptions partially turned under, so that only disconnected lines are visible: "His grim carniv'rous nature then shall cease./ And not one savage beast be seen to frown,/ A little child shall lead them all in love./ When man is led and moved by sovereign grace, . . ." (For complete verses see *Peaceable Kingdom* No. 4.) Reynolda House.

COMMENT: Though the child carries on serenely, the landscape is not a peaceable one, its blasted vegetation appearing to have passed through a whirlwind. One suspects there is a psychological significance here, reflecting the artist's reaction to the troubled climate of Quakerism during this period.

COLLECTIONS: Provenance unknown. Judge Potter, Philadelphia; Leonard C. Ashton, Paris Hill, Me.; Ferargil Galleries, New York, N.Y.; Frederick Newlin Price, New Hope, Pa.; Hartert Gallery, New York, N.Y.; Kennedy Galleries, Inc., New York, N.Y.; Reynolda House, Winston-Salem, N.C.

EXHIBITIONS: Ferargil Galleries, "Twenty-sixth Annual Exhibition of Early American Works" (New York, N.Y., 1946), no. 5; Ferargil Galleries (New York, 1951), no. 1; New York Historical Society (New York, July, 1960); Hirschl and Adler Galleries, "Reynolda House American Paintings" (New York, N.Y., November, 1970), cat. Barbara B. Lassiter, no. 7, p. 17 (col.).

Photograph courtesy Kennedy Galleries Inc., New York.

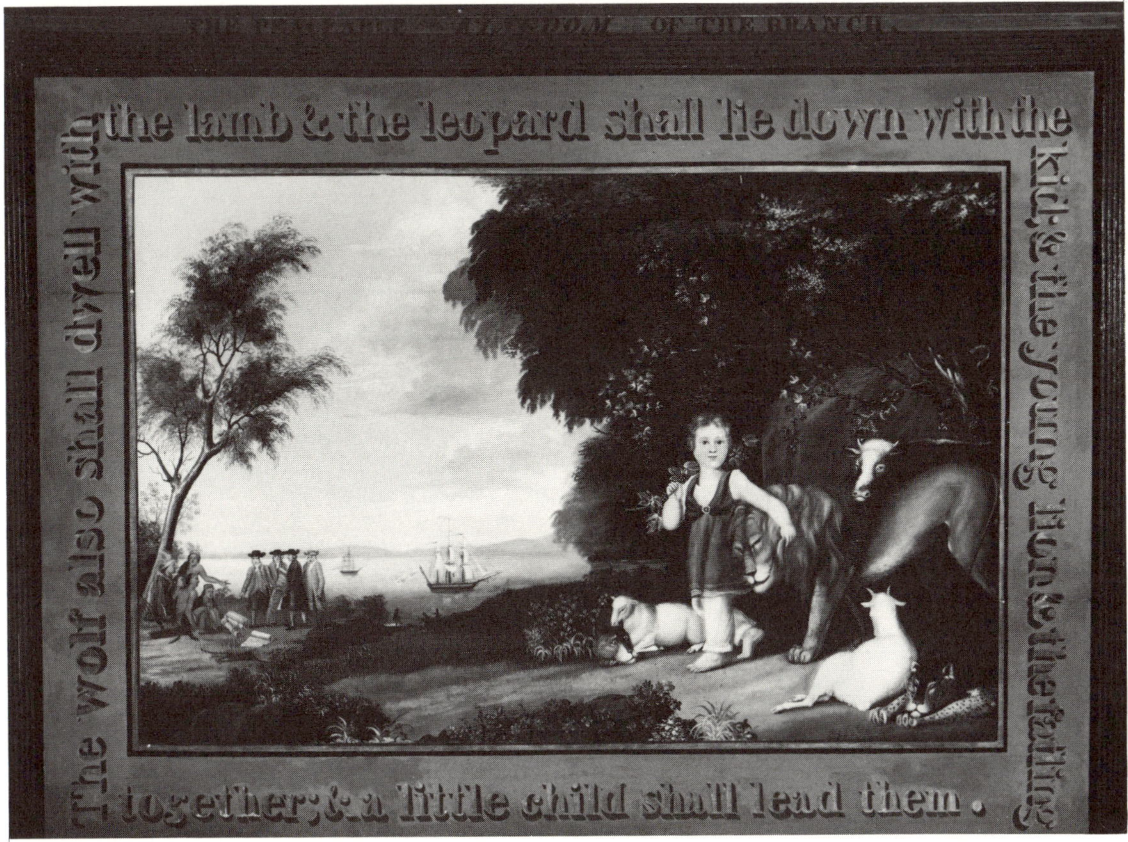

No. 6

PEACEABLE KINGDOM OF THE BRANCH, ca. 1825. Oil on wood panel, 33⅝ × 49½ inches. Bottom member of original reeded frame is missing, presumably because it was notched for use as a fireboard. Inscription on upper member: "THE PEACEABLE *KINGDOM* OF THE BRANCH." Biblical quotation surrounding the picture the same as that in *Peaceable Kingdom* No. 2 (omits calf). Private collection.

COMMENT: The pose of the Divine Child is that of No. 3, but the Natural Bridge has been replaced by a Delaware River landscape, and the simple pantaloon suit by a sumptuous and exotic costume. "Peace on Earth" proclaims the flag on the ship—a device carried over from Hicks's signpainting experience. In 1916 Harold Donaldson Eberlein and Abbot McClure included this in *The Practical Book of Early American Arts and Crafts* (Philadelphia: Lippincott), facing p. 262, noting, " 'The Peaceable Kingdom,' here reproduced in its fireboard form, is really a *chef d'oeuvre* of grotesquerie" (p. 270). Though this sounds disparaging, their inclusion of Hicks's work was in fact a harbinger of the folk art renaissance soon to come.

COLLECTIONS: This fireboard probably belonged to John H. Bunting, Hicksite member of Darby Meeting, an ancestor of Morgan Bunting of Darby, who is credited as owner by Eberlein and McClure; bequeathed to Mrs. Morgan Bunting, Philadelphia; to Eugene J. Sussel, Philadelphia; to a private collector.

EXHIBITIONS: AARFAC, "Edward Hicks" (1960), no. 6, p. 10, not ill.

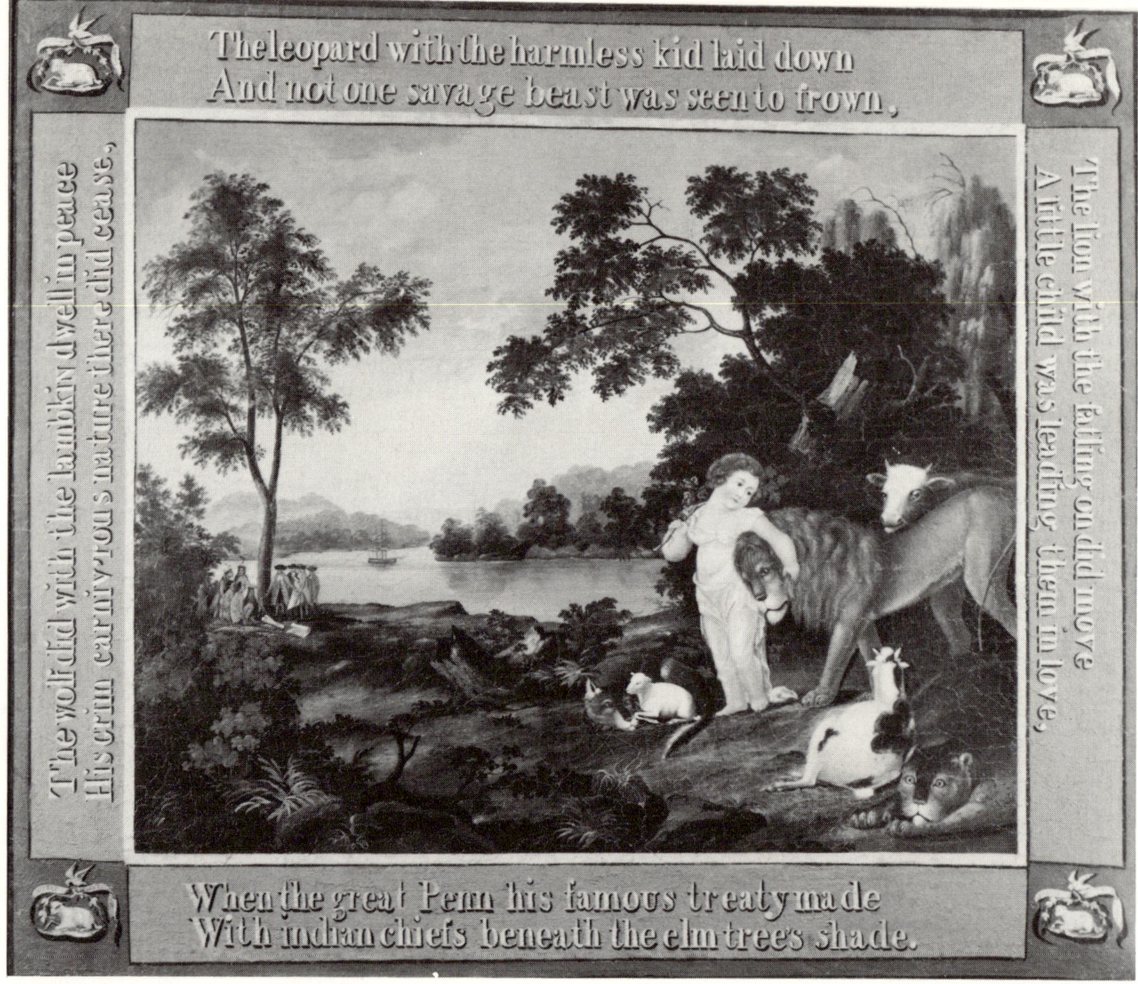

No. 7

PEACEABLE KINGDOM WITH RHYMED BORDERS, 1826. Oil on canvas, 32⅛ × 38⅛ inches. Prior to lining by the Los Angeles County Museum in 1969–70 an inscription on reverse read: "Edward Hicks, Painter to/ his Dear Cousin Sarah [illegible]/ 4$^{mo.}$ 1st 1826 New York." Surrounding poem differs from previous version in respect to fourth couplet:

When the great Penn his famous treaty made
With indian chiefs beneath the elm tree's
 shade.
Ariel B. Appleton.

COMMENT: The Delaware River landscape, partially veiled in mist, is framed with verses paraphrasing the biblical prophecy. Note emphasis on Penn in final couplet, a sign of Hicks's growing identification with the great Quaker leader. The earliest known *Kingdom* with a firm date.

COLLECTIONS: This may be the work referred to in a letter from the painter's cousin Silas Hicks of New York, whose wife was named Sarah. After thanking "Dear Coz Edward Hicks" for "the Painting thee was pleased to present us with," Silas adds that he is enclosing a check for $100.00 (letter of May 1, 1826, Hicks Collection, Alice Ford, *Edward Hicks: Painter of the Peaceable Kingdom* [Philadelphia: University of Pennsylvania Press, 1952], p. 49). To Ariel B. Appleton, Elgin, Ariz.

Photograph courtesy Christie, Manson & Woods International, New York.

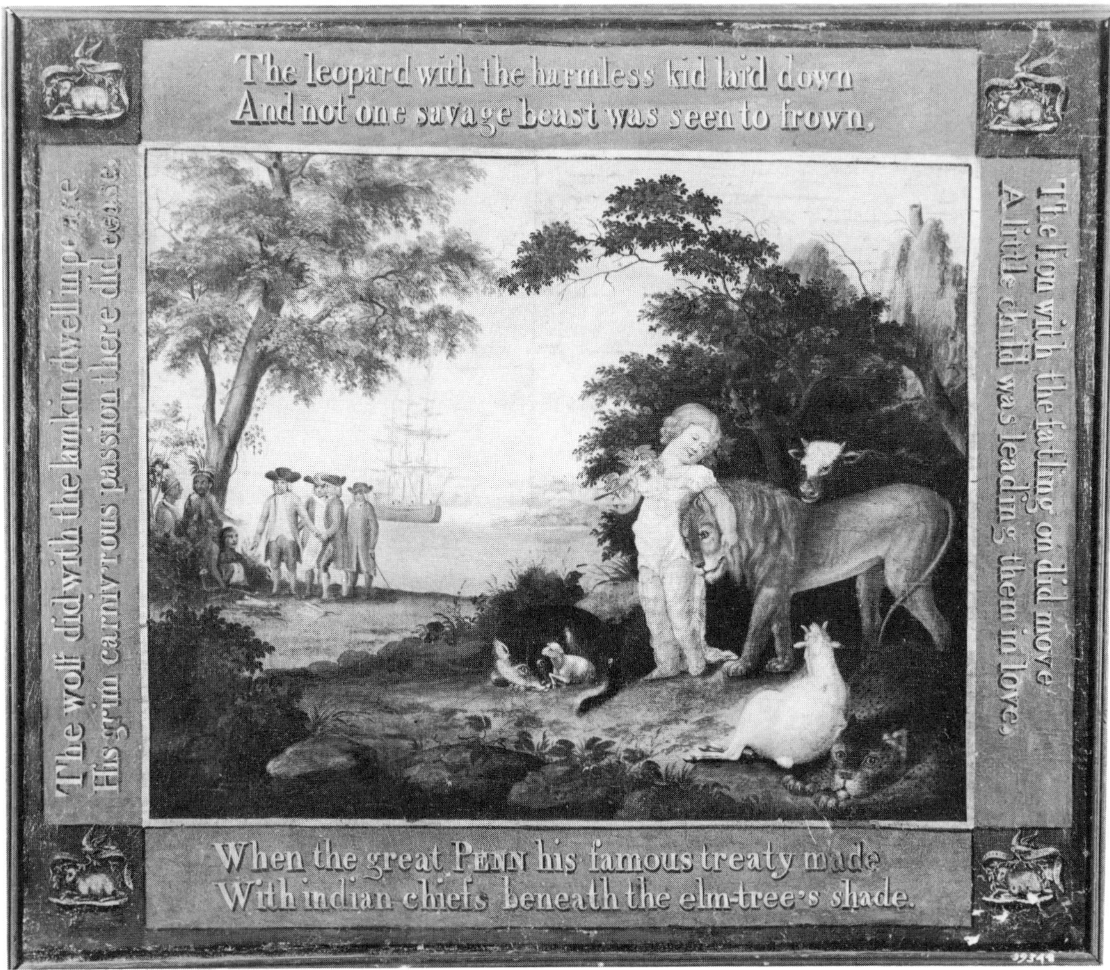

No. 8.

PEACEABLE KINGDOM WITH RHYMED BORDERS, ca. 1826. Oil on canvas, 30 × 36 inches. Original frame of black reeded molding. Private collection.

COMMENT: Shows increasing sophistication and delicacy of technique, both in the central composition with its diaphanously clad Divine Child, and in the marginal details. As in No. 7, the treatment of corner blocks suggests bas-relief, the words *Innocence*, *Meekness*, and *Liberty* here appearing on the banner above the lamb.

COLLECTIONS: One of a pair of works (the other since destroyed—see *Peaceable Kingdom* No. 55) given by the artist to Edward Lawrence of Lawrence, L.I.; by descent to his great-granddaughter, Hortense Howland Dixon of Lawrence; to a private collector.

EXHIBITIONS: Andrew Crispo Gallery, "Edward Hicks: A Gentle Spirit" (New York, 1975), no. 9, (col.).

Photograph courtesy Frick Art Reference Library.

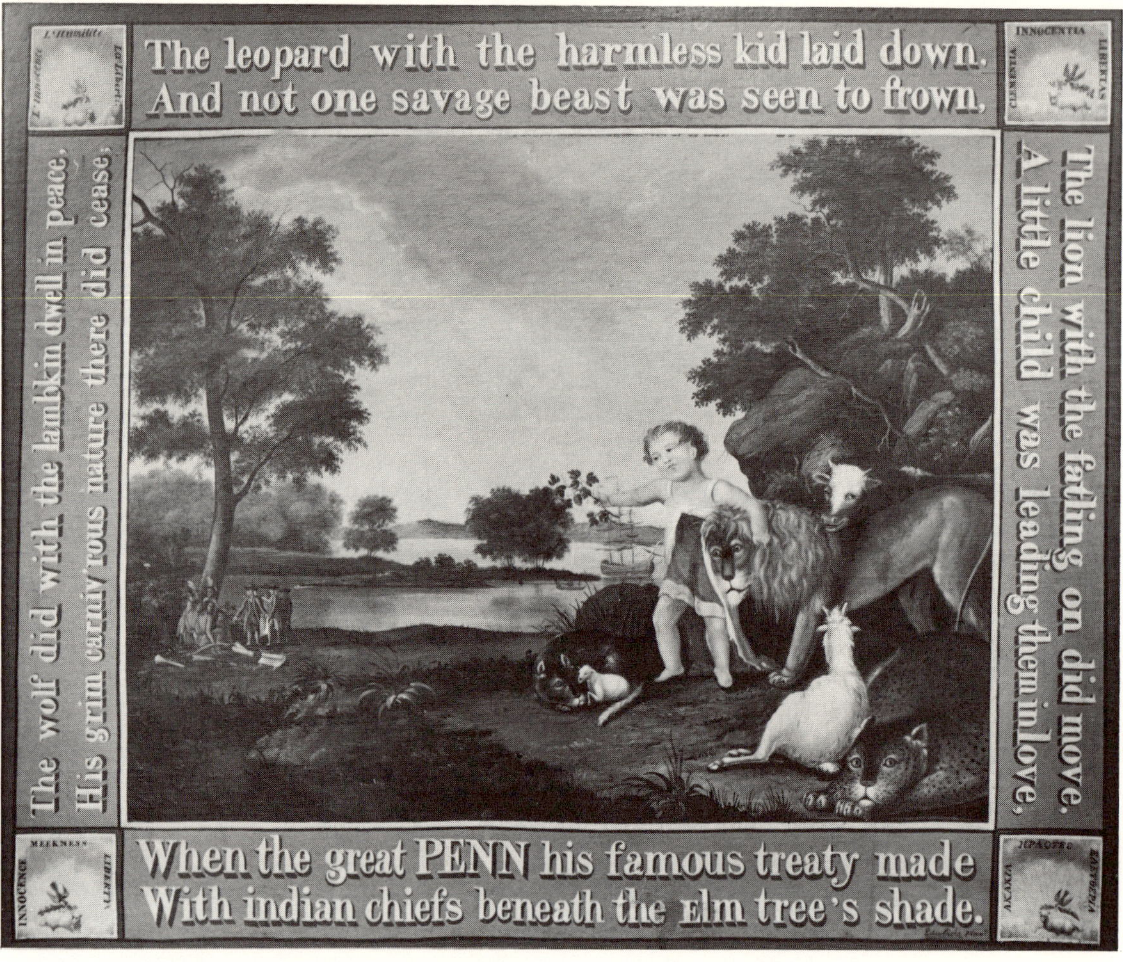

No. 9

PEACEABLE KINGDOM WITH RHYMED BORDERS, ca. 1826. Oil on canvas, 29 × 36 inches. Signed on lower right border, "Edw Hicks, Pinx^t." Friends Historical Library of Swarthmore College.

COMMENT: Considered a late version of an early type, this was long assumed to have been painted around 1840. But the recent discovery of a hitherto unknown *Peaceable Kingdom* (No. 7) of 1826, which this resembles in general form, leads us to assign this to the same approximate date.

COLLECTIONS: Original provenance unknown. Dr. Richard H. Harte (1855–1925) of Philadelphia was the first known owner. Though born in Rock Island, Ill., his middle name, Hickman, is found among Quakers of Chester and Delaware counties, Pennsylvania, suggesting that he may have inherited the canvas from Delaware Valley forebears. He gave it to Dr. Edward Martin, Media, Pa., "with the idea that it should come to Swarthmore College" (*The Phoenix*, 32 [1912–13]:1). Swarthmore College, Swarthmore, Pa.

EXHIBITIONS: AARFAC, "Edward Hicks" (1960), no. 9 p. 10 (not ill.); Carnegie/Corcoran, "Hicks, Kane, Pippin" (1966–67), p. 18; ACA Galleries, "Four American Primitives: Edward Hicks, John Kane, Anna Mary Moses, Horace Pippin" (New York, February 22–March 11, 1972), cat. Leon Anthony Arkus no. 9, ill.; Pennsylvania State University Museum, "Masterworks by Pennsylvania Painters" (University Park, Pa., 1972), no. 11; Galerie St. Etienne, "The Folk Art Tradition" (New York, November 17, 1981–January 9, 1982), cat. Jane Kallir, no. 24.

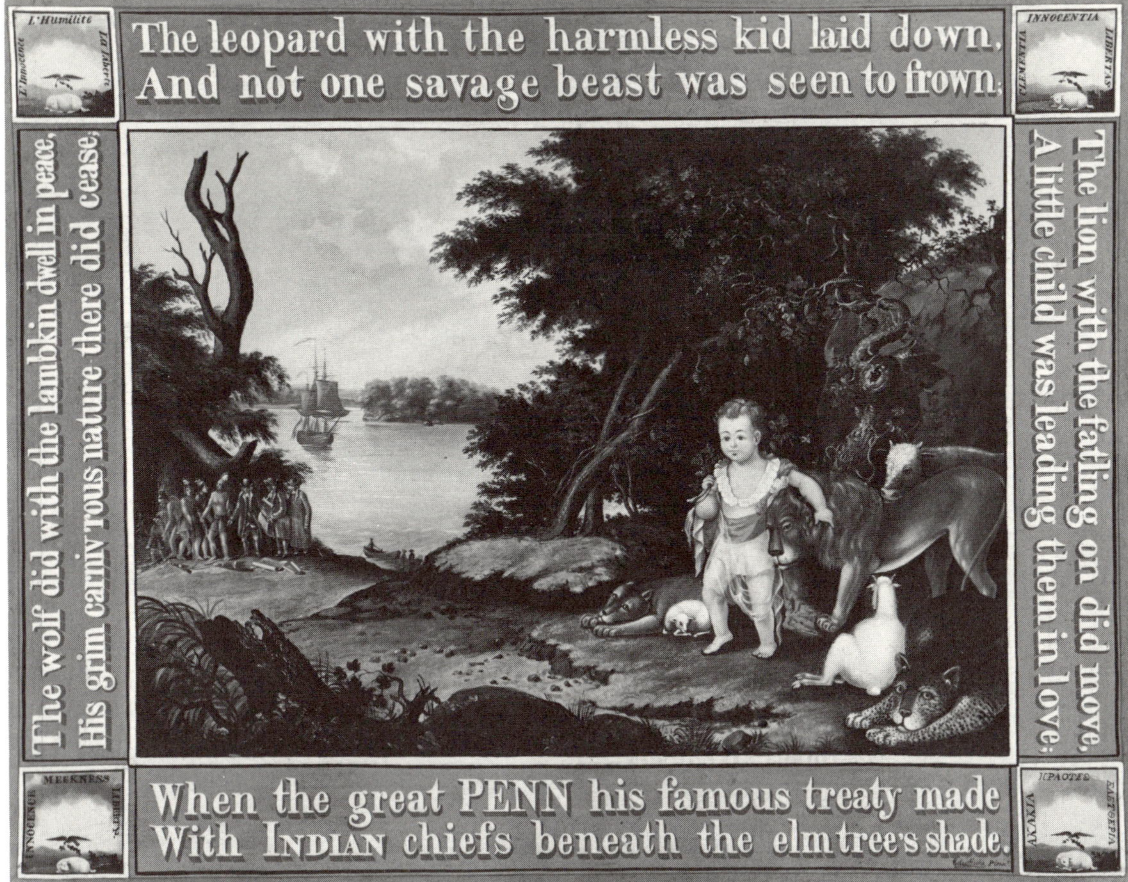

No. 10

PEACEABLE KINGDOM WITH RHYMED BORDERS, ca. 1826. Oil on canvas, 32¼ × 42 inches. Signed on border at lower right, "Edw Hicks Pinx^t." The Museum of Fine Arts, Houston, Bayou Bend Collection; gift of Miss Ima Hogg.

COMMENT: In spite of its cherubic child and gold-lettered border, this is a somewhat somber landscape because of its gray tones and dying vegetation. Note the crossed tree trunks inherited from Westall. They illustrate a diagonal line that recurs in varied forms throughout the *Kingdom* series. ·

COLLECTIONS: A friend of the painter's, Amos Campbell of Newtown, Pa. (later Woodbury, N.J.); by descent to his great-granddaughter, Mrs. Henrietta C. Collins, Haddonfield, N.J.; purchased by Robert Carlen, Philadelphia; Hirschl & Adler Galleries, New York; Ima Hogg, Houston, Tex.; Bayou Bend Collection, the Museum of Fine Arts, Houston, Tex.

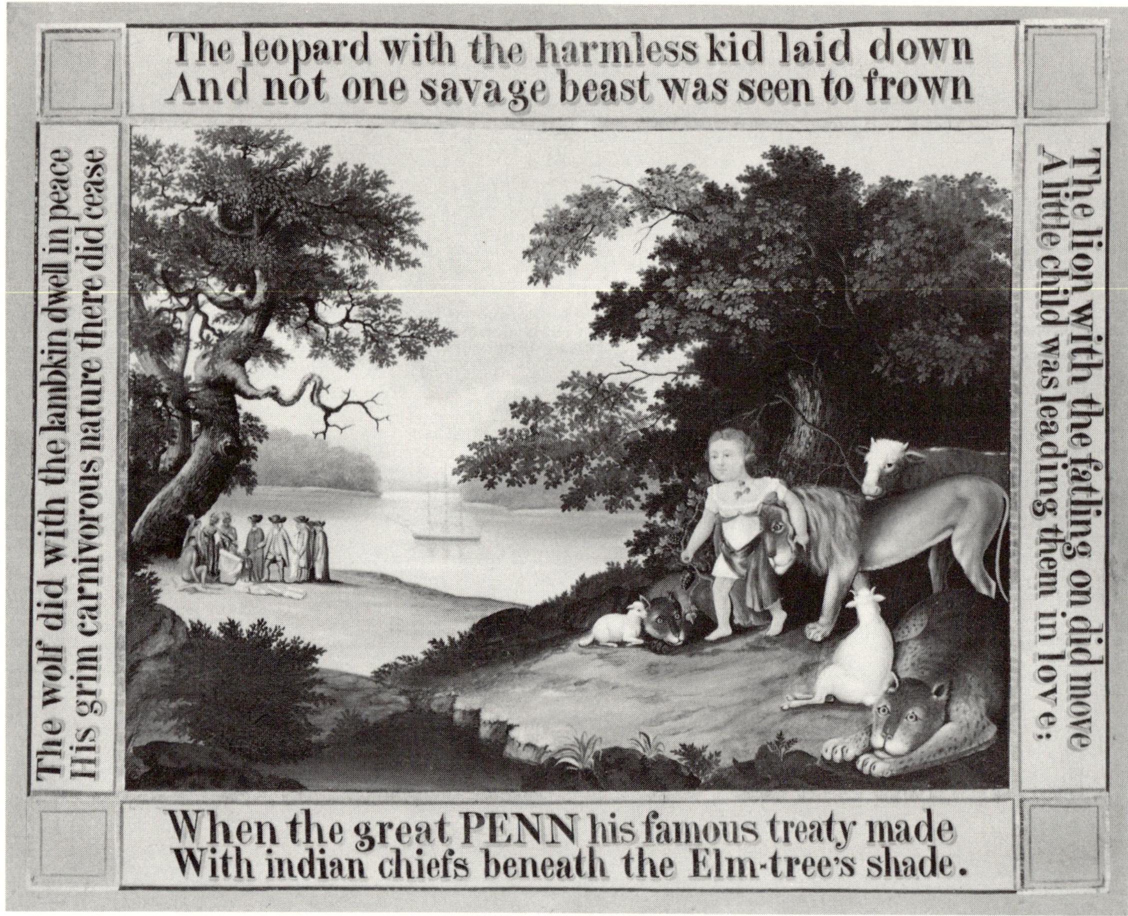

No. 11

PEACEABLE KINGDOM WITH RHYMED BORDERS, 1826. Oil on canvas, 32½ × 41½ inches. Inscribed on reverse: "Edw. Hicks painter/New-town Bucks County/ Penn^a 8 moth 26th." Philadelphia Museum of Art, bequest of Charles C. Willis.

COMMENT: Enlarged Treaty group shows Penn in his traditional blue sash (which does not appear in West's famous original), an Indian queen in leopard skin, and a Penn follower in a scarlet cloak. Above them spreads the large tree from Henry Tanner's 1822 engraving, which the artist also uses in his Niagara Falls compositions.

COLLECTIONS: Given by the painter to his friend Harrison Streeter of Fallsington, Bucks County, Pa.; to Charles C. Willis, Newtown, Pa.; to the Philadelphia Museum of Art, Philadelphia.

EXHIBITIONS: ACA Galleries, "Four American Primitives:" (New York, 1972), no. 1, fig. and detail; Allentown Art Museum, "Pennsylvania Folk Art" (Allentown, Pa., October 20–December 1, 1974, and William Penn Memorial Museum, Harrisburg, Pa., December 14, 1974–February 2, 1975), no. 89, rear cover (col.); Andrew Crispo Gallery, "Edward Hicks: A Gentle Spirit" (New York, 1975), no. 2 (col.).

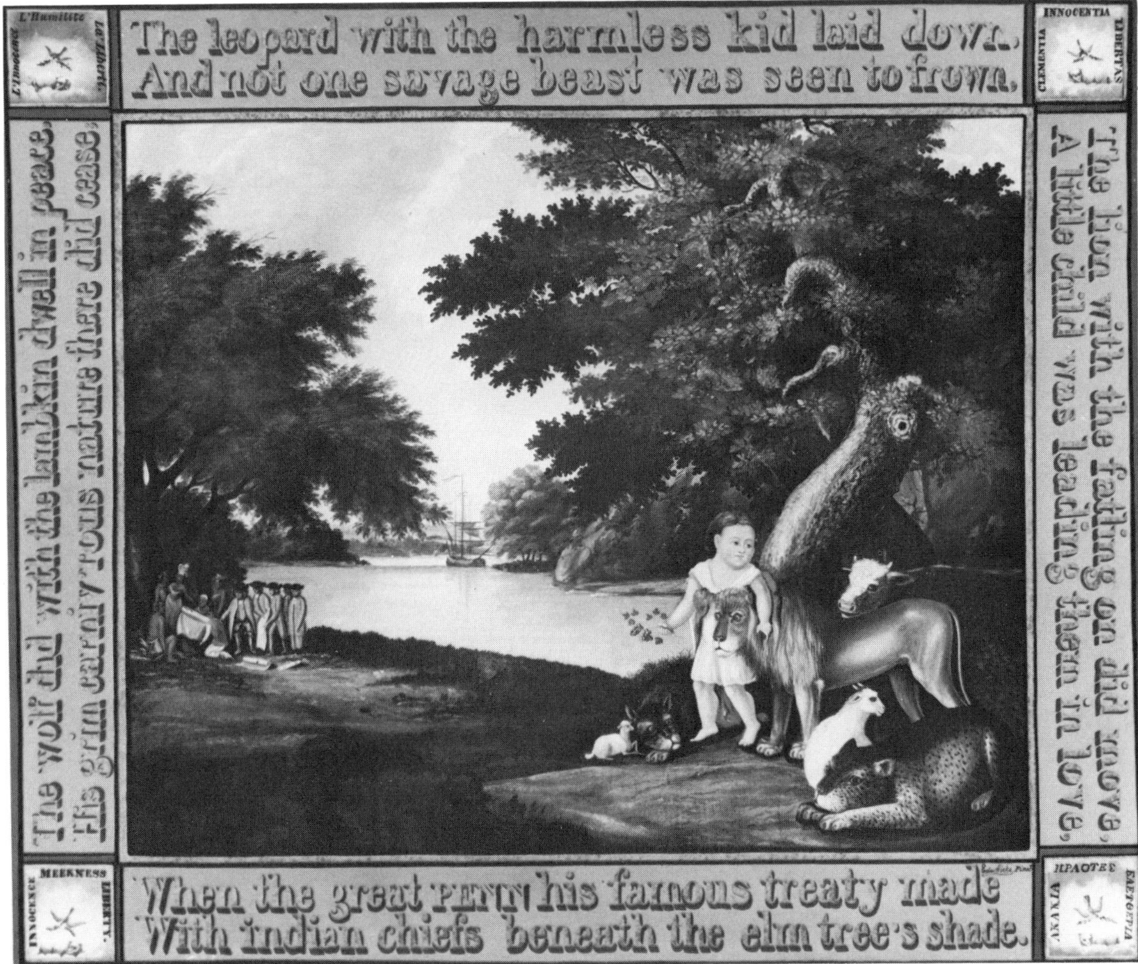

No. 12

PEACEABLE KINGDOM WITH RHYMED BORDERS, 1826–27. Oil on canvas, 29¼ × 35¼ inches. Signed on border at lower right, "Edw. Hicks Pinx^t." Abby Aldrich Rockefeller Folk Art Center.

COMMENT: Here the Indian queen is clad in white rather than leopard skin, and the tree from Tanner's engraving has been transferred to the right of the canvas. Behind it is the great rock, which is a frequent motif in the early *Peaceable Kingdoms*.

COLLECTIONS: Original provenance unknown. Acquired by Dr. Arthur Edwin Bye,* Holicong, Pa.; to Victor Spark, New York; to the Rhode Island School of Design, Providence, R.I.; to Abby Aldrich Rockefeller, New York; to the Abby Aldrich Rockefeller Folk Art Center, Williamsburg, Va.

EXHIBITIONS: AARFAC, "Edward Hicks" (1960), no. 6, p. 10 (not ill.); "American Folk Art from the AARFAC" (visiting Fort Worth Art Center, El Paso Museum of Art, and University of Texas Art Museum, Austin, Tex., May 14–September 15, 1962); the Jewish Museum, "The Hebrew Bible in Christian, Jewish and Muslim Art" (New York, February 18–March 24, 1963); University Art Center of the University of New Mexico, "The Animal Kingdom" (Santa Fe, N.M., February 11–April 28, 1968); Virginia Museum Artmobile Exhibition (September, 1968–September, 1970).

---

*A photograph of this work at the Mercer Museum Library, Bucks County Historical Society, Doylestown, Pa., is inscribed in Dr. Bye's handwriting, "Peaceable Kingdom/formerly in the collection of Dr. A. E. Bye."

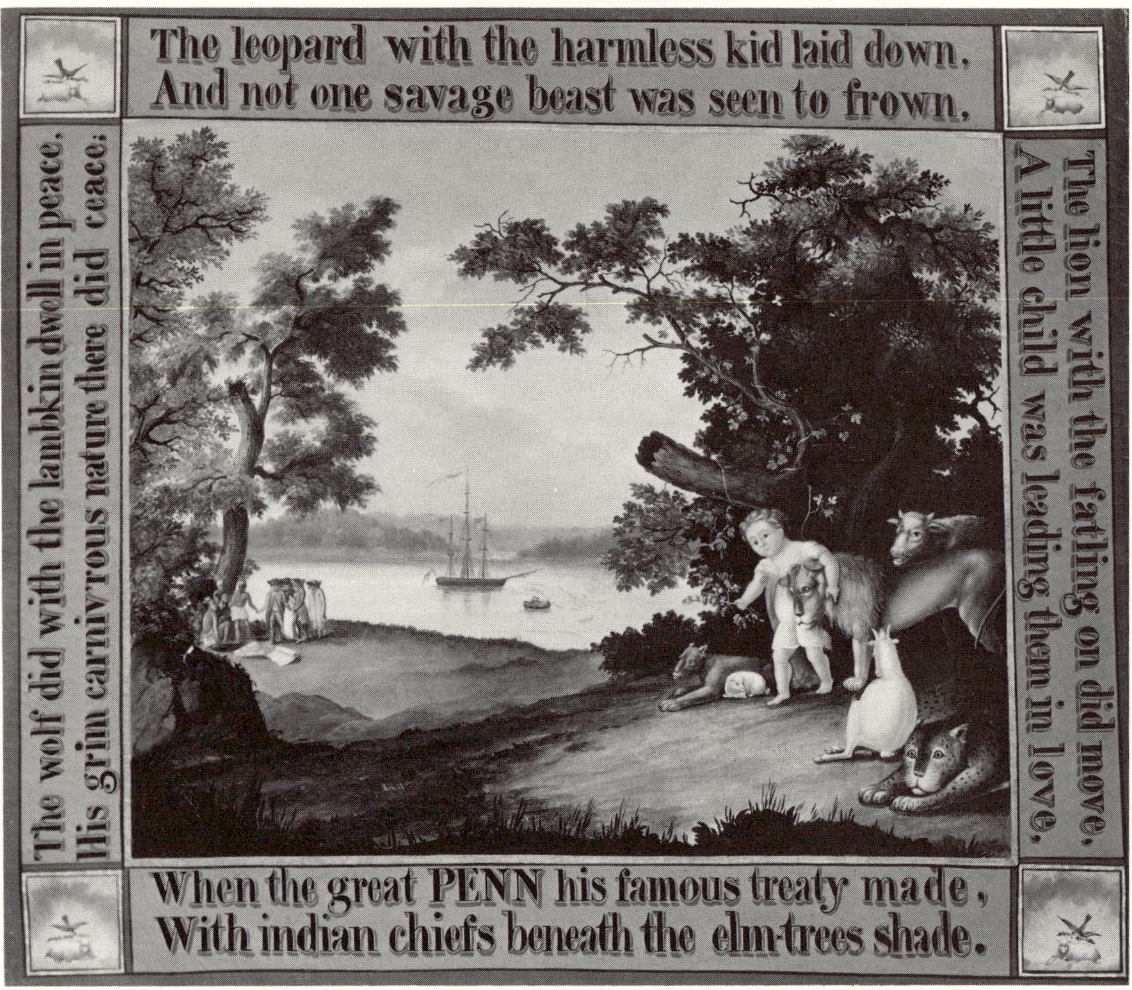

No. 13

PEACEABLE KINGDOM WITH RHYMED BORDERS, 1826–27. Oil on canvas, 30¼ × 36⅛ inches. Original molded mahogany veneer frame. Inscription on reverse of canvas: "Edw. Hicks To his adopped/ Sister Mary Leedom/ & her Daughters didecates/ this humble peice of his art/ of Painting." New York State Historical Association, Cooperstown.

COMMENT: Dove and lamb, possibly symbolizing the Holy Spirit and sacrifice of Christ, appear in the corner blocks without reference to *Innocence*, *Meekness*, and *Liberty*. The final couplet of Hicks's poem celebrates Penn's Treaty with the Indians as the realization of the peaceable kingdom on earth.

COLLECTIONS: Mary Leedom, Newtown, Pa.; to a daughter, Newtown; to her niece, Mrs. Mary A. Cadwallader; acquired by Carl Lindborg, Newtown Square, Pa.; to M. Knoedler & Co., New York; to Howard Lipman, Wilton, Conn.; New York State Historical Association, Cooperstown, N.Y.

EXHIBITIONS: Harry Shaw Newman Gallery, "Identified American Primitives" (New York, 1950); the Century Club (New York, January–February, 1952); Roberson Memorial Center, "Treasure House—New York State" (Binghamton, N.Y., December, 1954); Milwaukee Junior League, "Birds and Animals" (Milwaukee, Wis., October–December, 1957); Brussels International Exhibition, "American Primitive Art," Smithsonian Traveling Exhibition Service (Brussels, Belgium, April–October, 1958); AARFAC, "Edward Hicks" (1960), no. 8, p. 10 (not ill.); Historical Society of Talbot County, Easton, Md. (September, 1962), illustrating talk by Dr. Louis C. Jones; Carnegie/Corcoran, "Hicks, Kane, Pippin" (1966–67), ill. p. 7.

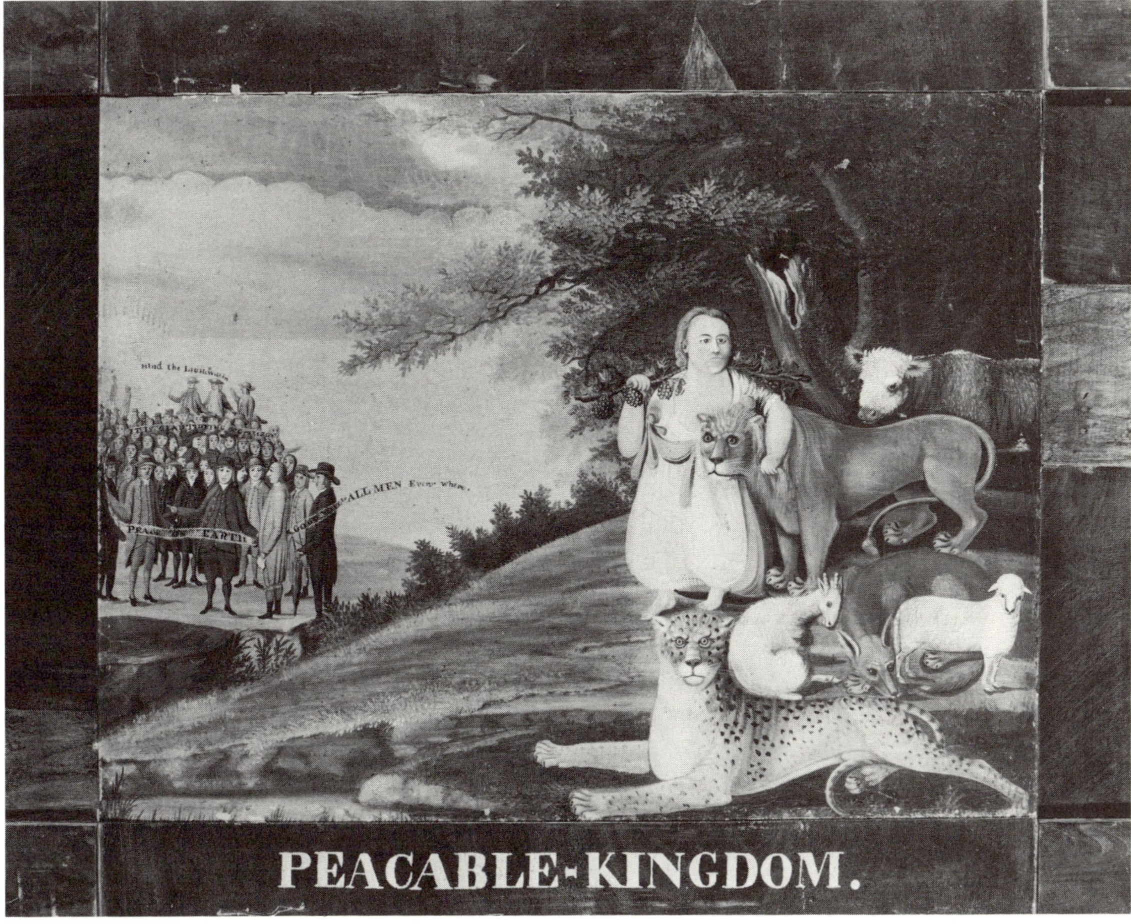

No. 14

PEACEABLE KINGDOM WITH QUAKERS BEARING BANNERS, ca. 1827–32. Oil on canvas, 17¾ × 23¾ inches. Original cherry veneer, block-cornered frame inscribed "PEACABLE-KINGDOM." Holger Cahill Collection.

COMMENT: Possibly the first painted of a new category reflecting the Quaker schism of 1827. Penn's Treaty is replaced by a pyramid of Quakers with Elias Hicks—controversial religious leader and cousin of the painter—in the foreground. Banner inscription combines Hicksite doctrine with the angel song announcing the birth of Christ from the Gospel of Luke: "Mind the LIGHT within IT IS GLAD TIDEING of Grate Joy PEACE ON EARTH GOOD WILL to ALL MEN Everywhere."

COLLECTIONS: Provenance unknown. Acquired by Edith Gregor Halpert from an individual in New York in 1933; purchased by Holger Cahill, New York; Holger Cahill Collection, New York. On extended loan to Smith College, Northampton, Mass.

EXHIBITIONS: AARFAC, "Edward Hicks" (1960), no. 15, p. 12, (not ill.); Carnegie/Corcoran, "Hicks, Kane, Pippin" (1966–67), p. 4; Andrew Crispo Gallery, "Edward Hicks: A Gentle Spirit" (New York, 1975), no. 4, ill.

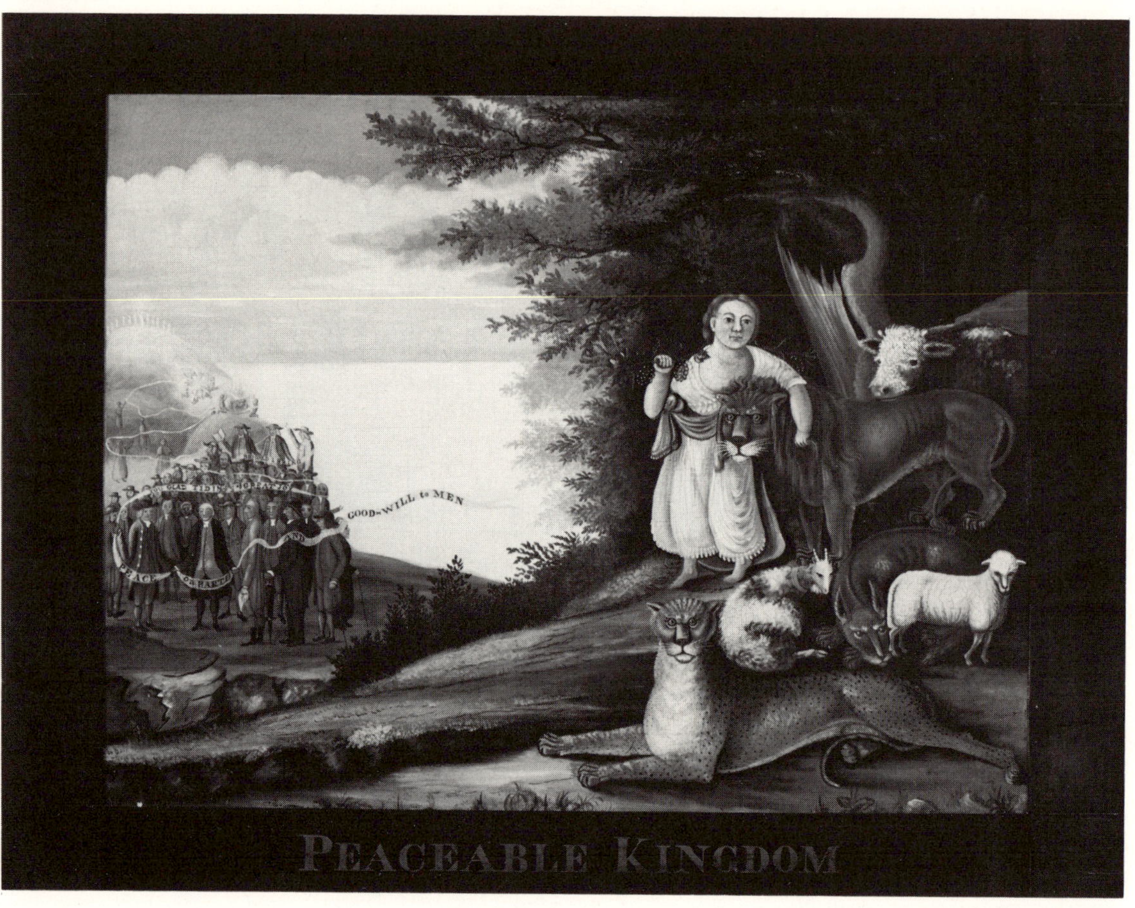

No. 15

PEACEABLE KINGDOM WITH QUAKERS BEARING BANNERS, 1827–32. Oil on canvas, 17½ × 23½ inches. Original cherry veneer frame with block corners, inscribed "PEACE-ABLE KINGDOM." Yale University Art Gallery; bequest of Robert W. Carle.

COMMENT: Thirteen rays of light on the mountain top were recognized as Christ and the Apostles by Alice Ford (*Edward Hicks, Painter of the Peaceable Kingdom* (Philadelphia: University of Pennsylvania Press, 1952), p. xii, note on Plate 3). From the central ray descends the banner that gives this category its name, the inscription here revised and spelling corrected: "BEHOLD I BRING YOU GLAD TIDINGS of GREAT JOY PEACE ON EARTH and GOOD-WILL TO MEN." Details of vegetation on the lower margin and lettering on frame are similar to those on *Penn Treaty* No. 86, also formerly owned by Robert Carle, the painter's great-grandson, suggesting that the two pictures may have been intended as a pair.

COLLECTIONS: Always in the Hicks family; Robert W. Carle, South Salem, Conn.; Yale University Art Gallery, New Haven, Conn.

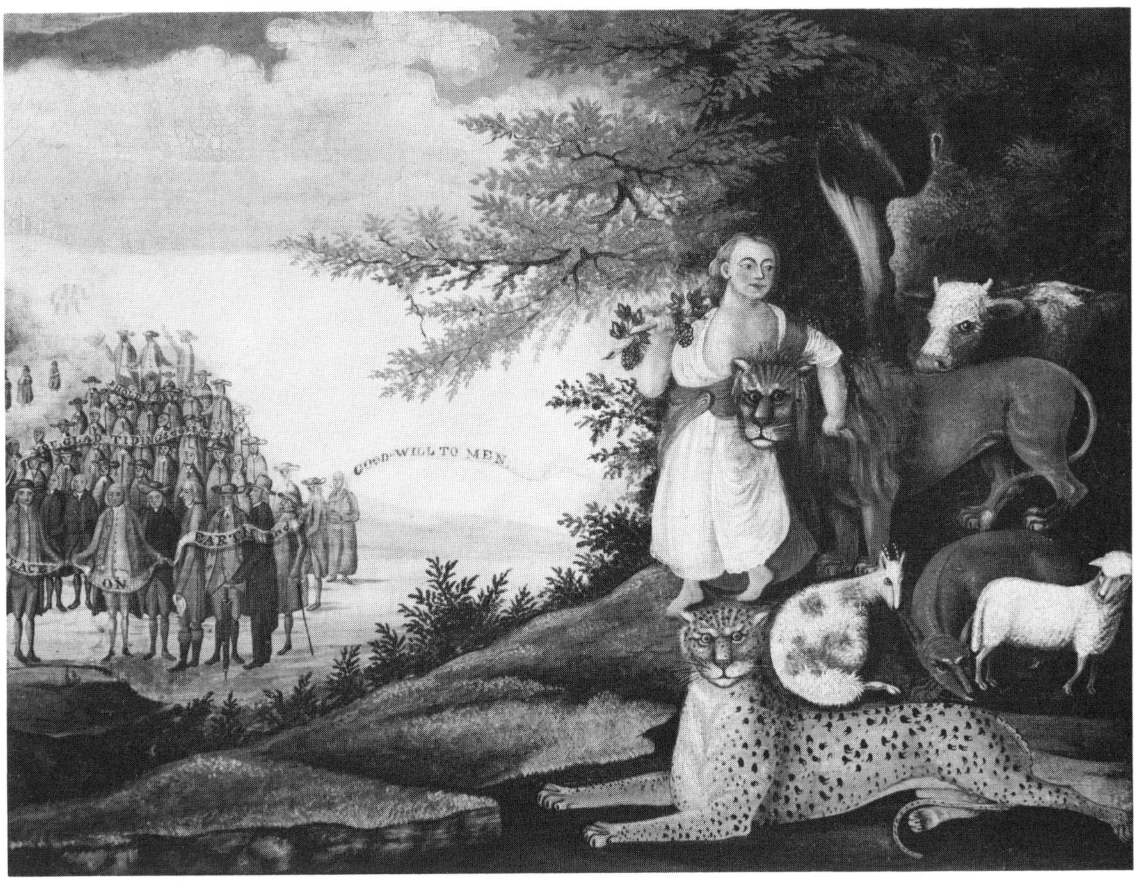

No. 16

PEACEABLE KINGDOM WITH QUAKERS BEARING BANNERS, 1827–32. Oil on canvas, 17¾ × 23¾ inches. (Nineteenth-century mahogany frame not original with painting.) Friends Historical Library of Swarthmore College; gift of William P. Sharpless.

COMMENT: The Divine Child is now a little girl in a long dress. Note signs of conflict: divided composition, cleft tree, and hostile faces of certain animals, though banner reads, "BHOLD [sic] I BRING YOU GLAD TIDINGS of GREAT JOY PEACE ON EARTH AND GOOD WILL TO MEN." Mary C. Black, curator of painting at the Rockefeller Collection in Williamsburg, perceived in these symbols of hostility a reflection of the Hicksite–Orthodox controversy ("& a Little Child Shall Lead Them," *Arts in Virginia* [1960]:24). Soon after, Dr. Frederick B. Tolles of Swarthmore College discovered a more specific source: a poem by Samuel Johnson, "To Edward Hicks on his proposition for painting an Historical piece commemorative of the progress of religious Liberty" (Tolles, "The Primitive Painter As Poet," *Bulletin of Friends Historical Association,* 50 [1961]: 12–30).

COLLECTIONS: Exact provenance unknown, but possibly inherited by William Sharpless, West Chester, Pa., or more probably by his wife, Frances Linton Sharpless (Swarthmore College, 1876), whose grandparents, John, Jr., and Jane Smith Linton, lived on a farm near Newtown, Bucks County and were distant relatives of the Dr. Morris Linton to whom Hicks gave the *Washington at the Delaware* now at Williamsburg. (See Morris Linton, "A Genealogy of the Descendants of John Linton (1662–1708) and Rebecca Delf and Their In-Laws," Historical Society of Pennsylvania, Philadelphia, 1:291 and 2:54.) Presented by William P. Sharpless to Swarthmore College, Swarthmore, Pa.

EXHIBITIONS: AARFAC, "Edward Hicks" (1960), no. 14, ill. p. 12; Carnegie/Corcoran, "Hicks, Kane, Pippin" (1966–67), ill. p. 3; University Art Museum, "The Hand and the Spirit" (Berkeley, Calif., 1972–73), no. 39, ill. p. 93; Andrew Crispo Gallery, "Edward Hicks: A Gentle Spirit" (New York, 1975), no. 3 (col.); Whitney Museum of American Art, "American Folk Painters of Three Centuries" (New York, February 25–May 18, 1980), ill. p. 90.

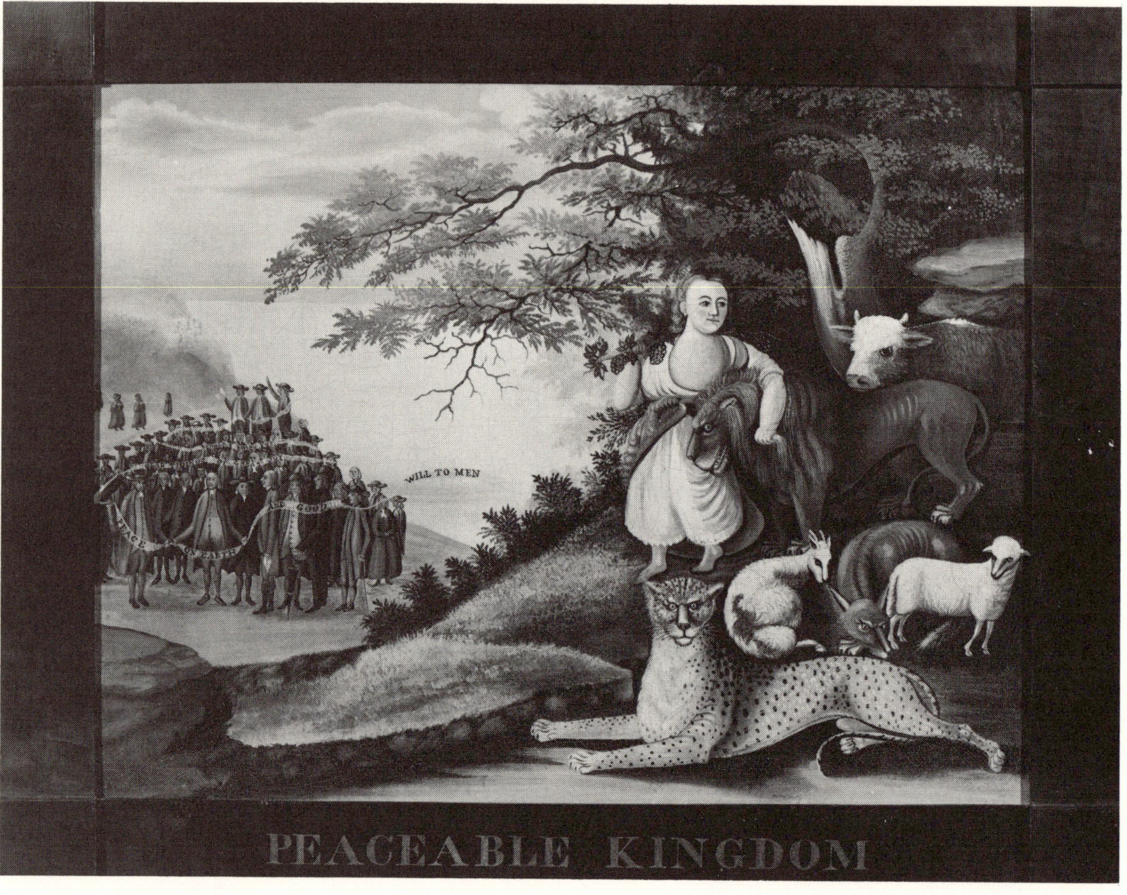

No. 17

PEACEABLE KINGDOM WITH QUAKERS
BEARING BANNERS, 1827–32. Oil on canvas,
17⅝ × 23⅝ inches. Original cherry veneer
frame with corner blocks, inscribed "PEACE-
ABLE KINGDOM." Courtesy of the San Antonio Museum Association, San Antonio,
Texas.

COMMENT: Three figures atop the Quaker pyr-
amid are recognizable: right to left: George
Fox—founder of Quakerism—preaching, Wil-
liam Penn extending arms in friendship, and
Robert Barclay expounding his book *The
Apology,* a classic defense of Quakerism. This
trio is not only mentioned in Samuel John-
son's poem, but many times in Hicks's own
Memoirs. Banner reads, "BEHOLD I BRING
YOU GLAD TIDINGS OF GREAT JOY PEACE
ON EARTH AND GOOD WILL TO MEN."

COLLECTIONS: Presumably the painter's son
Isaac (1809–98), Newtown, Pa.; his daughter
Sarah Worstall Hicks, Newtown; her cousin
Tacie Parry (Mrs. Robert R.) Willets, New
York; to her brother and his wife, Mr. and Mrs.
John Carle Parry, Wyncote, Pa.; to their son,
Edward Hicks Parry,* Wyncote, Pa., who in
joint ownership with his niece, Martha Parry
Hankin, sold it to Hirschl & Adler Galleries,
New York: to the Ewing Halsell Foundation,
San Antonio, Tex.; presented to the San An-
tonio Museum Association in memory of Eva
Halsell McCluskey.

EXHIBITIONS: Hirschl & Adler Galleries,
"Quality, An Experience in Collecting" (New
York, 1974), no. 21.

---

   *Wrote Edward Hicks Parry: "A younger sister
(Tacie) of my father John C. (grandson of EH) married Robert R. Willets of N.Y. and she and he on
one of their visits in Newtown in the late 80's or
very early 90's procured at least 3, and probably as
many more, P K's from Cousin Sarah W. Hicks. One
of these they gave my father and mother" (letter to
author, dated at Wyncote, Pa., November 2, 1974).

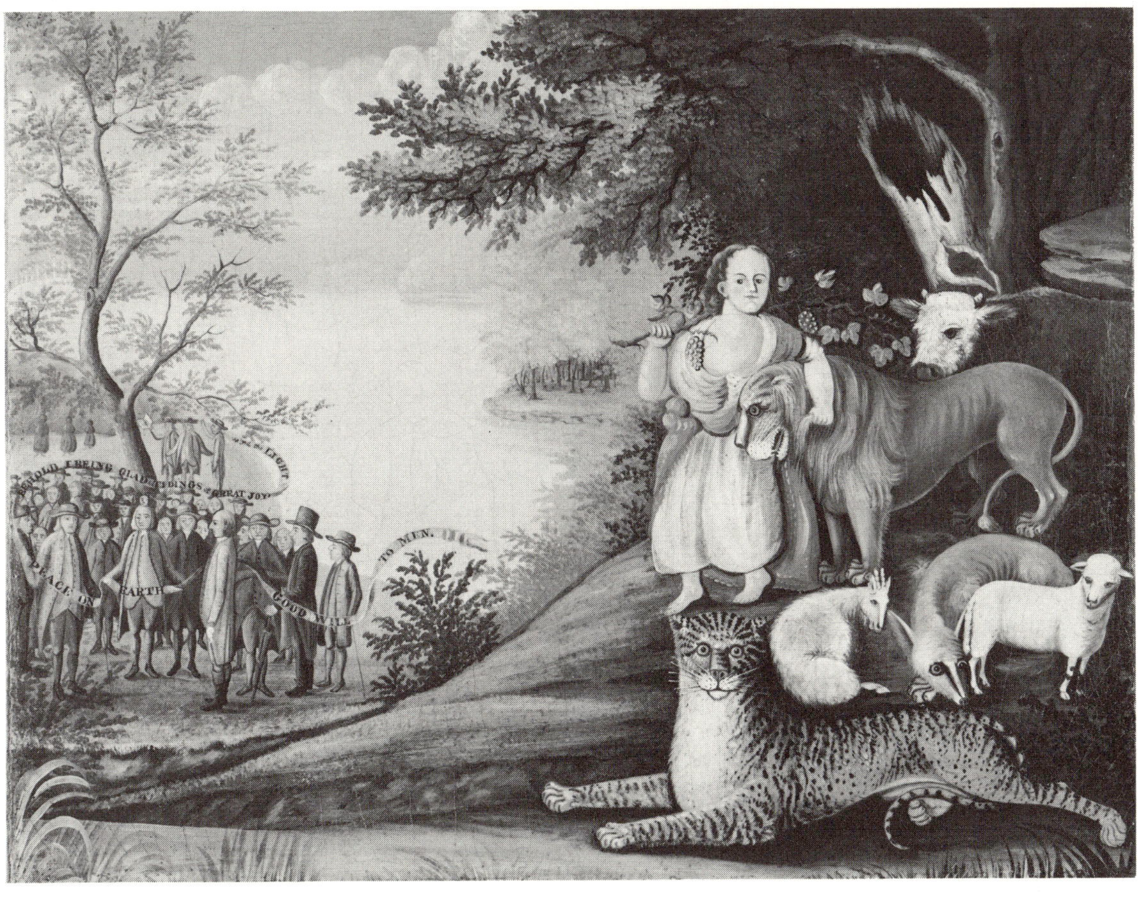

No. 18

PEACEABLE KINGDOM WITH QUAKERS BEARING BANNERS, 1830–32. Oil on canvas, 17⅝ × 23⅝ inches. Original cherry veneer frame with block corners. Courtesy, The Henry Francis du Pont Winterthur Museum.

COMMENT: The "Quaker *Kingdoms*," as these works are sometimes called, are not the earliest of Hicks's surviving canvases, and yet in certain respects they are the most primitive. This version is full of fifteenth-century survivals: linear tree, inscribed banners, heraldic leopard, and an unabashed mingling of Apostles and Quaker founders with the artist's own contemporaries. Likewise, the supernatural radiance from afar carries a didactic message, "Mind the LIGHT," as the banner twines about George Fox, continuing, "BEHOLD I BRING GLAD TIDINGS of GREAT JOY. PEACE ON EARTH GOOD WILL TO MEN."

COLLECTIONS: Provenance unknown. Mr. Henry Francis du Pont, Winterthur, Del. The Henry Francis du Pont Winterthur Museum, Winterthur, Del.

EXHIBITIONS: On loan to the Walters Art Gallery, New York, in 1944, when owned by Mr. du Pont (at which time it was conserved by David Rosen). Winterthur Museum, "Beyond Necessity: Art in the Folk Tradition" (Brandywine River Museum, Chadds Ford, Pa., September 17–November 16, 1977), catalogue by Kenneth Ames, no. 12 (not ill.).

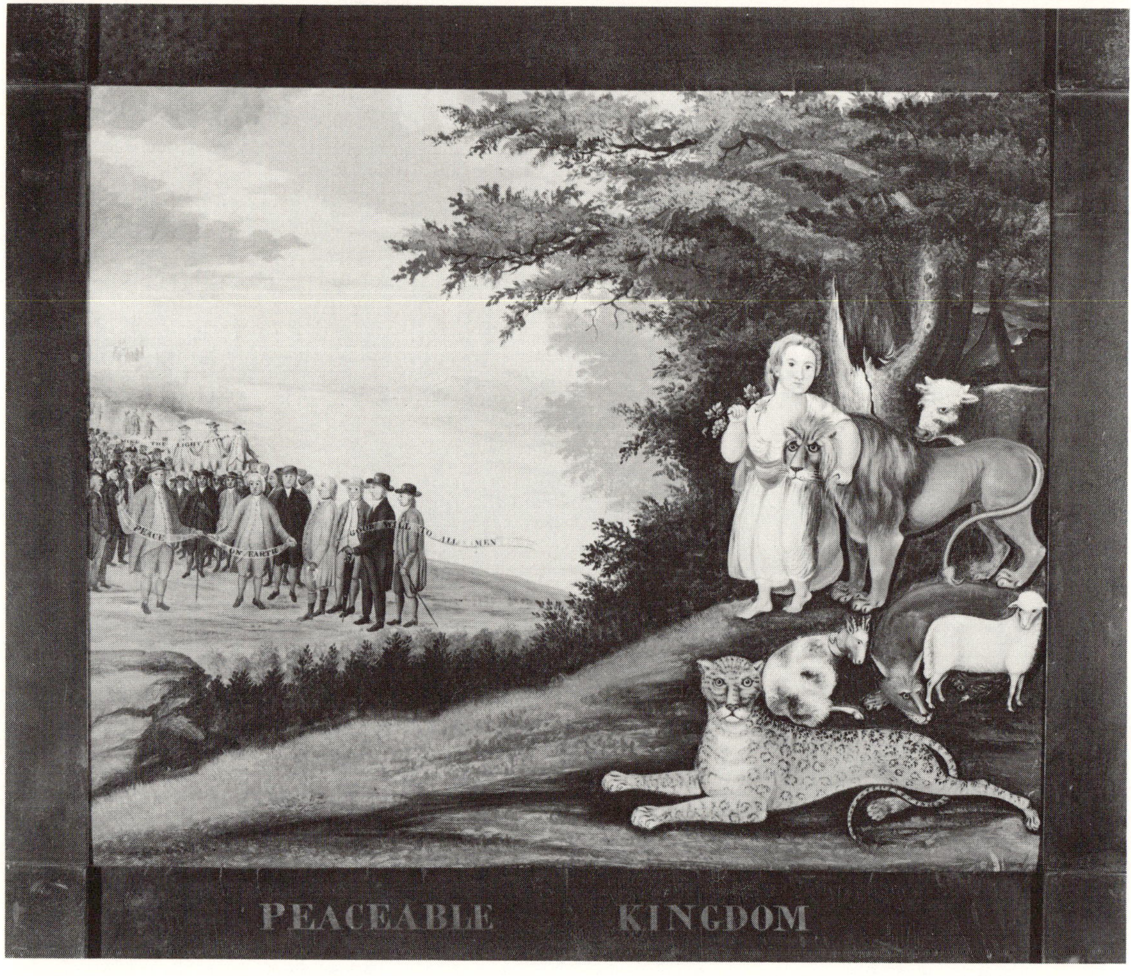

No. 19

PEACEABLE KINGDOM WITH QUAKERS BEARING BANNERS, 1830–32. Oil on canvas, 23½ × 30 inches. Original block-cornered cherry veneer frame inscribed, "PEACEABLE KINGDOM."* Private collection.

COMMENT: Here the message on the banner is further revised: "MIND THE LIGHT of Truth/ PEACE ON EARTH GOOD WILL TO ALL MEN." The influence of the Winterthur example is also seen in the hint of shore line and the flattening of the pyramid of Quakers by the emergence of the tree—although the tree itself has disappeared. Note the kid's buckled collar of light blue.

COLLECTIONS: For original provenance see note below. Acquired by Mrs. Edwin Lewis Read, Jr., Tucson, Ariz.; Hirschl & Adler Galleries, New York; to a private collector.

EXHIBITIONS: Hirschl & Adler Galleries, "Twenty-Five American Masterpieces" (New York, April 23–May 11, 1968), no. 9 (col.).

Photograph courtesy Hirschl & Adler Galleries, New York.

---

*A typed notation is fixed to the reverse. Neither type nor paper look old, suggesting a recently annotated copy of an old inscription, which reads:

PEACEABLE KINGDOM painted between 1825 and 1835 by Edward Hicks (1780–1849)

This particular canvas was painted by Hicks for his brother-in-law and was secured by the latter's niece in Ephrata, Pa. Hicks was a Quaker preacher who made his living as a coach and sign painter. His best-known canvases are of this same subject but a few others have been credited to him and were all Biblical subjects.

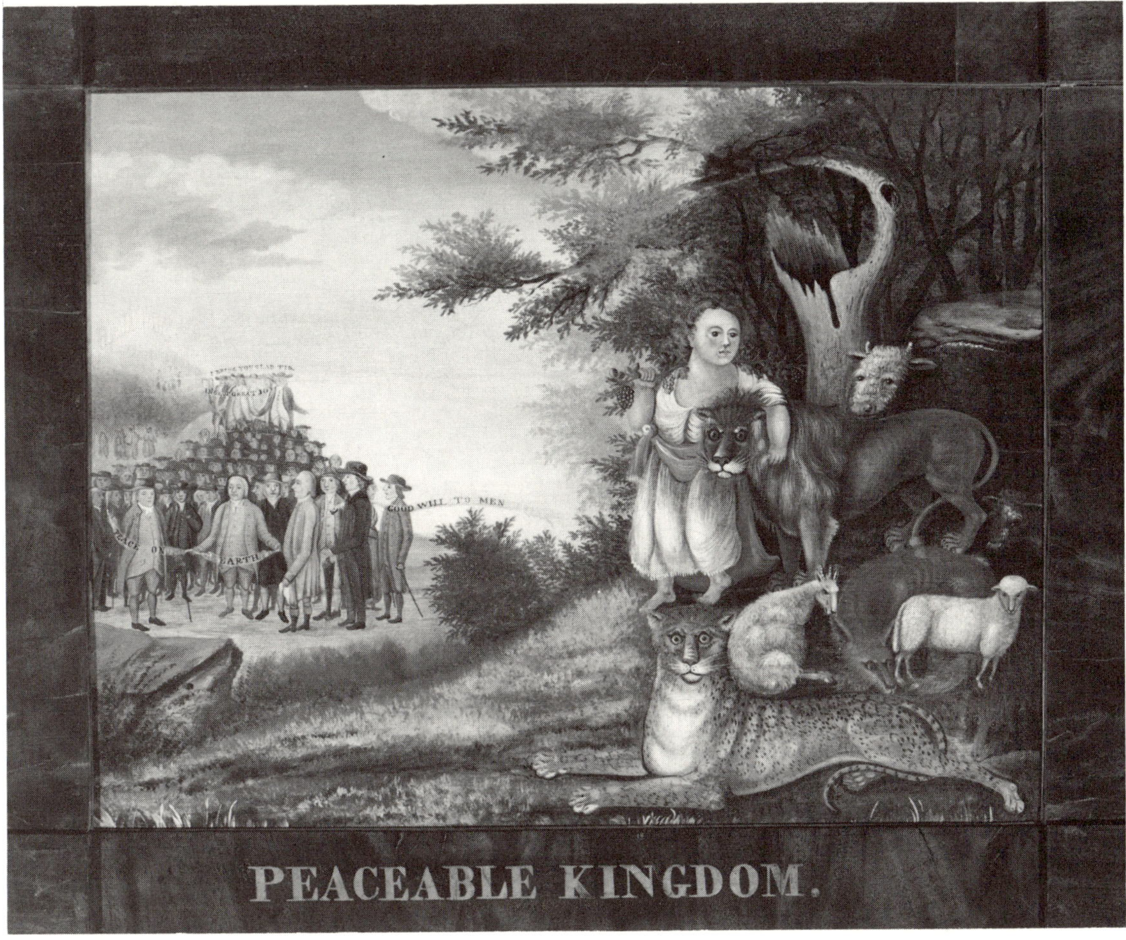

No. 20

PEACEABLE KINGDOM WITH QUAKERS BEARING BANNERS, 1832–37. Oil on canvas, 17½ × 23¾ inches. Original cherry veneer frame with block corners, lettered by artist, "PEACEABLE KINGDOM." Private collection.

COMMENT: This and two succeeding versions have heads of calf and bear cub on the right margin. This fourth pair of animals (Isaiah 11:7) entered the composition with the transitional *Kingdoms*, suggesting that this and the two above-mentioned canvases are late examples of their type. But the sequence of the *Kingdoms* is necessarily conjectural because of a lack of firm dates. Frederick Tolles identified the figure of Elias Hicks, in the front row holding a handkerchief, with a silhouette published by John Hopper in 1830, the date of Elias's death. But this discovery, though valid, raises a question. Does it mean that the painter did not begin his *Banners Kingdoms* till 1830? Or did Hopper borrow from Hicks? The inscription has become standardized: "I BRING YOU GLAD TID/ INGS OF GREAT JOY/ PEACE ON EARTH & GOOD WILL TO MEN."

COLLECTIONS: Descended in the Hicks family to Mrs. William P. Abendroth, Port Chester, N.Y. (see No. 54); to her son, William P. Abendroth, Jr., Berwyn, Pa.; Kennedy Galleries, New York; to private collector.

EXHIBITIONS: Kennedy Galleries, "American Naive and Folk Art of the Nineteenth Century" (New York, January, 1974), catalogue *Kennedy Quarterly*, vol. 13, cover (col.) and p. 55.

Photograph courtesy Kennedy Galleries, New York.

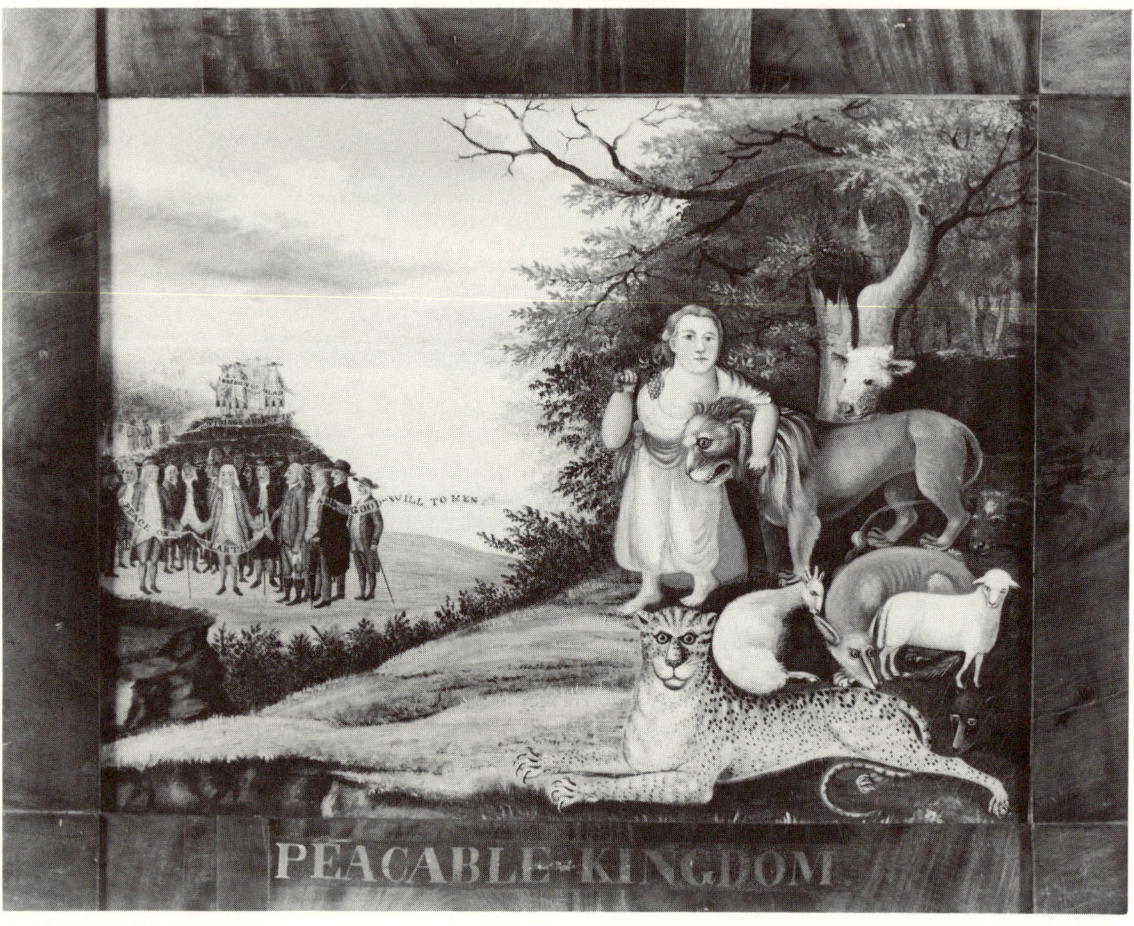

No. 21

PEACEABLE KINGDOM WITH QUAKERS
BEARING BANNERS, 1832–37. Oil on canvas,
18½ × 24 inches. Original cherry veneer
frame with block corners lettered by artist,
"PEACABLE-KINGDOM." Blount, Inc.

COMMENT. Here the eyes of the Divine Child
are strikingly blue. To the left of the Quakers
on the mountaintop is the funeral pyre of the
Spanish heretic, Michael Servetus, several
Protestant Reformers, and a shadowy host of
persecuted Huguenots—all mentioned in
Samuel Johnson's poem. Hicks, like Johnson
and their fellow Hicksites, saw the schism as
the culminating phase in the long struggle for
religious liberty. Banner reads: "I BRING YOU
GLAD/ TIDINGS of GREAT JOY/ PEACE ON
EARTH AND GOOD-WILL TO MEN."

COLLECTIONS: Original provenance unknown. Possibly owned by Miss Ellen
Stephens Davis, Norristown, Pa., who sold a
Peaceable Kingdom to Arthur Edwin Bye on
February 16, 1942, no description given. A
photo at the Bucks County Historical Society
shows that he owned this work, inscribed in

his hand, "Peaceable Kingdom/ formerly in
the Collection of Dr. A. E. Bye." We also know
that Bye had owned and sold eight works by
Hicks by May 22, 1942, in a letter to
Frederick B. Tolles, Friends Historical Li-
brary, Swarthmore, Pa. Process of elimination
suggests this to have been the *Kingdom* owned
by Miss Davis.* Dr. Arthur Edwin Bye,
Holicong, Pa.; Albert Duveen, New York; Mrs.
B. A. Behrend, Aiken, S.C.; to Hirschl & Adler,
New York; Thomas Laughlin, New York and
Aiken, S.C.; Acquavella Galleries, New York;
Kennedy Galleries, New York; to Blount, Inc.,
Montgomery, Ala.

EXHIBITIONS: Kennedy Galleries, "The
American View: Art from 1770 to 1978" (New
York, December 6, 1978–January 5, 1979).

---

*An entry in Hicks's diary reads, "Received the
affecting account of the death of Joseph Davis' wife,
Ellen, the once lovely daughter of my dear old
friend Stephen Stevens" (March 27–31, 1846,
Memoirs, p. 144). The deceased may have been the
grandmother of the Miss Davis who sold the *Peaceable Kingdom* to Dr. Bye.

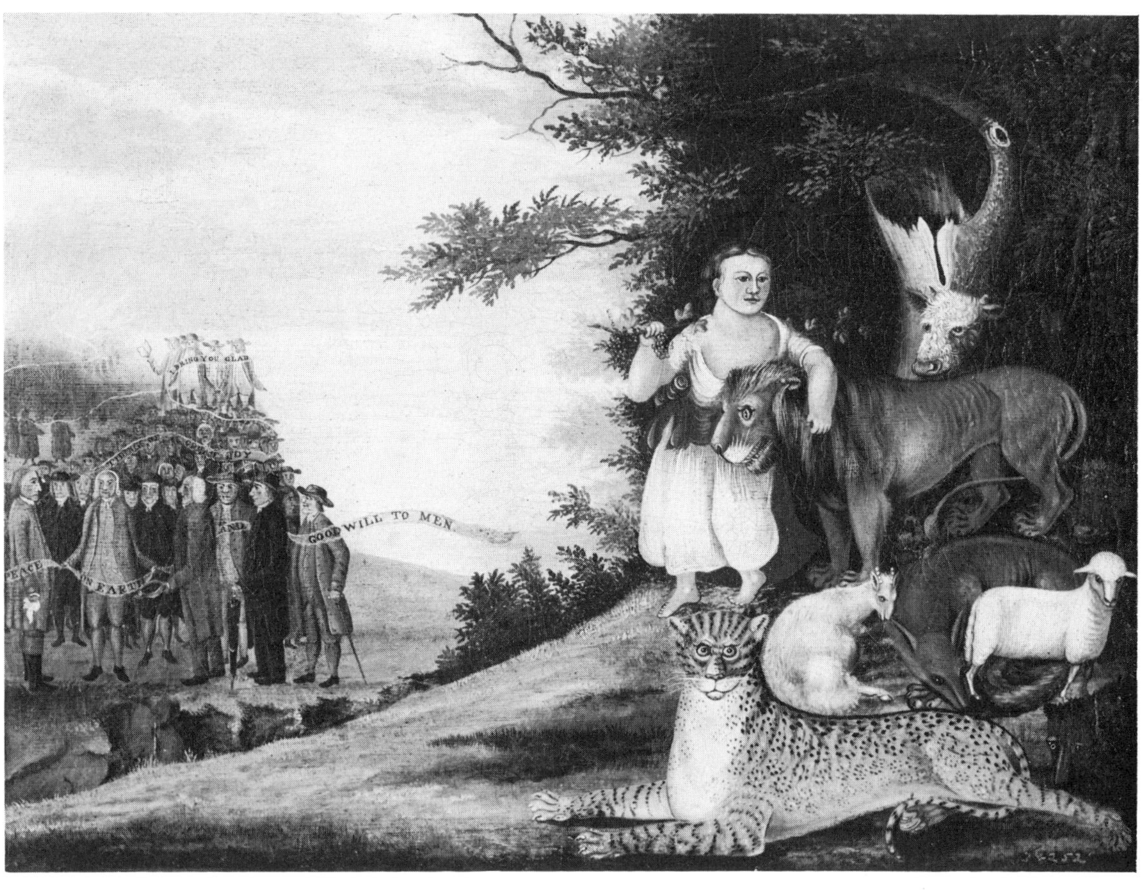

No. 22

PEACEABLE KINGDOM WITH QUAKERS BEARING BANNERS, 1832–37. Oil on canvas, 17½ × 23½ inches. Original mahogany veneer frame with corner blocks, lettered "PEACEABLE KINGDOM." Label on back reads, "Edward Hicks Phipps/ presented to him by his beloved uncle/ Edward Hicks in the year of our/ Lord 1837"* Private collection.

COMMENT: Foreground arrangement of figures has shifted, with Elias Hicks now at left, facing a white-haired patriarch with hat in hand. Above, a fourth figure has joined the trio on the mountaintop. Is it Isaac Penington, Quaker mystic and step-father-in-law of William Penn? (Johnson's poem does not mention him.) Banner reads, "I BRING YOU GLAD TIDINGS OF GREAT JOY / PEACE ON EARTH AND GOOD WILL TO MEN." The only *Banners Kingdom* with any pretensions to a date (see note below).

COLLECTIONS: Painted for Edward Hicks Phipps, Whitemarsh, Pa., born October 15, 1826, died September 25, 1849. The canvas was bought in the mid-1930s from Moore Price, New Hope, Pa., by Mrs. William Greenough Thayer, Jr., New York; a private collector.

EXHIBITIONS: Hospital of the University of Pennsylvania, "1976 Antiques Show" (Philadelphia, April 6–10, 1976), catalogue article by Mary Black, "Three Folk Artists and Their Description of Pennsylvania," pp. 34–38, plate 1 (col.).

Photograph courtesy Frick Art Reference Library.

----

*Formerly thought to be 1832 (Frederick Tolles, "The Primitive Painter as Poet," *Bulletin of the Friends Historical Association* 50(1961): 25). The label was probably placed on the painting some years after Phipps's death, which might account for the discrepancy in dating. Of the two dates, 1837 seems more likely, as Phipps was only six years old in 1832. The painter wrote in his diary for June 25, 1846: "Went to Whitemarsh to pay a social visit to my dear sister [in-law], Susan W. Phipps, and her husband and children; one of the most heavenly visits of the kind I ever paid. I say heavenly, for I have no recollection of ever feeling more Christian tenderness and love than I did towards my dear sister's interesting family of children" (*Memoirs*, p. 179).

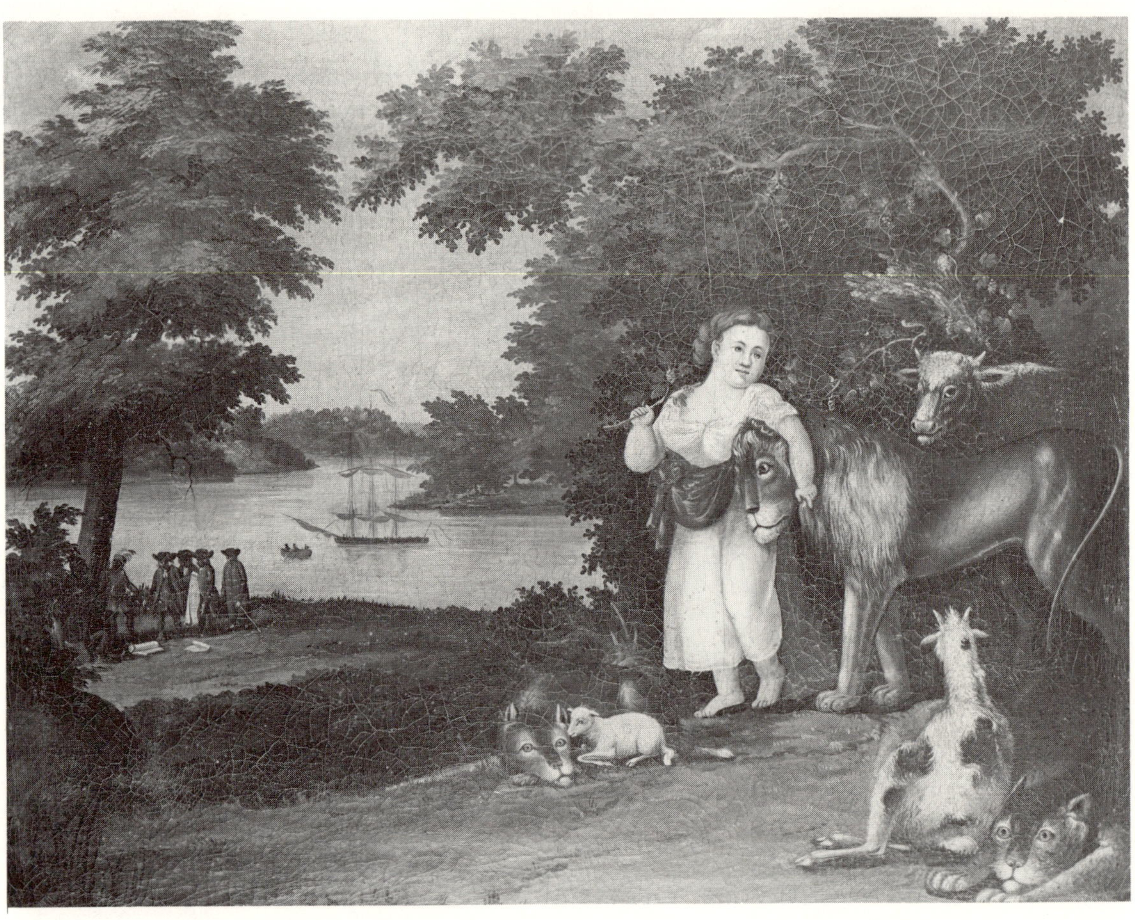

No. 23

PEACEABLE KINGDOM IN TRANSITION, 1830–32. Oil on canvas, 21¾ × 27½ inches. Gilt frame assumed to be original. Private collection.

COMMENT: This picture always hung in Edward Hicks's house. Essentially it is a *Border Kingdom* without the border, the Delaware River landscape providing a background for the same Divine Child whom we see in *Peaceable Kingdoms With Quakers Bearing Banners*. The girl's face is not unlike a small portrait titled "Little Sallie"—the painter's youngest daughter—done by cousin Thomas Hicks while an apprentice at Newtown. One wonders if she also served her father as a model.

COLLECTIONS: From the painter to his son Isaac Worstall Hicks, Newtown, Pa.; to his daughter Sarah Worstall Hicks, Newtown; to a private collector.

EXHIBITIONS: Newtown's 275th Anniversary (Newtown, Pa., June 2–13, 1959), no. 3 (cov. of cat. and reproduced on souvenir plate).

Photograph courtesy Frick Art Reference Library.

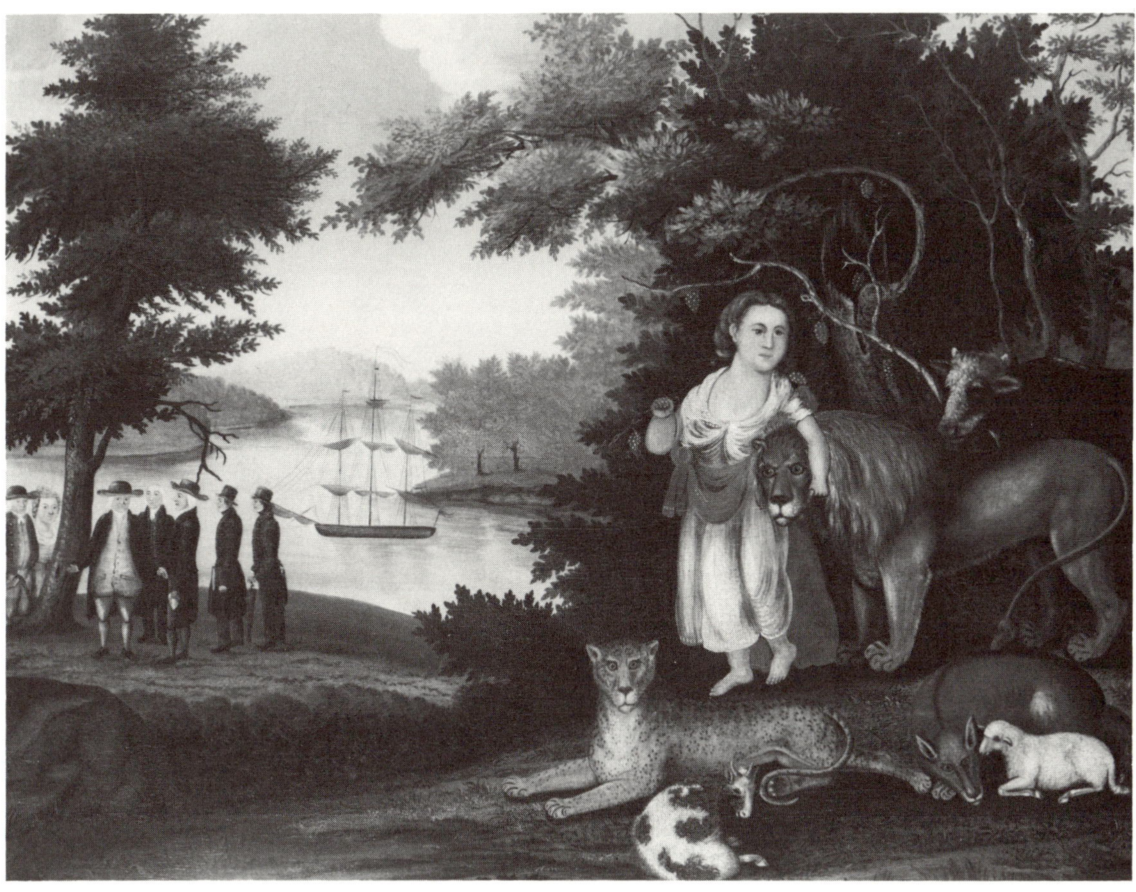

No. 24

PEACEABLE KINGDOM IN TRANSITION, 1830–32. Oil on canvas, 21¼ × 28 inches. Peter H. Tillou.

COMMENT: Landscape echoes No. 23, but figures are related to the *Banners Kingdoms*. The only ones identifiable are Penn and Elias Hicks, here wearing a hat, as in a painting by Jefferson Gauntt (fl. 1828) at the Friends Historical Library, Swarthmore College. Couple at left are curiously disproportioned (see John W. McCoubrey, "Three Paintings by Edward Hicks," *Yale University Art Gallery Bulletin* 25 [1959], 16–21).

COLLECTIONS: Inherited by Sarah W. Hicks, granddaughter of the painter; to Robert W. Carle, South Salem, Conn.; given by him to the Yale University Art Gallery, New Haven, Conn.; Peter H. Tillou, Litchfield, Conn.

EXHIBITIONS: Andrew Crispo Gallery, "Edward Hicks: A Gentle Spirit" (New York, 1975), no. 6 (col.).

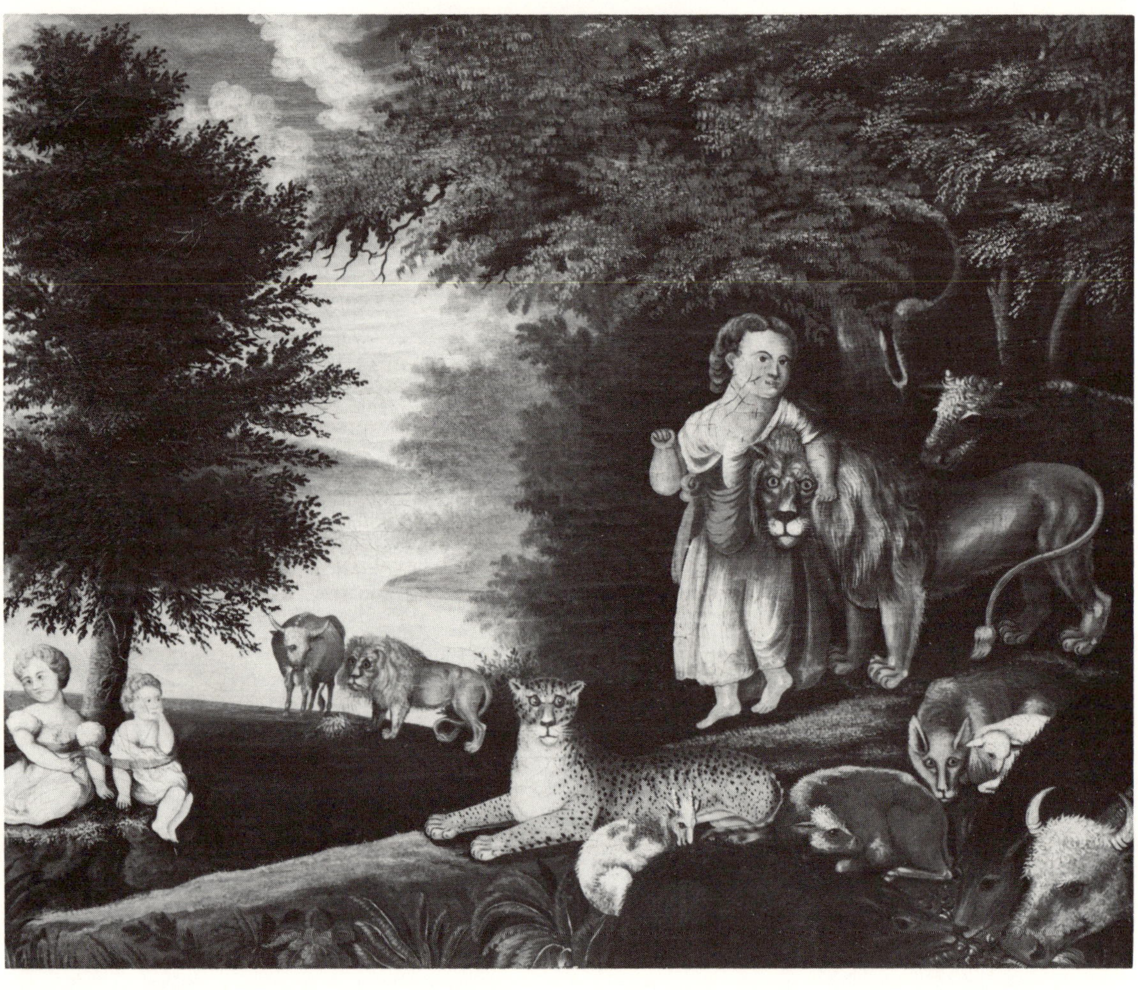

No. 25

PEACEABLE KINGDOM IN TRANSITION, 1830–32. Oil on canvas, 16½ × 19¾ inches. Original cherry veneer frame with block corners. Sidney Janis Collection.

COMMENT: The smallest of the *Kingdoms*, and one of the most important iconographically. Eight new figures appear, including a straw-eating lion and two extra children under tree to left. The Divine Child's grape branch has vanished, leaving her arm empty, but still bent in a carrying position.

COLLECTIONS: Daughter of the artist, Sarah Hicks Parry (1816–95), Horsham, Pa.; her daughter, Mrs. Susan Parry Harrar, Hatboro, Pa.; her husband, Mr. James F. Harrar, Hatboro, Pa.; sold to Mary B. Atkinson, a dealer in Doylestown, Pa.; to American Folk Art Gallery (Edith Gregor Halpert), New York; anonymous; Downtown Gallery (Edith Gregor Halpert), New York; Terry Dintenfass, New York; Sidney Janis, New York.

EXHIBITIONS: Museum of Modern Art, "Masters of Popular Painting" (New York, 1938), no. 118 (captioned American Folk Art Gallery); Carnegie/Corcoran, "Hicks, Kane, Pippin" (1966–67), p. 6; Andrew Crispo Gallery, "Edward Hicks: A Gentle Spirit" (New York, 1975), no. 8 (col.).

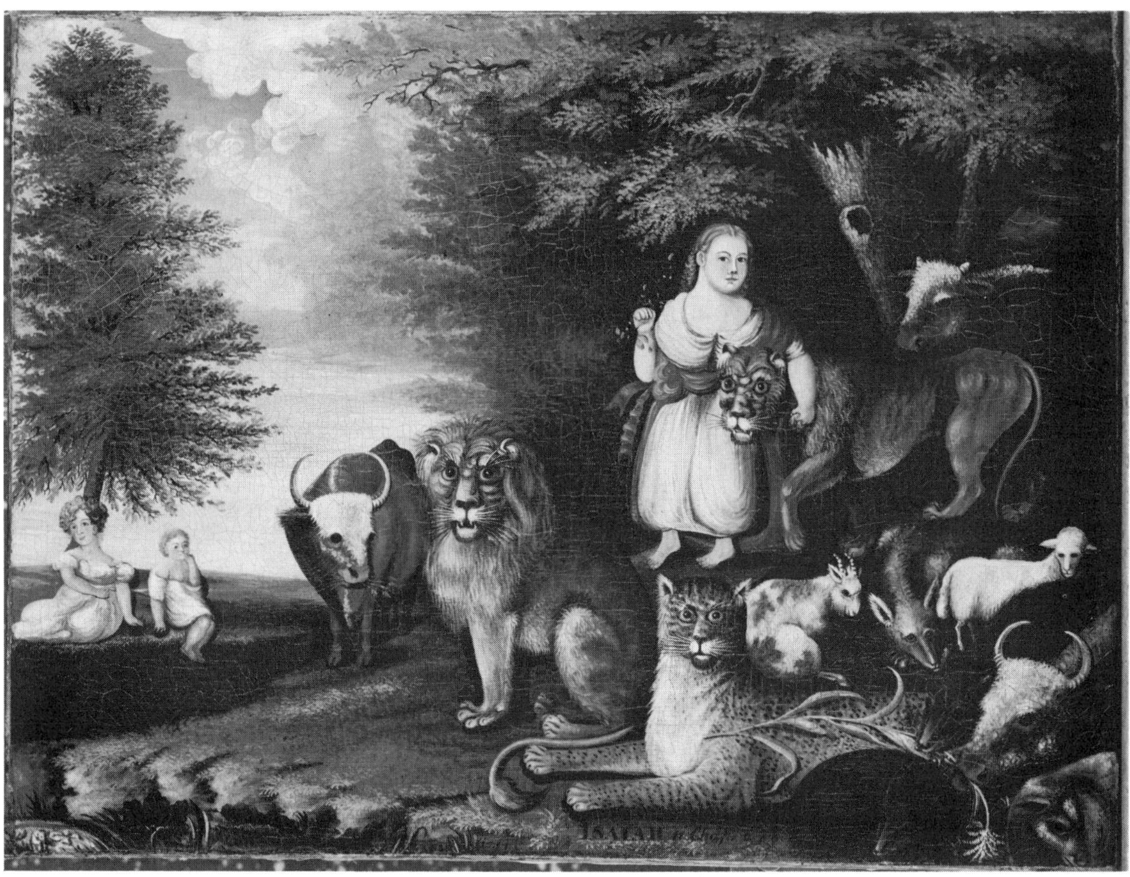

No. 26

PEACEABLE KINGDOM IN TRANSITION, 1830–32. Oil on canvas, 18 × 24 inches. Original 2½-inch beveled mahogany veneer frame with block corners. The Metropolitan Museum of Art, gift of Edgar William and Bernice Chrysler Garbisch, 1970.

COMMENT: The branch has returned, but bears olives instead of grapes. "ISAIAH 11 *Chap. 6 7 8*" beneath leopard's forepaw stresses the presence of *all* the creatures from verses 6, 7, and 8, including a fourth pair of animals, bear and cow, at lower right corner. Westall used only those from verse 6, omitting calf.

COLLECTIONS: Inherited by the Burton family of Edgely (near Tullytown in the area of Bristol), Bucks County, Pa., who sold it to the Robert Carlen Gallery, Philadelphia; to American Folk Art Gallery (Edith Gregor Halpert), New York; to Valentine Galleries, New York; to Col. Edgar William and Bernice Chrysler Garbisch, New York, who gave it to the Metropolitan Museum of Art, New York.

EXHIBITIONS: Milwaukee Institute of Art, "Primitive Art Exhibition" (Milwaukee, Wis., 1951); National Gallery of Art, "American Primitive Paintings from the Collection of Edgar William and Bernice Chrysler Garbisch" (Washington, D.C., Part 1, 1954; Part 2, 1957), not in cat.; American Federation of Arts traveling exhibition, "American Naive Painting of the Eighteenth and Nineteenth Centuries: 111 Masterpieces from the Collection of Edgar William and Bernice Chrysler Garbisch" (Paris, Berlin, Spoleto, Brussels, Madrid, Barcelona, Montreal, Washington, D.C., New York, Houston, West Point, N.Y., February 16, 1968–February 15, 1970), not in cat.; Bronx County Courthouse, "Paintings from the Metropolitan Museum of Art" (New York, 1971), no. 2; ACA Galleries, "Four American Primitives" (New York, 1972), no. 2, ill.; Metropolitan Museum of Art, "Recent Acquisitions 1967–72: The American Paintings and Sculpture Department" (New York, 1972); Andrew Crispo Gallery, "Edward Hicks: A Gentle Spirit" (New York, 1975), no. 7 (Col.); Queens Museum, "Cows" (New York, 1976); Everson Museum of Art, "The Animal Kingdom in American Art" (Syracuse, N.Y., February 5–April 2, 1978), no. 52.

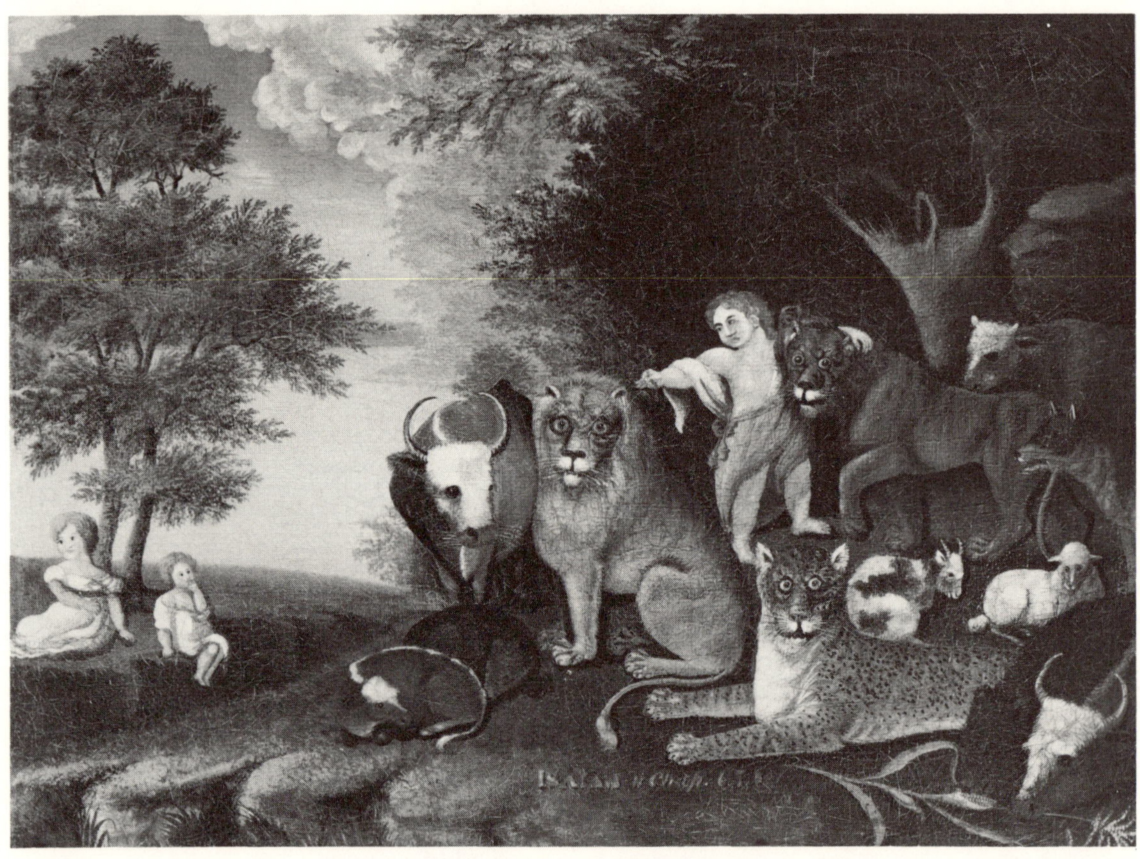

No. 27

PEACEABLE KINGDOM IN TRANSITION, 1830–32. Oil on canvas, 17½ × 23⅝ inches. Original black-painted, gold-lined frame with block corners. The Regis Collection.

COMMENT: Biblical inscription repeated. The Divine Child has been transformed into a little boy after a Rigaud print (Alice Ford, *Edward Hicks: Painter of the Peaceable Kingdom* (Philadelphia: University of Pennsylvania Press, 1952), pl. 22, p. 149), where the outstretched arm holds an olive branch of peace—more acceptable to Hicksite Friends than grapes, which symbolize the atonement of the Cross.

COLLECTIONS: Original provenance unknown. Mrs. John L. Robertson, Scranton, Pa.; to Mr. Sidney Janis, New York; Mr. and Mrs. Martin B. Grossman, New York; through Christie's, New York, to the Regis Collection, Minneapolis, Minn.

EXHIBITIONS: Carnegie/Corcoran, "Hicks, Kane, Pippin" (1966–67), no. 5; Andrew Crispo Gallery, "Edward Hicks: A Gentle Spirit" (New York, 1975), no. 5 (Col.); Everson Museum of Art, "The Animal Kingdom in American Art" (Syracuse, N.Y., 1978), no. 133, p. 105 (not ill.).

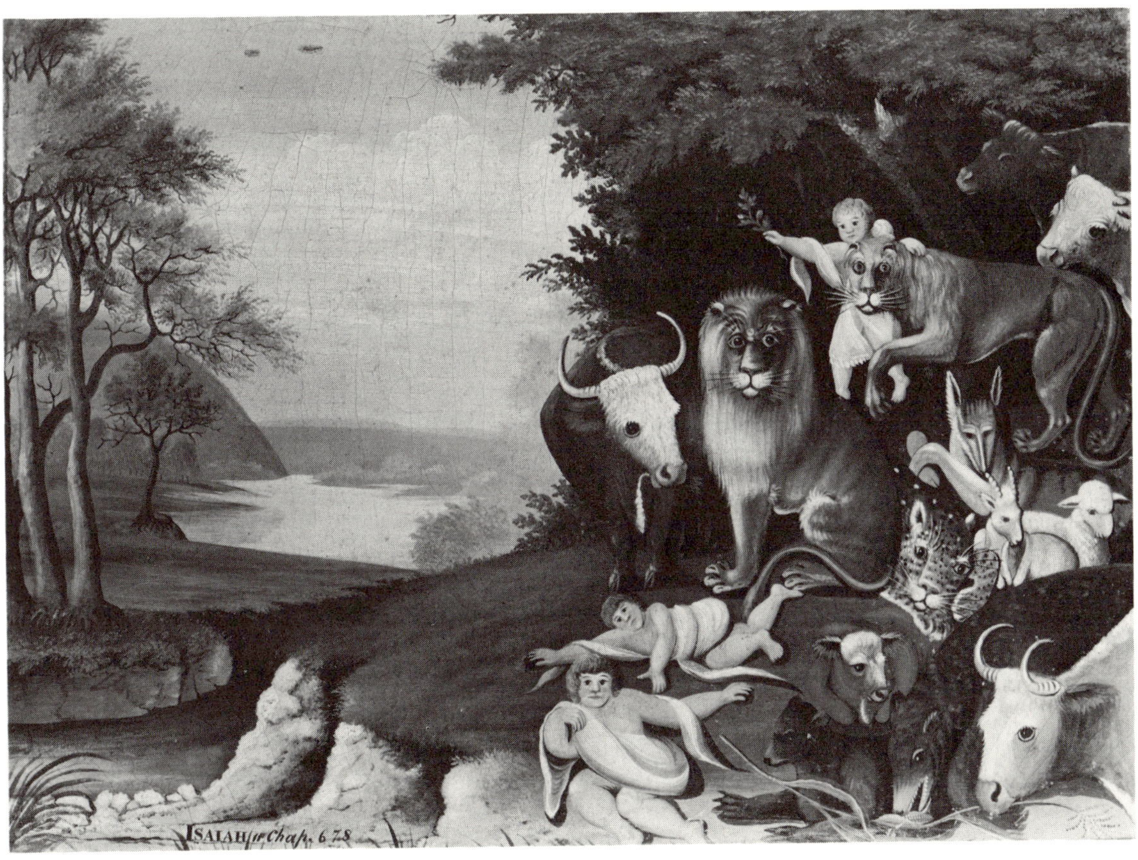

No. 28

PEACEABLE KINGDOM IN TRANSITION, 1830–32. Oil on panel, 17½ × 23½ inches. Scripps College, Claremont, Calif.

COMMENT: A curiously unbalanced composition, with all creatures, both human and animal, crowded to the right half of the canvas. The biblical reference at lower left links this to the two preceding *Kingdoms*, but the tree above introduces a new and important influence: *View on the Delaware* engraved by Asher B. Durand for *The American Landscape* in 1830, later published as *The Delaware Water Gap* (Oliver W. Larkin, *Art and Life in America* [New York: Rhinehart & Company, 1949], p. 143). See also John Durand, *The Life and Times of A. B. Durand* (New York: Charles Scribner's Sons, 1894), pp. 72–73.

COLLECTIONS: Original provenance unknown. Purchased by Robert Carlen Gallery, Philadelphia; to Hirschl & Adler Galleries, New York; in 1954 to M. Knoedler & Co., New York; to Bill Pearson, Pasadena, Calif.; given to Scripps College, Claremont, Calif.; lost in transit on its return from a loan exhibition in Arizona. Present location unknown.

Photograph courtesy Hirschl & Adler Galleries, New York.

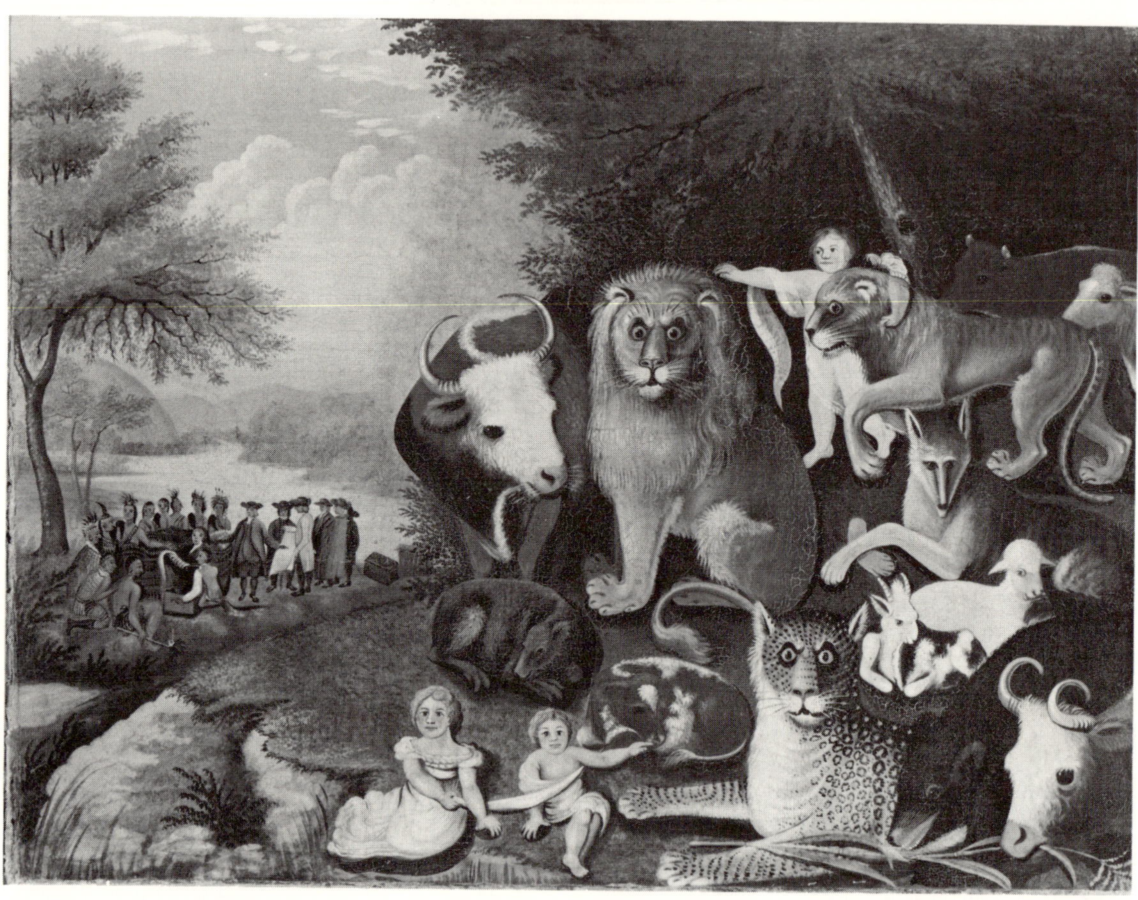

No. 29

PEACEABLE KINGDOM WITH SEATED LION, ca. 1833–34. Oil on canvas, 18 × 24⅛ inches. Plain frame of grained wood probably original. The Brooklyn Museum of Art; Dick S. Ramsay Fund.

COMMENT: A startling new category, dominated by straw-eating lion and ox and balanced by the return of Penn's Treaty, now enlarged, to the left of the composition. The staring eyes of lion and leopard may reflect the artist's sense of guilt in the wake of his activity in the religious schism.

COLLECTIONS: Provenance unknown. Yale University Art Gallery, Garvan Collection, New Haven, Conn.; Brooklyn Museum of Art, Brooklyn, N.Y.

EXHIBITIONS: Brooklyn Museum of Art, "American Paintings in the Brooklyn Museum Collection " (Brooklyn, N.Y., 1953), no. 35; AARFAC, "Edward Hicks" (1960), no. 16, p. 13 (not ill.); ACA Galleries, "Four American Primitives" (New York, 1972), no. 7, ill. and detail; Andrew Crispo Gallery, "Edward Hicks: A Gentle Spirit" (New York, 1975), no. 12 (Col.).

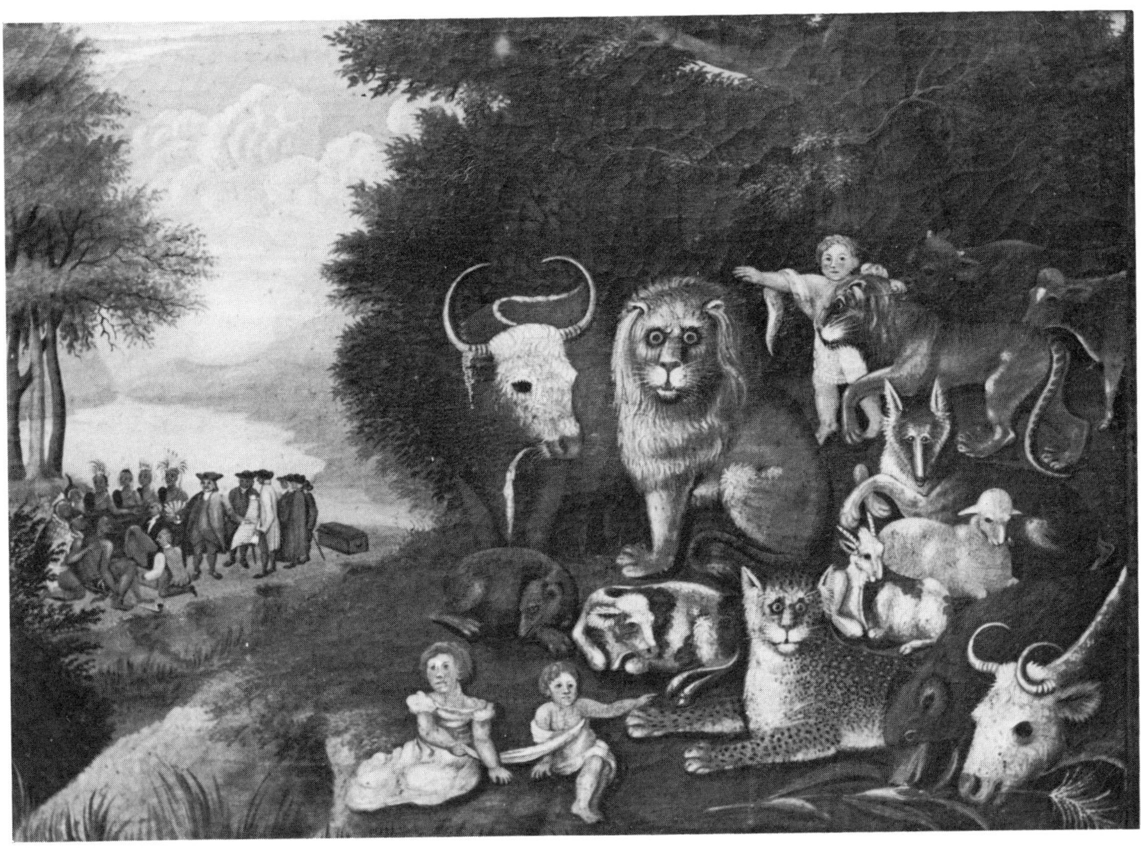

No. 30

PEACEABLE KINGDOM WITH SEATED LION, ca. 1833–34. Oil on canvas, 17½ × 23½ inches. Plain oak frame probably original. Randolph-Macon Woman's College Art Gallery; bequest of Phyllis Crawford.

COMMENT: Almost identical with the preceding and following canvases. This basic group of eleven animals and three children continues through the middle and late *Kingdoms*, with occasional additions. In the foreground are the "weaned child" and the "sucking child" of Isaiah 11:8 dressed entirely in white, as they usually are in these works of the mid–1830s.

COLLECTIONS: A family in New Jersey for generations; purchased by Lillian W. Boschen, a dealer in Freehold, N.J.; to Miss Phyllis Crawford, Santa Fe, N.M., who bequeathed it to Randolph-Macon Woman's College, Lynchburg, Va.

EXHIBITIONS: Andrew Crispo Gallery, "Edward Hicks: A Gentle Spirit" (New York, 1975), no. 13 (Col.).

Photograph courtesy Frick Art Reference Library.

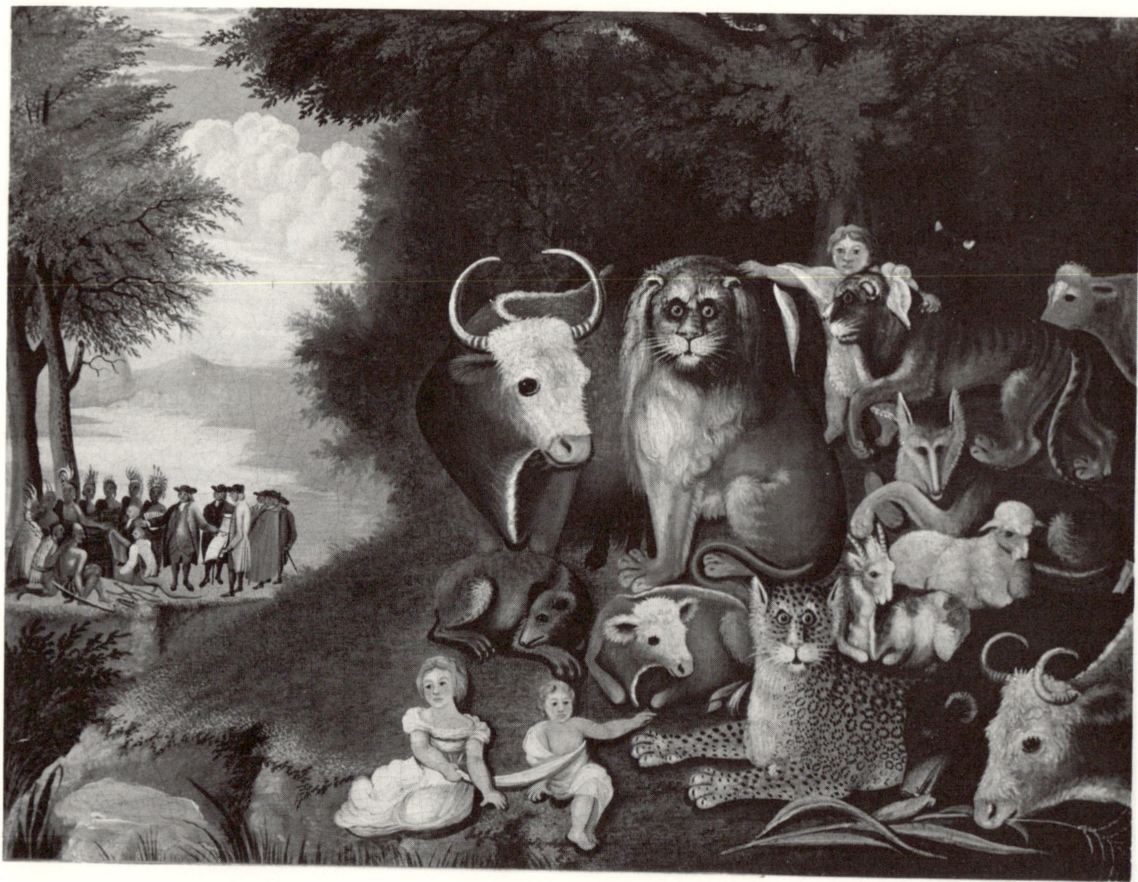

No. 31

PEACEABLE KINGDOM WITH SEATED LION, ca. 1833–34. Oil on canvas, 17½ × 23½ inches. Original block-cornered veneer frame. The Philadelphia Museum of Art; bequest of Lisa Norris Elkins.

COMMENT: Vivid color is confined to the Treaty group—of special interest to Friends, since concern for the American Indian was a traditional Quaker testimony. Here Hicks adds to West's design a legendary detail, the horned headdress of Chief Tammany, as glimpsed between the tree trunks (see Thomas Clarkson's *Memoirs of the Private and Public Life of William Penn* (London, 1813), 1:340].

COLLECTIONS: Provenance unknown. American Folk Art Gallery (Edith Gregor Halpert), New York (1938); to Elie Nadelman, Riverdale, N.Y. (1943); M. Knoedler & Co., New York (1943); Joseph Katz Co., New York (1944); M. Knoedler & Co., New York; William M. and Lisa Norris Elkins, Philadelphia (1945); bequeathed by Mrs. Elkins to the Philadelphia Museum of Art, Philadelphia, in 1950. On extended loan to the Governor's House, Harrisburg, Pa.

EXHIBITIONS: Museum of Modern Art, "Masters of Popular Painting" (1938), no. 117 (captioned American Folk Art Gallery); Carnegie/Corcoran, "Hicks, Kane, Pippin" (1966–67), no. 32, Brandywine River Museum, "Wildlife in America" (Chadds Ford, Pa., 1973).

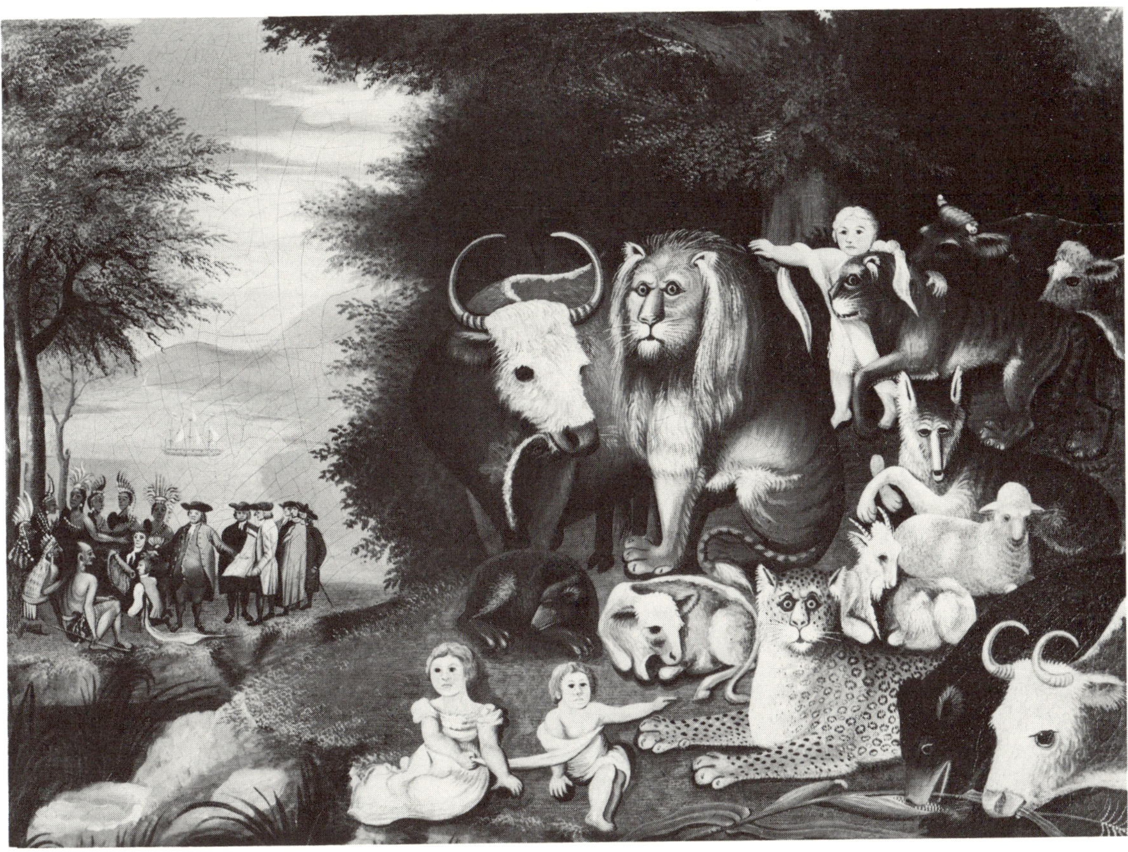

No. 32

PEACEABLE KINGDOM WITH SEATED LION, ca. 1833–34. Oil on canvas, 17¼ × 23¼ inches. Contemporary 19th-century veneer frame. Abby Aldrich Rockefeller Folk Art Center.

COMMENT: A popular canvas in the rediscovery of American Folk Art. Acclaimed by Fernand Léger, the French modern, it became the trademark of the growing movement ("Hicks called greatest in America by Léger," *Art Digest* 6 [1931]: 13). The lion's head has turned from full face to three quarters—a touch of naturalism. The only middle *Kingdom* in which a ship appears.

COLLECTIONS: Original provenance unknown. Acquired by American Folk Art Gallery (Edith Gregor Halpert), New York; Abby Aldrich Rockefeller, New York; the Museum of Modern Art, New York; the Metropolitan Museum of Art, New York; to the Abby Aldrich Rockefeller Folk Art Center, Williamsburg, Va.

EXHIBITIONS: Downtown Gallery, "American Ancestors" (New York, December 14–31, 1931), no. 1, p. 1; Detroit Society of Arts and Crafts (February, 1932); Albright Art Gallery (Buffalo, N.Y., July, 1932), no. 21, p. 31, ill. p. 66; Museum of Modern Art, "American Folk Art: The Art of the Common Man in America, 1750–1900" (New York, November 30, 1932–January 14, 1933, cat. Holger Cahill, no. 21; traveling section 1933–34: Philadelphia Museum of Art, Rhode Island School of Design (Providence, R.I.), Museum of Fine Arts (Boston), William Rockhill Nelson Gallery of Art (Kansas City, Mo.), Greenwich Society of Artists (Greenwich, Conn.), and Westchester Community Center (White Plains, N.Y.); Musée du Jeu de Paume, in collaboration with Museum of Modern Art, "Trois Siècles d'Art aux États Unis" (Paris, May–July, 1938), no. 69; Museum of Modern Art, "Art in our Time, An Exhibition to Celebrate the 10th Anniversary of the MOMA and the Opening of Its New Building" (New York, 1939), no. 6; Tate Gallery Exhibit prepared by the National Gallery of Art, Washington, D.C. (London, June–July, 1946); American Federation of Arts, "American Folk Art from the AARFAC," traveling exhibit (April 22, 1959–January 12, 1962), no. 19, p. 26 and frontispiece; the Jewish Museum, "The Hebrew Bible" (New York, 1963); Museum of Modern Art, "Art in Embassies" (Paris, March, 1963–

March, 1965, the loan of this particular paint-
ing extending to March, 1966; and Feb., 1967–
Jan., 1968); William Penn Memorial Museum
(Harrisburg, Pa., July 7–September 30, 1966);
AARFAC, "American Folk Art: The Exhibi-
tion of 1932" (Williamsburg, Va., January 16–
Mar. 3, 1968); Philbrook Art Center and
Oklahoma Art Center, "The American Realist
Tradition" (Tulsa, Okla., March 4–May 11,
1969).

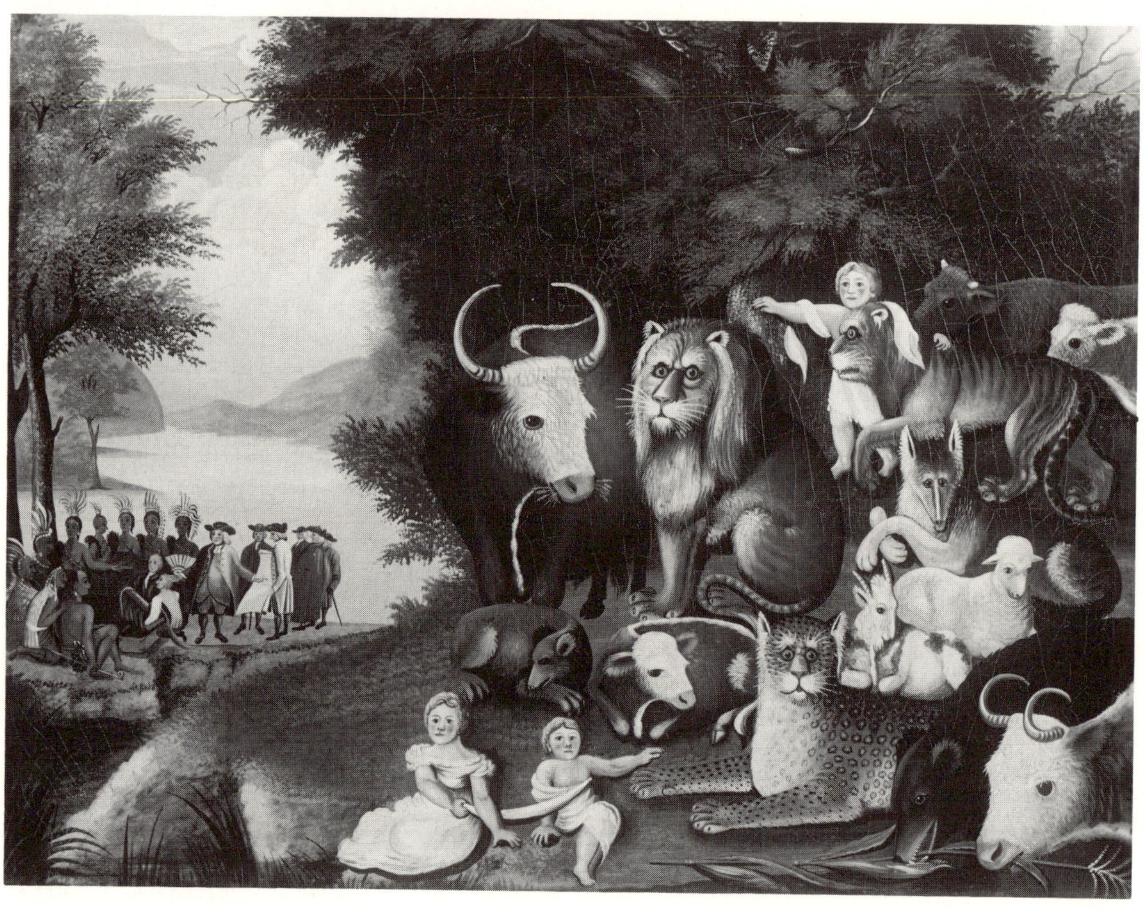

No. 33

PEACEABLE KINGDOM WITH SEATED
LION. ca. 1833–34. Oil on canvas, 17½ ×
23¹¹⁄₁₆ inches. Worcester Art Museum.

COMMENT: In this version the straw in the
lion's mouth is clearly delineated as grain. Being contrary to his natural appetite, it is a symbol of submission to the Divine will—the goal
of Quaker quietism (see E. P. Mather, "A
Quaker Icon," *The Art Quarterly* 36 [1973]:
91–92). One of the first of Hicks's works to be
acquired by an art museum, this is recorded in
Louisa Dresser's pioneer article, "The Peaceable Kingdom," *Worcester Museum Bulletin*
25 (1934): 25–30.

COLLECTIONS: Early provenance unknown.
American Folk Art Gallery (Edith Gregor Hal-
pert), New York; in 1934 to Worcester Art
Museum, Worcester, Mass.

EXHIBITIONS: Atwater Kent Museum: Friends
Historical Association Annual Meeting, "Exhibition of the Paintings of Edward Hicks"
(November 30–December 31, 1942); Sym-
phony Hall (Boston, March 12–27, 1948); the
Jewish Museum, "Encyclopedia of Paintings
by American Artists of the Eighteenth and
Nineteenth Centuries Depicting Old Testament Subjects" (New York, April 15–July 7,
1954); Corcoran Gallery of Art, "The American Muse" (Washington, D.C., April 4–May
17, 1959), no. 81; the Jewish Museum, "The
Hebrew Bible" (New York, 1963); no. 106;
Carnegie/Corcoran, "Hicks, Kane, Pippin"
(1966–67), p. 8; Ackland Art Center, "The Age
of Dunlap: The Arts of the Young Republic"
(University of North Carolina, Chapel Hill,
N.C., November 1–29, 1968); Worcester Art
Museum, "Art in America 1830–1950" (Worcester, Mass., January 9–February 23, 1969);
Museum of Art, "Art and the Excited Spirit:

America in the Romantic Period" (University of Michigan, Ann Arbor, Mich., March 19–May 14, 1972); Worcester Art Museum, "The Second Fifty Years: American Art" (Worcester, Mass., September 24, 1976–January 23, 1977), p. 27.

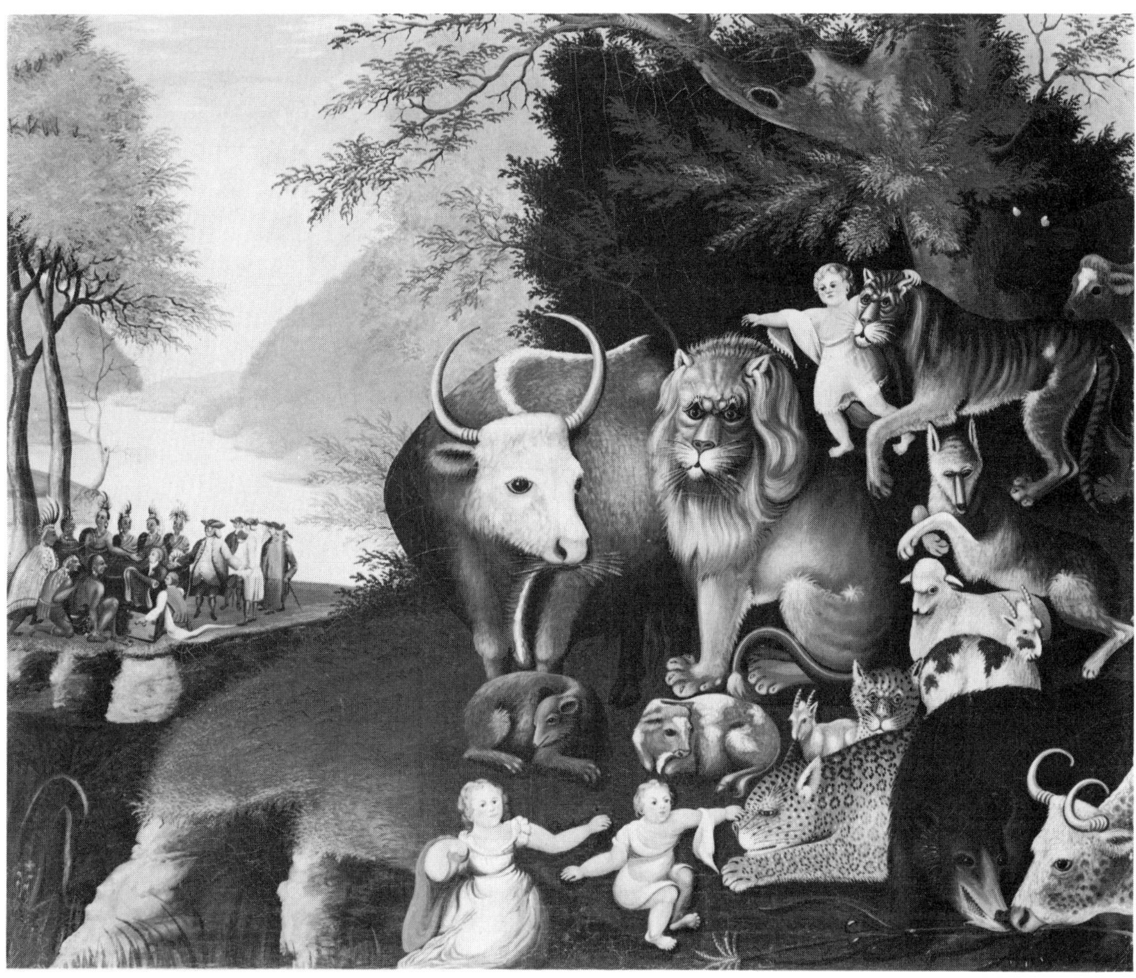

No. 34

PEACEABLE KINGDOM WITH SEATED LION, 1834. Oil on canvas, 30 × 35⅞ inches. Original 2½-inch black frame with gold-leaf beveled inner edge. National Gallery of Art, Washington: gift of Edgar William and Bernice Chrysler Garbisch.

COMMENT: The most highly evolved of the *Seated Lions*, having elements that foreshadow a departure in composition: enlarged canvas, doubling of leopard and kid, and the return of color to the costume of the "weaned child"—all are signals of change.

COLLECTIONS: From the artist to his friend Joseph Foulke (1786–1863); of Three Tuns, Pennsylvania—minister, teacher, and editor of the *Friends Almanac*; descended to his great-grandson, Thomas Foulke, Ambler, Pa.; to Robert Carlen Gallery, Philadelphia; to Edgar William and Bernice Chrysler Garbisch, New York, to the National Gallery of Art, Washington, D.C.

EXHIBITIONS: Robert Carlen Gallery, Philadelphia, "Hicks Centennial Exhibition" (no cat.; reviewed in *Philadelphia Inquirer*, January 9, 1949); Milwaukee Art Institute, "American Primitive Painting, 1750–1950" (Milwaukee, Wisconsin, February 24–March 25, 1951); National Gallery of Art, "American Primitive Paintings" (Washington, D.C., part 1, 1954; part 2, 1957), p. 76; American National Exhibition, "Early American Paintings" Sokoliki Park, Moscow, July 25–September 5, 1959); American Federation of Arts, "101 Masterpieces of American Primitive Painting from the Collection of Edgar William and Bernice Chrysler Garbisch" (New York, 1961–62), no. 53; traveling exhibition through United States (1962–64); Museum of Fine Arts, Inaugural Exhibition (St. Petersburg, Fla., February 7 –March 7, 1965), no. 6; Metropolitan Museum of Art, "Three Centuries of American Painting" (New York, April 9–October 1, 1965), cat. unnumbered; National Gallery of Art (September, 1966–February 15, 1967); American Federation of Arts, with Society of the Four Arts, "Fifty Masterpieces of Primitive Painting" (Palm Beach, Fla., March 4–26, 1967); American Federation of Arts, "Ameri-can Naive Painting of the Eighteenth and Nineteenth Centuries" (Europe and United States, 1968–70), pl. 49 (col.); M. Knoedler & Co., "What Is American in American Art?" (New York, 1971), no. 28, p. 51; National Gallery of Art, "American Naive Art: Selections from the Edgar William and Bernice Chrysler Garbisch Gift and Loans" (Washington, D.C., August 26, 1978–February 5, 1979).

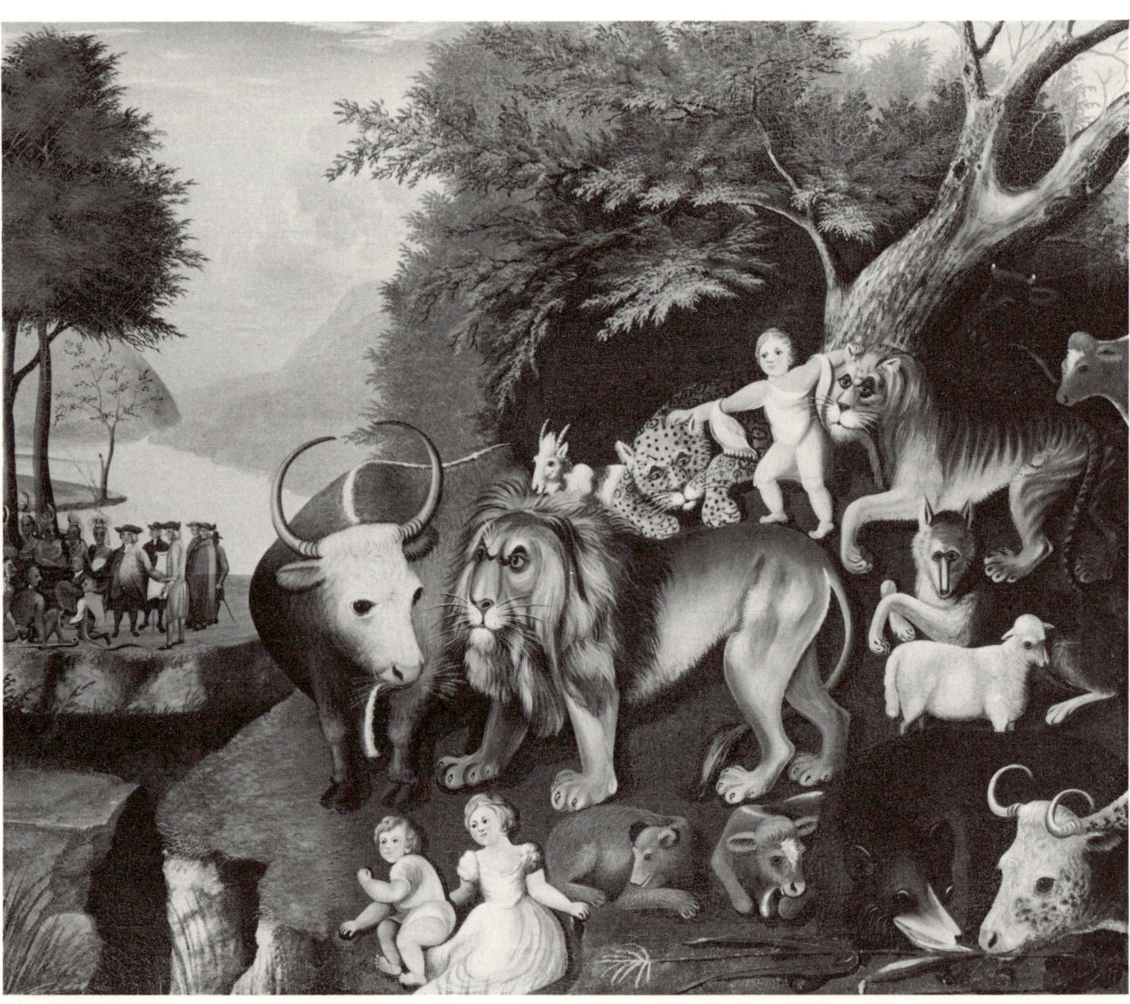

No. 35

PEACEABLE KINGDOM WITH LION IN PRO-FILE, ca. 1835. Oil on canvas, 29½ × 35¼ inches. Original black frame, with interior gold edging. Collection of Mr. and Mrs. Irwin Miller.

COMMENT: The lion now stands, a pose designated "Standing Lion in Profile" in the catalogue of the Williamsburg exhibition of 1960. The date then attributed to this category was 1840–45. But during the past twenty years many additional examples have surfaced, and a study of them now suggests 1835–40 as more likely. Durand's *Delaware Water Gap,* details of which appeared in No. 28, is here echoed in the total composition, and serves as background in all subsequent *Kingdoms.*

COLLECTIONS: Thomas Janney (1794–1879), Newtown, Pa., administrator of the painter's will (Alice Ford, *Edward Hicks: Painter of the Peaceable Kingdom* [Philadelphia: University of Pennsylvania Press, 1952], pp. 68 and 113). To his son, Emmor Kimber Janney, Philadelphia; to his son, Walter C. Janney, Bryn Mawr, Pa.; to Arthur J. Sussel, Philadelphia; to M. Knoedler & Co., New York; to Clifford Smith, New York; to M. Knoedler & Co., New

York; to Mr. and Mrs. Irwin Miller, Columbus, Indiana.

EXHIBITIONS: AARFAC, "Edward Hicks" (1960), no. 25, p. 16 (not ill.).

Photograph courtesy M. Knoedler & Co., New York.

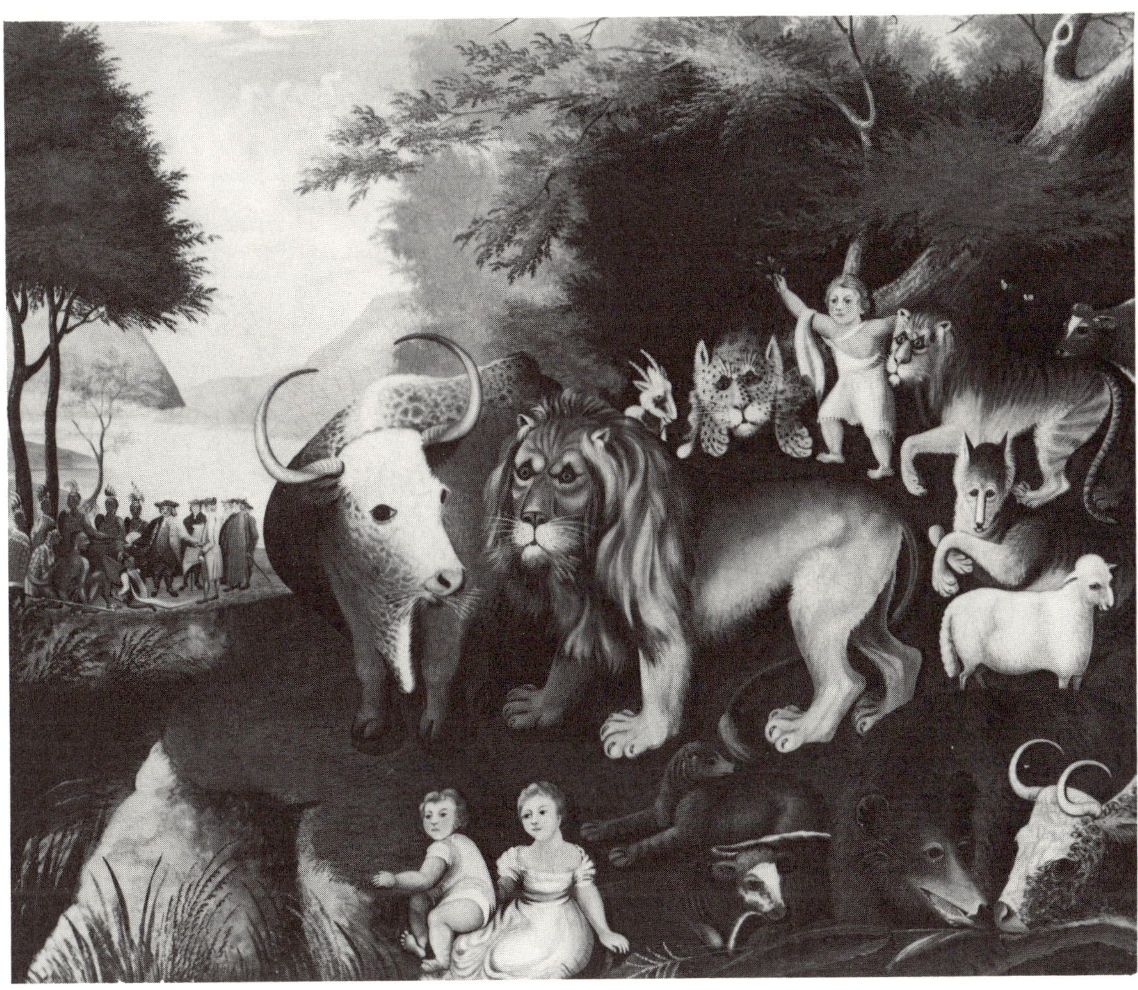

No. 36

PEACEABLE KINGDOM WITH LION IN PRO-FILE, ca. 1835. Oil on wood panel, 29 × 35¼ inches. Everson Museum of Art.

COMMENT: Very like no. 35—not surprisingly, since their original owners were related, and one work may have inspired the other. This differs from the previous version in that the Divine Child again holds an olive branch. Beneath his upraised arm appear only the head and front paws of the leopard, who seems to be almost extinguished by the surrounding landscape. But the lion is magnificient, his mane flamelike in form and color.

COLLECTIONS: Painted for the artist's friend Emmor Kimber (1775–1850), Kimberton, Pa., who is mentioned in Hicks's *Memoirs* (pp. 161 and 210). He was a Recorded Minister of the Society of Friends, founded a school for girls, and was active in the Underground Railroad, since Kimberton is near the Mason–Dixon Line in Chester County. Through the Massey family to Norris Barratt, Philadelphia; to his wife, Polly Barratt, Philadelphia; to M. Knoedler & Co., New York; to Everson Museum of Art, Syracuse, N.Y.

EXHIBITIONS: Everson Museum of Art, "The Animal Kingdom in American Art" (Syracuse, N.Y., 1978) no. 46 and cover (col.).

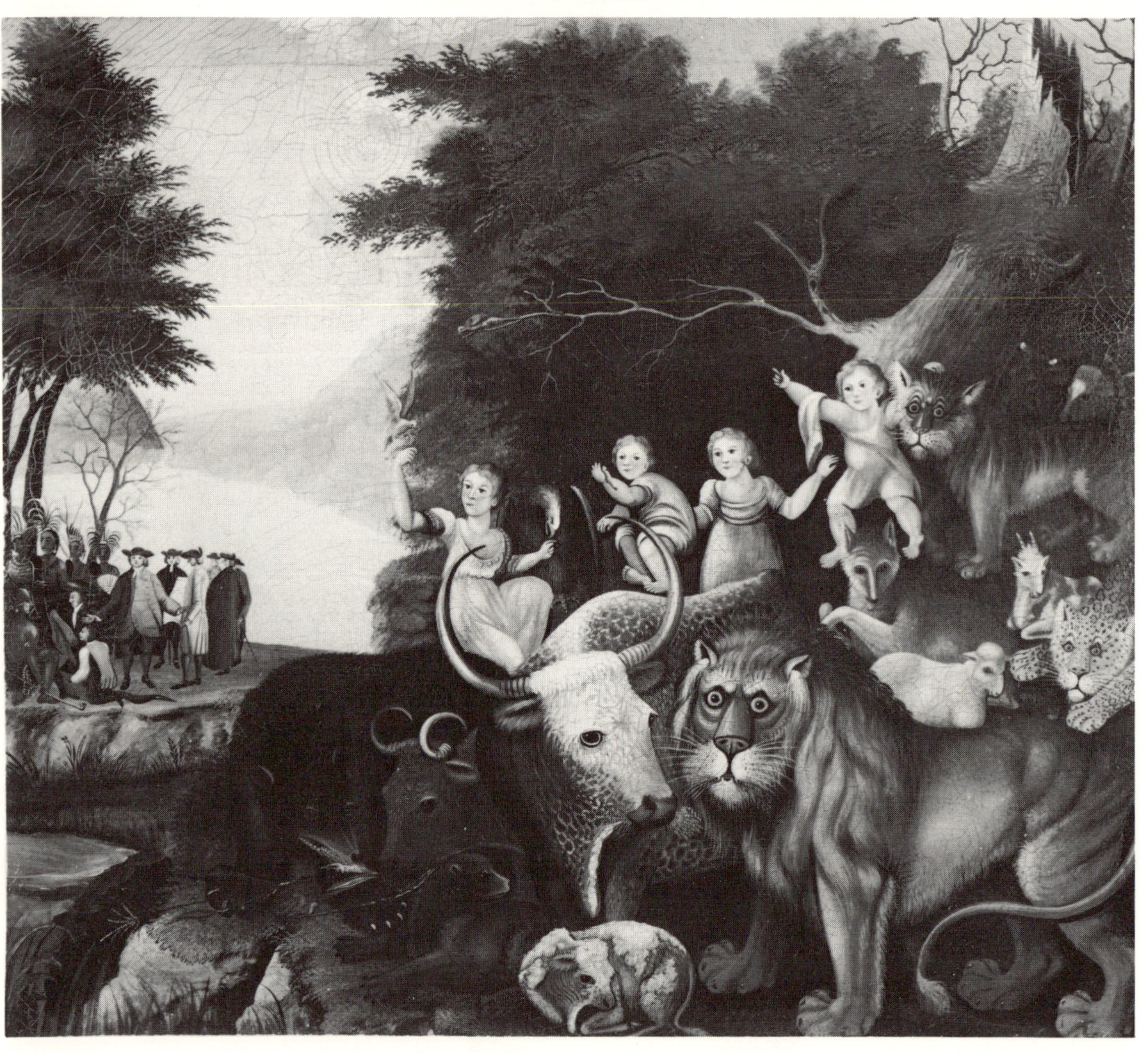

No. 37

PEACEABLE KINGDOM WITH LION IN PRO-FILE, ca. 1836. Oil on canvas, 30⅛ × 34½ inches. Original black frame, with interior gold edging. New York State Historical Association.

COMMENT: The figures shift to accommodate new characters: a white-robed maiden with dove and eagle, obviously drawn from some contemporary print of the goddess of youth, Hebe. This canvas unites an incredible diversity—idyllic charm, manic fear (in the eyes of leopard and lions), Hebrew prophecy, Quaker history, and a Greek goddess. Jean Lipman, a former owner of the work, sees design as the unifying agent ("The Composite Scene in Primitive Painting", *Gazette des Beaux-Arts* 29 [1946]: 126).

COLLECTIONS: Painted for a farmer near Newtown, Bucks County; to his great-grandson, still living on the same farm; to Wilbur T. Gracey, Bucks County, Pa.; Capt. Richard A. Loeb, Hampton, N.J.; to Albert Duveen, New York dealer; to Howard and Jean Lipman, Wilton, Conn.; to the New York State Historical Association, Cooperstown, N.Y.

EXHIBITIONS: Montclair Museum (Montclair, N.J. February, 1942); Loan Exhibition of Folk Art (Wilton, Conn., February, 1947); Harry Shaw Newman Gallery, "Identified American Primitives" (New York, 1950); the Century Club (New York, January–February, 1952); Cincinnati Art Museum, "Recent Rediscoveries in American Art" (Cincinnati, Ohio, October 3–November 6, 1955); M. Knoedler & Co., "The Art of the Pioneer" (New York, April, 1956); Wildenstein Gallery and American Federation of Arts, "The American Vision" (New York, October–November, 1957); Wildenstein Gallery, "Masters of Seven Centuries" (New York, February–March, 1962), ill.

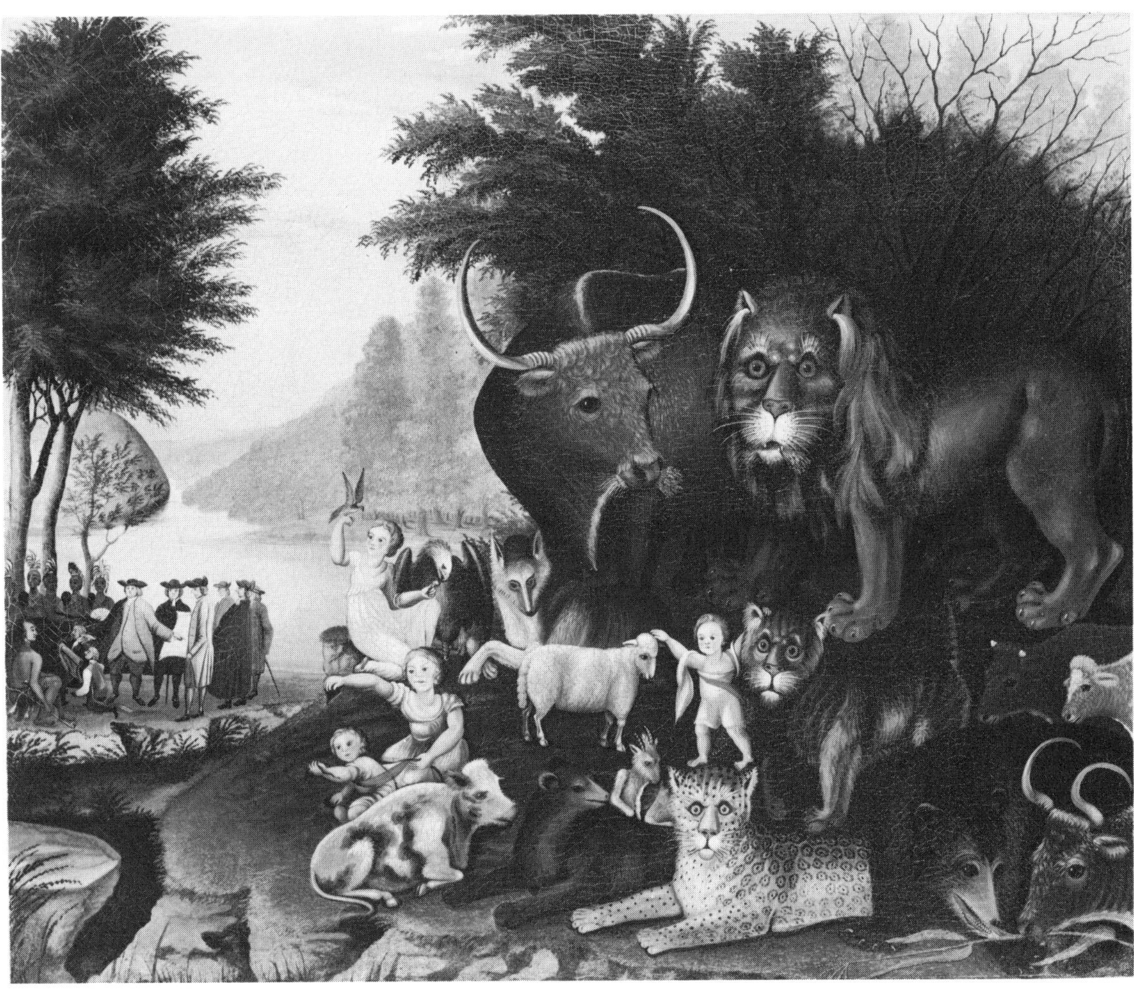

No. 38

PEACEABLE KINGDOM WITH LION IN PRO-
FILE, ca. 1836. Oil on canvas, 30 × 35¾
inches. Original frame, black with interior
gold edging, appears to have been enlarged.
Mr. and Mrs. Thomas M. Evans.

COMMENT: Ox and lion tower over the composition, sharing their meal of straw. The
story is told that while this canvas hung in the
classroom of Charles Kirk, Sandy Spring, Md.,
students poked holes in the eyes of certain
animals—since skillfully repaired. The outline of Hebe, with dove on her upraised right
hand and eagle feeding from her left, is here
clearly defined against the landscape. Hicks
also devoted an entire composition to this
trio, with the addition of a lamb. (See *Liberty,
Meekness, and Innocence,* No. 79).

COLLECTIONS: Painted for Benjamin Hallowell (1799–1877), president of the college
now University of Maryland, Baltimore, Md.;
to his son, Henry C. Hallowell, Sandy Spring,
Md.; given to first cousin, Charles F. Kirk,
Sandy Spring (1893); to son Rudolph and his
wife, Clara Kirk, Rutgers University, New
Brunswick, N.J., and later Ohio; purchased by
M. Knoedler & Co., New York; to Mr. and Mrs.
Thomas M. Evans of New York and Gaines-
ville, Va.

EXHIBITIONS: Carnegie/Corcoran, "Hicks,
Kane, Pippin" (1966–67), p. 9, ill.

Photograph courtesy M. Knoedler & Co., New
York.

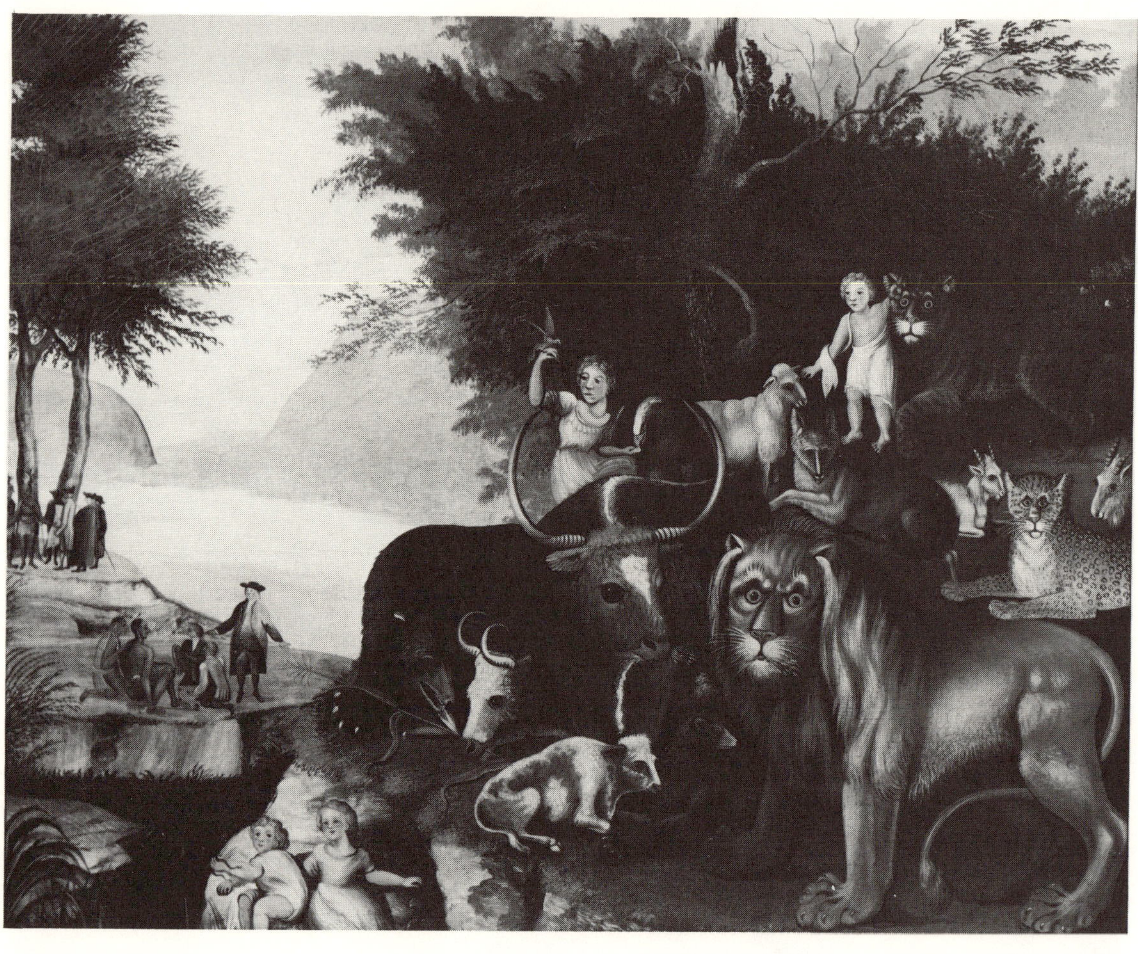

No. 39

PEACEABLE KINGDOM WITH LION IN PRO-
FILE, 1837. Oil on canvas, 28 × 35 inches.
Original black frame, with interior gold edging. The Mercer Museum, Bucks County Historical Society.

COMMENT: The artist continues to experiment. Here the Penn Treaty group appears on
two levels, a division unique in the *Peaceable
Kingdoms*. Two goat heads flank the leopard
at the right margin. As in all *Kingdoms* of the
latter 1830s, the "weaned child" at lower left
not only "plays on the hole of the asp" (Isaiah
11:8), but actually clutches the serpent in his
hand. His pose is obviously lifted from some
Bible engraving after Raphael's *Madonna
della Sedia*, but Hicks has made no attempt to
adjust the pose to present surroundings.

COLLECTIONS: Given by Hicks to his lawyer
friend, Abraham Chapman (1767–1856),
Doylestown, Pa.; presumably by inheritance
to Elizabeth Canby Jenks, Yardley, Pa., who in
1910 gave it to Henry Chapman Mercer,
Doylestown, Pa. (great-grandson of Abraham
Chapman), who gave it to the Mercer
Museum, Bucks County Historical Society,
Doylestown, Pa.

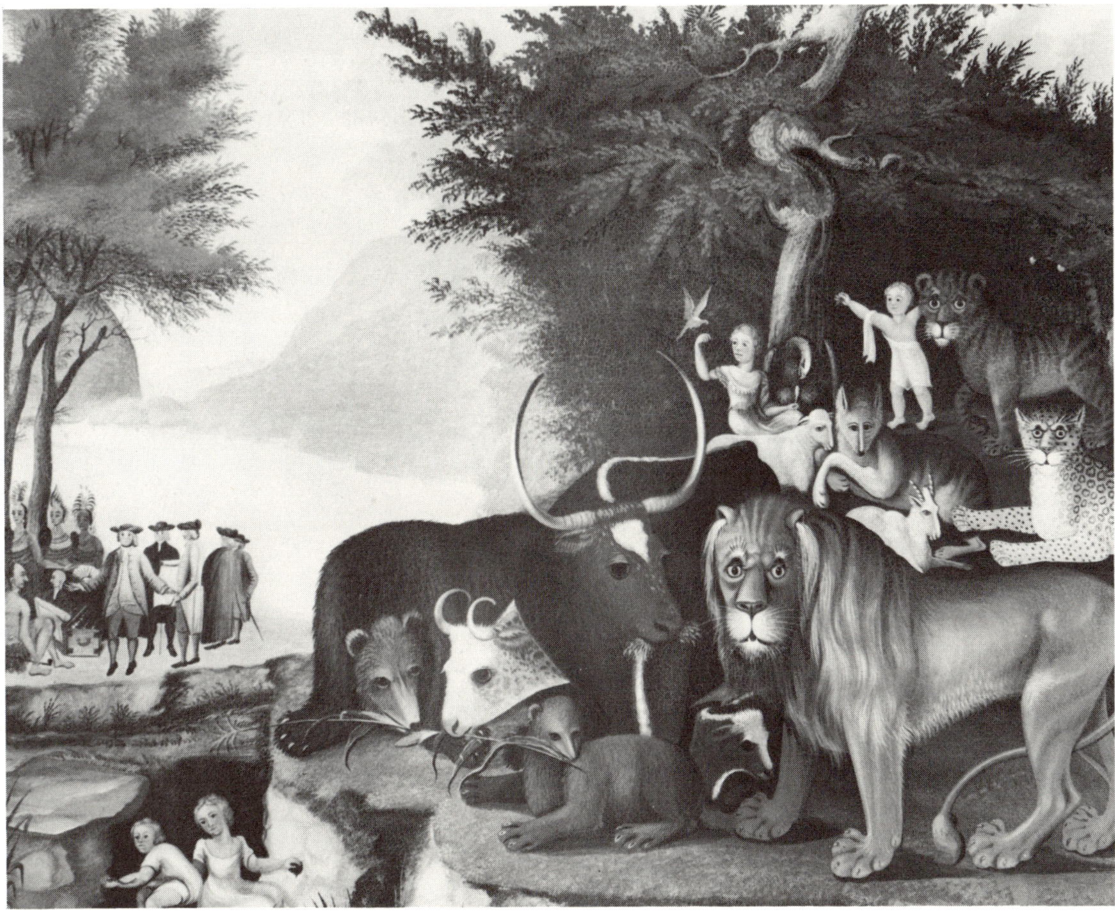

No. 40

PEACEABLE KINGDOM WITH LION IN PRO-
FILE, ca. 1837. Oil on canvas, 29 × 35¾
inches. Original black frame with gold inner
edging. Museum of Art, Carnegie Institute,
Pittsburgh: bequest of Charles Rosenbloom,
1974.

COMMENT: Similar to No. 39, but with the
Penn group united, as customary. One of
many examples that passed through the hands
of Dr. Arthur Edwin Bye, art historian and
antiquarian. A colleague, Edward R. Barnsley,
described the departure of this canvas from
the Bucks County historian's collection in a
letter to Robert W. Carle, great-grandson of the
painter: "Poor Bye almost cried when I took
away the best Peaceable Kingdom he had ever
seen. He has just fixed up his old house (built
ca. 1690–1700) and wanted to keep it. However, since he had told me some time ago it
was for sale, he had to let me have it. . . . The
painting is in its pristine condition, not even
having been dusted since it left the home of
the late Congressman Watson" (letter of
March 5, 1935, AARFAC files). The above-

mentioned transaction evidently did not go
through, for the picture remained in Bye's collection till 1940.

COLLECTIONS: First known owner, probably
by inheritance, Hon. Henry W. Watson, Langhorne, Pa.; to Arthur Edwin Bye, Holicong,
Pa.; to Charles J. Rosenbloom, Pittsburgh, Pa.,
who bequeathed it to the Museum of Art, Carnegie Institute, Pittsburgh.

EXHIBITIONS: Department of Fine Arts, Car-
negie Institute, "Survey of American Paint-
ing" (Pittsburgh, Pa.; October 24–December
15, 1940), no. 22 (captioned Dr. Arthur Edwin
Bye); Smithsonian Institution, Washingtion,
D.C., "American Primitive Art 1670–1954"
(City Art Gallery, Manchester, Eng., and
Whitechapel Art Gallery, London, June 3–
July, 1955), no. 30, plate E; Museum of Art,
Carnegie Institute, "Promised or Given"
(Pittsburgh, Pa., April 1–May 8, 1960).

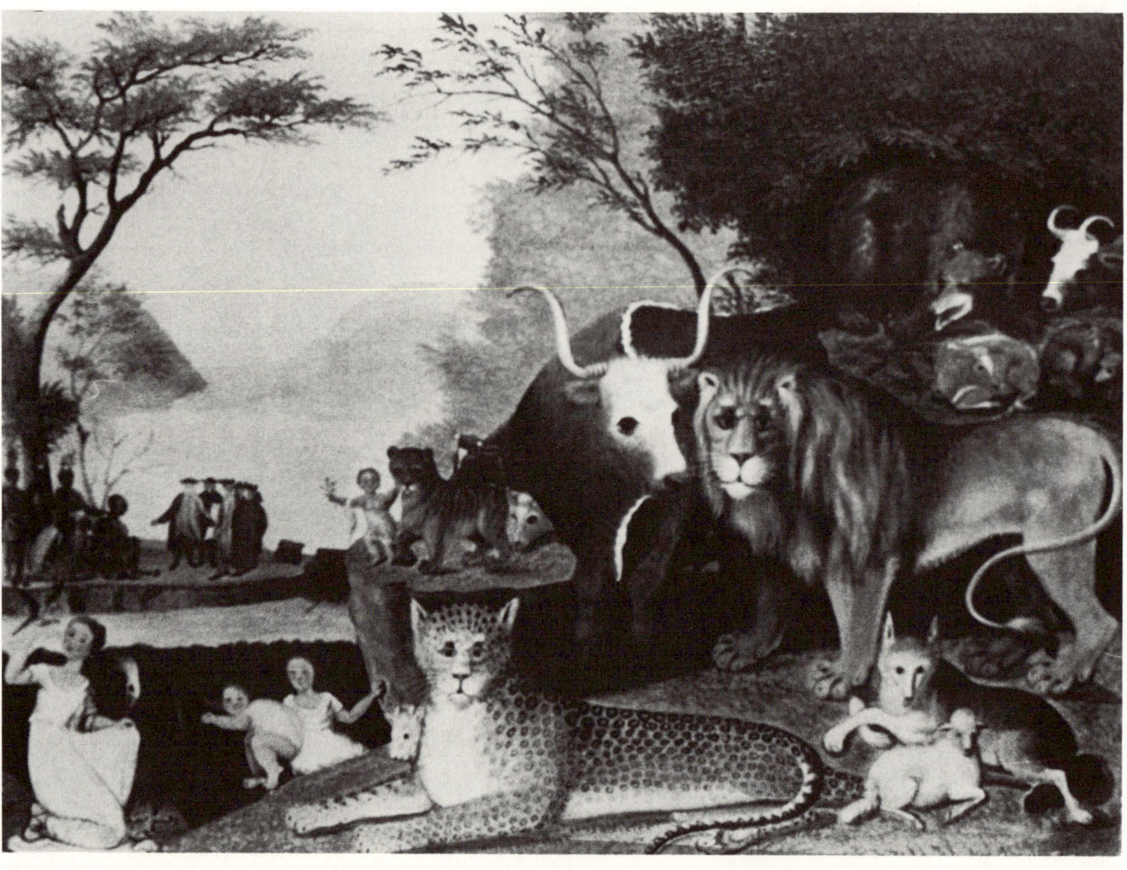

No. 41

PEACEABLE KINGDOM WITH LION IN PRO-
FILE, 1836. Oil on canvas, 17½ × 23¾
inches. Original black-painted, gold-lined
frame with corner blocks. Private collection.

COMMENT: The leopard makes a spectacular
return to the foreground, where it now
stretches at full length. There is also a renewed emphasis on the Divine Child and his
olive branch of peace. He and his cortège of
young animals—lion, calf, and fatling—are
here poised on the brink of a curious turf platform in the middle distance. One of many of
Hicks's canvases handled by Robert Carlen,
who has preserved valuable records of their
histories.

COLLECTIONS: Painted for John Lovett,
Penn's Manor, Bucks County, Pa.; acquired
from a descendant in New Jersey by Robert
Carlen Gallery, Philadelphia; to a private collector.

EXHIBITIONS: Robert Carlen Gallery,
Philadelphia, "Hicks Centennial Exhibition"
(no cat.—reviewed in *Philadelphia Inquirer*,
January 9, 1949).

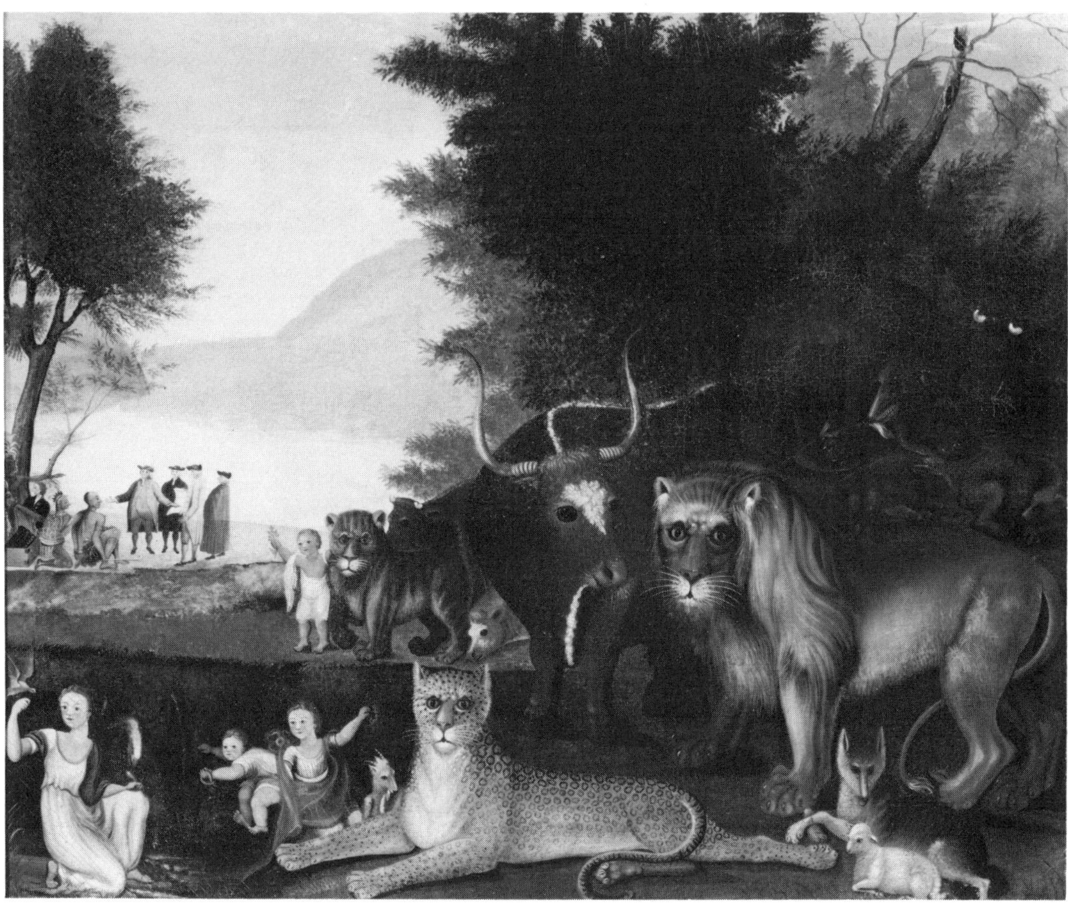

No. 42

PEACEABLE KINGDOM WITH LION IN PRO-FILE, 1837. Oil on canvas, 29 × 35¾ inches. Private collection.

COMMENT: Much like the preceding, but on a larger canvas. Probably one of two paintings referred to in a March 12, 1838, letter from Hicks to his friend Samuel Hart, the other work being the Chapman *Kingdom*, No. 39. "The object of my painting them," wrote the artist, "was to try to raise money to bear my expenses in my late journey" (Bucks County Historical Society files, quoted by Alice Ford, *Edward Hicks: Painter of the Peaceable Kingdom* (Philadelphia: University of Pennsylvania Press, 1952), p. 88). This ministerial travel of the previous year included Goose Creek Meeting, Loudon County, Virginia, where he preached his famous sermon on the Peaceable Kingdom. His canvases of the period illustrate it pictorially, with their four pairs of opposites: leopard and kid in the foreground, wolf and lamb to the right, above them the lion and docile ox, while lost in the shadow of the woods are the bear and cow sharing their cornstalk.

COLLECTIONS: Originally owned by Samuel Hart (1783–1863) of Doylestown, Pa., surveyor of Bucks County and justice of the peace; descended to Florence Hart (Mrs. T. F. Dixon) Wainwright, Villanova, Pa.; to Robert L. Montgomery, II, Big Flatts, N.Y.; to R. H. Love Galleries, Chicago, Ill.; to a private collector.

EXHIBITIONS: Carnegie/Corcoran, "Hicks, Kane, Pippin" (1966–67), no. 19; Andrew Crispo gallery, "Edward Hicks: A Gentle Spirit" (New York, 1975), no. 11; the Pennsylvania Academy of the Fine Arts, *In This Academy 1805–1876* (Philadelphia, 1976), no. 133.

Photograph courtesy R. H. Love Galleries, Chicago.

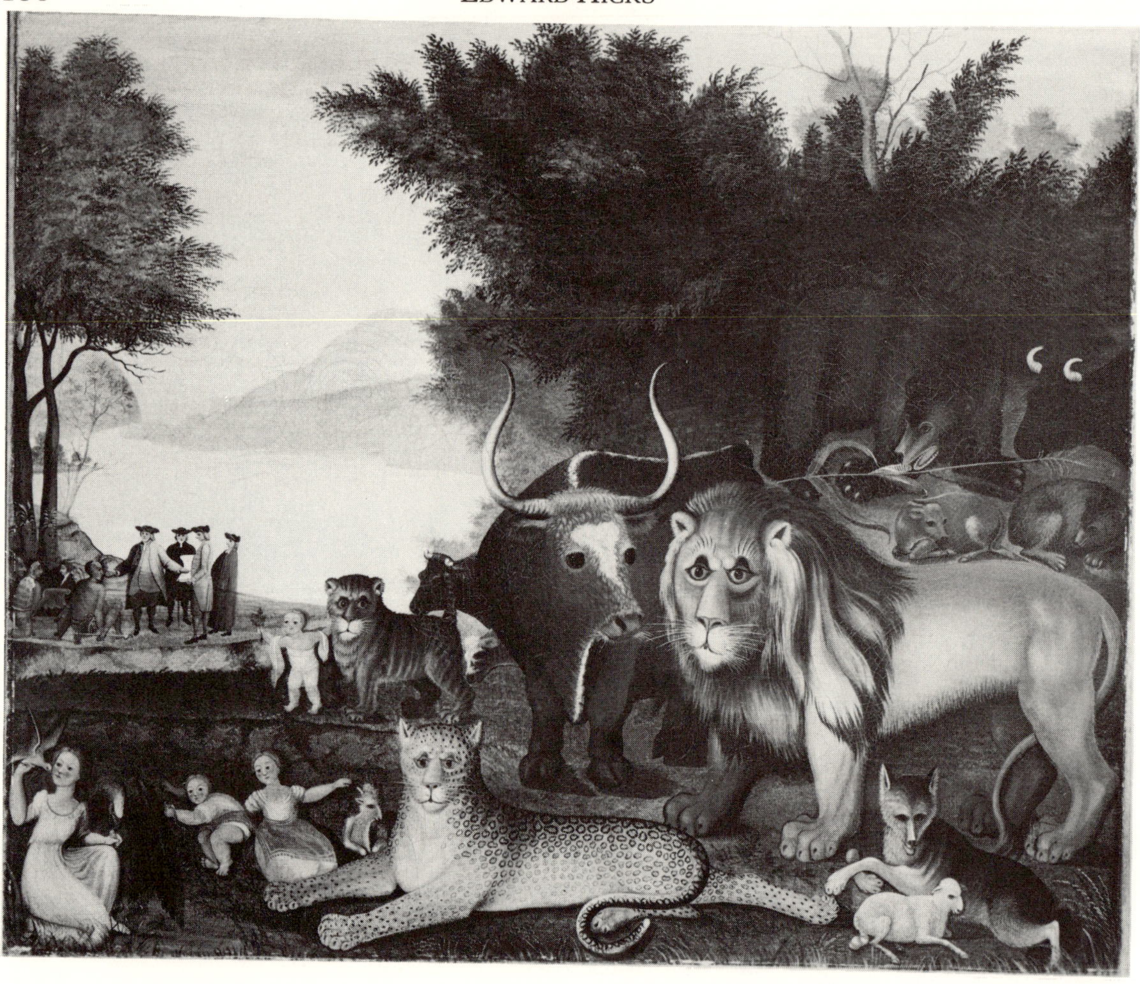

No. 43

PEACEABLE KINGDOM WITH LION IN PRO-
FILE, ca. 1837. Oil on canvas 29½ × 35¾
inches. Mr. Robert Lee.

COMMENT: The story of this *Kingdom* is
sparked with an interesting discovery. It was
auctioned early in 1980 with no record of its
original provenance. But within a year Ann
McCoy Weymouth and Kenneth C. Lindsey,
antique dealers of Chadds Ford, Pa., acquired
a pencil sketch of a lion and ox clearly linked,
through details in animals and background, to
this specific *Peaceable Kingdom*. Found between the leaves of an 1835 Bible belonging to
former attenders of Plymouth Meeting in
Montgomery County, it is unsigned. One

would, of course, like to believe that it was the
work of Hicks himself. But whether it can be
justly attributed to the painter or not, it is
helpful in suggesting a provenance otherwise
irretrievably lost.

COLLECTIONS: First recorded owner was
Mrs. T. Charlton Henry, Chestnut Hill, Pa.,
who bought it in Maine in the 1920s; to her
daughter, Mrs. Philip D. Armour, Coral
Gables, Fla.; auctioned by Samuel T. Freeman,
Philadelphia, to Robert Lee, Philadelphia.

Photograph courtesy Samuel T. Freeman &
Co., Philadelphia.

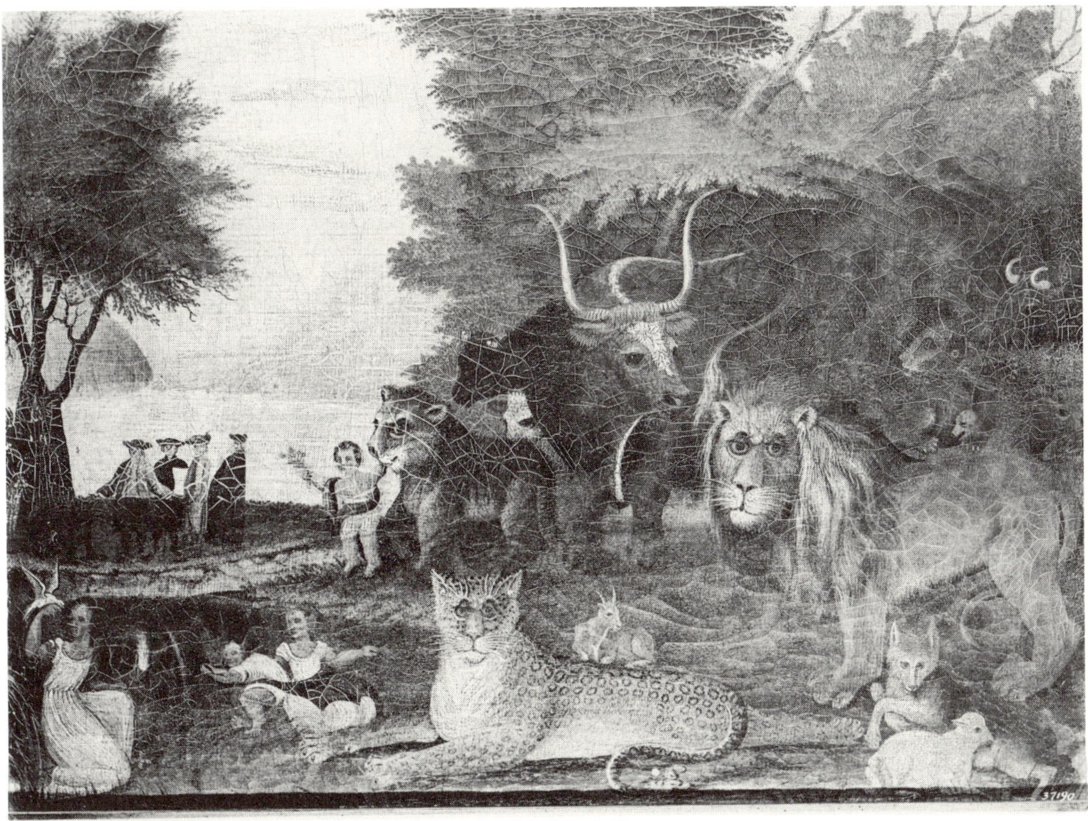

No. 44

PEACEABLE KINGDOM WITH LION IN PRO-
FILE, 1838–40. Oil on canvas, 17½ × 23½
inches. Original black, gold-lined, corner-
blocked frame made in Hicks's shop and decorated by him. Edwa Osborn.

COMMENT: This final phase of the *Middle
Kingdoms* does not emphasize the grain in the
lion's mouth, symbol of the self-denial of
Quaker quietism. Is the artist/preacher stressing another symbol of salvation, the olive
branch of reconciliation, which has returned
to the hand of the Divine Child? Note the lyre-
shaped horns of the ox—also the dispropor-
tionately large head of the young lion.

COLLECTIONS: Traditions vary as to whether
this was painted for Dr. A. H. Trego, the
Hicks's family physician, or for Dr. George T.
Heston, who lived at 212 South State Street,
Newtown, in an old stone house since razed.
Bequeathed by the doctor's widow to the
painter's grandson, William Penrose Hicks,
Newtown; to his daughter Hannah, Mrs. J.
Stanley Lee, Newtown; to Edwa Osborn.

EXHIBITIONS: "Newtown 275th Anniversary" (1959), no. 1 (not ill. in cat.).

Photograph courtesy Frick Art Reference Library.

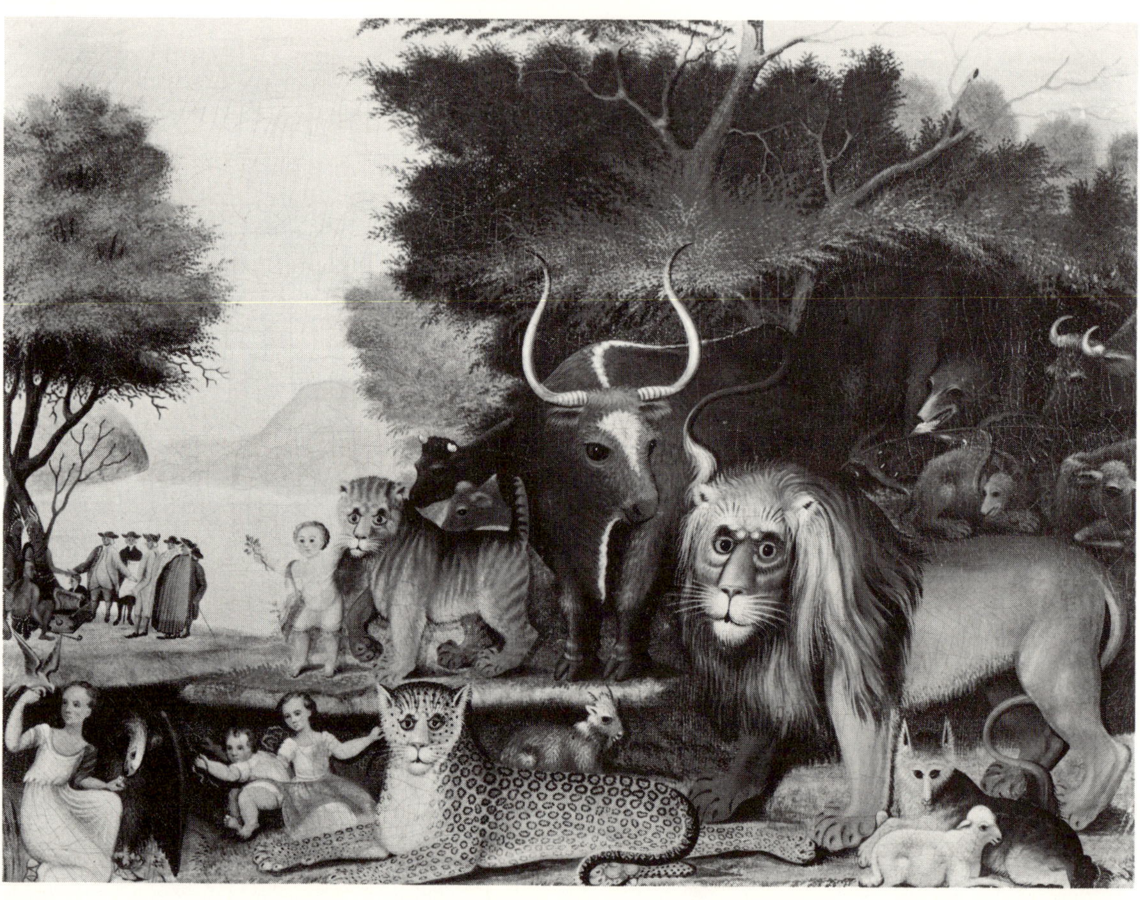

No. 45

PEACEABLE KINGDOM WITH LION IN PRO-
FILE, ca. 1838–40. Oil on canvas, 17¾ × 23¾
inches. Holger Cahill Collection.

COMMENT: Combines delicacy of technique
with deep psychological content. The lion, his
position lowly beside the ox, haunts us with
his wistful stare. One of the most frequently
reproduced of Hicks's works.

COLLECTIONS: Exact provenance unknown,
but from the area of Elmhurst, Long Island;
American Folk Art Gallery (Edith Gregor Halpert), New York to Holger Cahill Collection,
New York.

EXHIBITIONS: AARFAC, "Edward Hicks"
(1960), no. 26, p. 16 (not ill.); New York
Worlds Fair, arranged by Museum of Modern
Art, "Art in America: Four Centuries of Paint-
ing and Sculpture" (New York, April 22,
1964–October 17, 1965); Carnegie/Corcoran,
"Hicks, Kane, Pippin" (1966–67), no. 12; ACA
Galleries, "Four American Primitives" (New
York, 1972), no. 6 (ill. and detail); Whitney
Museum of American Art, "The Flowering of
American Folk Art" (New York, February 1–
March 24, 1974), no. 98, p. 74 (col.); travelling
exhibition (1974) to Virginia Museum of Fine
Arts, Richmond, Va.; to the Fine Arts
Museums of San Francisco: M. H. deYoung
Memorial Museum, San Francisco; Andrew
Crispo Gallery, "Edward Hicks: A Gentle
Spirit" (New York, 1975), no. 10 (col.).

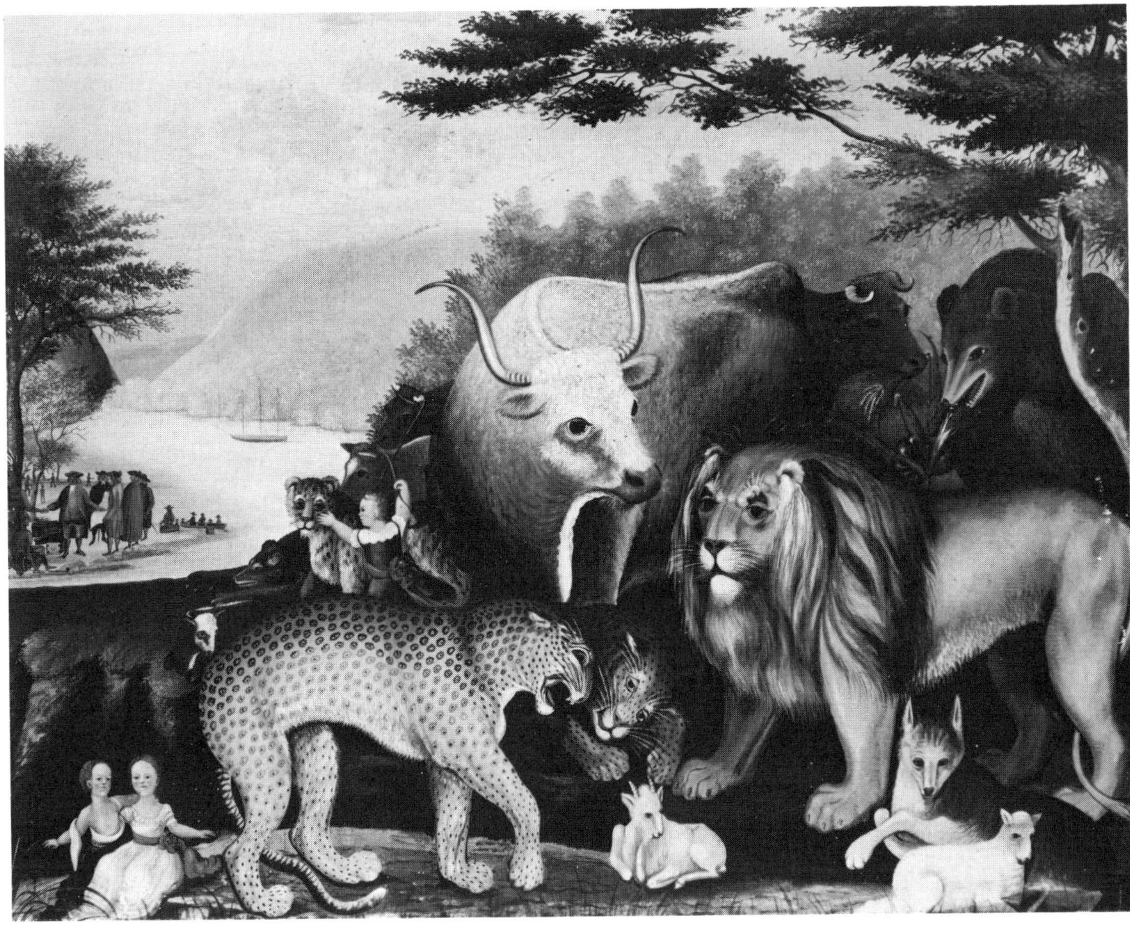

No. 46

PEACEABLE KINGDOM WITH ARCHING LEOPARD, ca. 1844. Oil on canvas, 24 × 31¼ inches. Original walnut frame. Private collection, present whereabouts unknown.

COMMENT: A new and menacing leopard arches above a crouching mate—not entirely to her dissatisfaction. The Divine Child represents reconciliation as he yokes the young lion, the calf, and the fatling together. This was accompanied by the artist's paraphrase of Isaiah 11:6–8 on a separate sheet, replacing the painted inscriptions of earlier versions:

> The wolf shall with the lambkin dwell in
>   peace,
> His grim carnivorous thirst for blood shall
>   cease,
> The beauteous leopard with his restless
>   eye,
> Shall by the kid in perfect stillness lie;
> The calf, the fatling, and young lion wild,
> Shall all be led by one sweet little child.
>
> The cow and bear shall quietly partake,
> Of the rich food the ear and cornstalk
>   make;

> While each their peaceful young with joy
>   survey,
> As side by side on the green grass they lay;
> While the old lion thwarting nature's law,
> Shall eat beside the ox the barley straw.
>
> The sucking child shall innocently play
> On the dark hole where poisonous reptiles
>   lay;
> The crested worm with all its venom then,
> The weaned child shall fasten in his den.
>
> The illustrious Penn this heavenly
>   kingdom felt,
> When with Columbia's native sons he
>   dealt;
> Without an oath a lasting Treaty made,
> In Christian Faith beneath the elm tree's
>   shade.

COLLECTIONS: Provenance unknown. Leonardo L. Beans, Trenton, N.J.; Sotheby Parke Bernet, New York; private collector.

EXHIBITIONS: "Newtown 275th Anniversary" (1959), no. 6 (not ill.); AARFAC, "Edward Hicks" (1960), no. 41, p. 19 (not ill.).

Photograph copyright Sotheby Parke Bernet, Inc., New York.

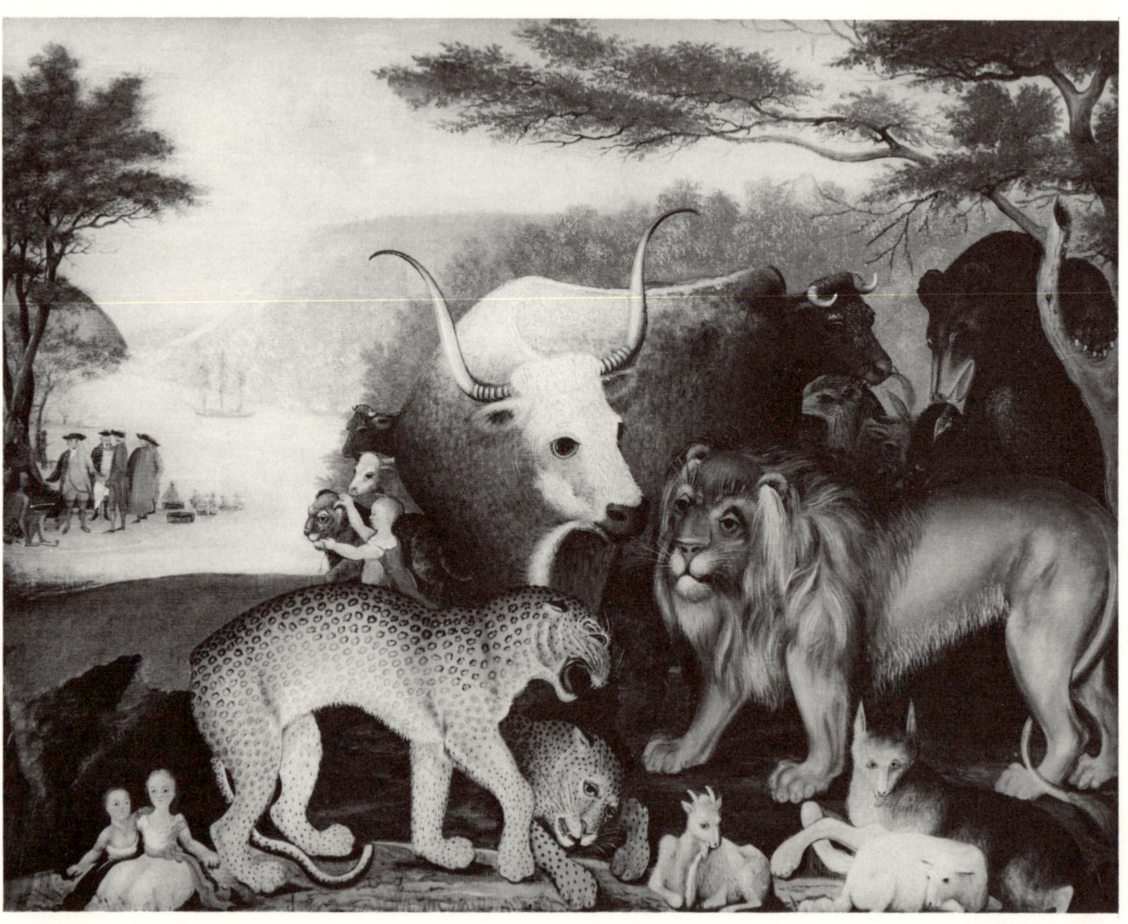

No. 47

PEACEABLE KINGDOM WITH ARCHING LEOPARD, 1844. Oil on canvas, 24 × 31¼ inches. Original frame by Edward Trego. Abby Aldrich Rockefeller Folk Art Center.

COMMENT: A massive triangle of leopard, lion, and ox, dominated by the ox. Uniquely well documented, this canvas was delivered to the purchaser by the artist's son, Isaac, with note dated 9 mo. 3. 1844 (Jane W. T. Brey, *A Quaker Saga* [Philadelphia: Dorrance & Co., 1967], pp. 479–80).

COLLECTIONS: Commissioned by Joseph Watson (1805–86), Langhorne, Pa.; to his elder daughter, Mary Elizabeth Watson, Langhorne, Pa.; her sister, Susanna Watson Hancock, Langhorne, Pa.; her great-niece, Jane Watson Taylor Brey, Germantown, Philadelphia; by Mabel Zahn of Charles Sessler, Inc., Phila., to Abby Aldrich Rockefeller Folk Art Center, Williamsburg, Va.

EXHIBITIONS: Friends Historical Association Annual Meeting at Atwater Kent Museum (Philadelphia, 1942); Germantown Friends School, *The Peaceable Kingdom Cantata* by Randall Thompson (Germantown, Pa., March 19, 1952); Philadelphia Yearly Meeting (Philadelphia, November 8–21, 1955, accompanying 1955 William Penn Lecture, November 13); Friends Neighborhood Guild, "Quaker Artists of America" (Philadelphia, March 17–April 9, 1957); on loan to United States Mission to the United Nations (New York, June 1, 1962–June 1, 1963); Time-Life Exhibition (New York, October 19–November 20, 1966); High Museum of Art Antiques Show (Atlanta, Ga., September, 1974), no. 111, p. 41 (not ill.), in conjunction with AARFAC traveling exhibition, "Folk Art in America: A Living Tradition"; Whitney Museum of American Art, "American Folk Painters of Three Centuries" (New York, 1980), p. 91 (col.).

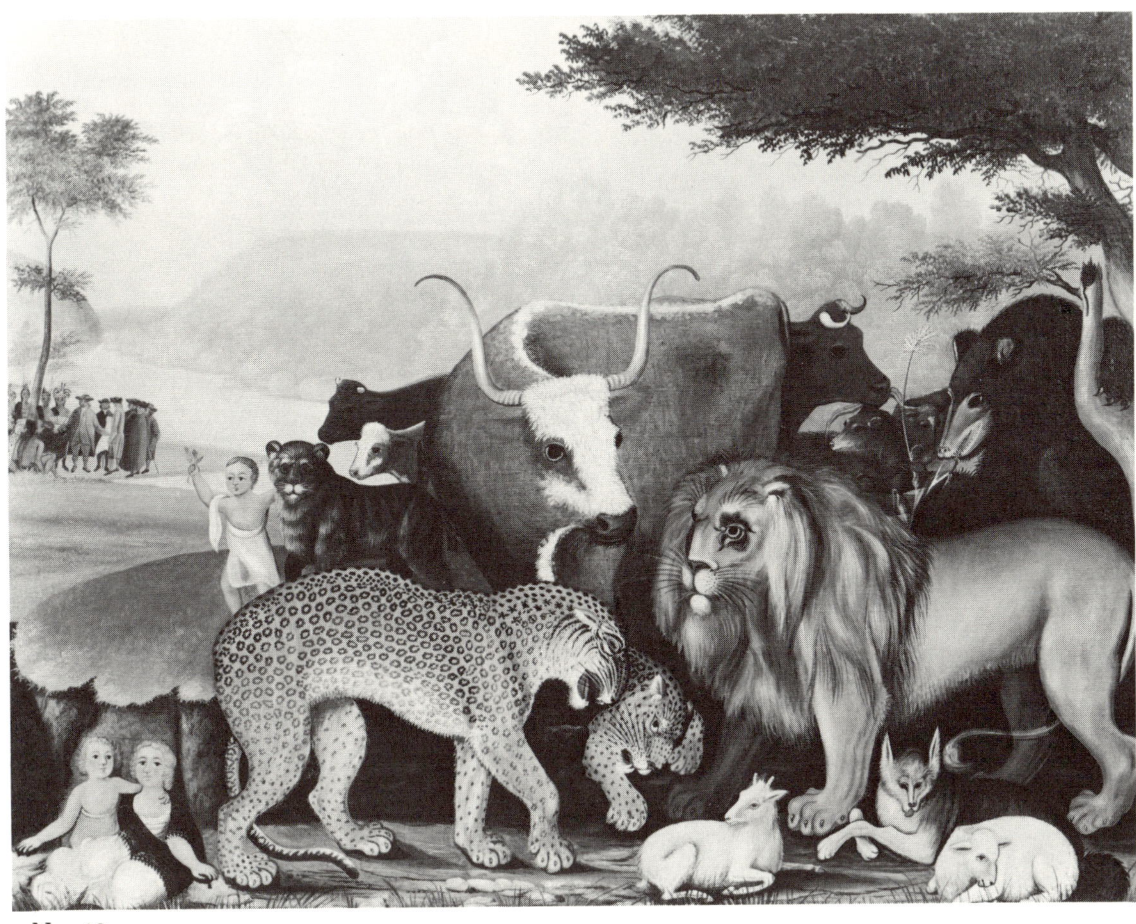

No. 48

PEACEABLE KINGDOM WITH ARCHING LEOPARD, 1844–46. Oil on canvas, 23⅞ × 31¼ inches. The Dallas Museum of Fine Arts; the Art Museum League Fund.

COMMENT: It is hard to tell where this fits in the *Kingdom* sequence. The olive branch in the hand of the Divine Child, as in the *Profiles*, suggests that it is the first of its category. On the other hand, the vivid color hints at a later date.

COLLECTIONS: Original provenance unknown. Said to have been found in Germantown, Philadelphia, off the stretcher and bought by a "runner" for $10.00. Acquired by Hirschl & Adler, New York; to David David, Philadelphia; to David Bakalar, Boston, Mass.; to Hirschl & Adler, New York; to the Dallas Museum of Fine Arts, Dallas, Tex.

EXHIBITIONS: "Selections from the Collection of Hirschl & Adler Galleries" (New York, 1963–64), no. 18, and cover (col.); *Hirschl & Adler Retrospective* (New York, November 8–December 1, 1973).

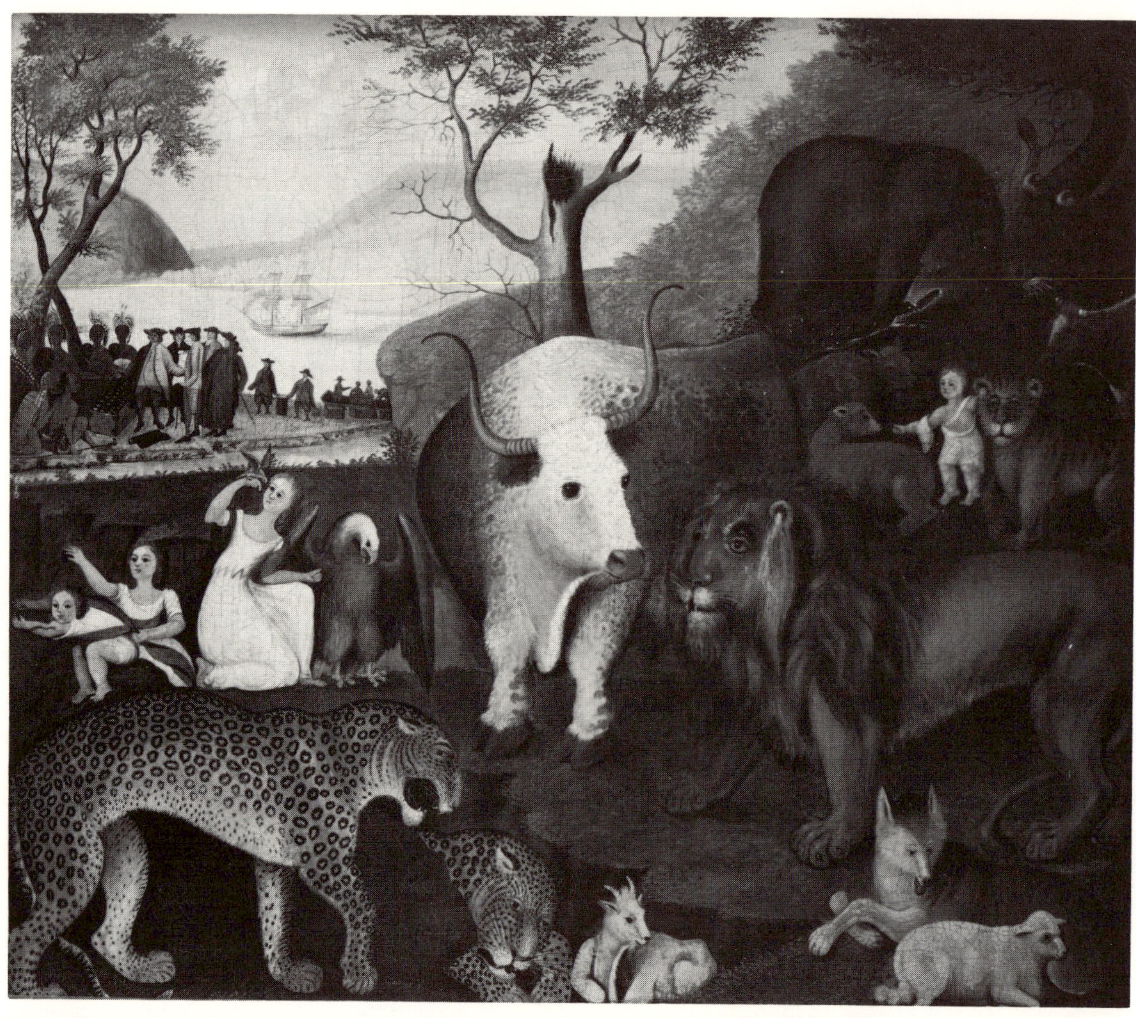

No. 49

PEACEABLE KINGDOM WITH ARCHING LEOPARD, ca. 1846. Oil on canvas, 25 × 28½ inches. Private collection.

COMMENT: A canvas somewhat different in proportions from others of its type. A late appearance of *Liberty*, *Meekness*, and *Innocence* illustrates the recurrence in the 1840s of motifs from Hicks's earlier works: This, like the looping of the red scarf about the "sucking child" and the asp in its hand, can be seen in No. 38 of the preceding decade.

COLLECTIONS: Original provenance unknown. Acquired by Downtown Gallery (Edith Gregor Halpert), New York; M. Knoedler & Co., New York; to Joseph Katz, New York; to M. Knoedler & Co., New York; to Martin Grossman, New York; to Hirschl & Adler, New York; to a private collector, New York.

EXHIBITIONS: AARFAC, "Edward Hicks" (1960), no. 40, p. 19 (not ill.); Carnegie/Corcoran, "Hicks, Kane, Pippin" (1966–67), p. 30; Princeton University Alumni, "American Art of the First Half of the Nineteenth Century" (Princeton, N.J., 1973), no. 34.

Photograph courtesy M. Knoedler & Co., New York.

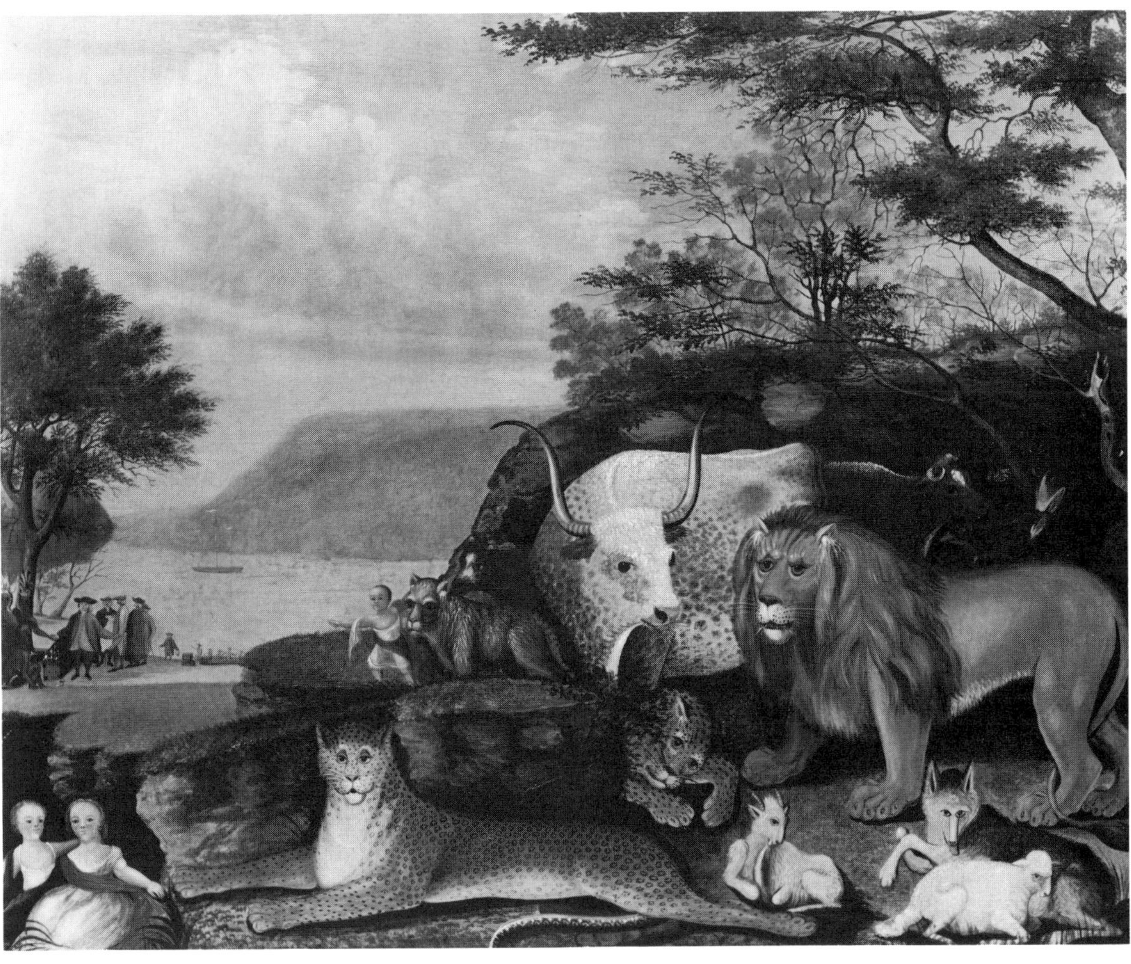

No. 50

PEACEABLE KINGDOM WITH SERENE LEOPARD, ca. 1845. Oil on canvas, 24½ × 30½ inches. Private collection, courtesy Andrew Crispo Gallery.

COMMENT: Unique in combining the crouching leopard of the previous category with a new and serene leopard extended across the foreground. One of the most colorful of the *Kingdoms.*

COLLECTIONS: Original provenance unknown. First known owner, Mary S. Paxson, Newtown, Pa., probably by inheritance, who gave it to Dr. Charles B. Smith, Newtown; by bequest to Friends Boarding Home, Newtown; acquired by Hirschl & Adler Galleries, New York; to a private collector, courtesy Andrew Crispo Gallery, New York.

EXHIBITIONS: Hirschl & Adler Galleries, "Quality: An Experience in Collecting" (New York, November 12–December 7, 1974), no. 20 (col.); Andrew Crispo Gallery, "Edward Hicks: A Gentle Spirit" (New York, 1975), no. 20, ill. and detail (col.); Baltimore Museum of Art, Baltimore, in collaboration with the White House, Washington, D.C., "200 Years of American Art" (shown during 1976 at Landes Museum, Bonn, Germany; Museum of Modern Art, Belgrade, Yugoslavia; Galleria Nazionale, Rome—cover of cat.; National Museum of Poland, Warsaw; Science Center, Baltimore, Md., January 16–February 6, 1977), no. 15.

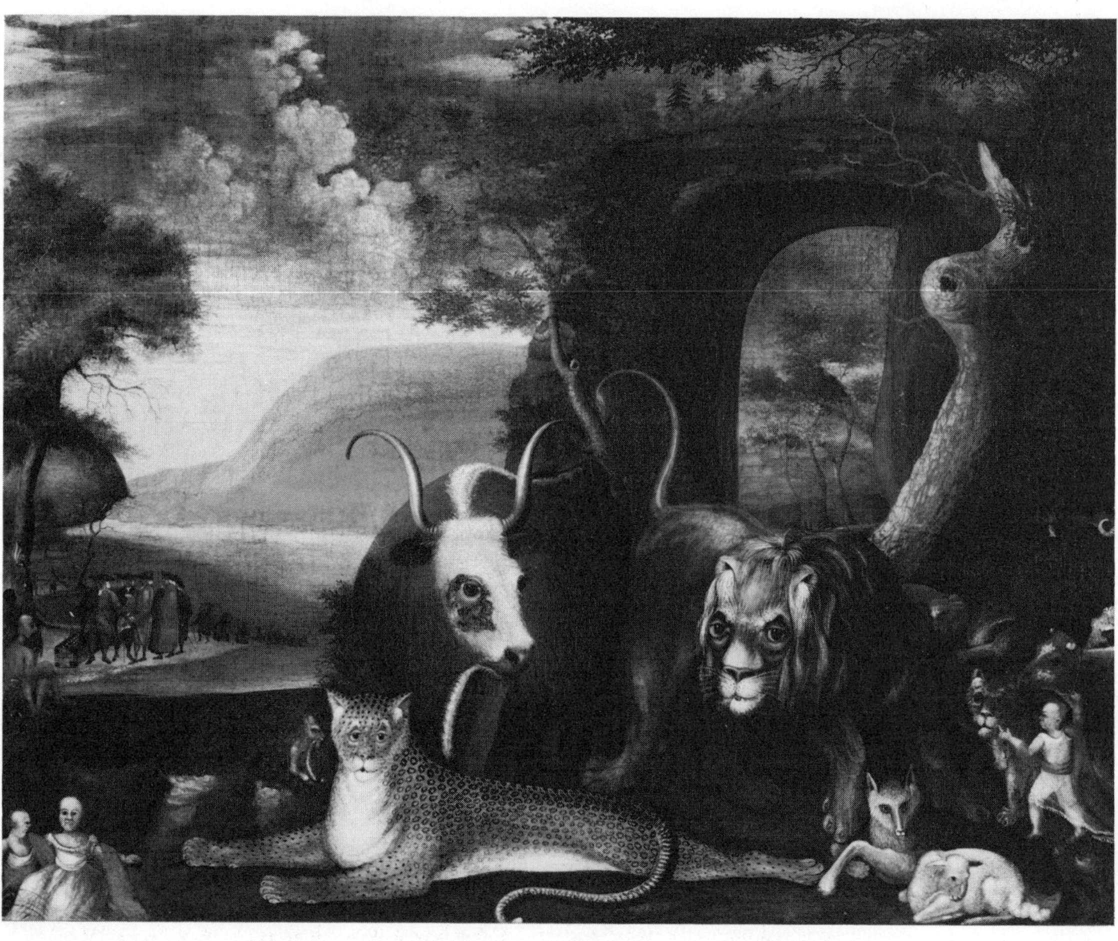

No. 51

PEACEABLE KINGDOM WITH SERENE LEOPARD, 1845. Oil on canvas, 24¼ × 31 inches. Inscription on stretcher reads, "Painted by Edward Hicks in the 65th year of his age. 1845." Frame probably original—the same as when acquired. Yale University Art Gallery; bequest of Robert W. Carle.

COMMENT: A rich vista into the painter's own mystical world, with the lion in a new, foreshortened pose against a landscape composed of earlier sources: the Natural Bridge of Virginia, the Delaware Water Gap, and Penn's Treaty (see Eleanore Price Mather, "In Detail: Edward Hicks's *Peaceable Kingdom,*" *Portfolio* [1980]: 34–39).

COLLECTIONS: The painter's son, Isaac W. Hicks, Newtown, Pa.; to his son, Edward Hicks, Newtown; acquired by the painter's great-grandson, Robert W. Carle, South Salem, Conn., who bequeathed it to the Yale University Art Gallery, New Haven, Conn. On extended loan to the American Embassy, London.

EXHIBITIONS: Pennsylvania Academy of the Fine Arts, Philadelphia, and Dickinson College, Carlisle, Pa., "Symbols of Peace: William Penn's Treaty with the Indians" (Philadelphia, May 12–September 26, 1976); cat. articles by Charles Coleman Sellers and Anthony N. B. Garvan, no. 23, plate 8.

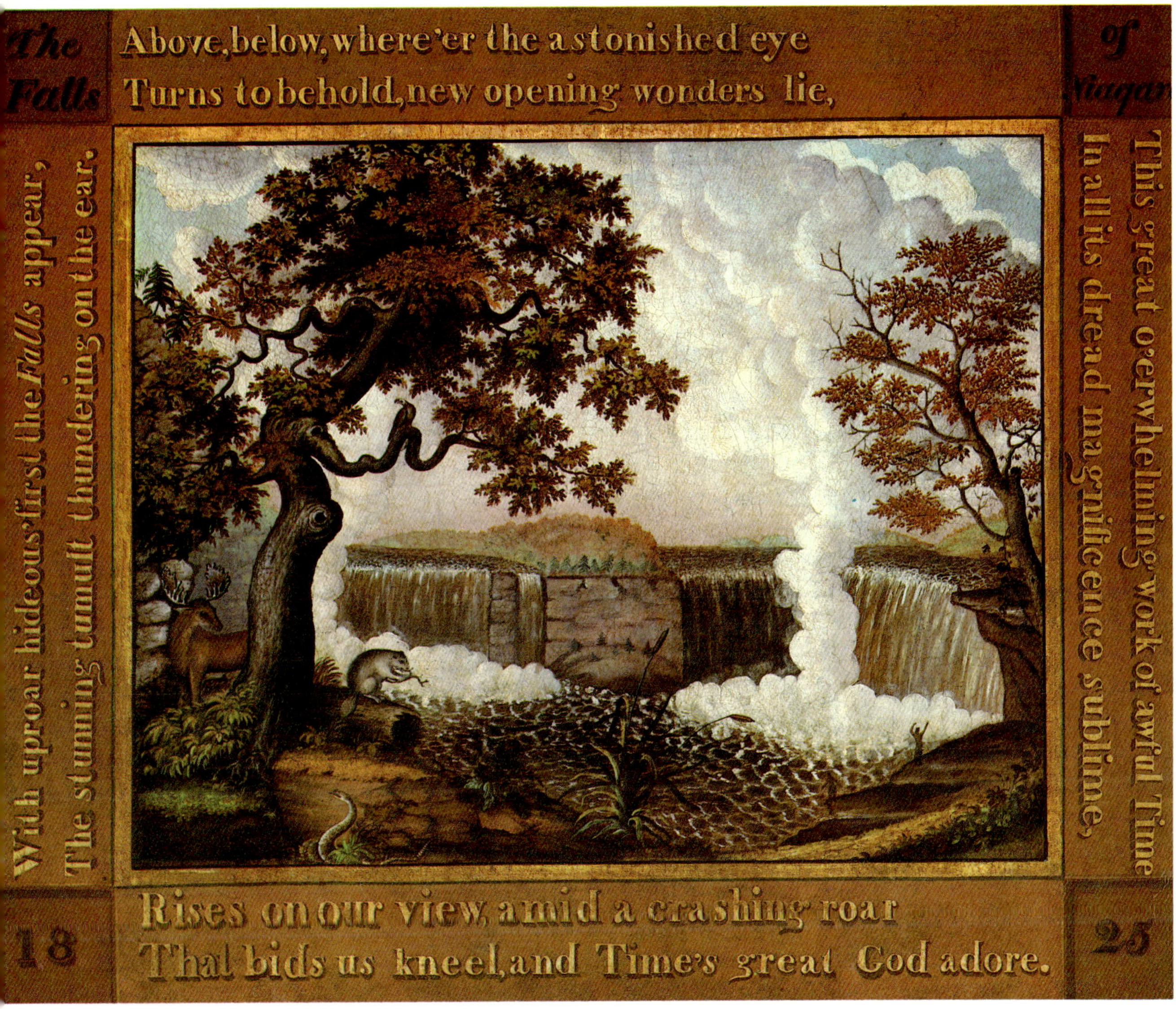

PLATE I. The Falls of Niagara, 1825. This romantic landscape, after an engraving by Henry Tanner, brings Hicks close in spirit to his academic contemporaries. Surrounding couplets are from "The Foresters" by Alexander Wilson, Scottish-born American ornithologist. (The Metropolitan Musum of Art; gift of Edgar William and Bernice Chrysler Garbisch 1962. Copyright 1981 by the Museum.)

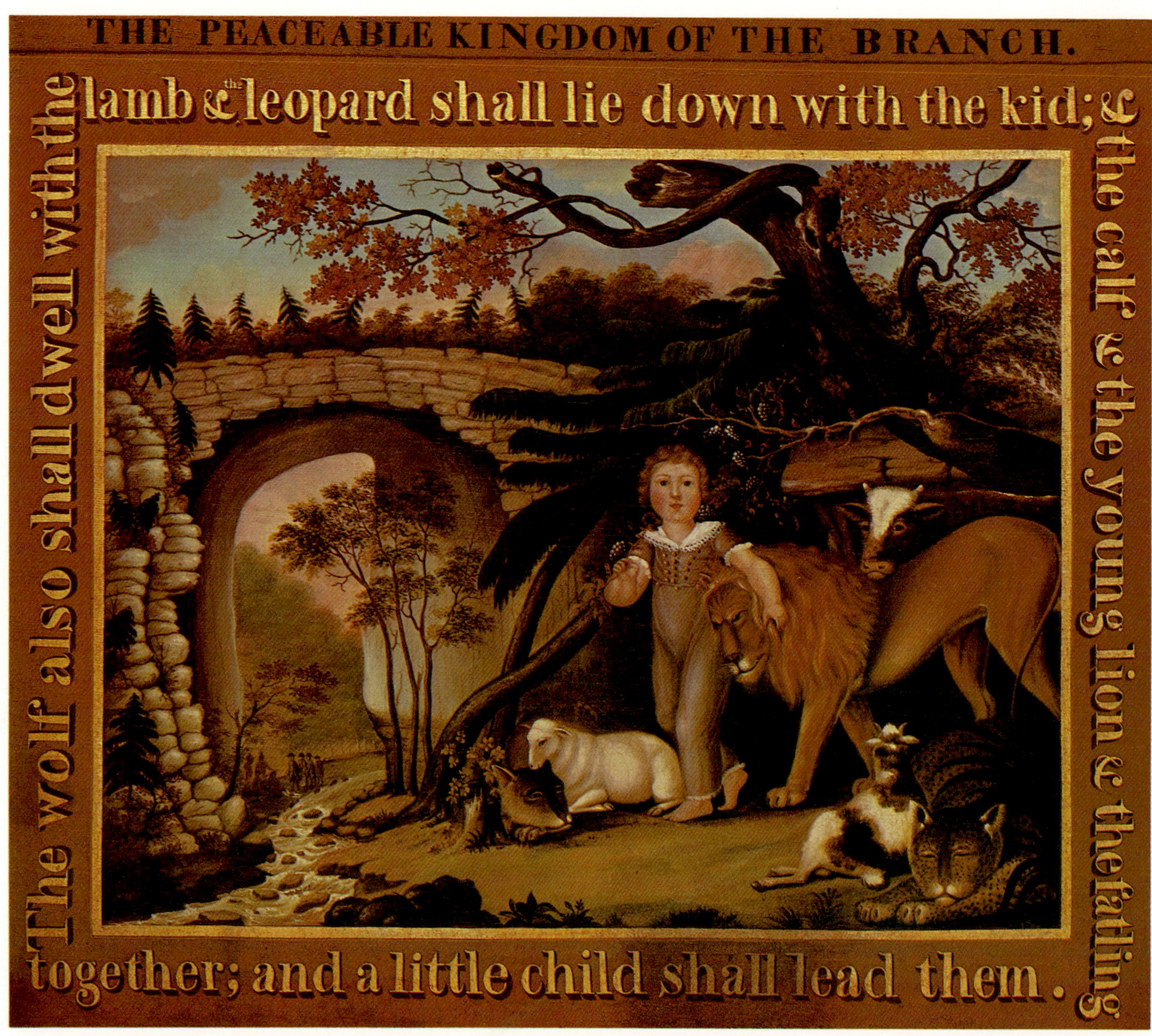

PLATE II. The Peaceable Kingdom of the Branch, 1825–26. Hicks borrowed the figures and their arrangement from a British illustrator, Richard Westall, but added features of his own: a neat pant suit of purplish hue, a small vignette of Penn's Treaty, and the Natural Bridge of Virginia from Tanner's engraving. (Abby Aldrich Rockefeller Folk Art Center, Williamsburg, Va.)

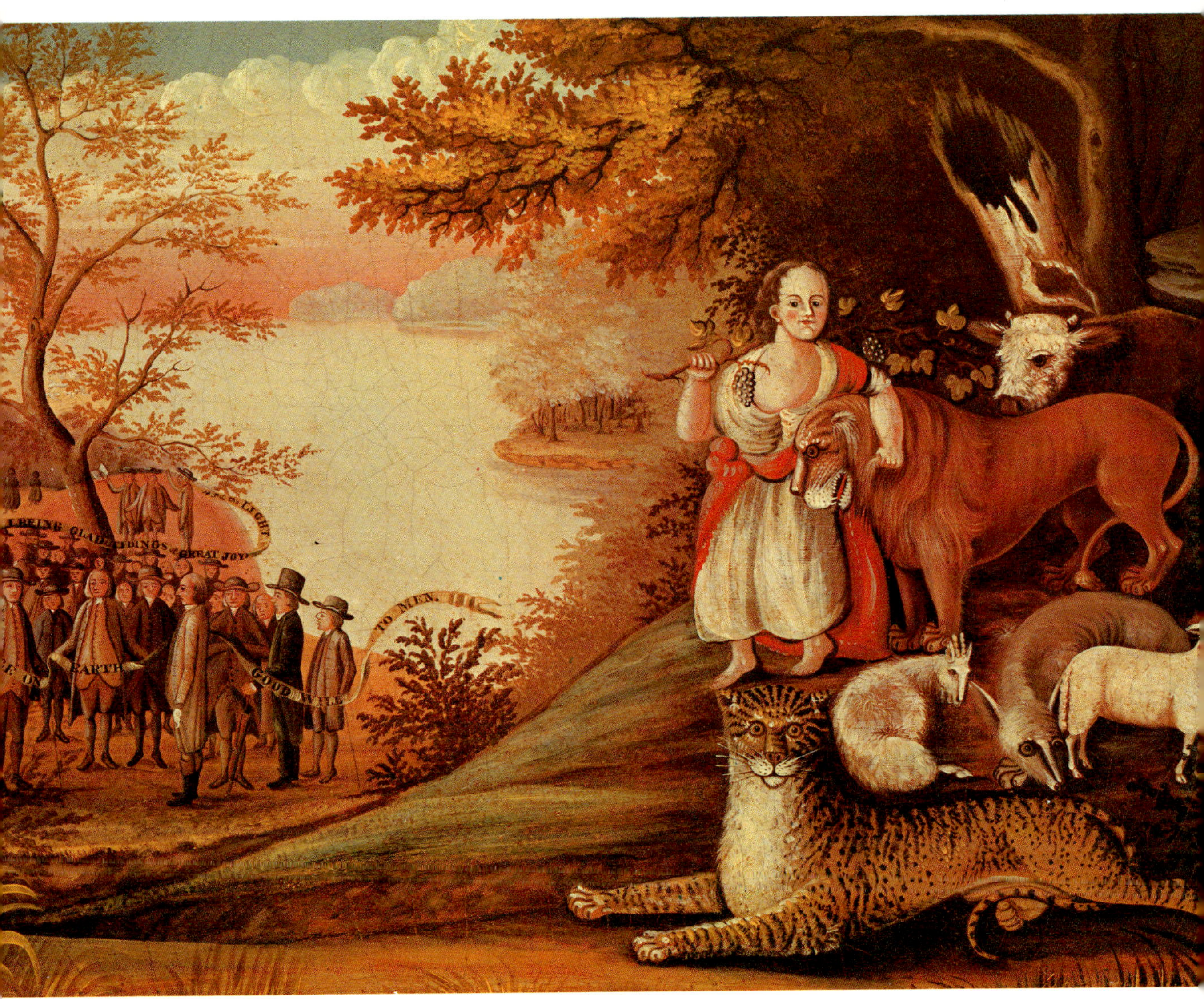

PLATE III. The Peaceable Kingdom With Quakers Bearing Banners, 1827–30. Two compositions within a single frame: the Westall nucleus to the right, a galaxy of eminent Quakers to the left. The tree that rises from their midst distinguishes this canvas from others of its type. (Courtesy of The Henry Francis du Pont Winterthur Museum.)

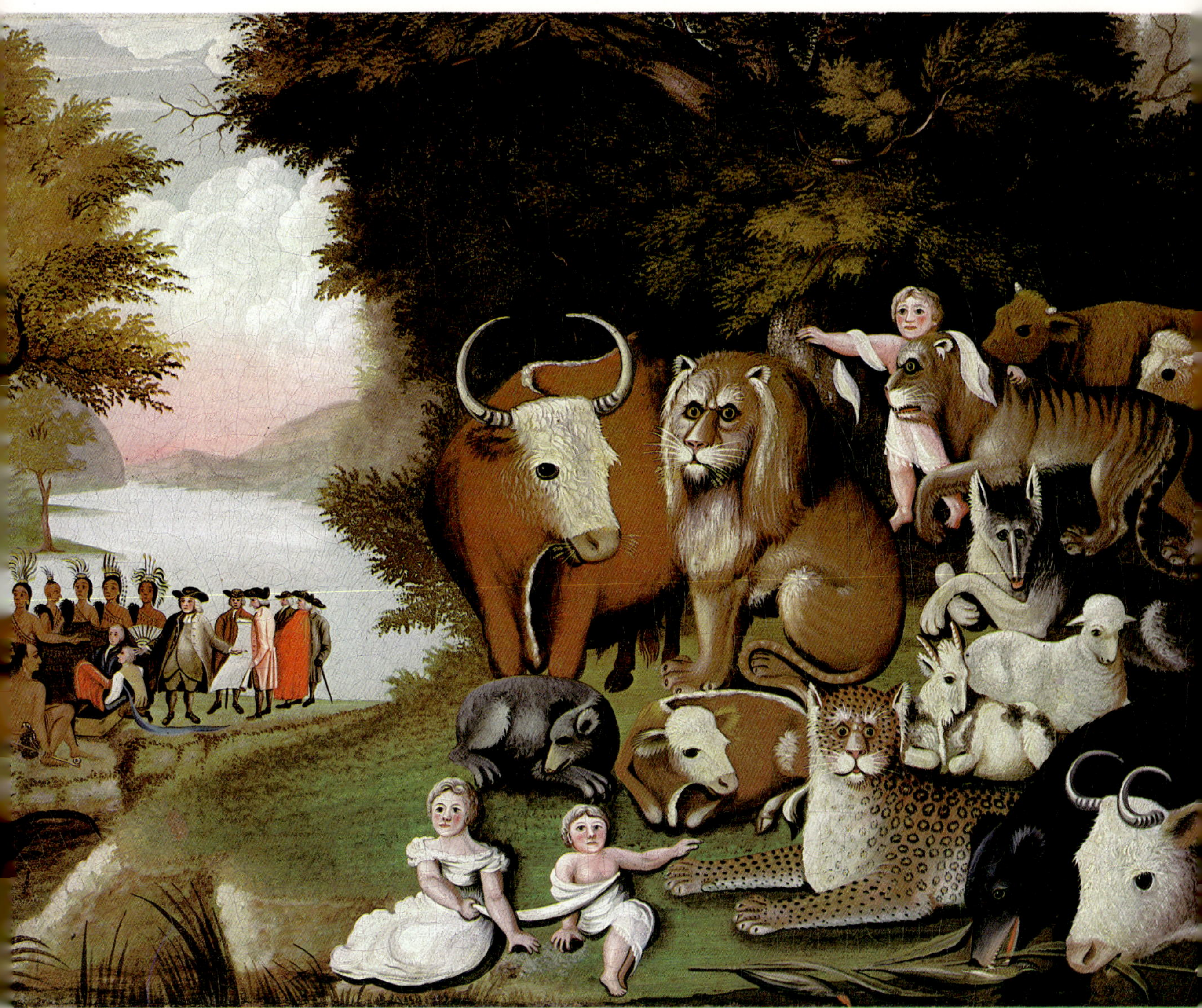

PLATE IV. The Peaceable Kingdom With Seated Lion, *ca. 1833. The artist's favorite subject in one of its most appealing phases. Centered in a seated lion, the composition introduces new figures from the biblical prophecy, including a bear and cow and two children (Isaiah 11:7–8). It also presents an expanded vignette of the Penn Treaty scene. (Worcester Art Museum, Worcester, Mass.)*

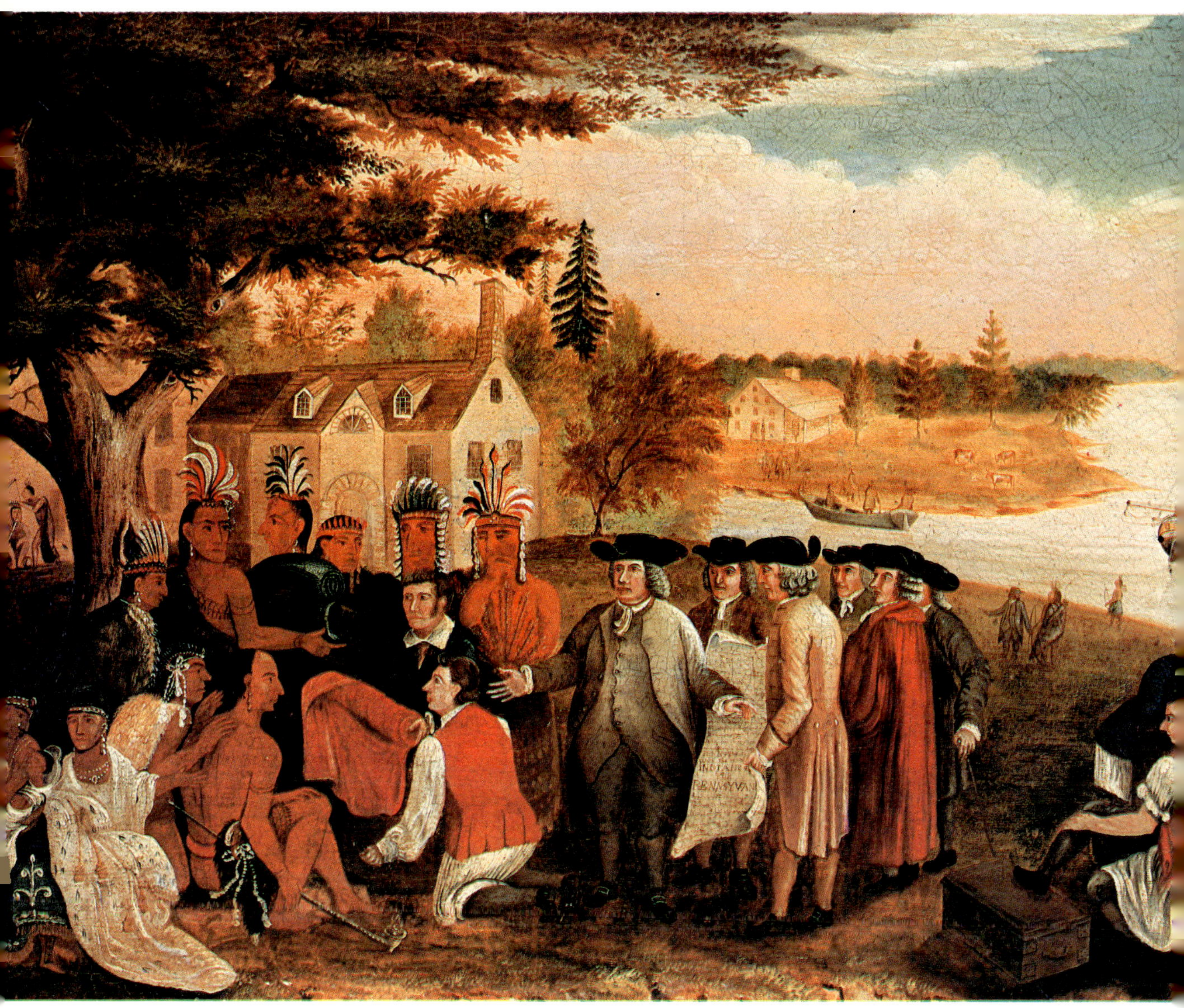

PLATE V. *Penn's Treaty, 1835–40. One of the artist's many tributes to his great hero, William Penn. Details indicate that this was copied from John Hall's 1775 engraving of William Penn's Treaty with the Indians by Benjamin West, but the brilliant colors are totally unlike the muted tones of West's original. (Mercer Museum of the Bucks County Historical Society, Doylestown, Pa.)*

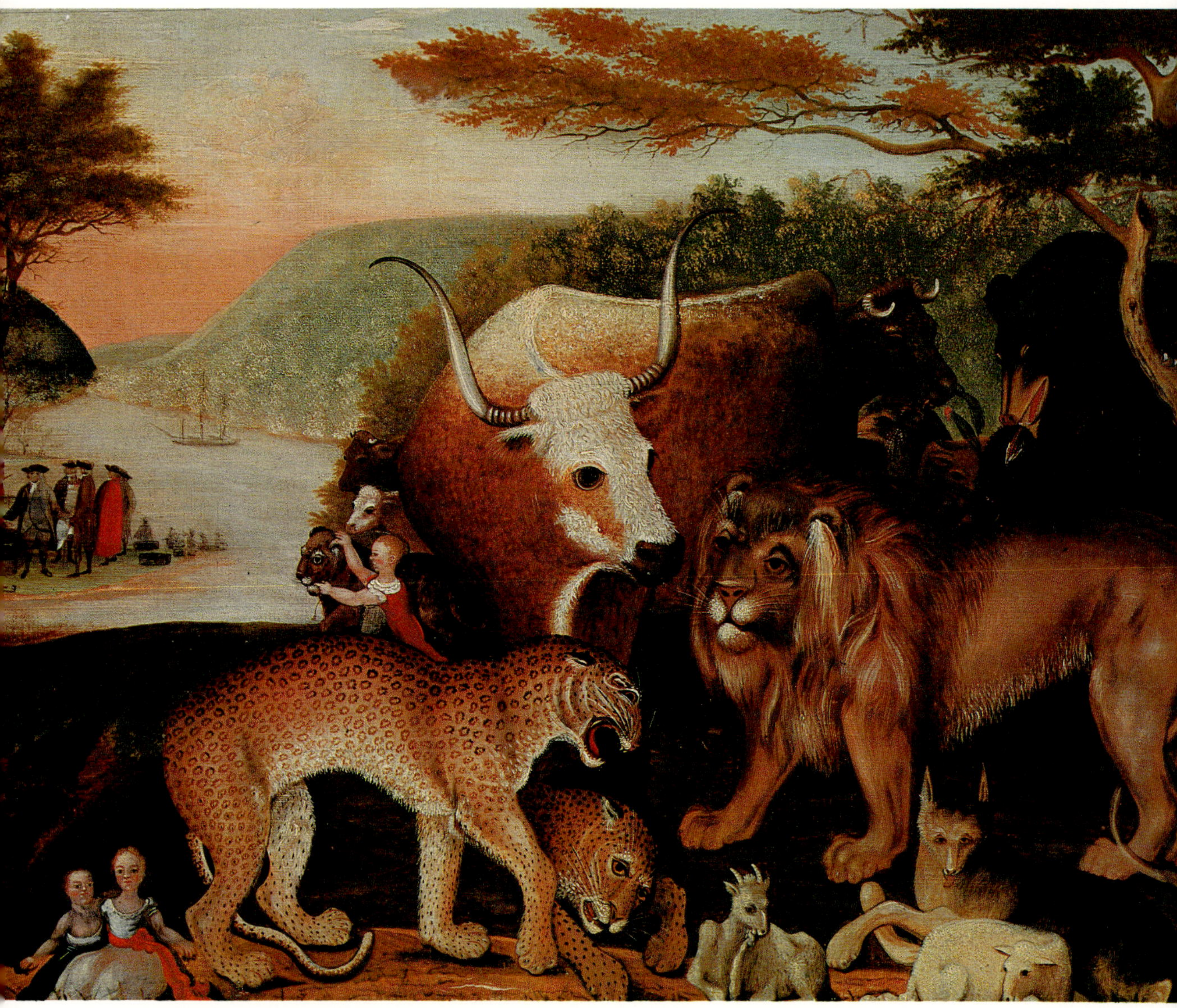

PLATE VI. The Peaceable Kingdom With Arching Leopard, 1844. This dynamic beast is a far cry from the dozing animal of Hicks's early Kingdoms. The ox, too, has become a dominant presence, while the Divine Child discovers a new function in yoking "the young lion, the calf, and the fatling together" (Isaiah 11:6). (Abby Aldrich Rockefeller Folk Art Center, Williamsburg, Va.)

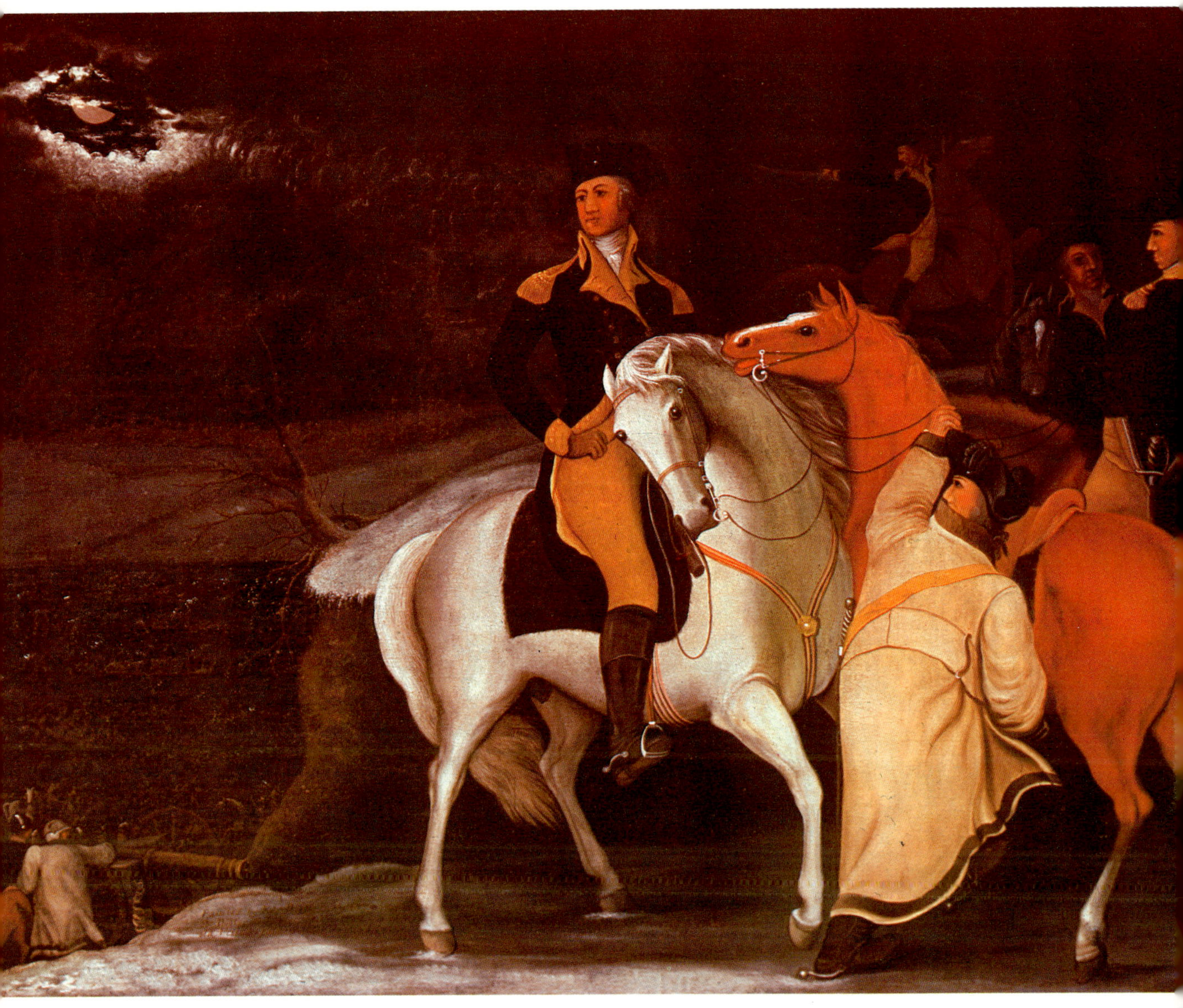

PLATE VII. Washington at the Delaware, 1848. A decorative canvas from the artist's last years that retai[n] primitive characteristics such as the gold-painted moon of his 1834 bridge signs. As a physic[al] likeness of Washington it is negligible, but as the collective image of a national hero, uns[ur]passed. (Abby Aldrich Rockefeller Folk Art Center, Williamsburg, Va.)

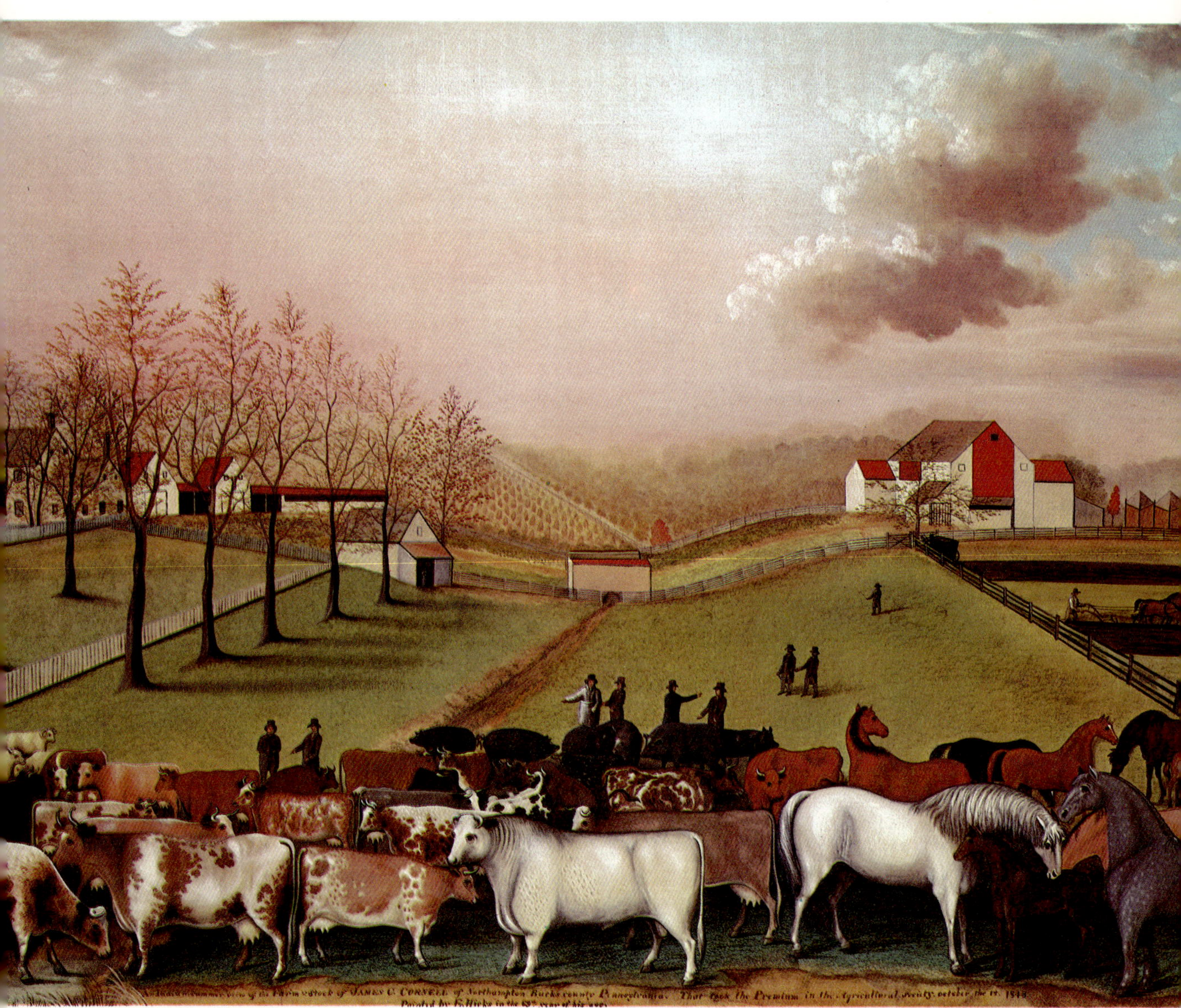

TE VIII. Cornell Farm, 1848. Inscribed, "An Indian summer view of the Farm & Stock of JAMES C. CORNELL of Northampton, Bucks County, Pennsylvania. . . ," this masterwork captures the bountiful mood of harvest time, as Cornell and his brothers survey their prosperous acres and prize-winning livestock. (National Gallery of Art, Washington, D.C.; gift of Edgar William and Bernice Chrysler Garbisch.)

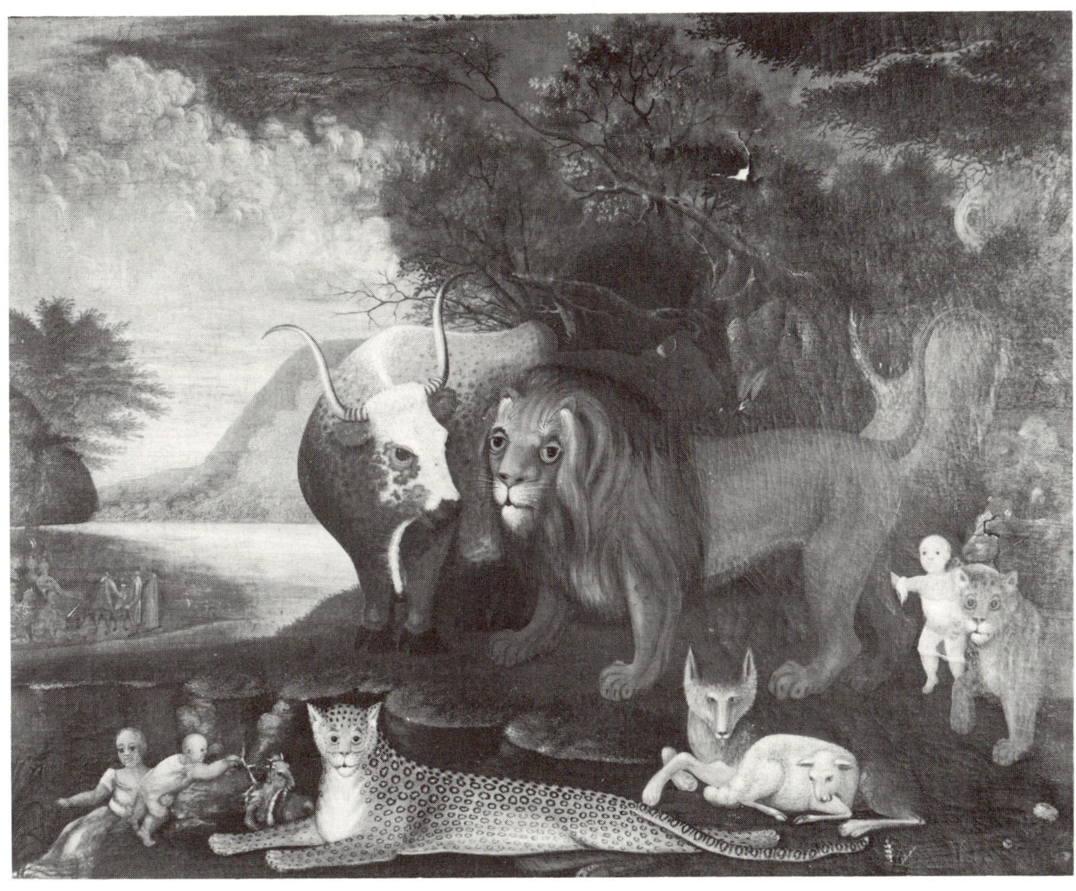

No. 52

PEACEABLE KINGDOM WITH SERENE
LEOPARD, ca. 1845. Oil on canvas, 23½ × 31
inches. Frame original, probably made by Edward Trego. Private collection.

COMMENT: Brooding shadow and rich color
relate this to No. 51, and make it an interesting
contrast to the brilliance of No. 50, with
which it shares certain elements: tumultuous
clouds, luxuriant foliage, and a silken
leopard. Note the rose and bud on the lower
right corner, a frequent motif in folk art portraits of the period.

COLLECTIONS: Made for the Pickering family near Bristol, Pa.* Descended to Henry Pickering, county surveyor of Lower Bucks
County, Woodbourne, Bucks Co., Pa.; Robert
Carlen, Philadelphia; Mrs. Theobald Clarke
(née Nevins, a distant relative of the painter's), Chestnut Hill, Pa.; her son, Anthony M.
Clarke, Philadelphia, Pa.; Robert Carlen,
Phila.; to a private collector.

EXHIBITIONS: Andrew Crispo Gallery, "Edward Hicks: A Gentle Spirit" (1975), no. 16.

---

*By tradition this was commissioned by a group
of people for presentation to a woman school su-
perintendent in the Newtown area.

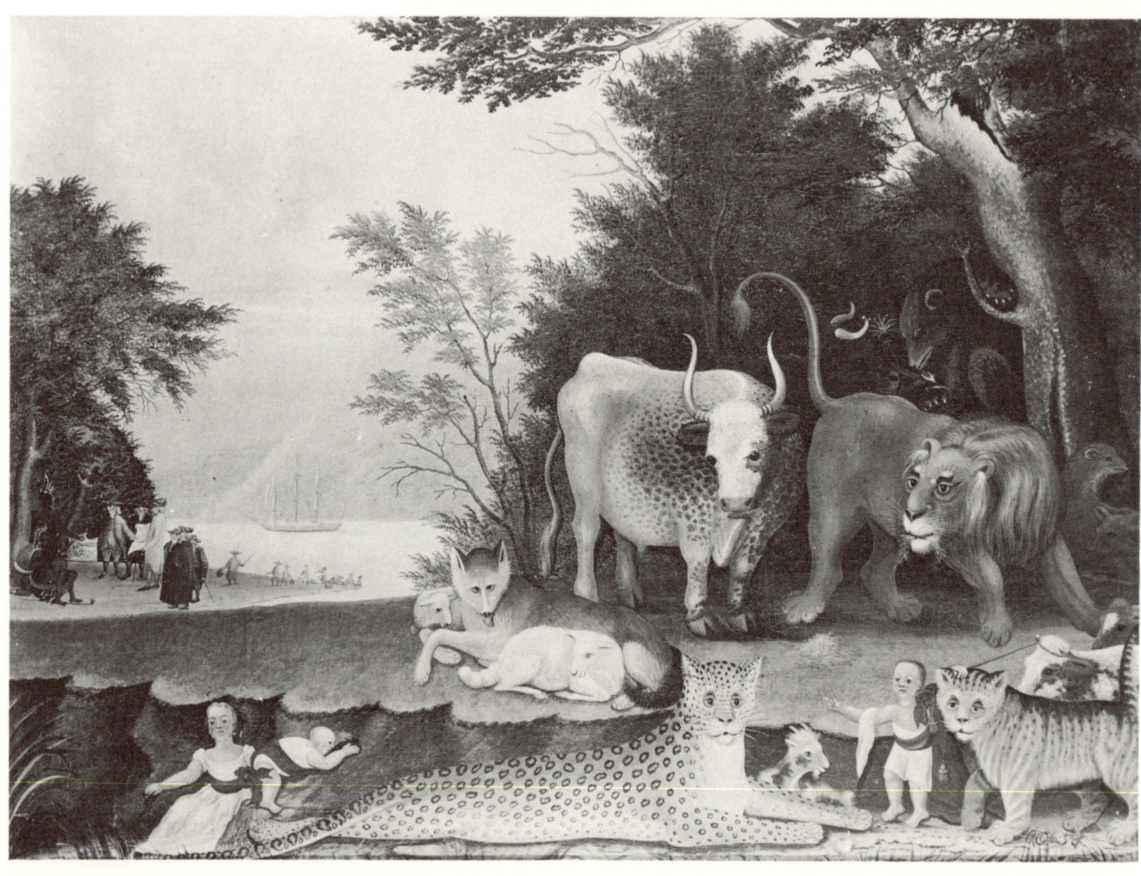

No. 53

PEACEABLE KINGDOM WITH SERENE LEOPARD, 1845–46. Oil on canvas, 23⅞ × 31⅞ inches. Name, "C. Vandegrift," reputedly written in pencil on reverse.* The Albright-Knox Art Gallery, Buffalo, N.Y.; James G. Forsythe Fund.

COMMENT: A canvas that clearly defines the tasseled cord with which the Divine Child is trying to yoke the fatling and the calf to their opposite, the young lion, and the straw in the mouth of the old lion, directly above. Of the latter's plunging pose Julius Held writes, "The type of this lion can actually be traced to Flemish artists under the influence of Rubens" ("Edward Hicks and the Tradition," *Art Quarterly* 14 [1951]: 126). Here the seductive leopard faces right instead of left.

COLLECTIONS: Painted for Dr. Thompson, Richboro, Pa.; to his daughter, Mrs. Martha Vandegrift, Wycombe, Pa.; bought by Harry C. Worthington, Doylestown, Pa.; sold to Col. Henry D. Paxson, Lahaska, Pa.; to Dr. Arthur Edwin Bye, Holicong, Pa.; to Joseph Downs, New York; to Dr. Arthur Edwin Bye, Holicong; to Julius Weitzner, New York; to George Keller, Bignou Gallery, New York; to the Albright-Knox Art Gallery, Buffalo, N.Y.

EXHIBITIONS: United States Section of the International Commission on Folk Arts, Exhibition of Folk Art (New York, 1935); Carnegie/Corcoran, "Hicks, Kane, Pippin" (1966–67), no. 10; Andrew Crispo Gallery, "Edward Hicks: A Gentle Spirit" (New York, 1975), no. 18 (col.).

Photograph courtesy Frick Art Reference Library.

————

*Noted by former owner, Col. Henry D. Paxson, Bucks County Historical Society files. The painting has since been relined, concealing any inscription.

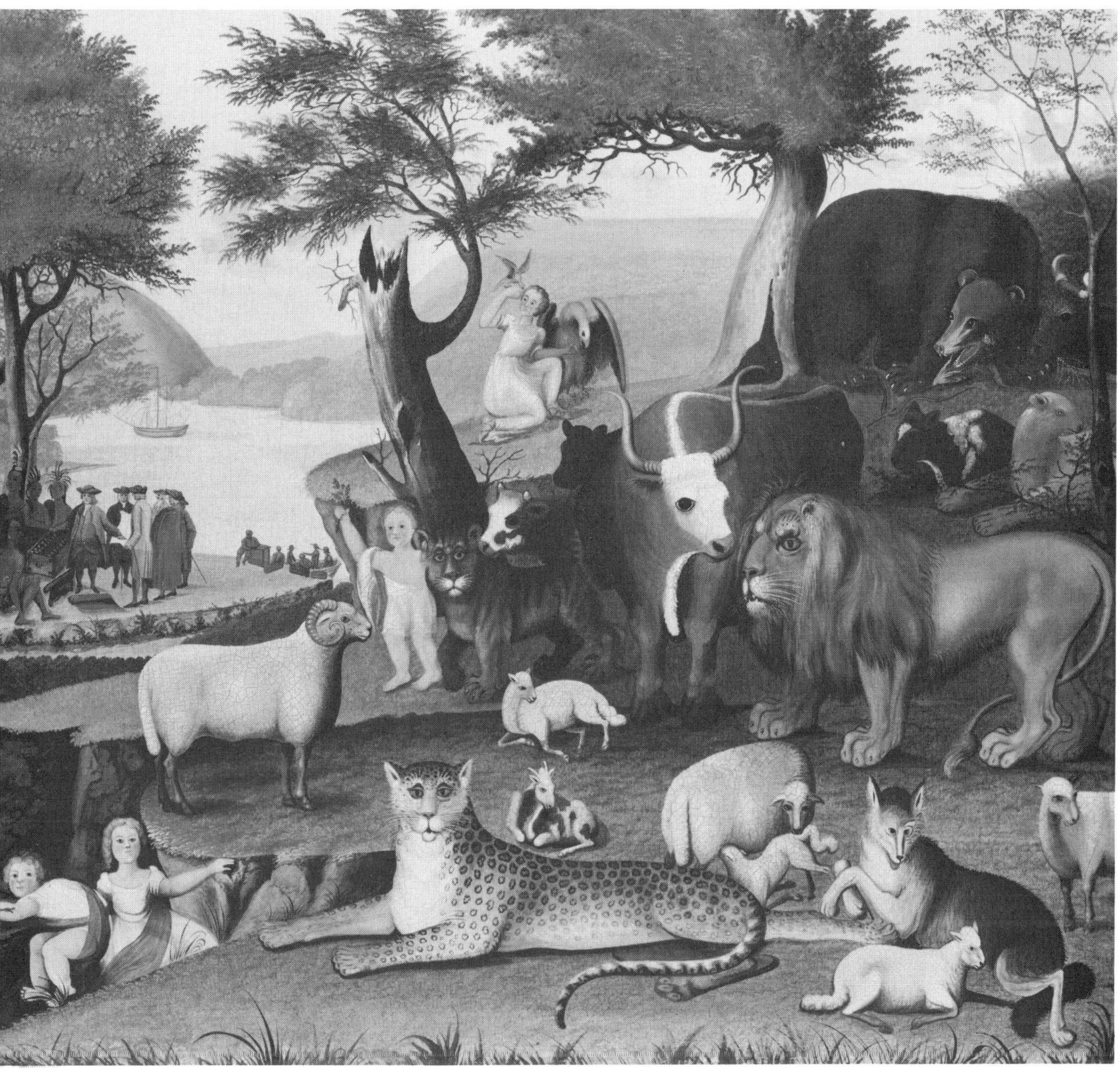

No. 54

PEACEABLE KINGDOM OF THE SERENE LEOPARD, ca. 1846. Oil on canvas 26 × 29½ inches. Private collection.

COMMENT: Finely preserved and unique in spatial concept. This obviously reflects the artist's interest in pastoral themes during the 1840s, having five extra sheep in poses that also appear in the Rockefeller version of *The Residence of David Twining.*

COLLECTIONS: Commissioned by Amos Willets (1792–1864), Quaker merchant of New York and descendant of the city's first English mayor, Thomas Willets. When his nephew, Robert R. Willets, married Tacie Parry, the art-ist's granddaughter, the heirs of Amos presented the couple with this canvas. It descended to their daughter, Mabel Willets (Mrs. William) Abendroth, Harrison, N.Y.; to her son, William Abendroth, Jr., Berwyn, Pa.; to Kennedy Galleries, New York; to a private collector.

EXHIBITIONS: Museum of Modern Art, "Masters of Popular Painting" (New York, 1938), no. 116.

Photograph courtesy Kennedy Galleries, Inc., New York.

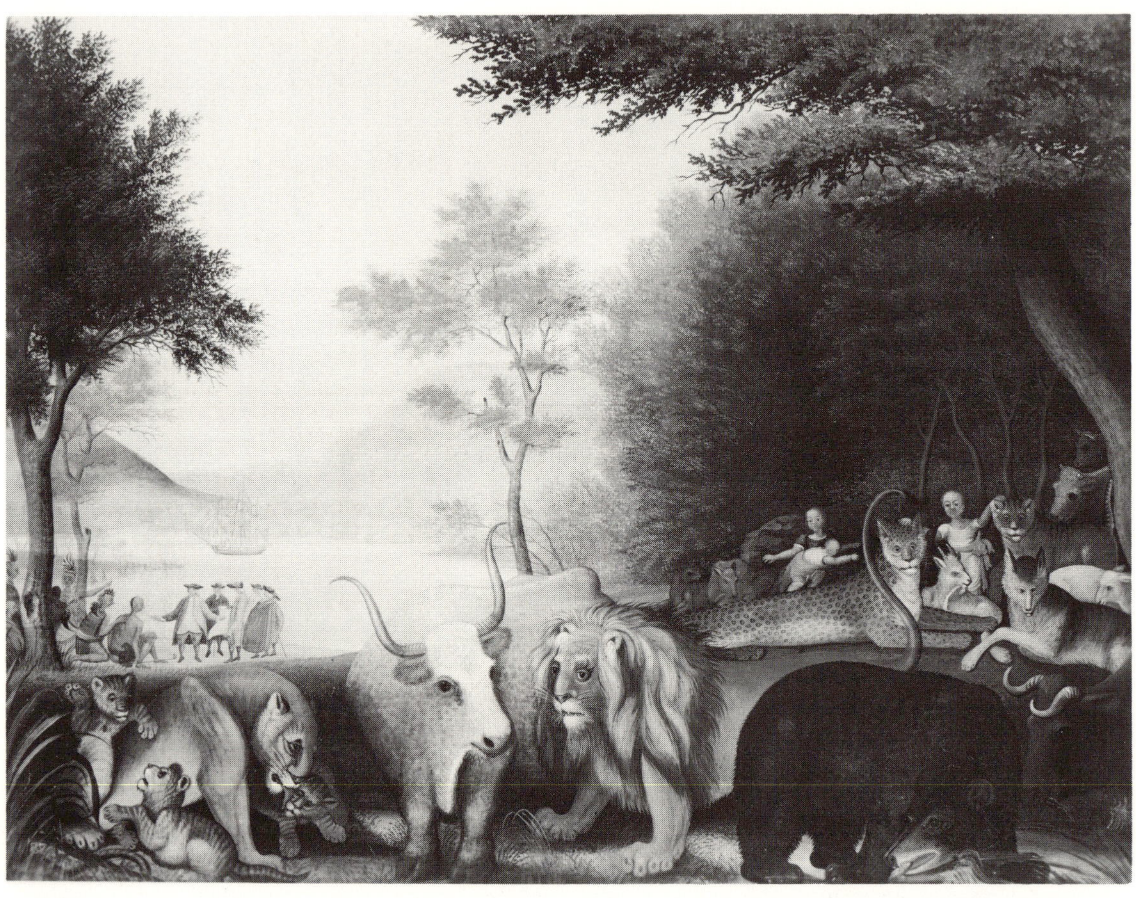

No. 55

PEACEABLE KINGDOM OF THE PENSIVE LION, 1845–46. Oil on canvas, 24 × 31¾ inches. Inscribed on stretcher, "Painted by Edward Hicks in the 66th year of his age." The Phillips Collection.

COMMENT: Ox and pensive lion dominate the foreground, the latter in profile with tail upraised. Lioness and three cubs in lower left corner. Evidently this motif had been on Hicks's mind for some years. In the 1820s he gave his friend Edward Lawrence of Long Island a *Border Kingdom* (No. 8) and another work, since destroyed. This, according to a former owner, Hortense Howland Dixon, "represented a large black lion roaring on the edge of a cliff, while the lioness crouched in a cave beneath with her cubs. I only remember bits of the verse in that one:

The great male Lion, terrible for blood
Walks out to view the vast, extended flood
· · · · · · [3 lines missing] · · · · ·
Perchance too near the female's den did creep.
Though grim her looks, her teeth in dread array
Her peaceful young ones o'er her body play."
(Letter to Dorothy Miller October 6, 1949.)

COLLECTIONS: Early provenance unknown. Downtown Gallery (Edith Gregor Halpert), New York; in 1939 acquired by the Phillips Collection, Washington, D.C.

EXHIBITIONS: Pan American Union (Washington, D.C., April–May, 1963); ACA Galleries, "Four American Primitives" (New York, 1972), no. 4; Andrew Crispo Gallery, "Edward Hicks: A :Gentle Spirit" (New York, 1975), no. 14 (col.)

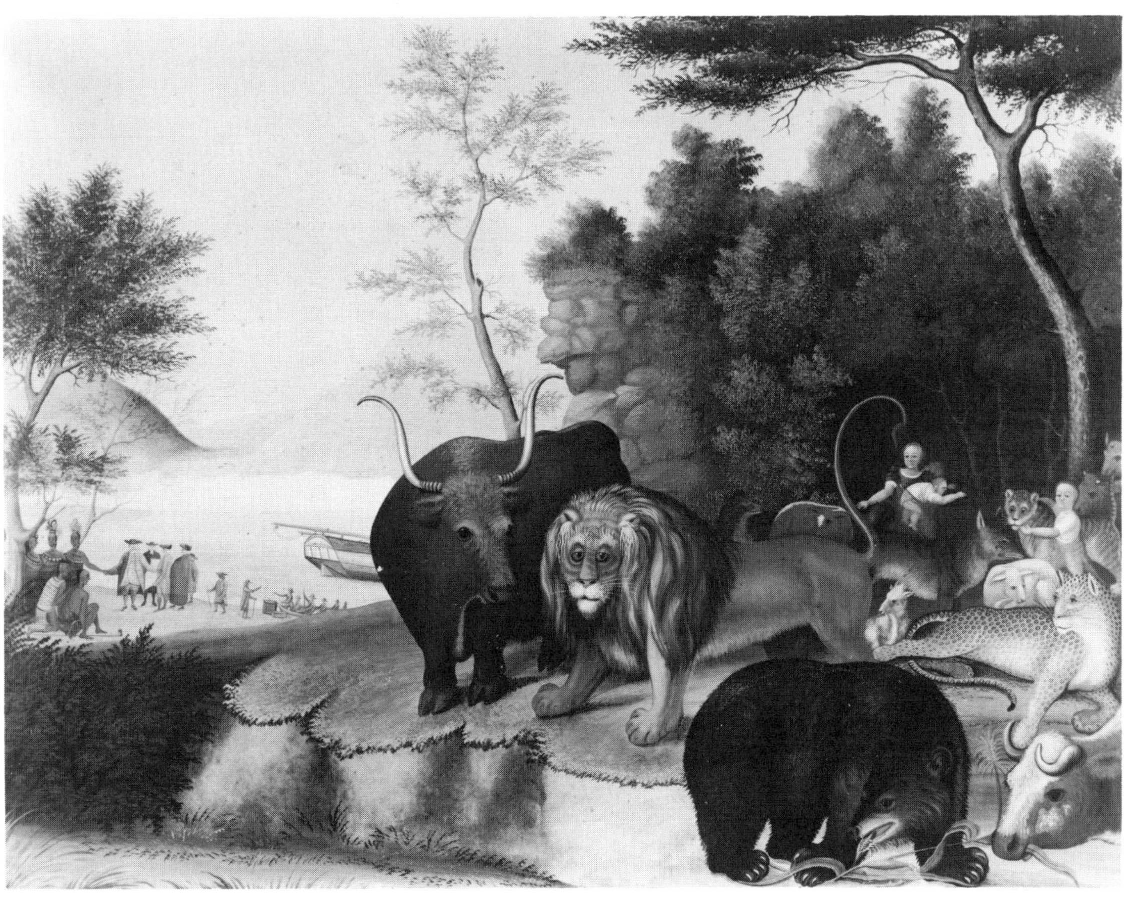

No. 56

PEACEABLE KINGDOM OF THE PENSIVE LION, 1846–47. Oil on canvas, 24 × 32 inches. Inscribed on reverse, "THE PEACEABLE KINGDOM, ISA^H. 11.6.7.8./ PAINTED BY EDWARD HICKS IN THE 67 YEAR OF HIS AGE." Slightly beveled black-painted frame with gold rabbit assumed to be original. Sidney Janis Collection.

COMMENT: Related to Nos. 55 and 58, though the lioness-with-cubs vignette in those works is here missing. The gold and green tones and the heraldic stance of the lion also recall Hicks's *Noah's Ark*. A princely leopard lounges to the right. The Isaiah citation on reverse is unique in late *Kingdoms*, but appears on the face of several versions of the early 1830s.

COLLECTIONS: Provenance unknown—presumably the Scull family of southern New Jersey. Given to the Vineland Historical Society, Vineland, N.J., by T. W. Scull; auctioned by Sotheby Parke Bernet, New York; to James Maroney, New York; to Sidney Janis, New York.

Photograph copyright Sotheby Parke Bernet, Inc., New York.

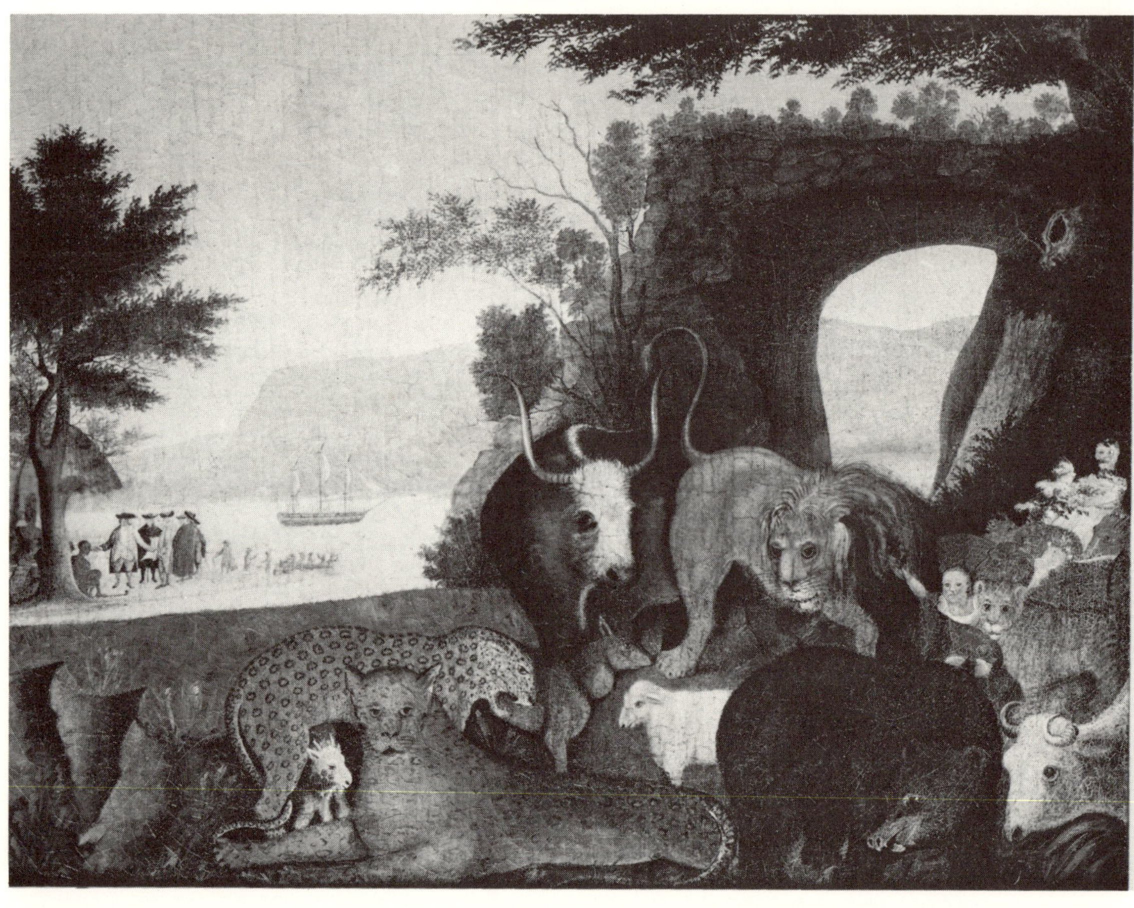

No. 57

PEACEABLE KINGDOM OF THE PENSIVE LION. 1846–47. Oil on canvas, 23¹¹⁄₁₆ × 31 inches. On reverse, "The Peaceable Kingdom/ Painted by Edward Hicks in his 67 year." Beveled soft wood frame, veneered with walnut, probably original. The Denver Museum of Art; gift of Charles Bayly, Jr.

COMMENT: A haunting composition uniting elements from both past and future against the symbolic background of the Natural Bridge. Here the arching and serene leopards meet one another, while the bridge becomes less of a natural wonder and more of a doorway opening upon another world.

COLLECTIONS: Provenance unknown. Owned jointly by M. Knoedler & Co. and Harry Shaw Newman, both of New York; purchased with funds from Charles Bayly, Jr., Denver, by the Denver Art Museum, Denver, Colorado.

EXHIBITIONS: The Columbus Gallery of Fine Arts, "Colonial Americas" [Columbus, Ohio, October, 1947); M. Knoedler & Co., "American Paintings of the Eighteenth and Early Nineteenth Centuries in Our Current Collections" (New York, 1948), no. 42; Carnegie/Corcoran, "Hicks, Kane, Pippin" (1966–67), no. 29; ACA Galleries, "Four American Primitives" (New York, 1972), no. 5, ill.

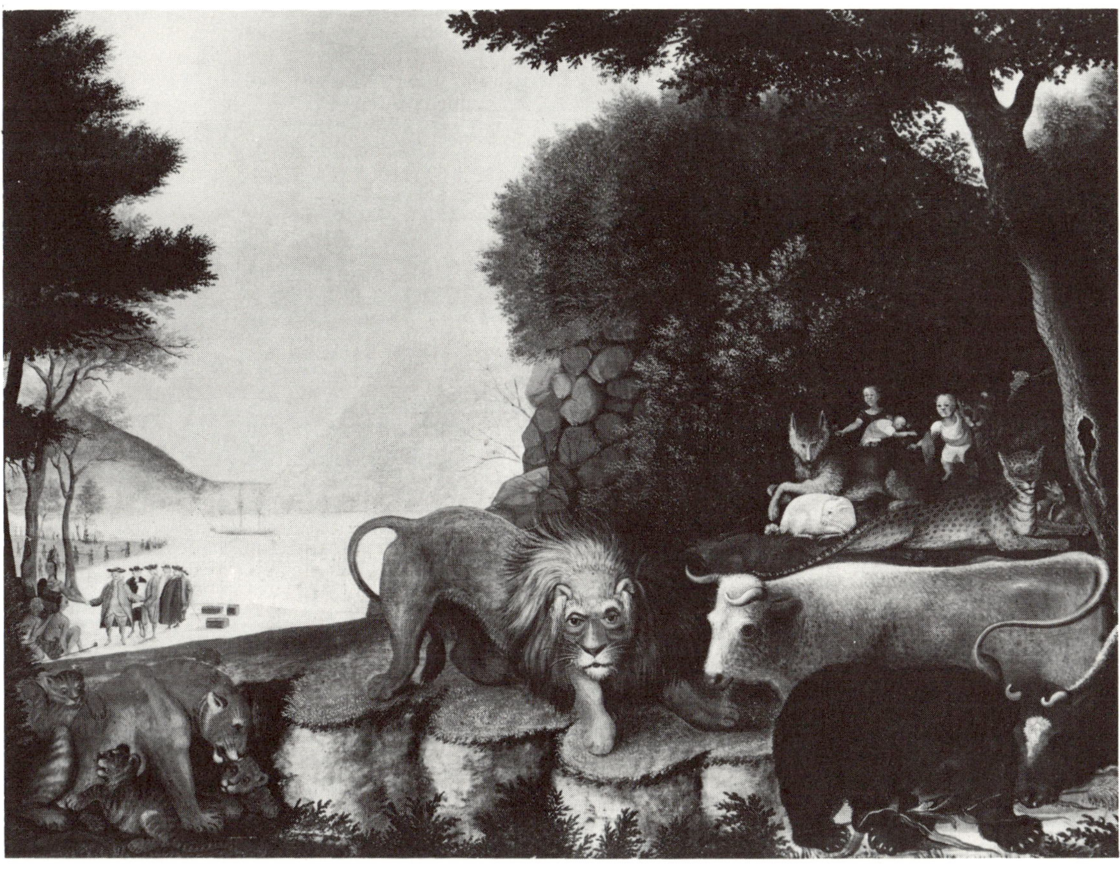

No. 58

PEACEABLE KINGDOM OF THE PENSIVE LION, 1847. Oil on canvas, 25 × 32½ inches. Stretcher inscribed, "Painted by EDWARD HICKS in the 67th Year of His Age." Curly maple frame not original. Private collection.

COMMENT: Here the composition belongs totally to the lion; all else is subordinate. The maternal tenderness of the lioness heightens the pathos of the old lion's face. Psychologically the most powerful of the *Kingdoms*.

COLLECTIONS: Exact provenance unknown. Found in Montgomery County by Robert Carlen, Philadelphia; to private collectors.

EXHIBITIONS: Robert Carlen Gallery, "Hicks Centennial Exhibition" (Philadelphia, 1949); Philadelphia Museum of Art, "Masterpieces from Philadelphia Private Collections" (Philadelphia, May 20–September 15, 1950), part 2, for cat. see *Bulletin* 45 (1950): no. 40; AARFAC, "Edward Hicks" (1960), no. 42, p. 19, not ill.; Carnegie/Corcoran, "Hicks, Kane, Pippin" (1966–67), no. 27; ACA Galleries, "Four American Primitives" (New York, 1972), no. 8; Andrew Crispo Gallery, "Edward Hicks: A Gentle Spirit" (New York, 1975), no. 17 (col.)

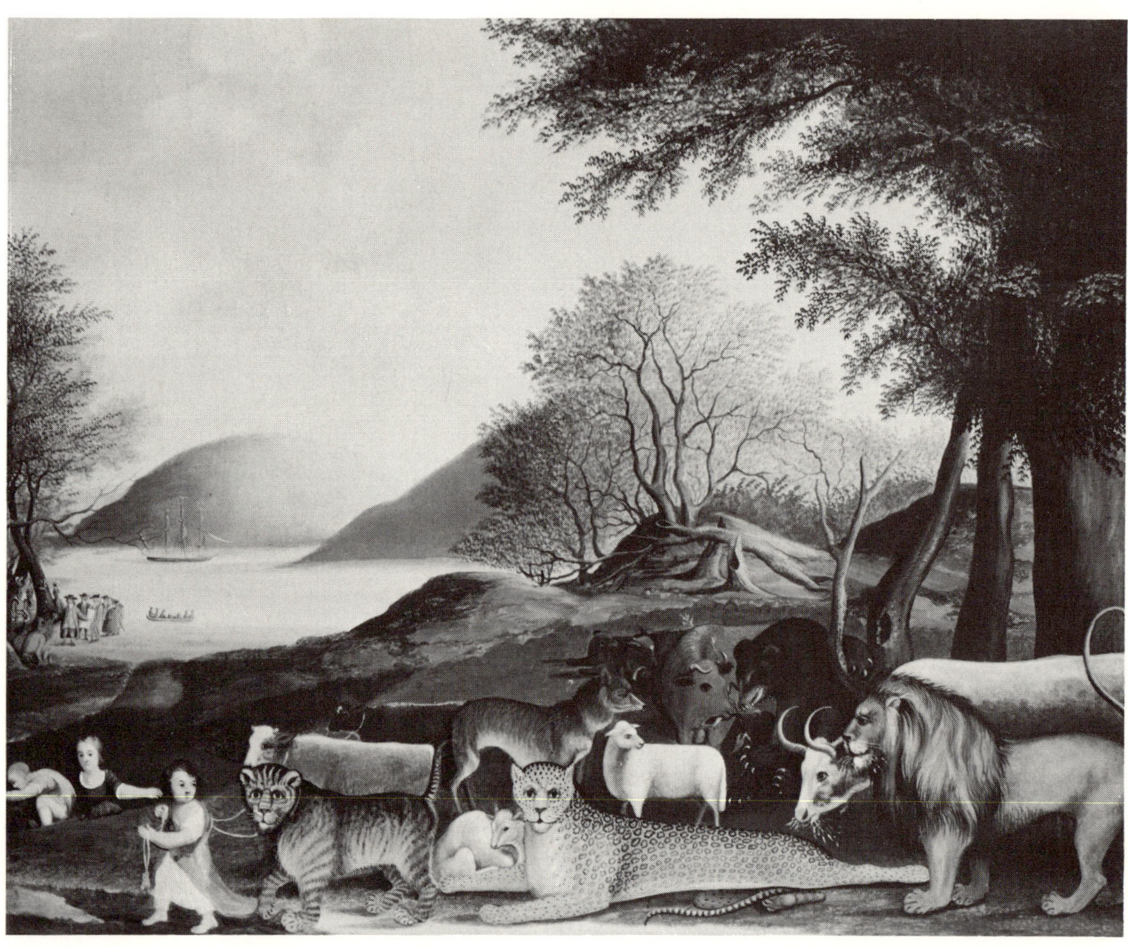

No. 59

PEACEABLE KINGDOM OF DEPARTURE, ca. 1849. Oil on canvas, 24 × 30¼ inches. Private collection, courtesy Galerie St. Etienne.

COMMENTS: Nearly identical with Hicks's final *Kingdom*. Against a background of autumnal foliage, the leopard is central, the lion and ox withdrawn to the right. The Divine Child, in the left foreground, has finally yoked the young lion, the calf, and the fatling together.

COLLECTIONS: Painted for Eliza Hough Jackson Bell (1813–1901), wife of Thomas C. Bell, Bayside, L.I. As a daughter of Halliday Jackson of Darby, Pa., she recalled in old age the Friends entertained in her father's hospitable home: John Comly, Edward Hicks, Joseph Foulke, Elias Hicks, Edward Stabler, Thomas Wetherald, etc. The painter said of her that "she was one of the women he could not speak of without shedding tears."* By descent to Miss Bell of Bayside, L.I.; Robert Carlen, Philadelphia; Mrs. William Elkins, Philadelphia; to M. Knoedler & Co., New York; Dr. Otto Kallir, New York; to a private collector, courtesy Galerie St. Etienne, New York.

EXHIBITIONS: The Galerie St. Etienne, New York, "American Primitives of Three Centuries" (New York, June 3–July 15, 1948) no. 4; AARFAC, "Edward Hicks" (1960), no. 39, p. 19; Carnegie/Corcoran, "Hicks, Kane, Pippin" Washington, D.C. (1966–67), no. 34; ACA Galleries, "Four American Primitives" (New York, 1972), no. 11, ill. and detail; University Art Museum, "The Hand and the Spirit" (Berkeley, Calif., 1972–73), no. 38, p. 89; Andrew Crispo Gallery, "Edward Hicks: A Gentle Spirit" (New York, 1975), no. 19 and cover; Galerie St. Etienne, "American Primitive Art" (New York, November 22, 1977– January 28, 1978), no. 15 and cover; Galerie St. Etienne, "The Folk Art Tradition" (New York, 1981–82), no. 26, pl. 9.

____

*Information from Robert Carlen, culled from Eliza Bell's diary in Archives of American Art, Smithsonian Institution, Washington, D.C., and Jackson family records at Friends Historical Library, Swarthmore College, Swarthmore, Pa.

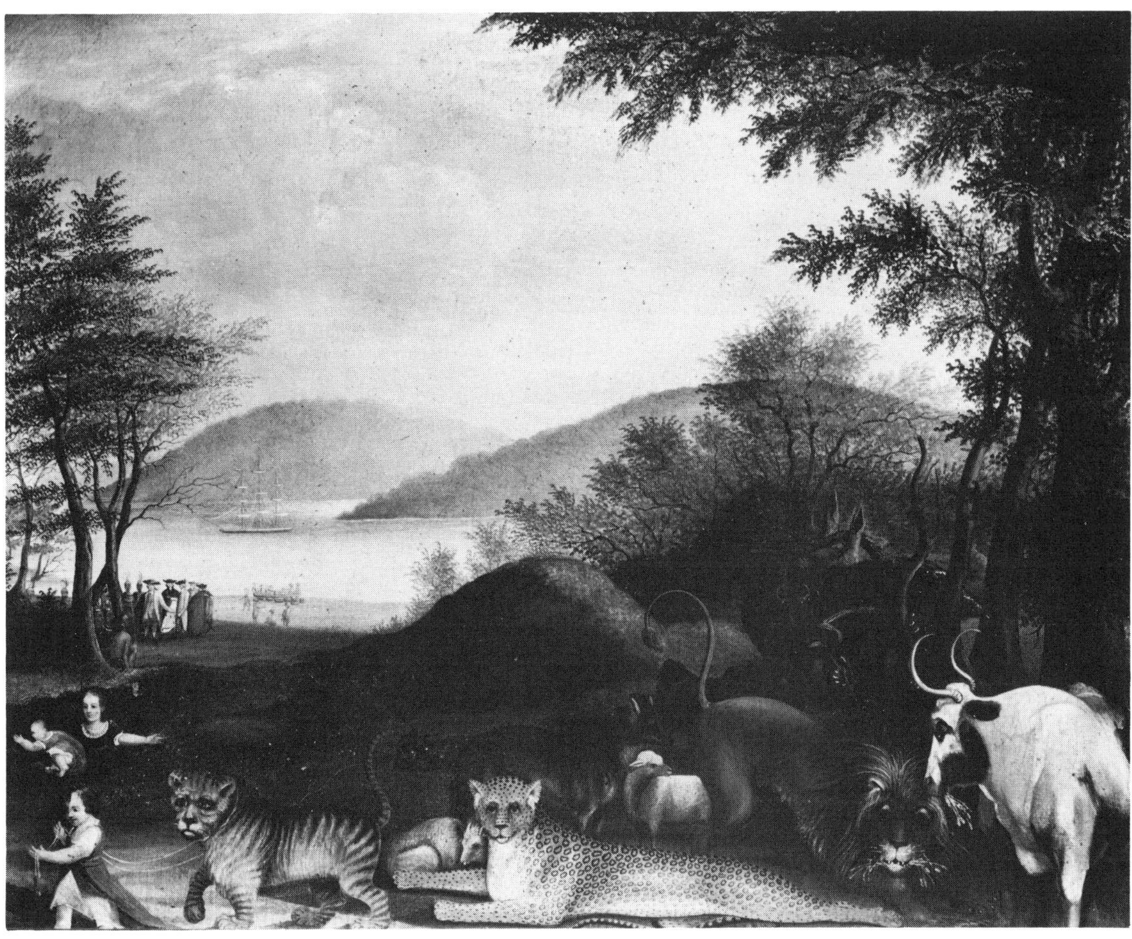

No. 60

PEACEABLE KINGDOM OF DEPARTURE, 1849. Oil on canvas, 24 × 30 inches. Gilt frame assumed to be original. Private collection.

COMMENT: The last canvas on Hicks's easel, painted for his favorite daughter, Elizabeth. Here the plunging lion returns like a dark ghost, chewing the straw of redemption, its pose derived from an Alexander Anderson wood engraving in an 1834 German Bible published in Philadelphia, probably for the Pennsylvania-German trade. Anderson was obviously inspired by, though he did not copy, Rubens's *Daniel in the Lions' Den,* discovered through the medium of some biblical engraving.

The night before his death the painter told his family that he had paid his last visit to his shop, and that his son, Isaac, could put the finishing touches to this *Kingdom* (Alice Ford, *Edward Hicks: Painter of the Peaceable Kingdom* [Philadelphia: University of Pennsylvania Press, 1952], p. 114). But by local tradition the final details were completed by Jonathan Trego, Newtown portrait painter.

COLLECTIONS: Apparently Elizabeth Hicks did not take this with her when she went to Baltimore as the wife of Richard Plummer. It remained in Newtown, presumably in the home of her brother, Isaac; to his daughter Sarah Worstall Hicks; to a private collector.

EXHIBITIONS: Museum of Modern Art, "Masters of Popular Painting" (New York, 1938), no. 122A; Newtown's 275th Anniversary (1959), no. 5 (not ill.); AARFAC, "Edward Hicks" (1960), no. 43 (not ill.).

OTHER WORKS

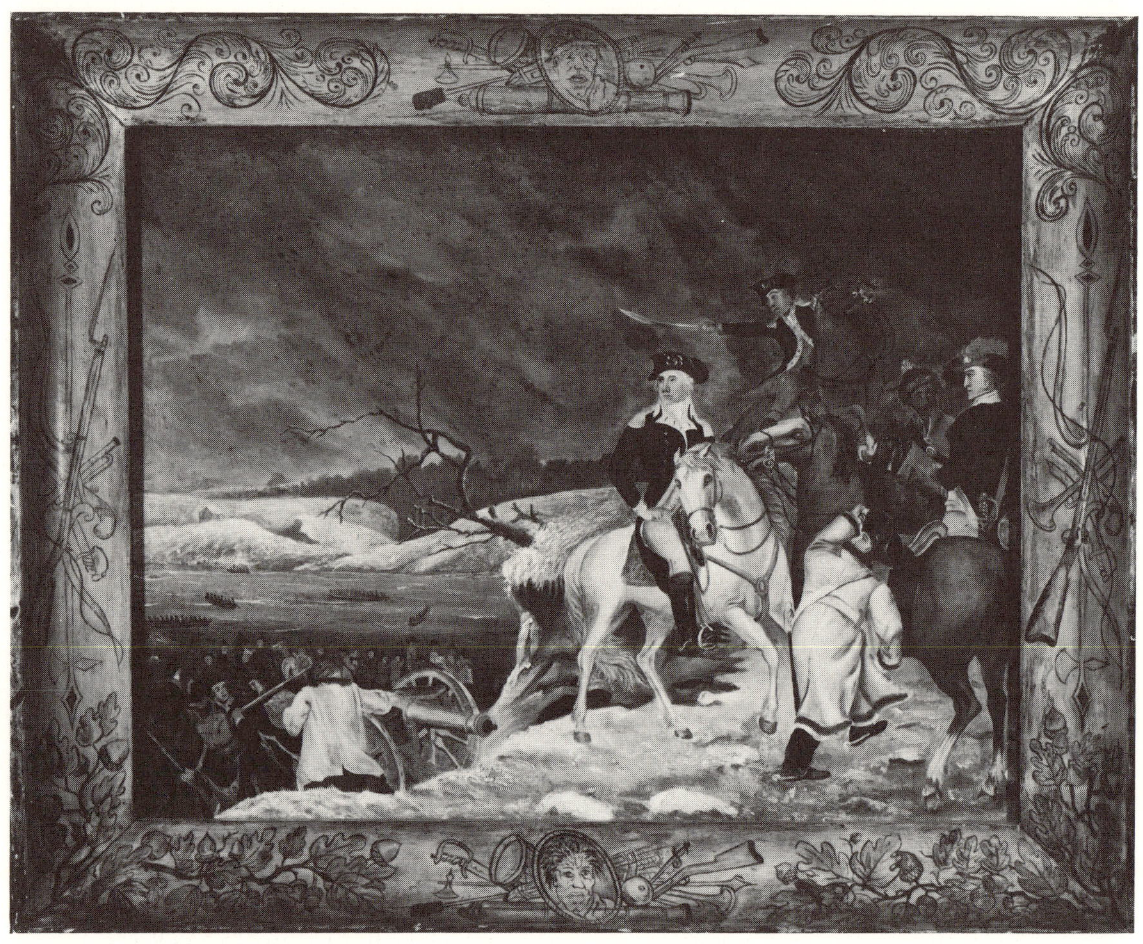

No. 61

WASHINGTON AT THE DELAWARE , ca. 1825. Oil on wood, 17 × 21½ inches. On back: "Washington Crossing Delaware/E.H. 1817 Phila. Pa." Original decorated wooden frame, etched with acorn and oak leaf motif. Mr. and Mrs. John A. Harney.

COMMENT: Inspired by Thomas Sully's 1819 *Washington at the Passage of the Delaware*, now in the Boston Museum of Fine Arts, probably after the George S. Lang engraving. A former owner, Leonardo Beans, in his pamphlet *The Life and Work of Edward Hicks* (Trenton, N.J., 1951), p. 14), asserted that this preceded the version by Sully, who was the copier. Though not impossible, this seems unlikely.

The picture's chief claim to authenticity lies in its frame, the acorn and leaf motif on which closely resembles the design sketched on the back of a love letter from Catharine to Isaac Hicks, the artist's parents, found among his effects after his death (Alice Ford, *Edward Hicks: Painter of the Peaceable Kingdom* [Philadelphia: University of Pennsylvania Press, 1952], pp. 28 and 117).

COLLECTIONS: Early provenance unknown. Leonardo L. Beans, Trenton, N.J.; to Mr. and Mrs. John A. Harney, Trenton, N.J.

EXHIBITIONS: AARFAC, "Edward Hicks" (1960), no. 20, p. 14 (not ill.).

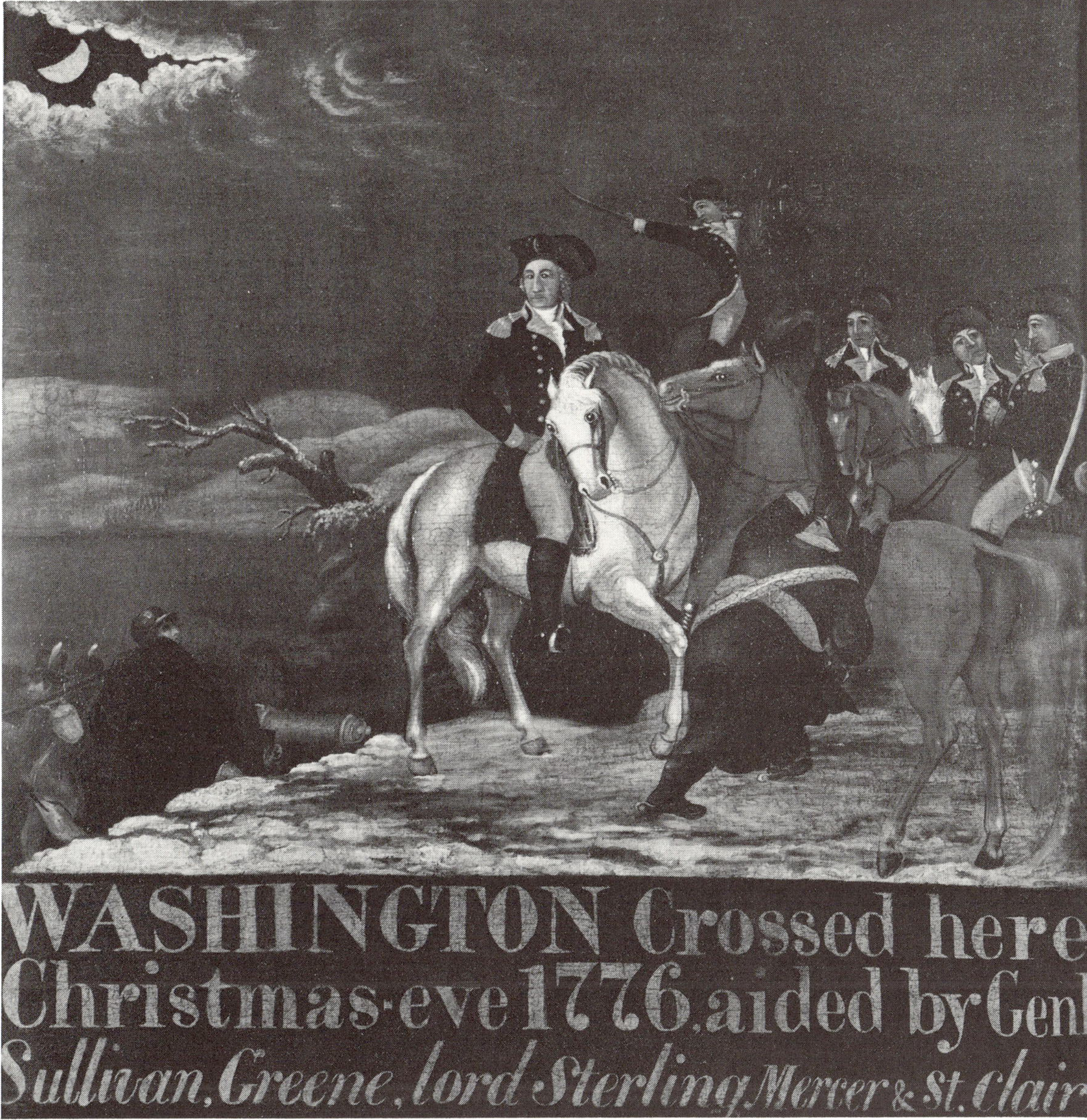

No. 62

WASHINGTON AT THE DELAWARE*, 1834. Oil on wood signboard, 32 × 31½ inches, including original frame. Inscription at bottom reads, "WASHINGTON Crossed here/ Christmas-eve 1776, aided by Genl^s/ *Sullivan, Greene, lord Sterling Mercer & St. Clair.*" Private collection, courtesy Andrew Crispo Gallery.

COMMENT: Hicks's patriotic subjects adhere more closely to their borrowed sources than do most of his works. But to Sully's composition he here adds a crescent moon and an extra mounted officer to the right. This sign hung at the New Jersey end of a bridge across the Delaware that was opened January 1, 1834. It was swept away by flood seven years later on January 8, 1841.

COLLECTIONS; Rescued from the flood, it hung in the bar of Alexander Nelson's New Jersey tavern. Years later it turned up in Macy's Store, New York; sold by owner, William Secord, New York, to Robert Friedenberg, a New York dealer; to Harry Shaw Newman, New York; to George G. Frelinghuysen, Morristown, N.J.; to Mr. and Mrs. Bertram K. Little, Brookline, Mass.; to a private collector, courtesy Andrew Crispo Gallery, New York.

EXHIBITIONS: Macy Galleries, "An Exhibition in Honor of the Bicentenary of the Birth of George Washington" (New York, February, 1932), no. 5 and cover (captioned as by "Benjamin Hicks of Newtown"); Newark Museum,

____

*Better known as *Washington Crossed Here.*

"Owned in New Jersey: Paintings and Decorative Arts" (Newark, N.J., October 24–December 1, 1946), no. 4; Smithsonian Institution, Washington, D.C., for the United States Information Services: (1)"Primitive Painters from the Seventeenth Century to Today," shown at Kunstmuseum Luzern, Lucerne, Switzerland (1954), no. 29, p. 18; (2) "American Folk Art from 1670 to Today," shown at Österreichisches Museum für Angewandte Kunst (Vienna, 1954), no. 25, p. 15; (3) "American Primitive Art 1670–1954," shown at City Art Gallery, Manchester, Eng., and Whitechapel Art Gallery, London (1954), no. 29; AARFAC, "Edward Hicks" (1960), no. 21, p. 14 (not ill.); Carnegie/Corcoran, "Hicks, Kane, Pippin" (1966–67), p. 11; AARFAC, "Land and Seascape as Observed by the Folk Artist," from Bertram K. and Nina Fletcher Little Collection (Williamsburg, Va., January 13–May 11, 1969), no. 23, p. 17 (ill.); Galerie St. Etienne, "The Folk Art Tradition" (New York, 1981–82), no. 25, not in cat.

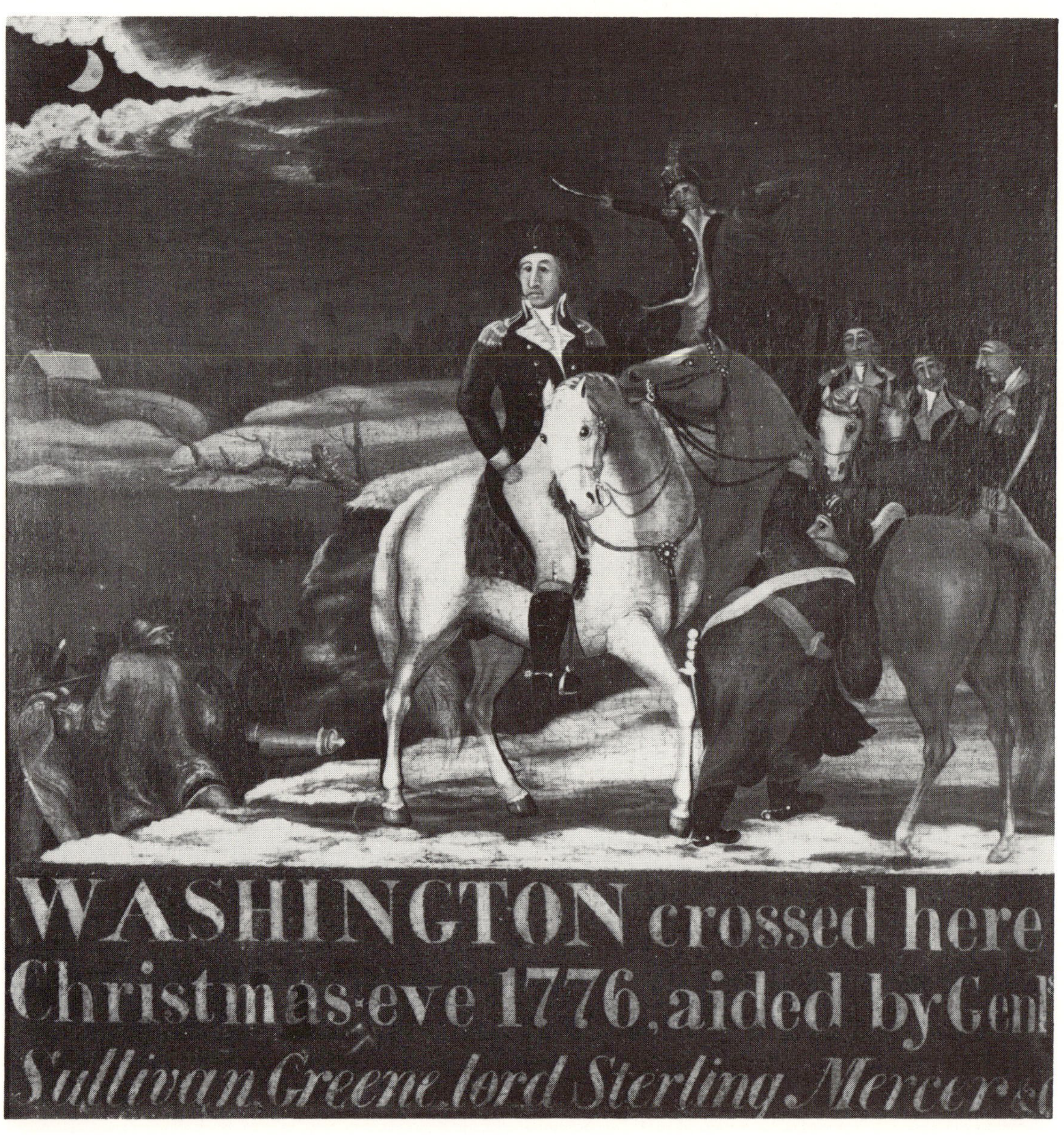

No. 63

WASHINGTON AT THE DELAWARE, 1834. Oil on wood signboard, 33¾ × 33¼ inches, including original frame. Inscription at bottom reads, "WASHINGTON crossed here/ Christmas-eve 1776, aided by Genl^s / *Sullivan, Greene, lord Sterling Mercer &*" (inscription curtailed by frame). The Mercer Museum of the Bucks County Historical Society.

COMMENT: Similar to No. 62, but placed at the Pennsylvania terminus of the bridge. Rescued from the flood by Dr. Huston Thompson, Taylorsville, who carried it to safety. Washington's crossing of the Delaware to capture the Hessians at Trenton was a local event to the citizens of Newtown, where Washington and his staff spent the preceding night, and to which they returned after the victory. The crossing actually took place on Christmas night, not eve (see B. F. Fackenthal, Jr., "Paintings and Other Works," *Bucks County Historical Society Papers* [1935; reprint ed., Doylestown, Pa., 1941], p. 8).

COLLECTIONS: Discovered in a loft in Taylorsville, at the Pennsylvania end of the bridge; given by the owner, James B. Jamison, Taylorsville, to Henry Chapman Mercer, Doylestown, Pa., who gave it to the Mercer Museum of the Bucks County Historical Society, Doylestown.

EXHIBITIONS: Exhibited in Trenton, 1876, on the Centennial anniversary of the battle.

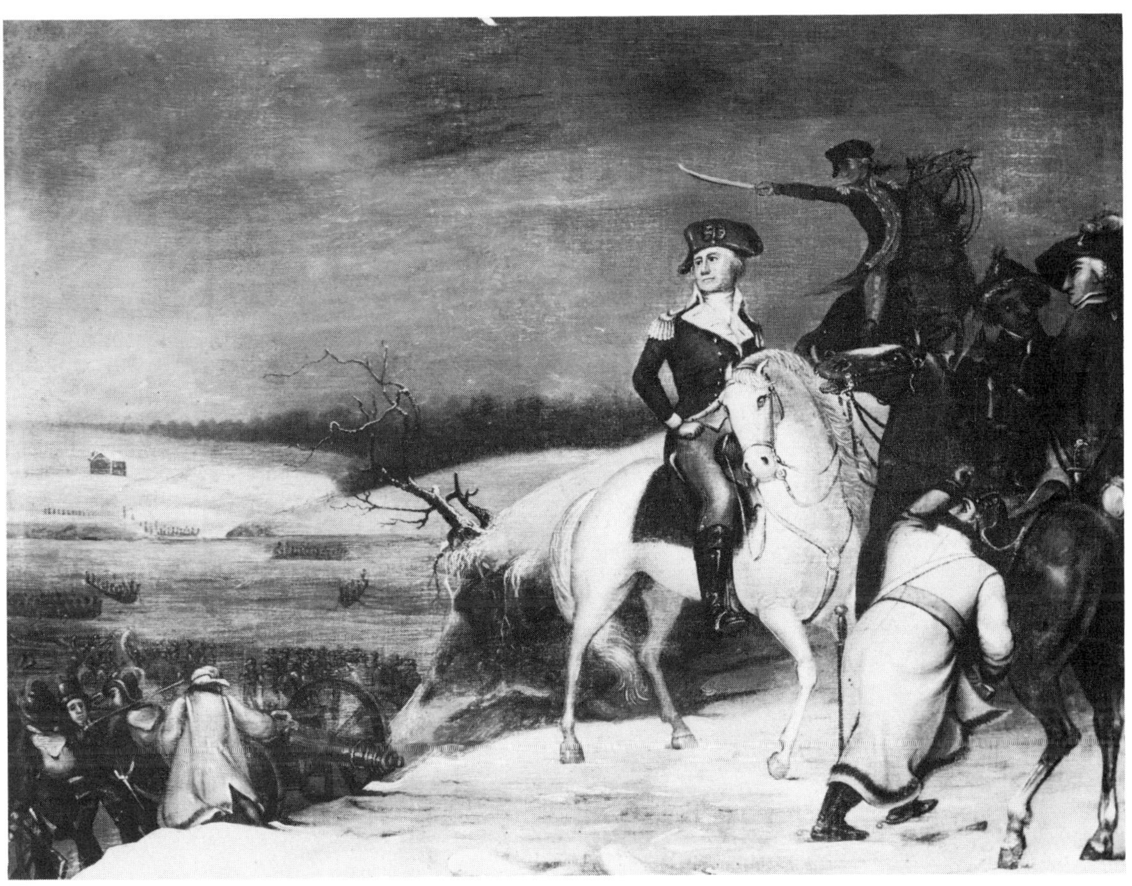

No. 64

WASHINGTON AT THE DELAWARE, 1837–40. Oil on canvas, 17¼ × 23¼ inches. Veneer frame with corner blocks probably original. The Mercer museum of the Bucks County Historical Society.

COMMENT: Closer to the Sully original, with its moonless sky and the presence of the black man among the officers. Shows increasing sophistication of technique, particularly in the face of Washington. For Sully's work see Edgar P. Richardson, who notes that it was ordered by the state of North Carolina, but due to its large size—12 × 17 feet—no space could be found for it in the state capitol and it was left on the artist's hands (*American Romantic Painting*, ed. Robert Freund [New York: E. Weyhe, 1944], fig. 33 and p. 47).

COLLECTIONS: Given by the artist to his good friend Abraham Chapman, "father of the Bucks County bar"; to his son, the Hon. Henry Chapman, Doylestown, Pa.; to his son, Arthur Chapman, Esq.; to his nephew, Henry Chapman Mercer, who gave it to the Mercer Museum of the Bucks County Historical Society, Doylestown, Pa.

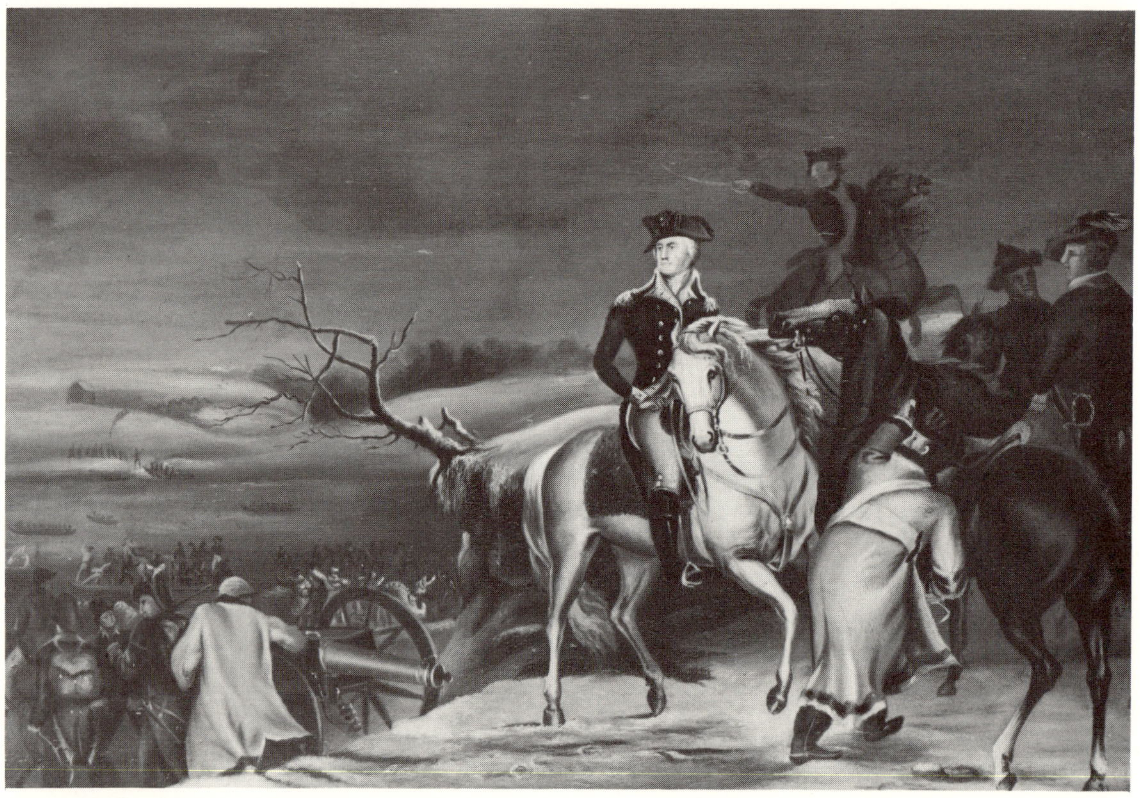

No. 65

WASHINGTON AT THE DELAWARE, 1837–40. Oil on panel, 14¾ × 20 inches. Inscribed on reverse, "Washington Passing the Delaware/ Evening Previous to the Battle of Trenton Dec 25 1776/ E.H.," surrounded by brush flourishes. Stained wood frame with black-painted corner blocks presumably original. Mr. H. Richard Dietrich, Jr.

COMMENT: In spite of the initials "E.H." on the reverse, the authenticity of this and the two succeeding paintings is somewhat uncertain, since we know little of the provenance of any of them. But the compositions closely resemble *Washingtons* by Hicks, and the inscription on the reverse of this, though unlike that of any other in format, is a plausible variant.

COLLECTIONS: Original provenance unknown. To Leonardo L. Beans, Trenton, N.J.; to a private collector; to Clarence Prickett, dealer of Yardley, Pa.; to Mr. H. Richard Dietrich, Jr., Philadelphia.

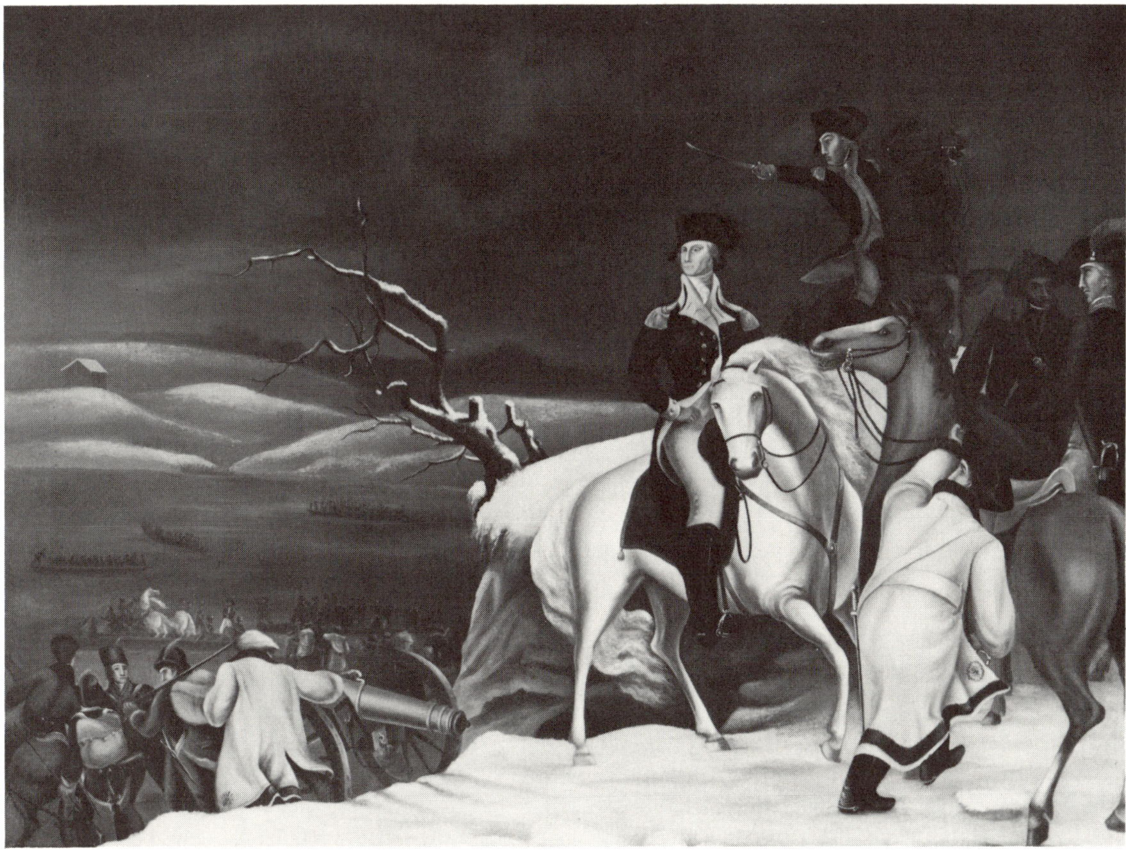

No. 66

WASHINGTON AT THE DELAWARE, 1840–
49. Oil on canvas, 36 × 49 inches. Mr.
H. Richard Dietrich, Jr.

COMMENT: All three of these attributions
share with Hick's established versions certain
details not found in Sully's original, such as
the house on the hillside, at left, and Washington's hand closed in a fist rather than with
fingers extended. The faces of subordinate
figures are here very similar to the Garbisch
canvas at the National Gallery. But note an
oddity: the curiously elongated neck of Washington!

COLLECTIONS: Original provenance un-
known; to Bihler and Coger Antiques, Ashley
Falls, Mass.; in 1966 sold to Mr. H. Richard
Dietrich, Philadelphia.

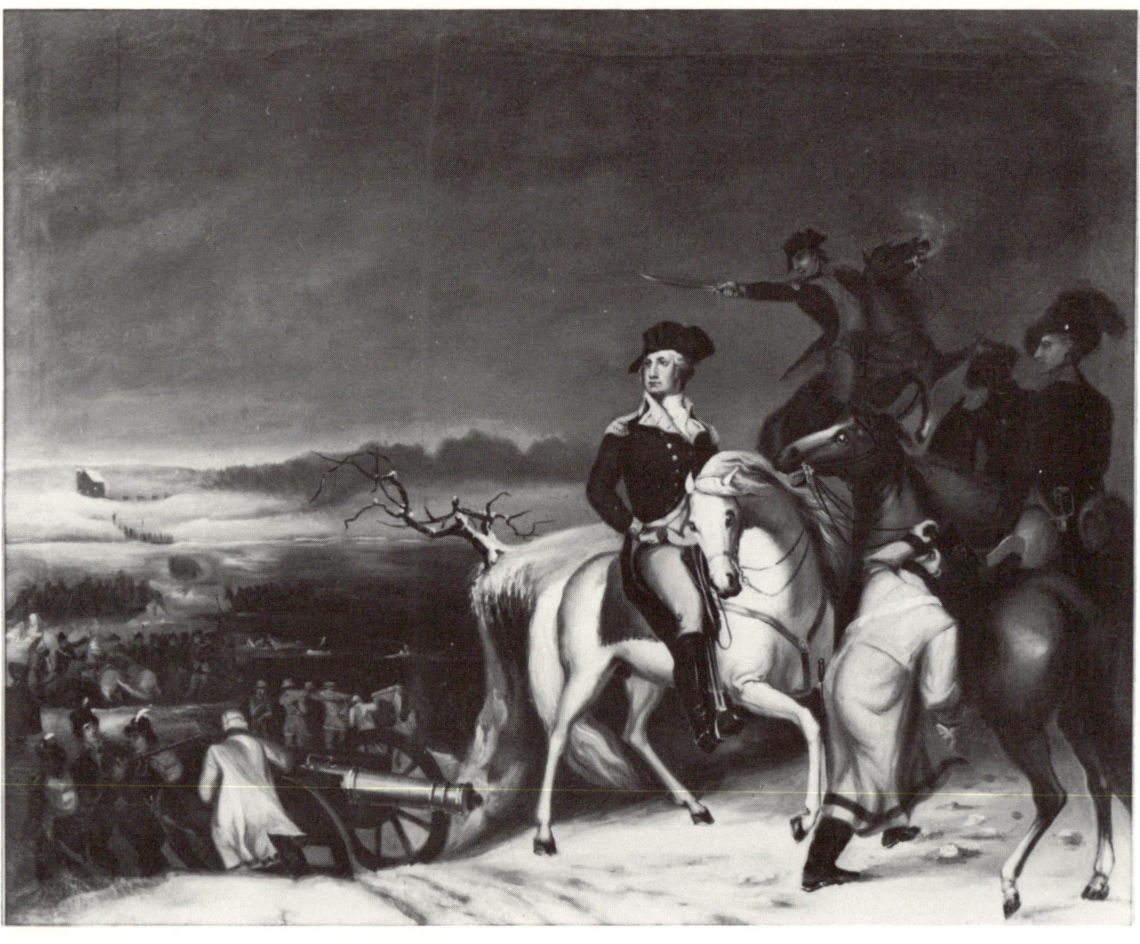

No. 67

WASHINGTON AT THE DELAWARE, 1840–49. Oil on canvas, 37½ × 47⅝ inches. The Edison Institute—Henry Ford Museum, Dearborn, Michigan.

COMMENT: The light on the distant hillside recalls Sully, but, as in all these adaptations, the hero's general bearing reflects the sober resolution of Gilbert Stuart's famous portrait rather than the studied and somewhat self-conscious attitude presented by Sully.

COLLECTIONS: Provenance unknown. Acquired by Stalker and Boos, auctioneers of Birmingham, Mich.; sold in 1972 to the Edison Institute—Henry Ford Museum, Dearborn, Mich.

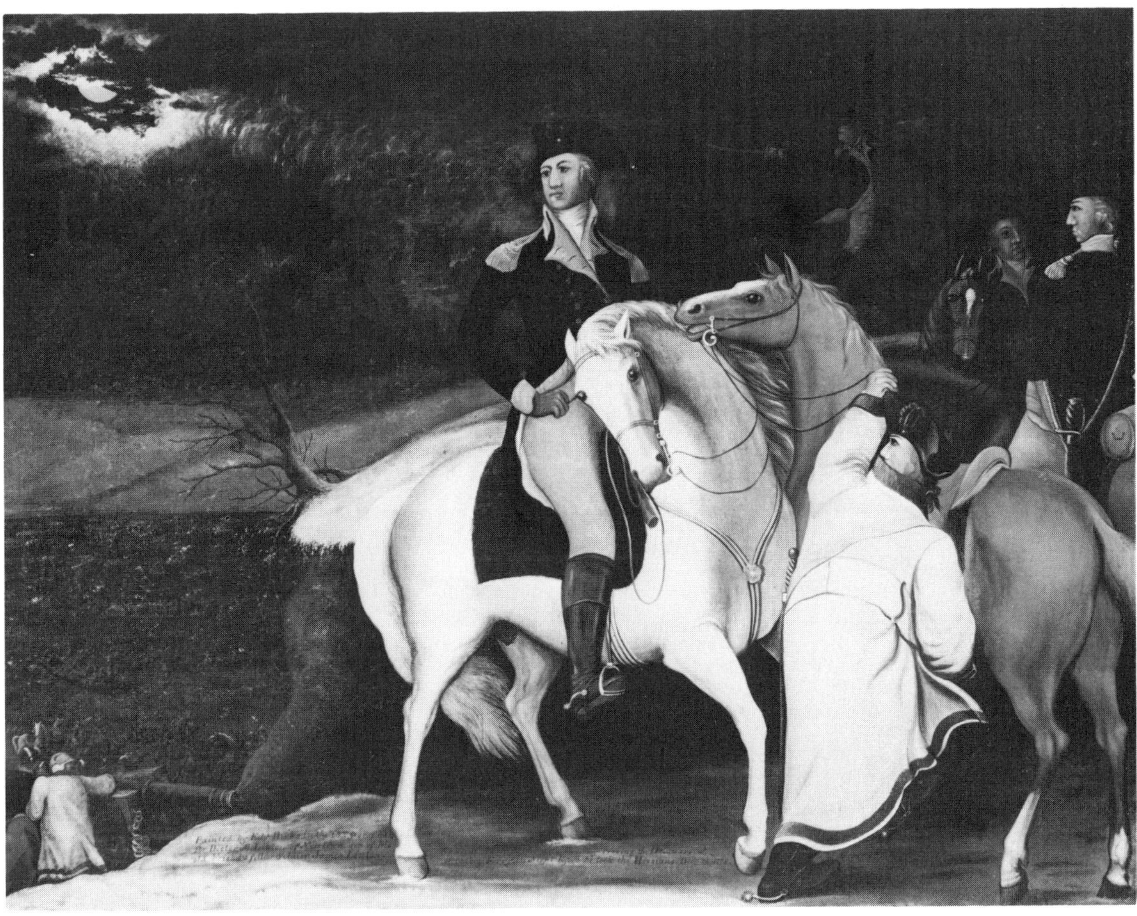

No. 68

WASHINGTON AT THE DELAWARE, 1848–
49. Oil on canvas, 36⅛ × 47⅜ inches. Inscribed at lower left: *"Painted by Edw. Hicks
in the 69th year of his age/ for Doctor M. Linton of Newtown, son of his/ old Friend & fellow Soldier, James Linton."* and at lower
center: *"George Washington with his army
crosing [sic] the Delaware/ at McConkey Ferry
the night before he took the Hessians, Dec. 25,
1776."* Abby Aldrich Rockefeller Folk Art
Center.

COMMENT: Shows simplification and subordination of detail. The figure of Washington,
here centered and proportionately larger than
in other versions, achieves an almost mythic
power. For a less favorable critique see
Stuart P. Feld, "The tradition of the primitive
imagination—denied," *Antiques* 83 (1963):
100.

COLLECTIONS: Dr. Maurice Linton, dentist
of Newtown; his nephew, Henry Ridge,* Langhorne, Pa.; to M. Knoedler & Co., Inc., New
York; to the Abby Aldrich Rockefeller Folk
Art Center, Williamsburg, Va.

EXHIBITIONS: AARFAC, "Edward Hicks"
(1960), no. 19, p. 14; Museum of Texas Tech-
nical College, "The Symbols of American
Heritage" (Lubbock, Texas, 1961); "American
Folk Art from the AARFAC," shown at Min-
neapolis Institute of Fine Arts (1962) and
Cummer Gallery of Art, Jacksonville, Fla.
(1964); Loan exhibition from the AARFAC,
Texas traveling exhibit shown at Fort Worth,
Austin, and El Paso (1962); William Penn
Memorial Museum (Harrisburg, Pa., 1966);
Museum of Early American Folk Art, *Time-
Life* Exhibition (New York, October 19–
November 20, 1966); Andrew Crispo Gallery,
"Edward Hicks: A Gentle Spirit" (New York,
1975), no. 34 (col.); Yorktown Victory Center
(Yorktown, Va., April 1–October 31, 1976);
Southern Alleghenies Museum of Art, "Penn-
sylvania Decorative and Functional Folk Art"
(Loretto, Pa., 1978), (ill.); Yorktown Victory
Center, "Patriotic Folk Art" (Yorktown, Va.,
November 19, 1979–May 31, 1980), ill.

---

*Ridge wrote, "Both my sister and I distinctly
remember this painting without a frame before it
was sent to our attic fifty odd years ago. . . . It is very
likely that Hicks did this work for my great uncle,
Dr. Linton, in payment for a medical bill and did
not include a frame" (letter to Mitch Wilder of
M. Knoedler & Co., May 29, 1957, AARFAC files).

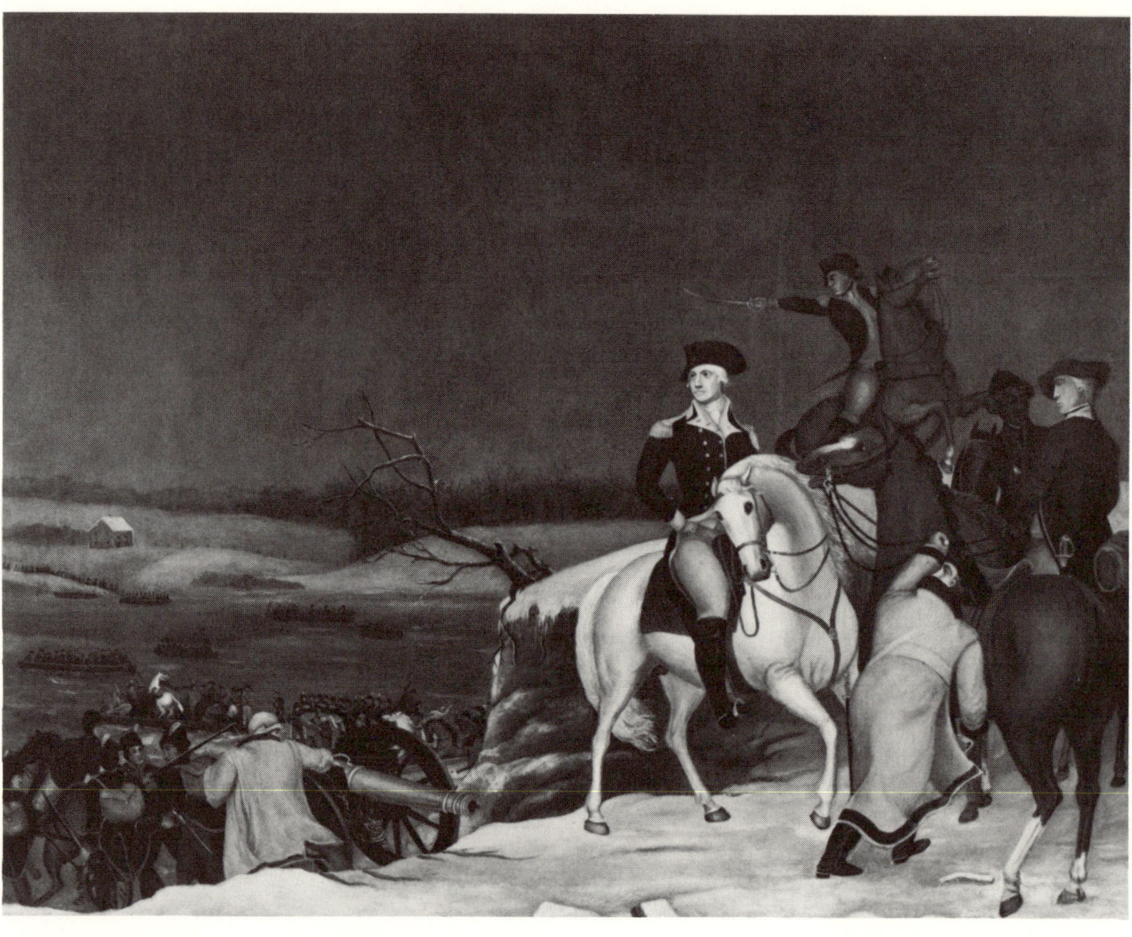

No. 69

WASHINGTON AT THE DELAWARE, 1849. Oil on canvas, 28 × 35¾ inches. Date "1849" inscribed on reverse. The Chrysler Museum, Norfolk, Virginia; gift of Edgar William and Bernice Chrysler Garbisch.

COMMENT: Painted a year after the Rockefeller version, this illustrates a complete departure from it in treatment, for instead of eliminating details the artist here renders the embarking soldiers figure by figure, the feathers on their hats being individually visible. As likenesses of Washington, this and No. 64 are the best examples.

COLLECTIONS: Provenance unknown. Collection of Edgar William and Bernice Chrysler Garbisch, who donated it to the Chrysler Museum, Norfolk, Va.

EXHIBITIONS: Andrew Crispo Gallery, "Edward Hicks: A Gentle Spirit" (New York, 1975), no. 33; Chrysler Museum, "Three Hundred Years of American Art in Norfolk" (Norfolk, Va., March 1–July 4, 1976), cat. by Dennis R. Anderson, p. 44.

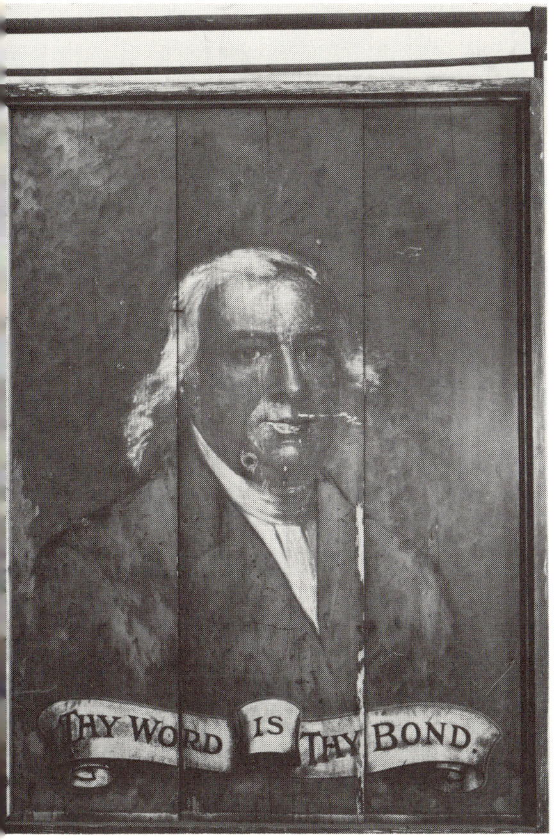

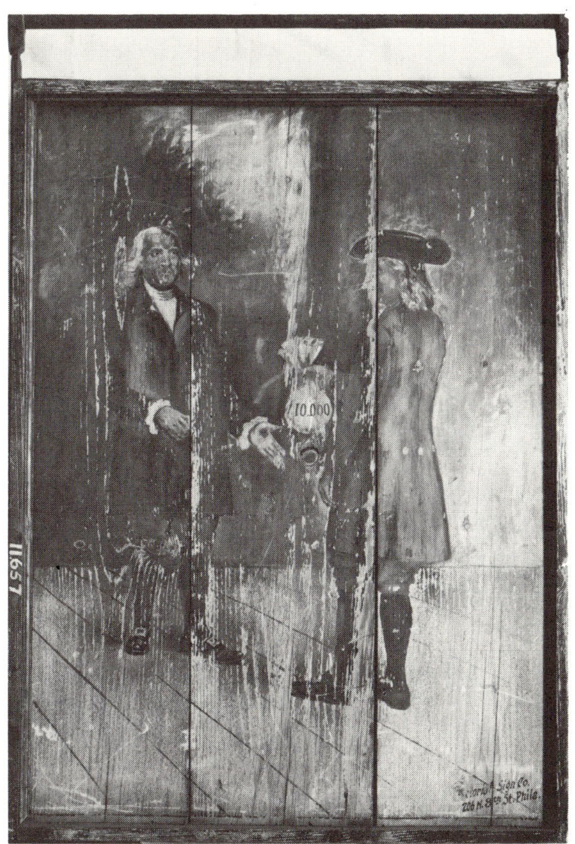

ROBERT MORRIS
A Distinguished Member of the Illustrious Congress of 1776 for whose financial labors, next to Washington, America is indebted for turning the tide of success in the American Revolution, in taking the Hessians at Trenton on Christmas Morning 1776, reviving the desponding cause of Liberty and Independence

Washington needs $10,000 -
You must let me have this money.
My note and my honor will be your only security
Robert: Thee Shall Have It.

No. 70, 71, 72, 73

ROBERT MORRIS SWINGING SIGN, ca. 1825. Oil on board 48 × 36 inches; pendant 10 × 36 inches. Beneath a bust-length portrait of Morris is a scroll inscribed, "THY WORD IS THY BOND." Pendant board reads, "ROBERT MORRIS/ a Distinguished Member of the Illustrious Congress of 1776 for/ whose financial labors, next to Washington, America is indebted/ for turning the tide of success in the American Revolution, in taking/ the Hessians at Trenton on Christmas Morning 1776, reviving/ the desponding cause of Liberty and Independence."

On reverse: Morris stands with hands outstretched to receive a bag marked "$10,000" from a man with back to viewer. In lower left corner is stenciled "Pictorial Sign Co./ 206 North 8th St. Phila." Pendant reads, "Washington needs $10,000/ You must let me have this money/ My note and my honor will be your only security/ Robert: Thee Shall Have It." Iron frame and mounting of sign original. The Mercer Museum of the Bucks County Historical Society.

COMMENT: The attribution of the sign to Hicks has been questioned because of the stenciled name of a Philadelphia sign company, but this may well have been a shop to which the sign was sent for repair. The authenticity of the work is supported by a quotation from the *Doylestown Democrat*, June 8, 1875: "An old sign, which swings back and forward in front of the Carlisle Hotel in Morrisville, is commemorative of Robert Morris. It was painted by Edward Hicks, a Bucks County Quaker. The old sign has been swinging to and fro, for more than half a century, without a touch from vandal hands. On one side Morris was represented talking to a friend, and telling him of the distressed state of Washington's army, and of the immediate necessity of $10,000" (discovered by Terry McNealy, Librarian, Mercer Museum BCHS files).

The friend was a Philadelphia Quaker, as described in Charles Goodrich's *The Lives of the Signers of the Declaration of Independence,* a book we know Hicks owned and annotated. However, since the book was published in 1829 and the sign very possibly made at the time of Lafayette's triumphal tour of 1824–25, which included Morrisville, the painter may have acquired the story from a local version.

Other arguments for authenticity: the use of the plain language, the mistake in date on the pendant as in the artist's early Washington signs, and the appeal of the subject matter to Hicks, suggesting Quaker support of the famous crossing of the Delaware (see text, p. 61).

The model for the bust appears to have been Gilbert Stuart's portrait, or the one after Stuart by Bass Otis, retouched by Sully, now at the Historical Society of Pennsylvania, Philadelphia (Nicholas B. Wainwright, *Paintings and Miniatures at the Historical Society of Pennsylvania*, rev. ed. [Philadelphia: Historical Society of Pennsylvania, 1974]).

COLLECTIONS: Carlisle Hotel, Morrisville, Bucks County, Pa.; to William F. Diener, Philadelphia (1917); to the Mercer Museum of the Bucks County Historical Society, Doylestown, Pa.

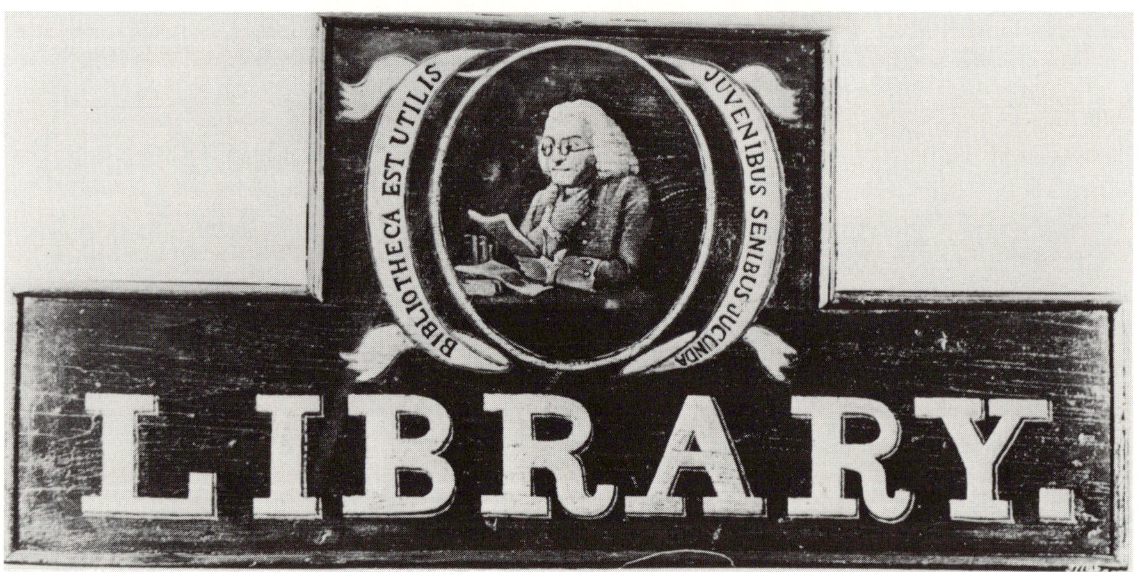

No. 74

NEWTOWN LIBRARY SIGN, 1825. Oil on wood, 17¾ × 37½ inches. Benjamin Franklin in a green coat is portrayed sitting at a table reading, his chin resting on the thumb of his right hand, the portrait encircled with ribbons inscribed, "BIBLIOTHECA EST UTILE" and "JUVENIBUS SENIBUS JUCUNDA."* On a broader surface below is written "LIBRARY." in large capitals. Narrow molded frame original. The Newtown Library Company.

COMMENT: Hicks was paid $1.00 for this sign. The likeness of Franklin is after David Martin's 1767 "thumb portrait," now at the Pennsylvania Academy of the Fine Arts. Founded in 1760, the Library Company was housed in the artist's own time on land donated by his father, Squire Isaac Hicks, who received a life membership in appreciation.

COLLECTIONS: Commissioned by the Newtown Library Company, Newtown, Pa., and still in its possession.

EXHIBITIONS: AARFAC, "Edward Hicks (1960), no. 11 (not. ill.); Carnegie/Corcoran, "Hicks, Kane, Pippin" (1966–67), p. 2; Andrew Crispo Gallery, "Edward Hicks: A Gentle Spirit" (New York, 1975), no. 22 (ill.).

---

*"Books are useful to the young and the old" (Edna Pullinger, *Newtown's First Library Building*, vol. 1 [Newtown, Pa., Newtown Library Company, 1976], p. 6).

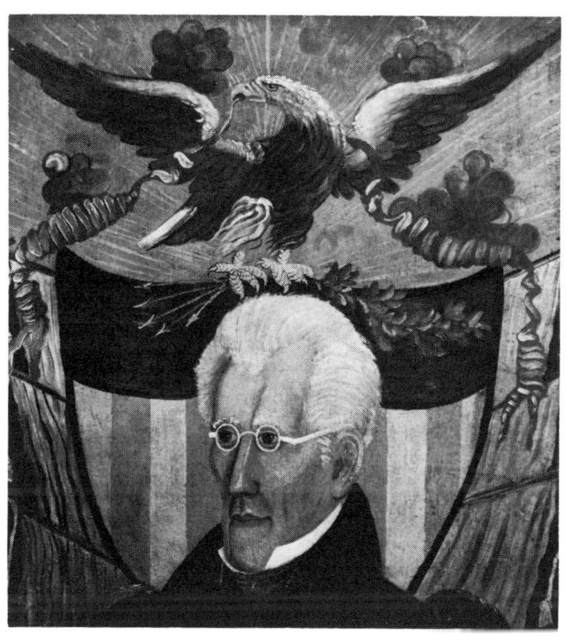

No. 75

ANDREW JACKSON, ca. 1835. Oil on carriage cloth, mounted on wood panel, 21½ × 20 inches. Private collection.

COMMENT: Found rolled up in Hicks's workshop after his death, this was mounted and framed in relatively recent times by J. Stanley Lee, husband of the painter's great-granddaughter, Hannah. The source was a T. Illman print of Hoppner Meyer's drawing after an oil portrait by Ralph E. W. Earl (Alice Ford, *Edward Hicks: Painter of the Peaceable Kingdom* [Philadelphia: University of Pennsylvania Press, 1952], pp. 83 and 146). Earl married the niece of Jackson's wife and portrayed "Old Hickory" many times. Hicks added the shield and American eagle. Its arrows and olive branch appear repeatedly in the popular art and signcraft of the period.

COLLECTIONS: From the painter's son, Isaac W. Hicks, Newtown, Pa., to his daughter, Sarah Worstall Hicks, Newtown; to J. Stanley and Hannah Hicks Lee, Newtown; to a private collector.

EXHIBITIONS: Newtown's 275th Anniversary (1959), no. 2 (not ill.); AARFAC, "Edward Hicks" (1960), no. 12, p. 12 (not ill.).

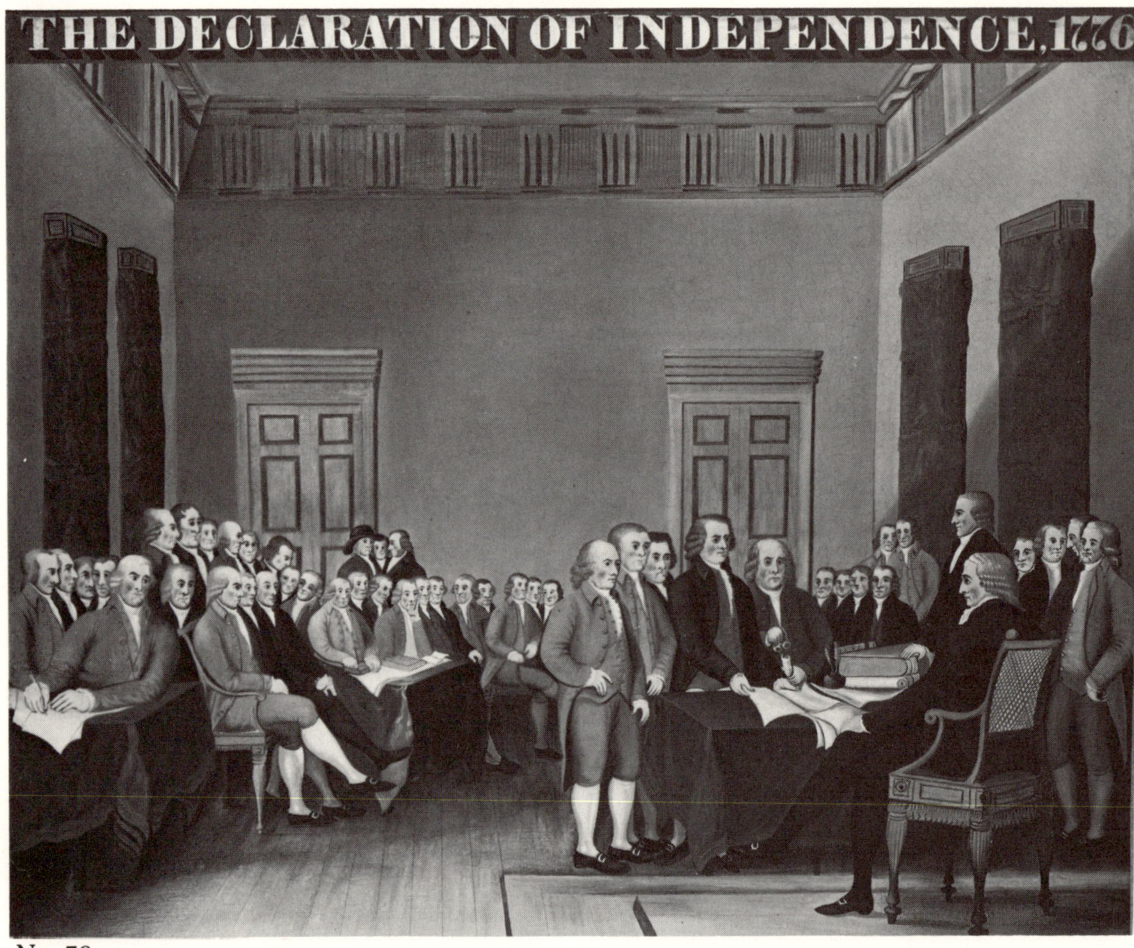

No. 76

THE DECLARATION OF INDEPENDENCE, 1840–44. Oil on canvas, 26¼ × 29¾ inches. Inscribed at top of canvas, "THE DECLARATION OF INDEPENDENCE, 1776." Birds-eye maple frame probably original. The Chrysler Museum, Norfolk, Virginia; gift of Edgar William and Bernice Chrysler Garbisch.

COMMENT: This is ultimately derived from John Trumbull's *Declaration of Independence* in the Rotunda of the Capitol, Washington,* but Alice Ford has suggested an immediate source in an engraving by Illman and Pilbrow used as a frontispiece for Charles A. Goodrich's 1829 *Lives of the Signers to the Declaration of Independence*—the leaf significantly missing from the painter's own well-worn copy of the book (*Edward Hicks: Painter of the Peaceable Kingdom* [Philadelphia: University of Pennsylvania Press, 1952], p. 66).

COLLECTIONS: Presumably inherited by Horace Burton of Edgely, near Bristol, Bucks County (Col. Henry D. Paxson noted on a file card for the *Declaration* now at AARFAC but then owned by Edward Hicks, the painter's grandson, that a similar work belonged to Horace Burton; Bucks County Historical Society files). To Robert Carlen Gallery, Philadelphia; to Edith Gregor Halpert, New York; M. Knoedler & Co., New York; Joseph Katz Co., New York; M. Knoedler & Co; to Edgar William and Bernice Chrysler Garbisch, New York, who gave it to the Chrysler Museum, Norfolk, Va.

EXHIBITIONS: Andrew Crispo Gallery, "Edward Hicks: A Gentle Spirit" (New York, 1975), no. 24; Chrysler Museum, "Three Hundred Years of American Art at Norfolk" (Norfolk, Va., 1976), p. 44.

---

*One of four panels commissioned in 1817 but not completed till 1824. Trumbull had begun work on the subject as early as 1787 in the studio of Benjamin West, London, producing a small two-by-four-foot study now in the Yale University Art Gallery. See Edgar P. Richardson, *Painting in America* (New York: Thomas Y. Crowell Co., 1956), p. 201.

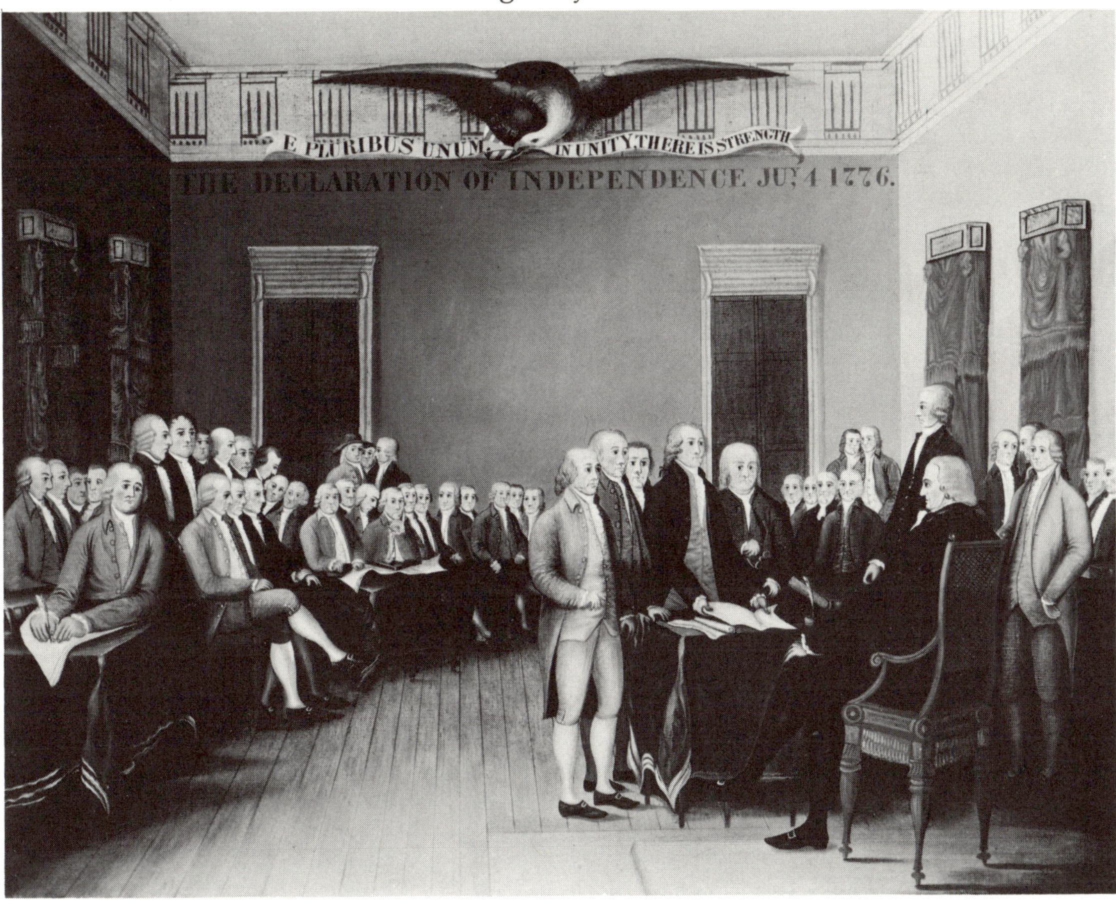

No. 77

THE DECLARATION OF INDEPENDENCE, 1840–44. Oil on canvas, 24 × 31¾ inches. Above the familiar scene of the founding fathers an eagle with wings outspread holds in his beak an American shield and a ribbon lettered, "E PLURIBUS UNUM. IN UNITY THERE IS STRENGTH," and beneath the cornice molding, "THE DECLARATION OF INDEPENDENCE Ju.ʸ 4 1776." Nineteenth-century contemporary veneered frame probably original. Abby Aldrich Rockefeller Folk Art Center.

COMMENT: Authorities differ as to the aesthetic merit of Hicks's *Declarations*. Jean Lipman considered this version to be superior not only to the engraved source, but also to Trumbull's original, its excellence residing in "the lucid tonal design, which bears no relationship whatsoever to the engraving Hicks copied" ("Print to Primitive," *Antiques*, 50 [1946]: 41–43).

COLLECTIONS: From the painter to his son, Isaac Hicks, Newtown, Pa.; to his son, Edward Hicks, Newtown, Pa.; to his daughter, Mary Barnsley Hicks Richardson, Sweet Briar, Va.; to Capt. Richard A. Loeb, Hampton, N.J.; to Mr. and Mrs. Howard Lipman, Wilton, Conn.; to a dealer, Mary Allis, Southport, Conn.; to M. Knoedler & Co., Inc., New York; to the Abby Aldrich Rockefeller Folk Art Center, Williamsburg, Va.

EXHIBITIONS: Friends Historical Association Annual Meeting, Atwater Kent Museum (Philadelphia, November 30–December 31, 1942); Cincinnati Museum, "Rediscoveries in American Painting" (Cincinnati, Ohio, October–November, 1955); AARFAC, "Edward Hicks" (1960), no. 27, p. 16 (not. ill.); Texas Technological College, "Symbols of Our American Heritage" (Lubbock, Texas, September 28–October 31, 1961); Carnegie/Corcoran, "Hicks, Kane, Pippin" (1966–67), p. 17; AARFAC, "Folk Art in America: A Living Tradition" (preview at Williamsburg, traveling 1974–75 to Atlanta, Ga., St. Petersburg, Fla., Columbia, S.C., West Palm Beach, Fla., Raleigh, N.C., New Orleans, La., Charlotte, N.C., Peoria, Ill., and Little Rock, Ark.), no. 57, p. 59, ill. p. 15.

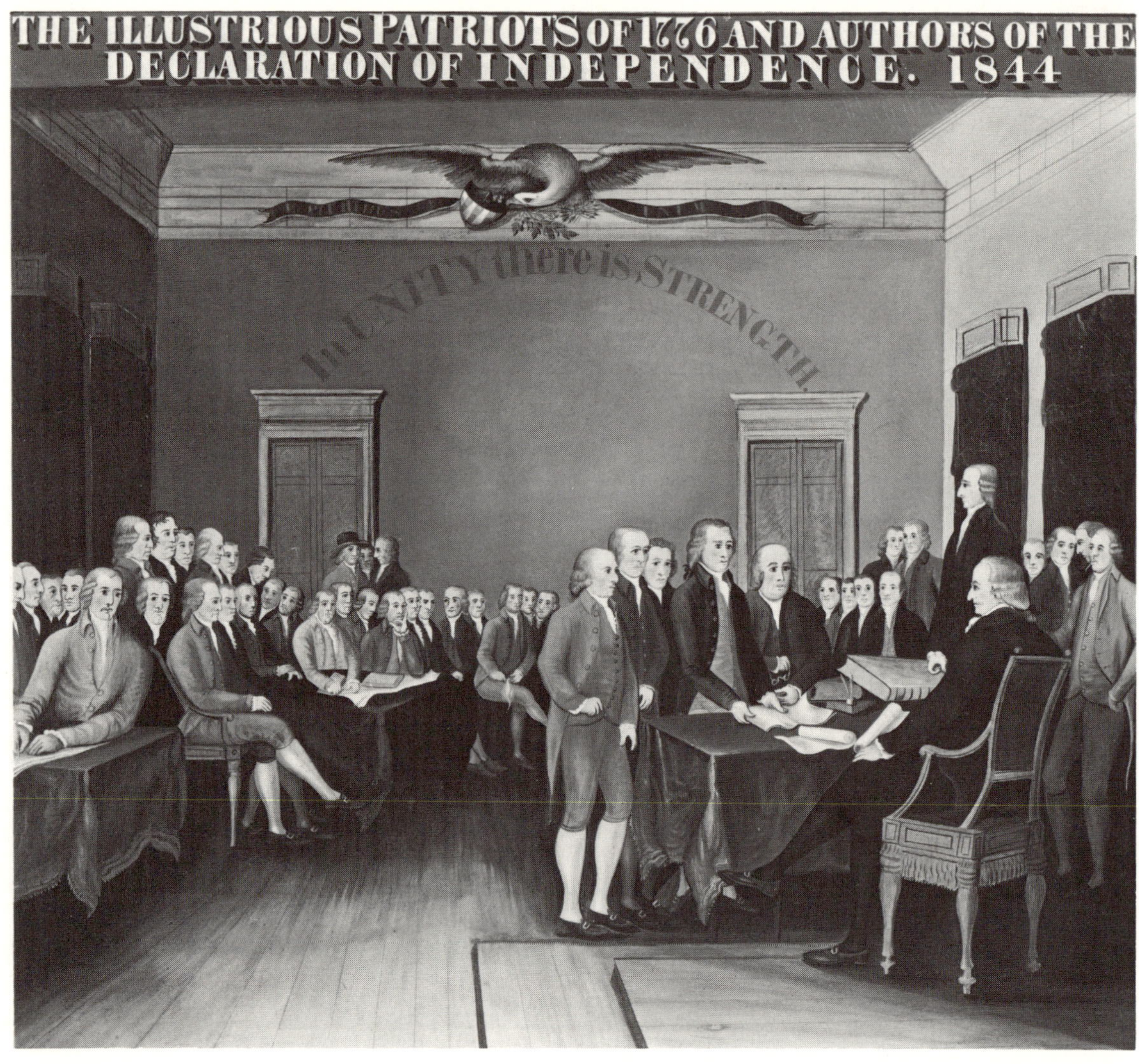

No. 78

THE DECLARATION OF INDEPENDENCE, 1844. Oil on canvas, 26 × 30 inches. Lettered at top: "THE ILLUSTRIOUS PATRIOTS OF 1776 AND AUTHORS OF THE DECLARATION OF INDEPENDENCE. 1844." Shield and eagle similar to No. 77, with ribbon inscribed, "E PLURIBUS UNUM," and on the wall beneath, in a curved line, "In UNITY there is STRENGTH." Curly maple veneer frame with cherry corner blocks probably original. Collection of Hirschl and Adler Galleries.

COMMENT: The only one of Hicks's *Declarations* with a firm date, and possibly the last painted, since the lettered inscriptions are the most highly evolved. More subdued in color than the other two versions, this has black curtains at the windows instead of red.

COLLECTIONS: Provenance unknown. Estate of Leonardo L. Beans. Auctioned at Sotheby Parke Bernet, New York, to Hirschl & Adler Galleries, Inc., New York.

EXHIBITIONS: Andrew Crispo Gallery, "Edward Hicks: A Gentle Spirit" (New York, 1975), no. 25 (col.).

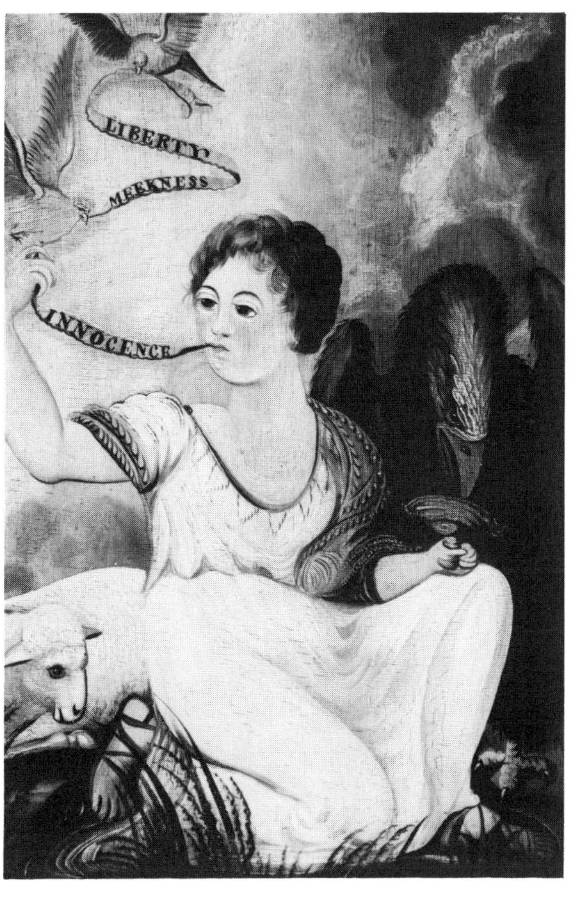

No. 79

LIBERTY, MEEKNESS, AND INNOCENCE, ca. 1835. Oil on Wood, 14 × 9¾ inches. A ribbon, supported by two doves on the wing and the upraised hand of a kneeling girl, is inscribed, "LIBERTY," "MEEKNESS," and "INNOCENCE." Heavy molded wood frame probably original. Private collection.

COMMENT: The neoclassical maiden and eagle of liberty formed a popular combination in early nineteenth-century America. Lamb, doves, and inscription were added by Hicks, and were used by him in the decorated corner blocks of his *Peaceable Kingdoms with Rhymed Borders*, while the constellation as a whole, minus the lamb, appears as a vignette in a number of later *Kingdoms*.

COLLECTIONS: Provenance unknown. Acquired by dealer, Marian Conrad Beans, Newtown, Pa.; Museum of Modern Art, New York; Robert W. Carle, South Salem, Conn.; to a private collector.

EXHIBITIONS: AARFAC, "Edward Hicks" (1960), no. 24, p. 15 (not ill.); Carnegie/Corcoran, "Hicks, Kane, Pippin" (1966–67), p. 15 (ill.).

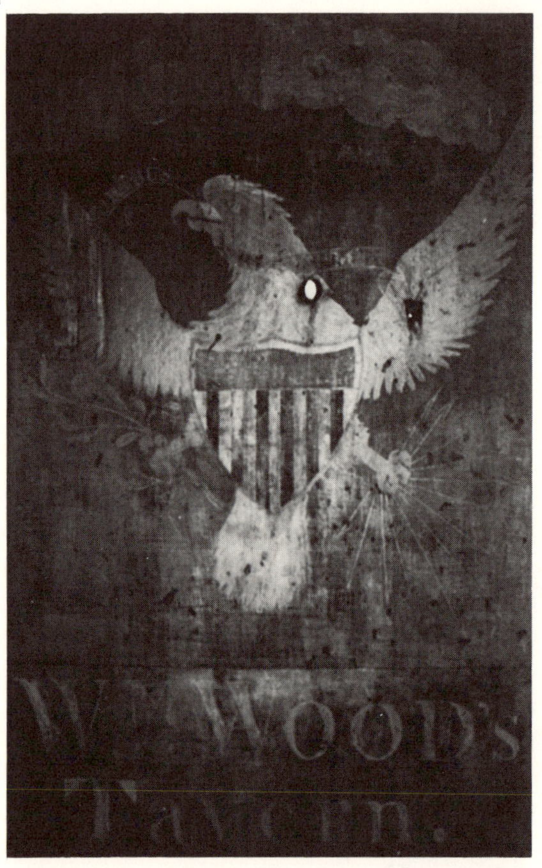
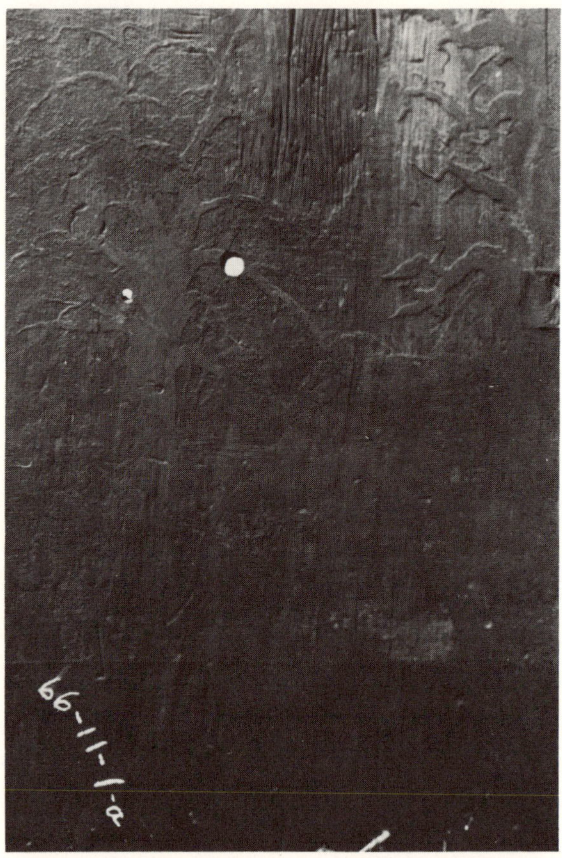

No. 80, 81

WM. WOOD TAVERN SIGN, 1844–47. Oil on wood, 29½ × 43½ inches. Shows eagle with outspread wings, beak holding a streamer inscribed, "E PLURIBUS UNUM," claws grasping olive branches and arrows. Inscription at base reads, "WM WOOD's/Tavern." Mounting and chains original. Historic Fallsington, Inc.

COMMENT: Attribution to Hicks rests on details such as the inscribed band at base of board, also seen in his Washington bridge signs and certain easel pictures, and in the treatment of eagle and other American symbols, as in his *Andrew Jackson*. But unlike the naturalistic bird of the Jackson portrait, this creature—similar to that on the seal of the President of the United States—is the spread eagle of European heraldry, the national motto and striped shield transforming it into a patriotic emblem.

"The reverse side," wrote Leonardo L. Beans, a former owner, "once had a very interesting painting in the nature of a farm scene, but probably showing the tavern with horses tied outside" (*The Life and Work of Edward Hicks* [Trenton, N.J.: Privately printed, 1951], p. 30). Though the paint has almost disappeared from this side, a marked weathering of the background (presumably less thickly painted) has produced an embossed effect that indicates the design. Close examination reveals two trees, with a bird on the branch of one. No trace of farm or tavern remains.

COLLECTIONS: Painted for William Wood of New Jersey. Acquired by Leonardo L. Beans, Trenton, N.J. For some years on loan to, and now the property of, Historic Fallsington, Inc., Fallsington, Bucks County, Pa., where it is exhibited in the Stagecoach Tavern.

Photographs by Robert W. Mather.

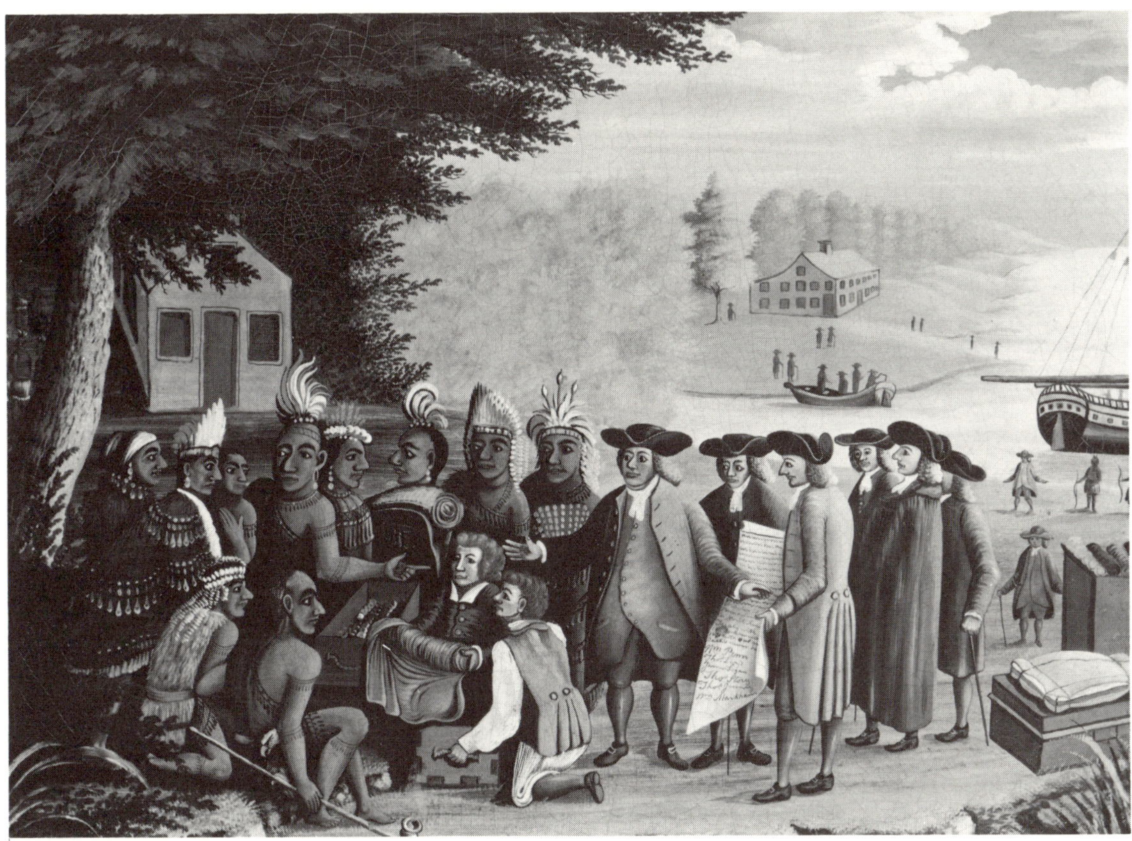

No. 82

PENN'S TREATY, 1830–35. Oil on canvas, 17⅝ × 23¾ in. Written on scroll within painting: "Charter of/ Pennsylvania/ in North America/ Treaty with/ the Indians in —/ 1681 without an oath & never broken/ Wm. Penn/ Thos. Lloyd/ James Logan/ Thos Story/ Thos Janney/ Wm. Markham." Original block-cornered veneered frame, 2½ in. wide, stenciled in gold, "PENN'S *TREATY*," made in the painter's shop by Hicks himself or his assistant, Edward Trego. Abby Aldrich Rockefeller Folk Art Center.

COMMENT: Derived from Benjamin West's *William Penn's Treaty with the Indians* (1771) through John Hall's engraving (published by John Boydell, 1775). Because Hicks copied from the engraving all his versions reverse West's composition.

COLLECTIONS: Provenance unknown. Purchased from New York dealer (name unknown) by Charles Montgomery; to the Halladay-Thomas Collection, Sheffield, Mass.; to Abby Aldrich Rockefeller Folk Art Center, Williamsburg, Va.

EXHIBITIONS: Carnegie Institute, "American Provincial Paintings From the Collection of J. Stuart Halladay and Herrel George Thomas" (Pittsburgh, Pa., April 24–June 1, 1941) and at the Whitney Museum of American Art (New York, October 27–November 19, 1942), no. 3; "Early American Paintings," Halladay-Thomas Collection, shown at Hudson Park Library (New York, March 1–April 30, 1946); "American Provincial Paintings 1680–1880," Halladay-Thomas Collection, shown at the Art Museum (New Britain, Conn., November, 1947), no. 93, and at Syracuse Museum of Fine Arts (Syracuse, N.Y., January 23–February 22, 1949), no. 4; "American Provincial Paintings 1700–1860," Halladay-Thomas Collection, shown at Albany Institute of History and Art (Albany, N.Y., October, 1949), no. 12; AARFAC, "Edward Hicks" (1960), no. 22, p. 15 (not ill.); "American Folk Art from AARFAC" at the American Museum in Britain (Claverton Manor, Bath, Eng., March 9–November 1, 1961); "Loan Exhibition from the AARFAC," Texas traveling exhibit (Fort Worth, El Paso, and Austin, 1962); "American Folk Art from the AARFAC," shown at Museum of New Mexico (Santa Fé, N.M., January 1–April 17, 1963), Minneapolis Institute of Arts (Minneapolis, Minn., May 19–July 1, 1964), and at Cummer Gallery of Art (Jacksonville, Fla., December 1, 1964–January 3, 1965); exhibition at William Penn Memorial Museum (Harrisburg, Pa., 1966); Andrew Crispo Gallery, "Edward Hicks: A Gentle Spirit" (New York, 1975), no. 30 (col.); Whitney Museum of American Art, "American Folk Painters of Three Centuries" (New York, 1980), p. 90 (col.).

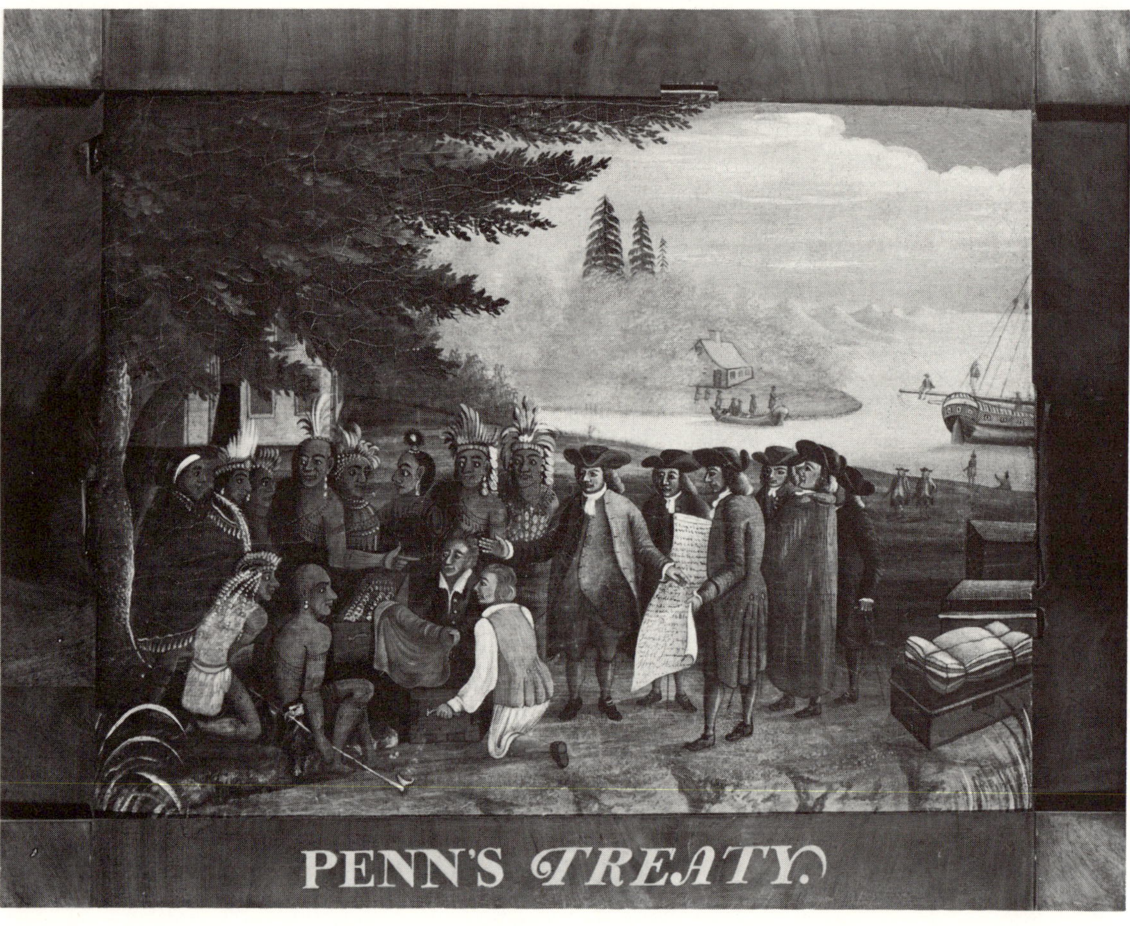

No. 83

PENN'S TREATY, 1830–35. Oil on canvas, 17¼ × 23¼ inches. Letters on the scroll are largely illegible, but close scrutiny reveals a few words: "Treaty with the Indians"/ "1681"/ "made not to be broken." The signatures are clearly inscribed beneath: "William Penn/ Thos Lloyd/ James Logan/Thos. Story/ Thomas Janney/ Wm. Markham." Original veneered frame with block corners, stenciled in gold: "PENN'S TREATY," probably made in Hicks's shop. Mr. and Mrs. Meyer P. Potamkin.

COMMENT: Very similar to the preceding. To West's design Hicks has added details from two engravings by T. H. Mumford, *Penn Landing at Chester* and *Penn Landing at Blue Anchor Inn* (Philadelphia), in John Fanning Watson's *Annals of Philadelphia*, vol. 1 Philadelphia, 1857), facing p. 127, sources that he scrambled freely. For the history behind West's painting see Charles Coleman Sellers's essay, "The Beginning," in *Symbols of Peace*, catalog for Bicentennial Exhibition at the Academy of the Fine Arts (Philadelphia, 1976).

COLLECTIONS: Probably acquired by Dr. David Hutchinson (grandson of David and Elizabeth Twining), though the first recorded owner is his son, James Pemberton Hutchinson (1843–1901), Newtown, Pa.; to Thomas Ross, Doylestown, Pa.; purchased by Robert Carlen Gallery, Philadelphia; to Mr. and Mrs. Meyer P. Potamkin, Philadelphia.

EXHIBITIONS: Bucks County Bicentennial Celebration (Doylestown, Pa., August 31– September 2, 1882), cat. ed. Henry C. Michener, listed as owned by J. Pemberton Hutchinson; Newark Museum, "American Primitives . . . an Exhibition of Nineteenth-Century Folk Artists" (Newark, N.J., November 4, 1930–February 1, 1931), no. 56, p. 66, listed as owned by Thomas Ross; Robert Carlen Gallery, "Edward Hicks Centennial" (Philadelphia, 1949); Carnegie /Corcoran, "Hicks, Kane, Pippin" (1966–67), p. 20; ACA Galleries, "Four American Primitives" (New York, 1972), no. 10; Andrew Crispo Gallery, "Edward Hicks: A Gentle Spirit" (New York, 1975), no. 29 (col.).

Photograph courtesy Hirschl & Adler Galleries, New York.

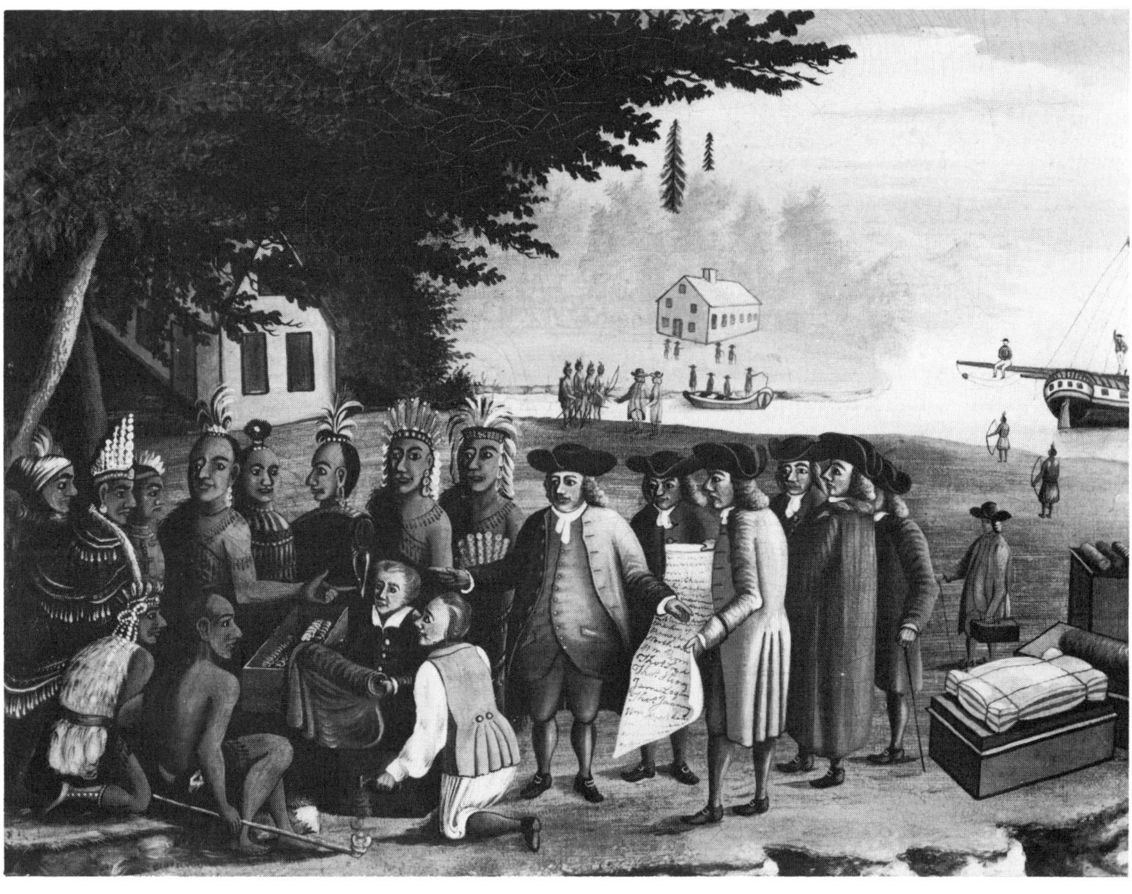

No. 84

PENN'S TREATY, 1830–35. Oil on canvas, 17¾ × 24 inches. Top lines on scroll suggest writing, but are not decipherable. Below Penn's left hand is written, "Charter of/ Pennsylvania/ North America." Beneath are signatures: "Wm Penn/ Thos Loyd/ Thos Story/ James Logan/ Thos Janney/ Wm Markham." Original veneered corner-blocked frame inscribed in gold: "PENN'S *TREATY*." The Thomas Gilcrease Institute of American History and Art, Tulsa, Oklahoma.

COMMENT: The Indian motif is stressed by a pair of aborigines with bows from Mumford's Philadelphia *Landing* and a group of four seen chatting with two Quakers in the middle distance. Penn's ship, the *Welcome* (its gun ports suggesting a frigate rather than a ship of peace), comes from Mumford's Chester *Landing*.

COLLECTIONS: Early provenance unknown. American Folk Art Gallery, New York; Downtown Gallery (Edith Gregor Halpert), New York; purchased by Thomas Gilcrease, Claremore, Okla.; given by him to the Thomas Gilcrease Institute of American History and Art, Tulsa, Okla.

EXHIBITIONS: Downtown Gallery (New York, March, 1941), listed as owned by American Folk Art Gallery; Grand Central Galleries, "Parade of Patriots" (Hotel Gotham, New York, 1942).

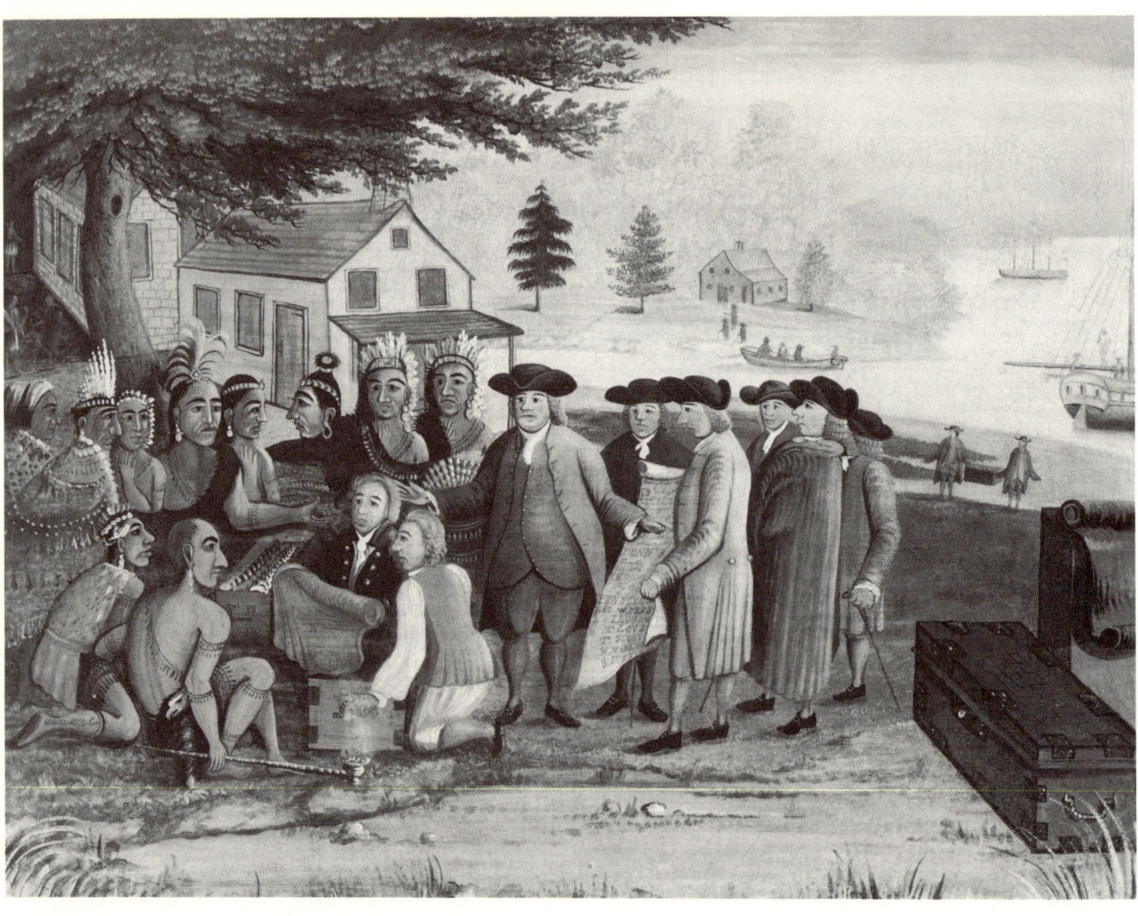

No. 85

PENN'S TREATY, 1830–35. Oil on canvas, 17½ × 23½ inches. Scroll inscription illegible except for names in capitals: "PENN'S", "INDIANS," "PENNSYLVANIA," and the signers: "W. PENN," "J. LOGAN," "T. LOYD" (sic), "T. STORY," "W. MARKHA(M)," and "S. JENNINGS." Original block-cornered veneer frame, stenciled in gold, "PENN'S TREATY." Private collection.

COMMENT: This finely preserved example, like West's original and all its derivatives, portrays an event for which there is no historical documentation. Though records exist of a number of Penn's negotiations with the Indians, this famous gathering at Shackamaxon, in what is now North Philadelphia, is supported only by tradition. But fact or fiction, it is part of Western culture.

COLLECTIONS: The first recorded (and probably original) owner was John Ruddle of Bucks County, who came to Pennsylvania in 1820 and married a Quaker, Hannah Prior; to their son, George Ruddle of the Lehigh Valley; to his daughter, Eliza Ruddle, Mauch Chunk, Pa.; to Kennedy Galleries, Inc., New York; to a private collector. On extended loan to the White House, Washington, D.C.

EXHIBITIONS: Andrew Crispo Gallery, "Edward Hicks: A Gentle Spirit" (New York, 1975), no. 32 and detail (col.).

Photograph courtesy Kennedy Galleries, Inc., New York.

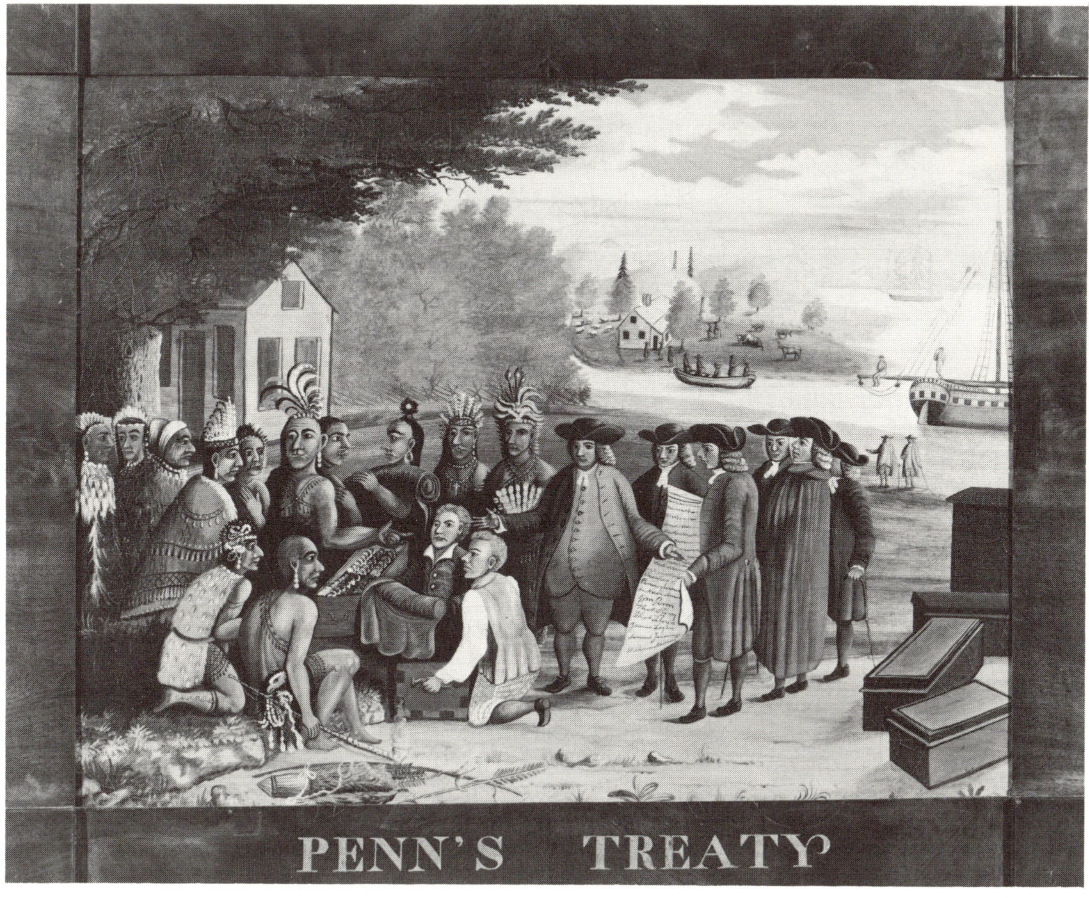

No. 86

PENN'S TREATY, 1830–35. Oil on canvas, 17¾ × 23¾ inches. Scroll inscribed: "Pennsylvania In North America," "Wm. Penn," "Thos. Story," "Thos. Lloyd," "James Logan," "Samuel Jennings," "William Markham." Original cherry veneer frame with block corners and title in gold: "PENN'S TREATY." Private collection.

COMMENT: Unlike other early versions, this shows the quiver of arrows that appears in the foreground of West's painting. In the distance stands the house of Robert Wade, a British Quaker already settled in the Chester area before Penn arrived. In front of his house are his sheep and cattle.

COLLECTIONS: Descended in the artist's family to great-grandson, Robert W. Carle, South Salem, Conn.; given by him to Yale University Art Gallery, New Haven, Conn.; to a private collector; sold to Hirschl & Adler Galleries, New York; to a private collector.

EXHIBITIONS: United States Section of the International Commission on Folk Art, Exhibition of Folk Art (New York, 1935); Carnegie/Corcoran, "Hicks, Kane, Pippin" (1966–67), p. 16; Hirschl & Adler Galleries, "American Folk Art" (New York, November 26–December 29, 1977), no. 31, p. 27 (col.).

Photograph courtesy Hirschl & Adler Galleries, New York.

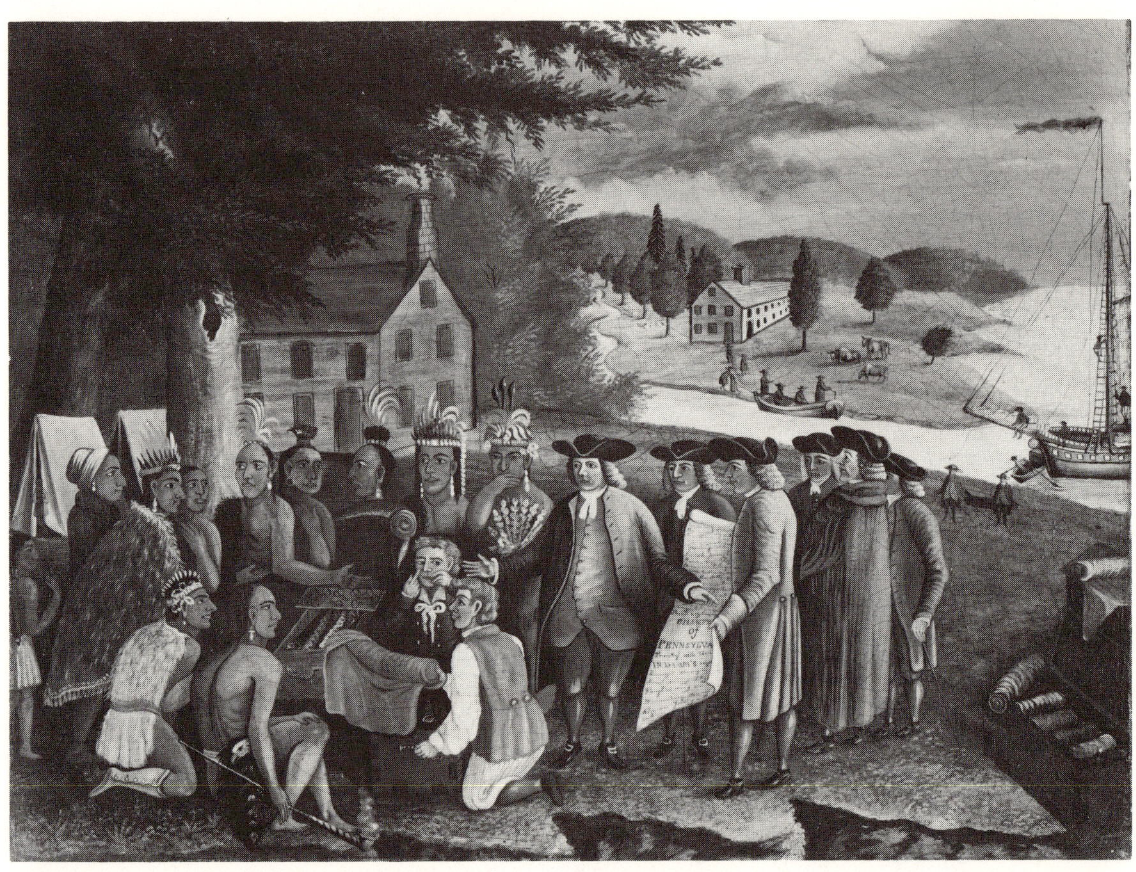

No. 87

PENN'S TREATY, ca. 1835. Oil on canvas, 17¾ × 23⅝ inches. Scroll inscribed: "CHARTER of PENNSYLVANIA Treaty with the INDIANS," followed by undecipherable writing. The Museum of Fine Arts, Houston, Bayou Bend Collection; gift of Miss Alice C. Simkins.

COMMENT: Unique in portraying an English servant demonstrating a jews-harp. A tray of these small instruments lies across the open chest. They were a recorded item of barter with the Indians. Hicks may have learned of them in *Life of William Penn* (Philadelphia: H. C. Carey & I. Lea, 1822) by Mason L. Weems ("Parson" Weems, presumed inventor of Washington's cherry tree), which lists 100 jews-harps as part of Penn's payment for his land (p. 163).

COLLECTIONS: Provenance unknown. First identified owner, Jacob Paxson Temple, Tanguy, Chester County, Pa.; sold through Anderson Galleries, New York, to Will E. Hogg, New York (1922); to his wife, Alice Nicholson Hogg, later Mrs. Harry Hanszen, Houston, Tex.; to her niece, Alice C. Simkins, Houston, who gave it to the Museum of Fine Arts, Houston, Bayou Bend Collection.

EXHIBITIONS: Museum of Fine Arts, Houston, "American Art 1845–1945" (Houston, Texas, January 4–March 18, 1979).

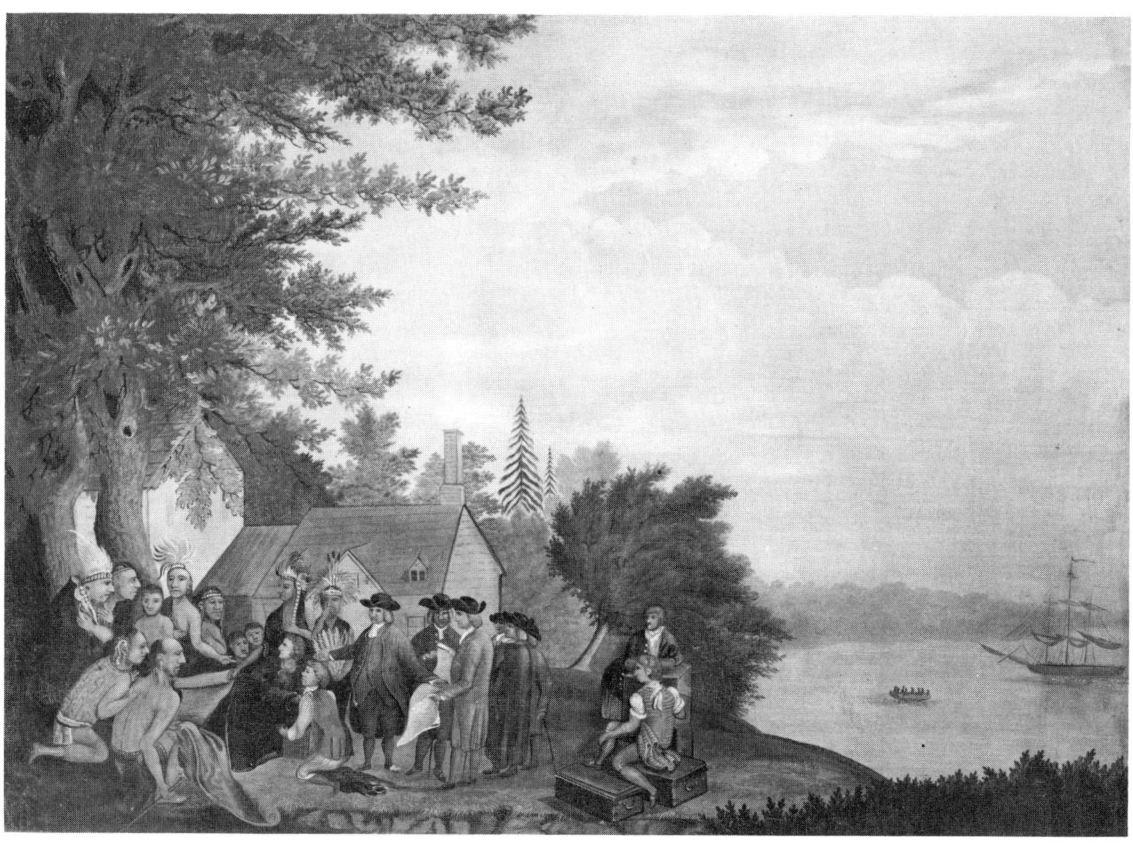

No. 88

PENN'S TREATY, 1835–40. Oil on canvas, 20⅝ × 27¾ inches. Private collection, present whereabouts unknown.

COMMENT: The influence of the Boydell-Hall engraving becomes evident in the more open treatment, in details of foliage and buildings, and in the addition of two British sailors to the right. The upper of these two figures was by tradition West himself. The same tradition identified the man with the scroll as James Logan, Penn's secretary, the man with the cloak as Thomas Lloyd, deputy-governor, and the individual behind Penn as Thomas Story, Quaker minister. These attributions are incorrect historically—none of the three was on this side of the ocean at the time of the treaty—but since their names appear on certain of Hicks's canvases, we gather that he leaned on the tradition as a source (see Ellen Starr Brinton's detailed study of West's original and its derivations, "Benjamin West's Painting of Penn's Treaty With the Indians," *Bulletin of the Friends Historical Association,* 30 [1941]: 116).

COLLECTIONS: Original provenance unknown; acquired by Harry Shaw Newman, New York, in 1944; to a private collector.

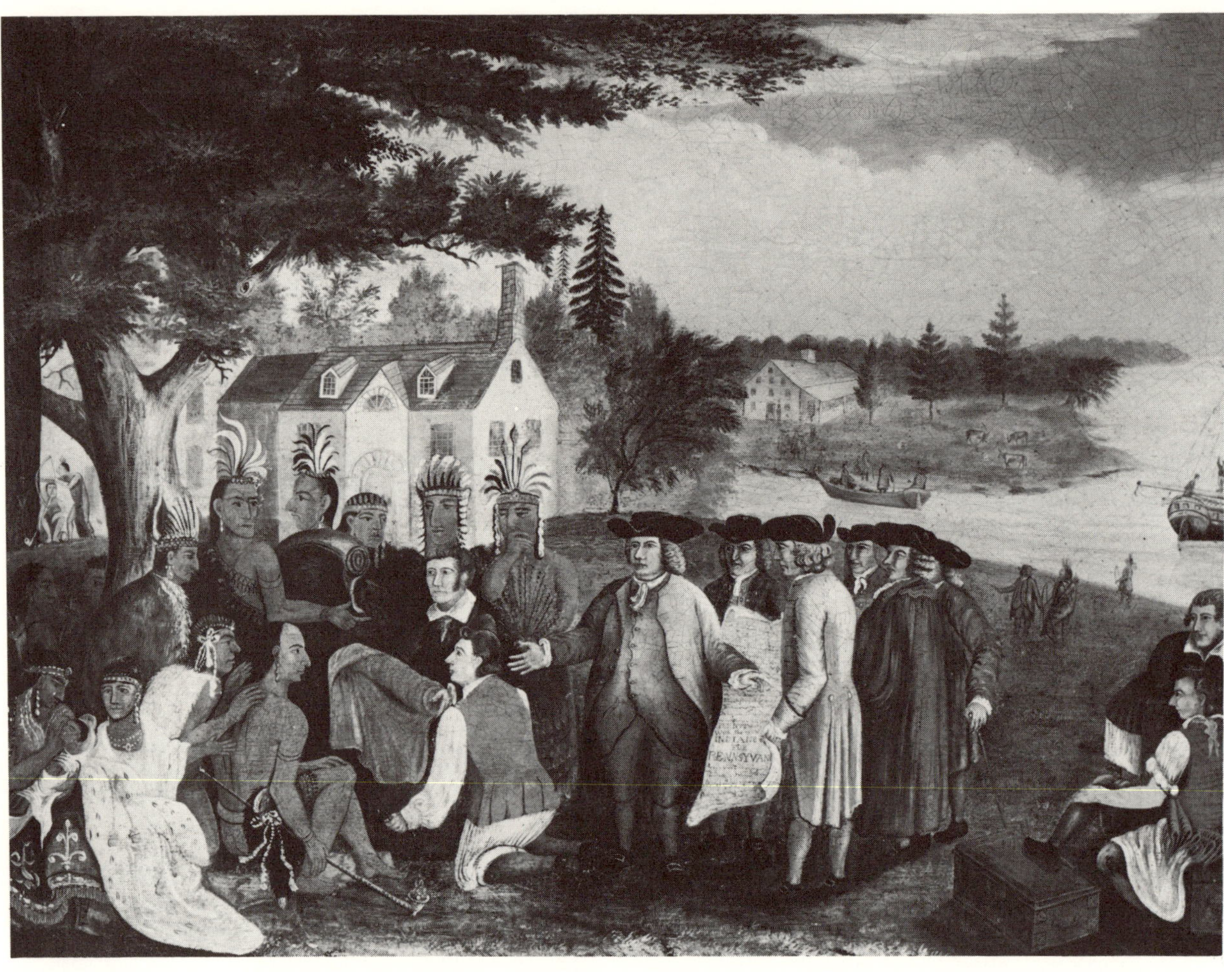

No. 89

PENN'S TREATY, 1835–40. Oil on canvas, 21¼ × 28 inches. Scroll reads: "PENN'S Treaty with the INDIANS FOR PENNSYLVANI(A)." Original cherry veneer frame inscribed in gold: "PENN'S TREATY." The Mercer Museum of the Bucks County Historical Society.

COMMENT: Two female figures at left—the squaw with papoose being modeled on West's wife, according to one tradition (Brinton, "Benjamin West's Painting of Penn's Treaty," p. 116)—bring the composition very close to West's original. But Hicks's colors are brighter than West's, possibly due to Parson Weems's description of the scene: "Here the English sailors, with their usual alacrity, opened out their ready bales of cloths, their 'true *blues*,' and fiery *crimsons*, and *flaming reds*, stretching them along in all their dazzling colors on the grass" (Mason Weems, *Life of William Penn* [Philadelphia, 1822], pp. 154–155). Directly above the Indian maiden stands the sachem, presumably the celebrated Tamany, chief of the Delawares. Here he wears a feathered headdress rather than the horn shown in certain *Peaceable Kingdoms*. Next to him, with arm extended, is the spokesman who acts as intermediary between Tamany and Penn.

COLLECTIONS: Given by the painter to Wilhelmina, daughter of Abraham Chapman, who became Mrs. Mathias Morris, Doylestown, Pa.; to her daughter, Mary Ann (Mrs. John Chester) Lyman, Boston, Mass.; to her daughter, Marian Lyman; to Henry Chapman Mercer, who gave it to the Mercer Museum of the Bucks County Historical Society, Doylestown, Pa.

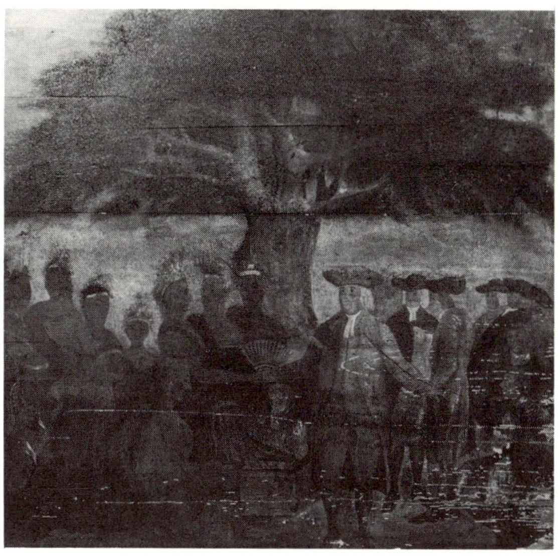

No. 90

PENN TREATY SWINGING SIGN, 1844. Oil on wood, 57 inches square. Delaware County Historical Society.

COMMENT: Though badly weathered, the sign is a significant variant on the Treaty theme. It hung in front of an old 1747 tavern in Chester, Pa. Originally known as the Pennsylvania Arms, the inn was renamed the Washington House because George Washington stopped there in 1777 to write his report to the Continental Congress after the disastrous Battle of Brandywine. In 1844 it became a temperance hotel. An earnest temperance advocate, Samuel West (probably a remote relative of Benjamin the artist), paid Hicks to paint the sign, which West presented to the new landlord (Henry Graham Ashmead, *History of Delaware County* [Philadelphia: L. H. Everts & Co., 1884], p. 368).

It differs from Hicks's other *Treaties* in having the tree in the middle. The reverse, defaced by exposure to the Delaware River, reveals dimly the usual arrangement with the tree to the extreme left and in the background details from the Mumford engravings. Hicks is said to have painted another Penn Treaty sign that was mounted on top of a pole in front of Samuel Willet's tavern in Buckingham, Bucks County, and while it remained the inn was known as "The Sign of Penn's Treaty."*

COLLECTIONS: Samuel West, Chester, Pa.; to Edward E. Flavill, owner of the Washington House in 1844; through subsequent owners to William Band, who in 1920 presented the sign to the Delaware County Historical Society, now housed in the Wolfgram Memorial Library, Widener College, Chester, Pa.

Photograph by Flynn Photography Ltd.

*See Warren S. Ely, "Bogart's Inn: An Old Hostelry," *Bucks County Historical Society Papers* 3(1901): 96–106.

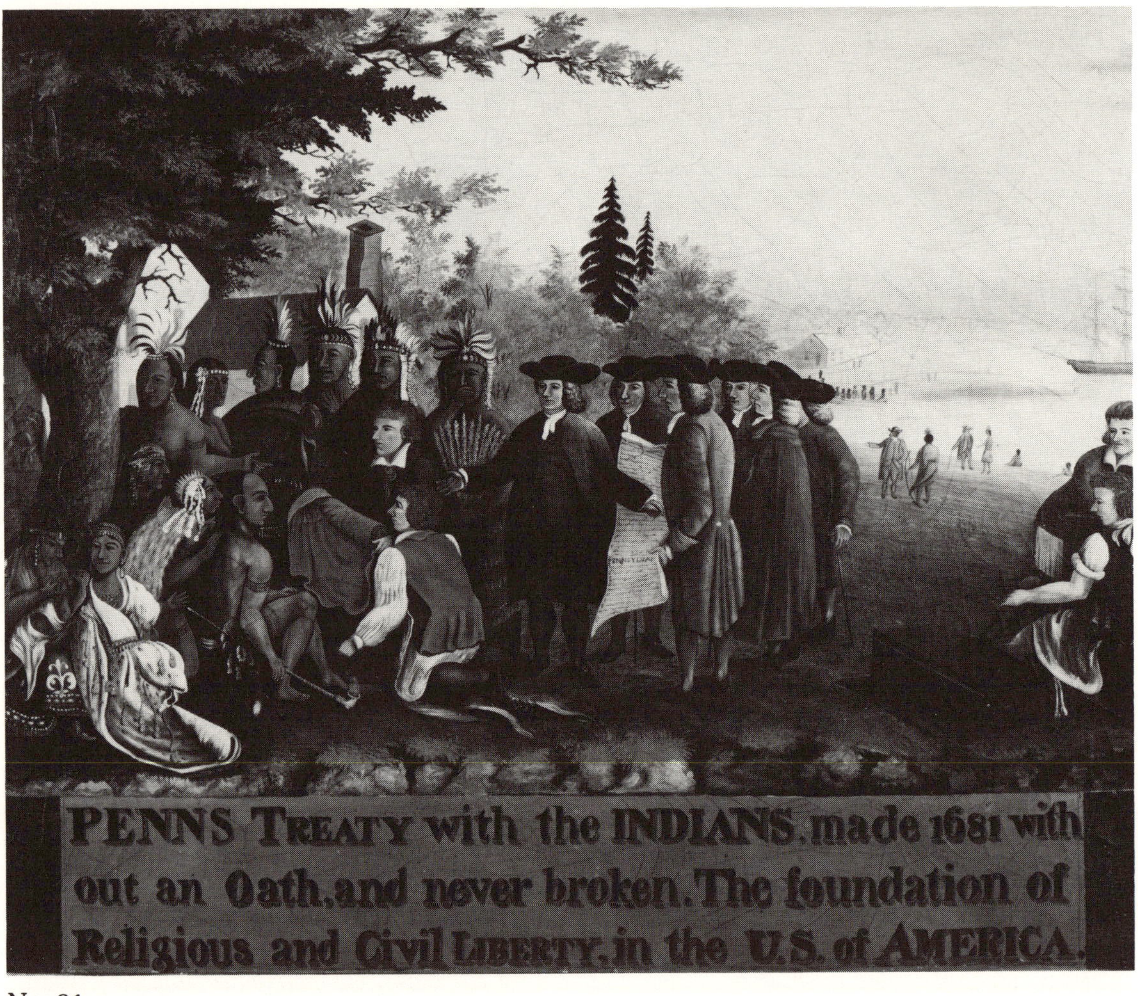

No. 91

PENN'S TREATY, 1840–44. Oil on canvas, 25 × 30½ inches. Lettered at base of canvas: "PENN'S TREATY with the INDIANS, made 1681 with/out an Oath and never broken. The foundation of/Religious and Civil LIBERTY, in the U.S. of AMERICA." Courtesy Shelburne Museum, Shelburne, Vermont.

COMMENT: The statement inscribed on the scroll in earlier *Treaties* is here lettered at the bottom of the canvas. The treatment of the composition is more mature in its subordination of detail, but there is a curious omission: Chief Tamany is missing. In consequence, the Indian spokesman appears to be addressing an invisible person. At one point in the life of this picture the top portion of the canvas was turned over an inch to fit an existing frame, but this condition was corrected by Dr. Arthur E. Bye.

COLLECTIONS: Probably painted for Dr. David Hutchinson, Newtown, Pa., whose mother, Sarah Twining Hutchinson, was the eldest daughter of David and Elizabeth Twining; to his son, Edward Stanley Hutchinson of Newtown; to his daughter, Helen (Mrs. Martin) Caples, Princeton, N.J.; to her three children, including Mary Lloyd (Mrs. M. W.) Barrett, Norfolk, Va., who negotiated for herself, brother, and sister in selling the work to Dr. Arthur E. Bye, Holicong, Pa.; to the Downtown Gallery (Edith Gregor Halpert), New York; to the Shelburne, Museum, Shelburne, Vermont.

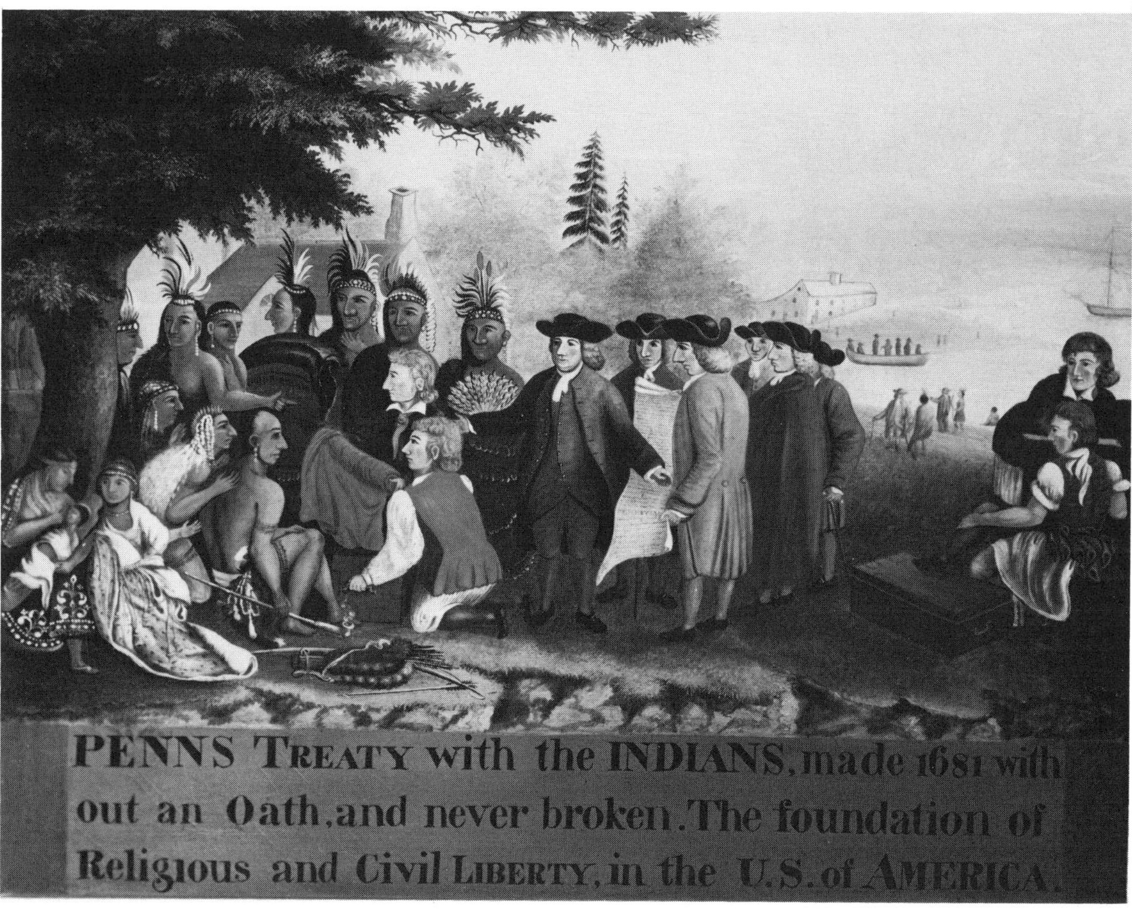

No. 92

PENN'S TREATY, 1840–44. Oil on canvas, 24¼ × 30⅛ inches. Lettered at base, "PENN'S TREATY with the INDIANS, made 1681 with/out an Oath and never broken. The foundation of Religious and Civil LIBERTY, in the U.S. of AMERICA." On the scroll is inscribed the word, "PENNSYLVANIA." Original 1½-inch-wide half-round brown-painted molded frame. National Gallery of Art, Washington; gift of Edgar William and Bernice Chrysler Garbisch.

COMMENT: Very like the preceding, but the absent sachem has returned, his profile emerging from behind the tree, and Hicks has introduced into the foreground a curious snakelike object that is unique in these *Treaties*, along with West's bow and quiver of arrows. He also elaborates on West by adding meticulously detailed ornament to the squaw's skirt and by clothing the maiden beside her in ermine laden with gold tassels.

COLLECTIONS: Original provenance unknown. Acquired by M. Knoedler & Co., New York; to Col. Edgar William and Bernice Chrysler Garbisch, New York; given by them to the National Gallery of Art, Washington, D.C.

EXHIBITIONS: National Gallery of Art, "American Primitive Paintings" (Washington, D.C., part 1, 1954; part 2, 1957); p. 77; American Federation of the Arts, "American Naive Painting of the Eighteenth and Nineteenth Centuries"—Garbisch Collection (Europe and United States, 1968–70), pl. 66 (col.); Chrysler Museum of Art, "The New World, 1620–1970" (Provincetown, Mass., June 12–July 29, 1970), no. 14; Andrew Crispo Gallery, "Edward Hicks: A Gentle Spirit" (New York, 1975), no. 31 (col.); National Gallery of Art, "American Naive Art,"—Garbisch Collection (Washington, D.C., 1978–79).

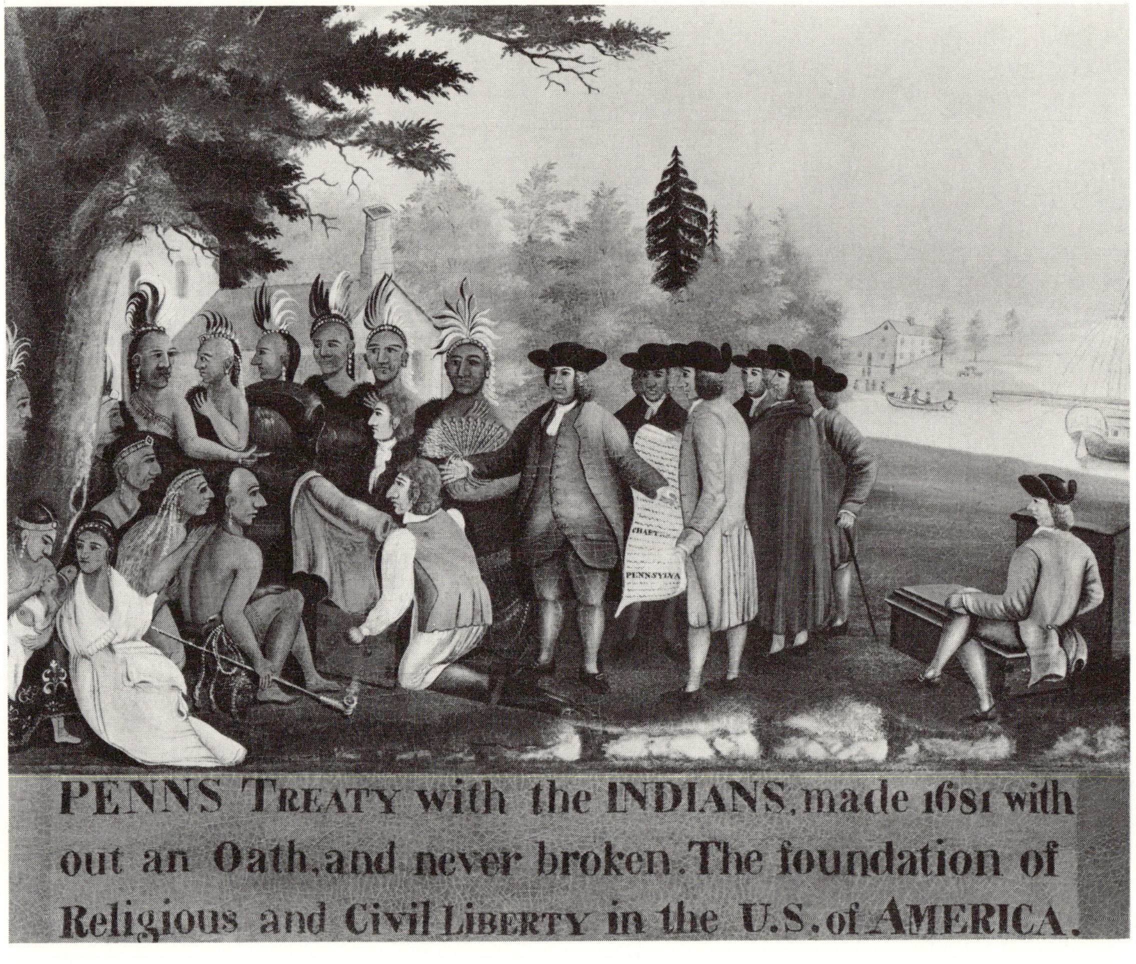

No. 93

PENN'S TREATY, ca. 1846. Oil on canvas, 24 × 30 inches. Lettered at base of canvas: "PENNS TREATY with the INDIANS, made 1681 with/out an oath, and never broken. The foundation of/Religious and Civil LIBERTY in the U.S. of AMERICA." Written on scroll: "PENNSYLVANIA" and "CHARTER." The Dietrich Brothers Americana Corporation of Philadelphia.

COMMENT: The word *Charter* on the scroll, as on several earlier *Treaties,* refers to Penn's 1701 Charter of Privileges, which granted to Pennsylvania's colonists a degree of liberty unusual for the times. Was this canvas painted for a Friend with a strong testimony for simplicity? The ermine and gold tassels have been removed and the two sailors replaced with a gray-clad Quaker. For the social impact of West's *Treaty* see Anthony B. Garvan, "Consequences," in catalogue of *Symbols of Peace,* the Bicentennial Exhibition at Philadelphia, in which this painting appeared.

COLLECTIONS: Original provenance unknown. Acquired by David David, Inc., Philadelphia; to Hirschl & Adler Galleries, New York; to the Dietrich Brothers Americana Corporation of Philadelphia.

EXHIBITIONS: Hirschl & Adler Galleries, "Plain and Fancy/A Survey of American Folk Art" (New York, April 30–May 23, 1970) no. 22 (col.); Allentown Art Museum, "Pennsylvania Folk Art" (Allentown, Pa., 1974, and William Penn Memorial Museum, Harrisburg, Pa., 1974–75), no. 92, p. 32; Andrew Crispo Gallery, "Edward Hicks: A Gentle Spirit" (New York, 1975), no. 28 (not ill.); The Pennsylvania Academy of the Fine Arts and Dickinson College, "Symbols of Peace: William Penn's Treaty with the Indians" (Philadelphia, May 12–September 26, 1976), no. 16, pl. 7.

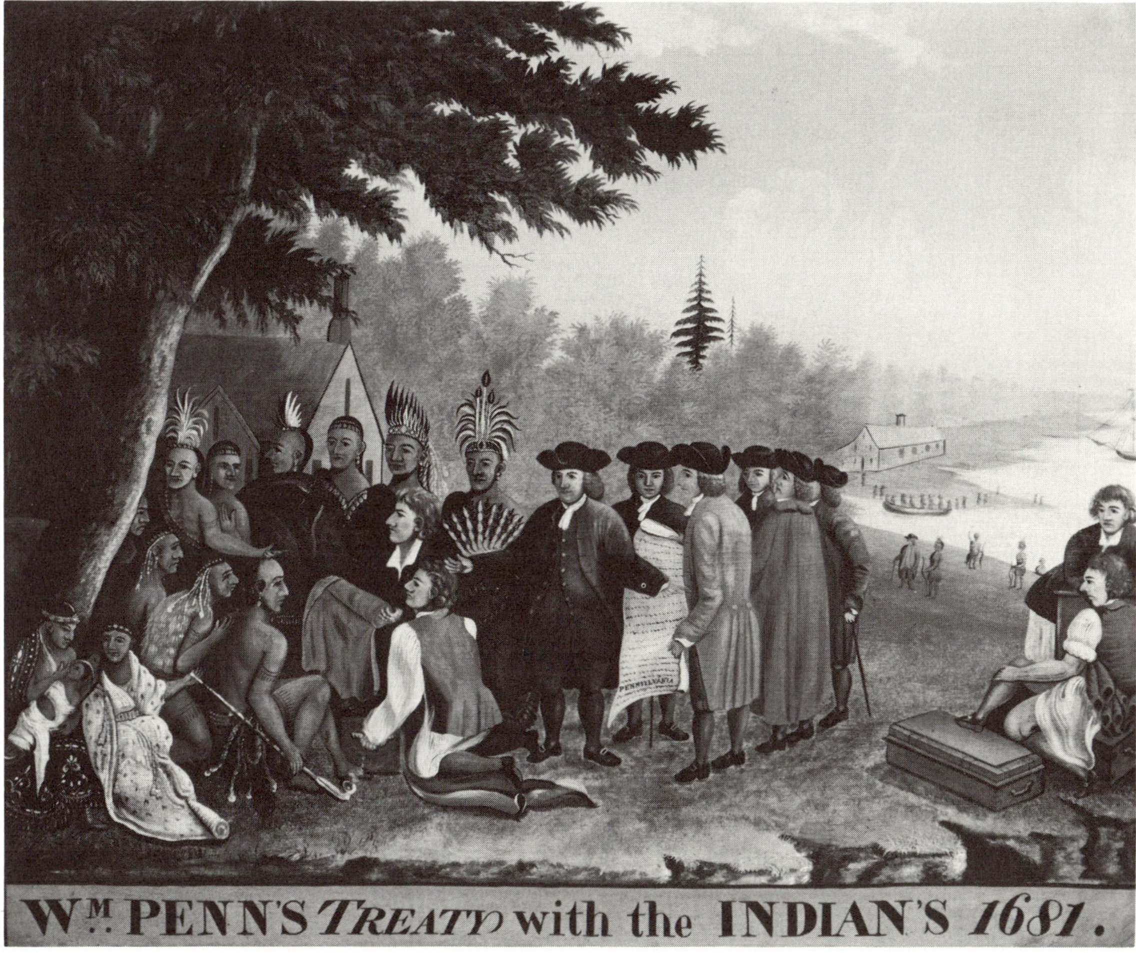

No. 94

PENN'S TREATY, 1847. Oil on canvas, 24¾ × 29¾ inches. Lettered at base: "Wᴹ PENN'S TREATY with the INDIAN'S 1681." On the scroll is inscribed: "PENNSYLVANIA." Curly maple frame not original. Private collection.

COMMENT: Similar to Shelburne and Garbisch versions, but here the reduction of the lettered caption to a single line concentrates attention on the composition and on the color, which is vivid and rich. The date 1681, as in other *Treaty* inscriptions, is an error—it could be no earlier than 1682, the date of Penn's arrival.

COLLECTIONS: Painted for Edward Leedom (brother of David and Charles), Bristol, Pa.; to his great-granddaughter, Mrs. Dora Leedom Cadwallader; purchased by Robert Carlen, Philadelphia; to private collectors. On extended loan to the State Department, Washington, D.C.

EXHIBITIONS: Robert Carlen Gallery, "Edward Hicks Centennial Exhibition" (Philadelphia, 1949); Philadelphia Museum of Art, "Masterpieces from Philadelphia Private Collections" (Phila., May 20–September 15, 1950), no. 38 (not ill.), part 2, for cat. see *Bulletin* 14 (1950); AARFAC, "Edward Hicks," (1960), no. 23, p. 15; Carnegie/Corcoran, "Hicks, Kane, Pippin" (1966–67), p. 28.

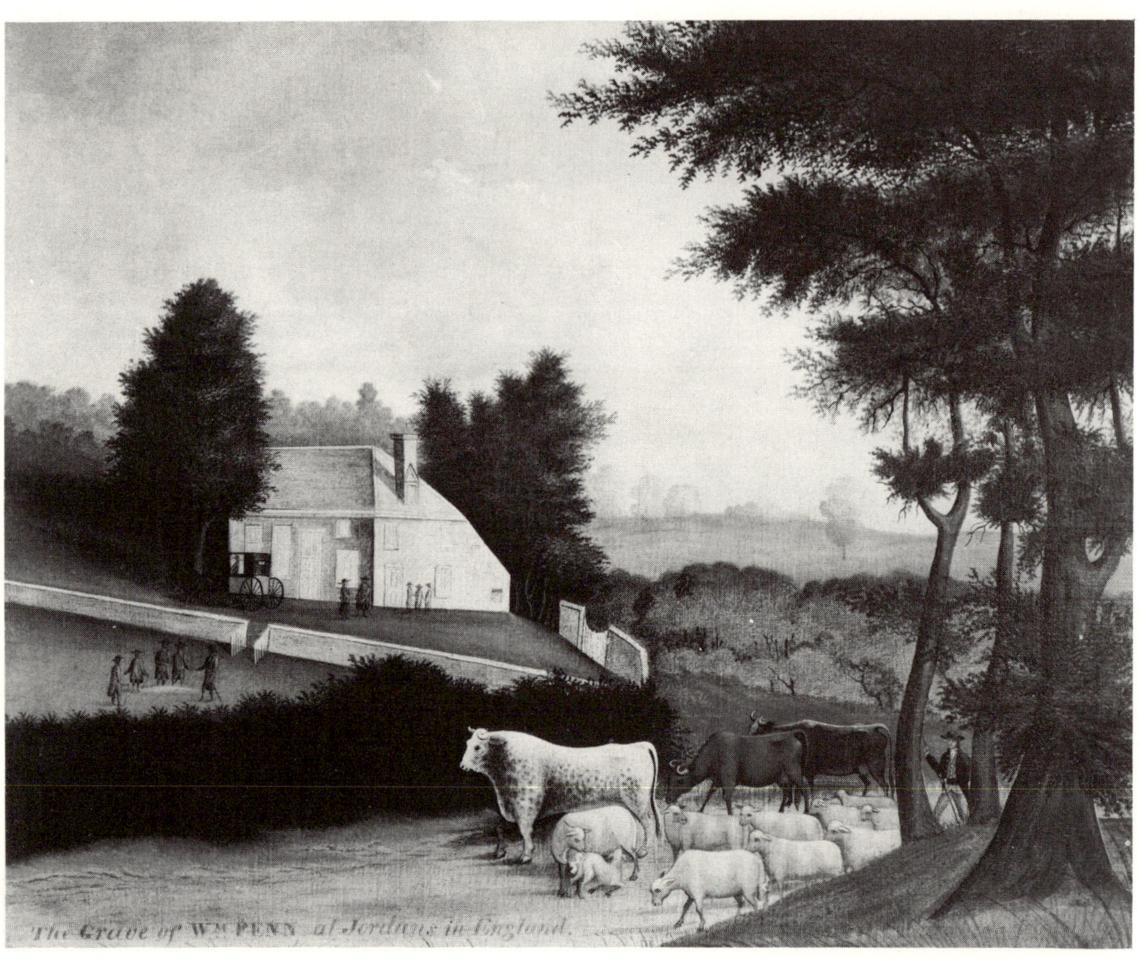

No. 95

THE GRAVE OF WILLIAM PENN, 1847. Oil on canvas, 24 × 30 inches. Inscription on lower left margin of canvas: *"The Grave of* WM PENN *at Jordans in England."* Stenciled on top stretcher on reverse, "Painted by E. Hicks in his 68th year,/ For his friend Ann Drake." Label on reverse reads: "Found in Newtown." Original mahogany veneer frame, 3½ inches wide. Abby Aldrich Rockefeller Folk Art Center.

COMMENT: Hicks derived his composition from Paul Gauci's lithograph after a painting by the Dutch artist Hendrik Frans de Cort. The original is now at the Historical Society of Pennsylvania, Philadelphia, the gift of Granville Penn, descendant of the Founder.

COLLECTIONS: Painted for Ann Drake, Newtown, Pa.; purchased early in the 1930s by Edith Gregor Halpert (Downtown Gallery), New York; to Mrs. John D. Rockefeller, Jr., New York, who gave it to the Abby Aldrich Rockefeller Folk Art Center, Williamsburg, Va.

EXHIBITIONS: Detroit Society of Arts and Crafts (Detroit, Mich., 1932); Albright Art Gallery (Buffalo, N.Y., 1932); Museum of Modern Art, "American Folk Art: The Art of the Common Man in America" (New York, Philadelphia, Providence, R.I., Boston, Kansas City, Mo., Greenwich, Conn., White Plains, N.Y., 1932–34), no. 22; Museum of Modern Art, "Masters of Popular Painting" (New York, 1938), no. 119, ill.; AARFAC Traveling Exhibition, 1958–60; AARFAC, "Edward Hicks" (1960), no. 34, p. 18 (not ill.); AARFAC Traveling Exhibition (March 9, 1961–March 20, 1966); American Museum in Britain, "American Folk Art from the AARFAC" (Bath, England, 1961); "American Folk Art from the AARFAC" (Santa Fe, N.M., Minneapolis, Minn., and Jacksonville, Fla., 1963–65); AARFAC Traveling Show (Hendrix College, Conway, Ark., September 10–November 20, 1965); Southern Allegheny Museum of Art, "Pennsylvania Decorative and Functional Folk Art" (Loretto, Pa., October 14–December 3, 1978), ill.

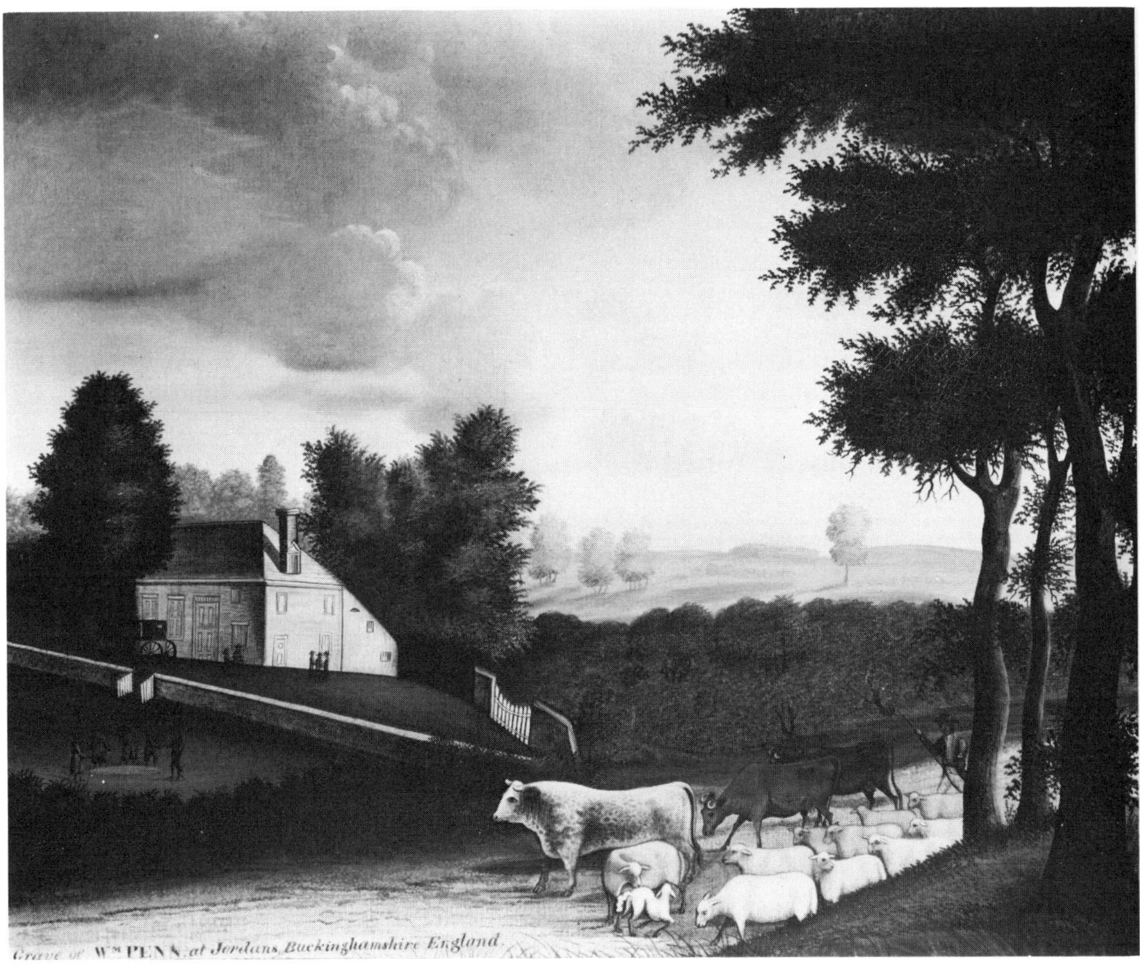

No. 96

THE GRAVE OF WILLIAM PENN, 1847. Oil on canvas, 24 × 30 inches. Lettered on lower left margin of canvas: *"The Grave of* Wᴹ *PENN at Jordans, Buckinghamshire England."* Stenciled on reverse: "Painted by E. Hicks in the 68th year of his age For his friend Elizabeth Cary, 1847." Label on back reads: "From Ann Cary to Sallie Hicks." Original stained wood frame. Private collection.

COMMENT: Almost identical with the preceding version. At first glance these works may be seen as literal landscapes, but the bull that Hicks has introduced as leader of flock and herd probably has a certain symbolic significance, whether conscious or unconscious.

COLLECTIONS: Painted for Elizabeth Cary, Newtown, Pa. Returned to Hicks family as a gift from the Carys; Sarah Worstall Hicks (the painter's granddaughter), Newtown, Pa.; to a private collector.

EXHIBITIONS: Sesquicentennial, Philadelphia, Pennsylvania Academy of the Fine Arts, "A Gallery of National Portraiture and Historic Scenes" (June 13, 1926–October 10, 1926), no. 9; Newtown's 275th Anniversary (1959), no. 4, p. 5; AARFAC, "Edward Hicks" (1960), no. 33 (not ill.).

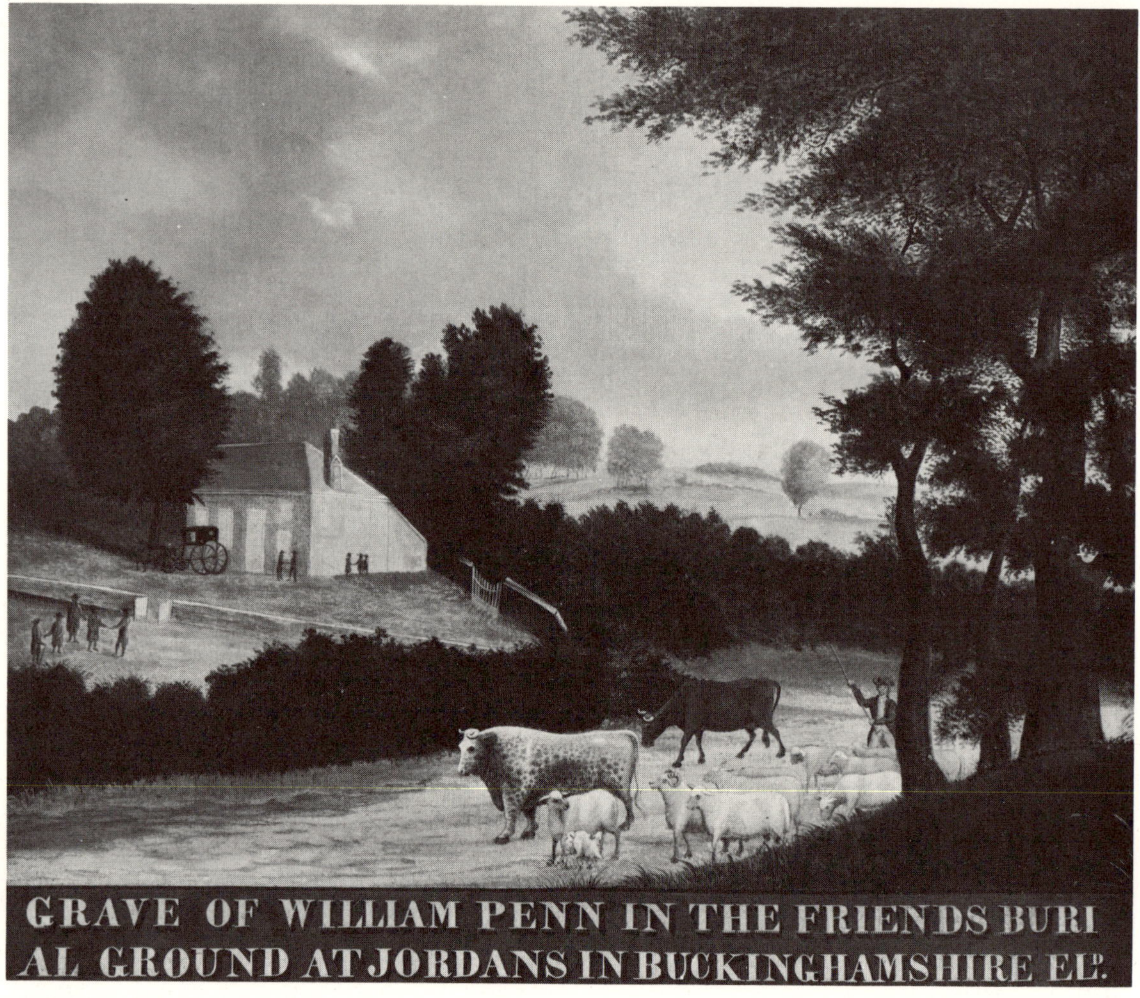

No. 97

THE GRAVE OF WILLIAM PENN, 1847. Oil on canvas, 25¾ × 29⅞ inches. Inscribed at base of canvas, in boldly lettered capitals: "GRAVE OF WILLIAM PENN IN THE FRIENDS BURI/AL GROUND AT JORDANS IN BUCKINGHAMSHIRE EL^D." Inscription on reverse reads (top stretcher): "Painted by Edward Hicks in the 68th year of his age/for his old friend Job Roberts Esq. the practical," continuing on bottom stretcher: "farmer of Montgomery County, Pennsylvania aged 91 /Painted A.D. 1847.)" Flat, undecorated wood frame about 5 inches wide, with rose-headed nails showing on reverse, may be original. Yale University Art Gallery; gift of Robert W. Carle.

COMMENT: The boldly lettered base border, like those on the late *Treaties*, reflects Hicks's signpainting experience. As in the two preceding listings, the artist adds to de Cort's composition the nursing ewe and lamb of his farmscapes and pastorals, but here a ram also joins the herd. Job Roberts (1756–1851), for whom the work was painted, was a noted local character—justice of the peace, pioneer agriculturist, and author of *The Pennsylvania Farmer* (1804).

COLLECTIONS: Job Roberts, Whitpain, Pa.; to Mary Beans, Jenkintown, Pa. (presumably by inheritance); purchased by Robert Carlen Gallery, Philadelphia; to Hirschl & Adler Galleries, New York; purchased by the painter's great-grandson, Robert W. Carle, South Salem, Conn., who gave it to the Yale University Art Gallery, New Haven, Conn.

EXHIBITIONS: Philadelphia Museum of Art, "Masterpieces from Philadelphia Private Collections" (Philadelphia, 1950), no. 39 (not ill.); Carnegie/Corcoran, "Hicks, Kane, Pippin" (1966–67) p. 26; Andrew Crispo Gallery, "Edward Hicks: A Gentle Spirit" (New York, 1975), no. 27 (ill.).

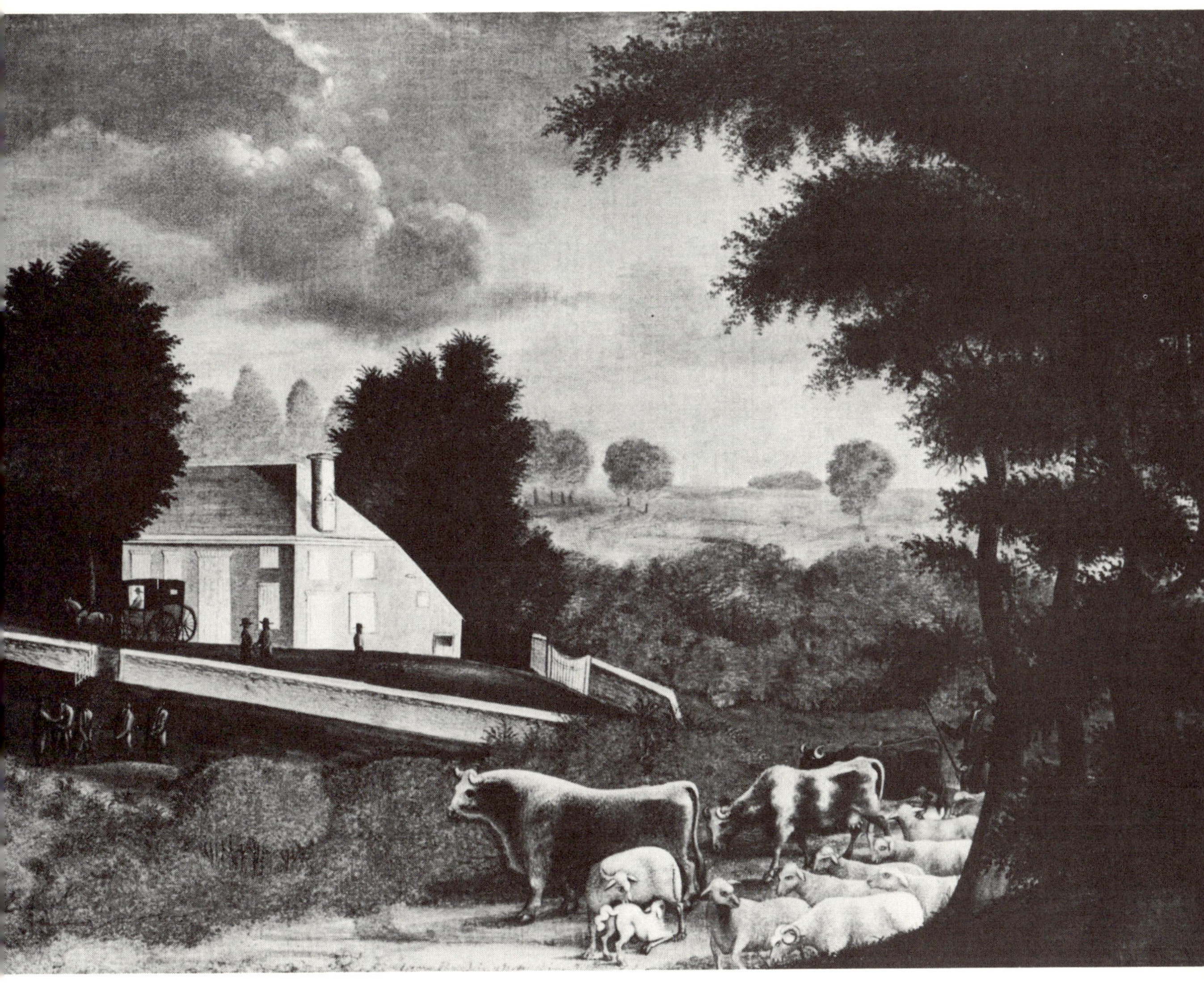

No. 98

THE GRAVE OF WILLIAM PENN, 1847. Oil on canvas, 23½ × 31¼ inches. Inscription on lower left margin is undecipherable except for the word *Buckinghamshire*. Inscribed on reverse, on top and bottom stretchers: "PAINTED BY EDW. HICKS IN THE 68TH YEAR OF HIS AGE/ FOR HIS FRIEND JOSHUA LONGSTRETH OF PHILADA." Molded frame of birds-eye maple, with gilt inner frame, probably original. Private collection, courtesy Andrew Crispo Gallery.

COMMENT: The artist had several contemporaries named Joshua Longstreth. This one was probably the father-in-law of his friend Richard Price. In a letter to the latter Hicks refers to this elderly Friend as "having a taste for farming and cattle," and describes the print source of these works as "the handsomest English landscape I ever saw" (Newtown, undated, FHL). That it was the final resting place of his great hero, Penn, increased its appeal. The bull's darkening coat may reflect the painter's sense of his own approaching death.

COLLECTIONS: Painted for Joshua Longstreth, Philadelphia; in 1920s sold to Mr. and Mrs. Owen Winston, New York, through Edward Hicks Carle (brother of Robert W. Carle); to their son, John Winston, Gladstone, N.J.; to his wife, Mrs. John Winston, Gladstone, N.J.; to their daughter, Mrs. David Callard, Bethesda, Md.; auctioned through Christie's, New York, to a private collector, courtesy Andrew Crispo Gallery, New York.

EXHIBITIONS: United States Section of the International Commission on Folk Art, Exhibition of Folk Art (New York, 1935); Whitney Museum of American Art, "A Century of American Landscape Painting 1800–1900" (New York, January 19–February 25, 1938), p. 25 (captioned "The Home of William Penn"); Squibb Art Gallery, "American Painting: A Gathering from Three Centuries," organized by the Historical Society of Princeton (Princeton, N.J., October 5–31, 1975), no. 29.

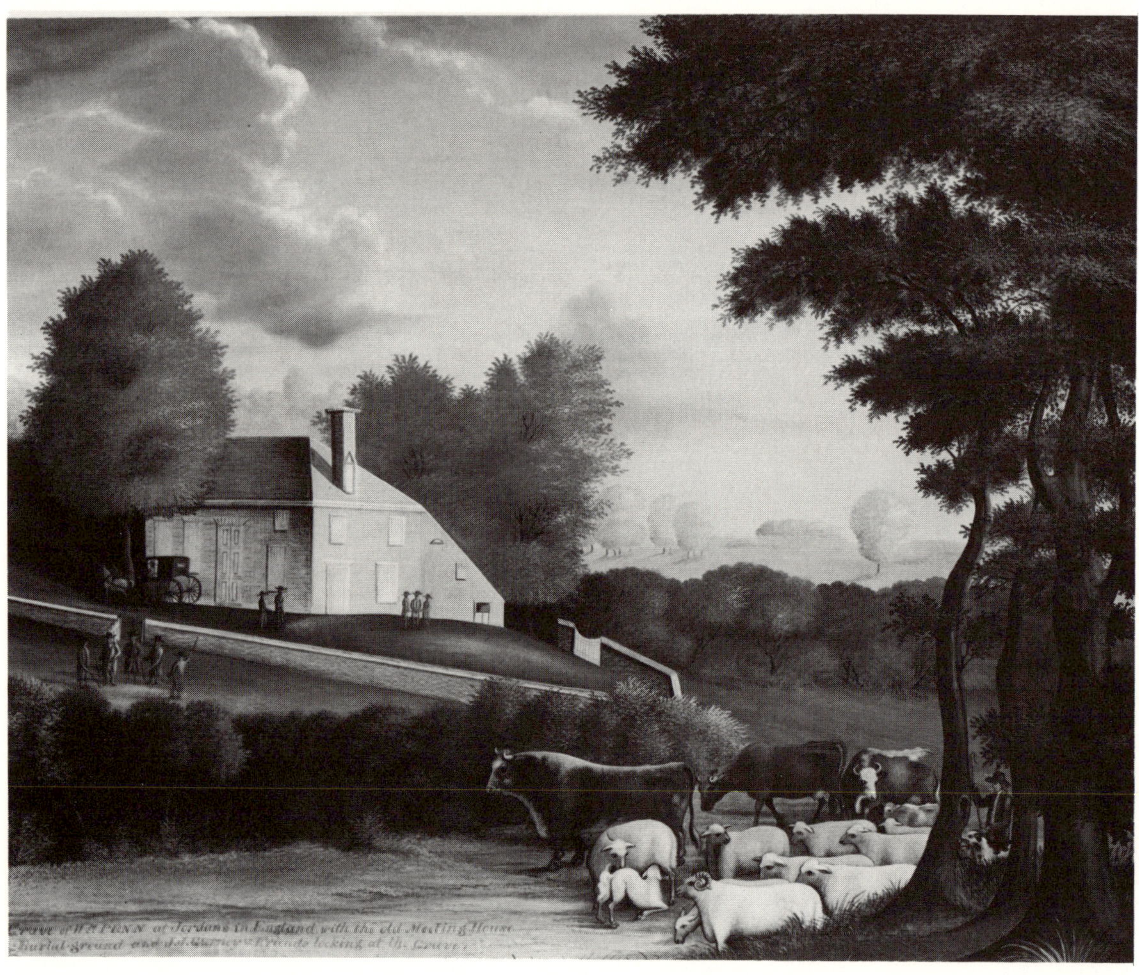

No. 99

THE GRAVE OF WILLIAM PENN, 1847. Oil on canvas, 24 × 30 inches. Inscribed at lower left margin of canvas: *"Grave of WM. PENN at Jordans in England with the old Meeting House/ & Burial. ground and J. J. Gurney & Friends looking at the Grave."* Stenciled on stretcher: "Painted by Edw. Hicks in his 68th year, for his/ Friend William H. Macy of New York 1847." Handwritten label on stretcher reads: "Presented to/ George Macy/ from/ his grandmother/ E. L. Macy." Molded gilt frame presumably original. Collection of the Newark Museum; gift of Mr. and Mrs. Bernard M. Douglas.

COMMENT: The reference to J. J. Gurney, prominent British Quaker, is an error. DeCort had intended to portray the French philosopher Montesquieux. But like all Hicks's historical errors, the mistake is inconsequential in the context of his work, for this is one of the most moving of his canvases, yet still has a light touch—the shepherd's dog with a basket in his mouth, seen through tree trunks at right.

COLLECTIONS: William H. Macy, New York; to his wife, Eliza L. (Jenkins) Macy; to her grandson, George Macy, to Mary Allis, Southport, Conn., dealer; to Mr. and Mrs. Bernard M. Douglas, Stockton, N.J., who gave it to the Newark Museum, Newark, N.J.

EXHIBITIONS: ACA Galleries, "Four American Primitives" (New York, 1972), no. 3 (ill.); Andrew Crispo Gallery, "Edward Hicks: A Gentle Spirit" (New York, 1975), no. 26 (col.); M. Knoedler & Co., "Aspects of a Collection: Eighteenth- and Nineteenth-Century Paintings from the Newark Museum" (New York, April 6–30, 1977); Everson Museum of Art, "The Animal Kingdom in American Art" (Syracuse, N.Y., 1978), no. 53, p. 53 (ill.)

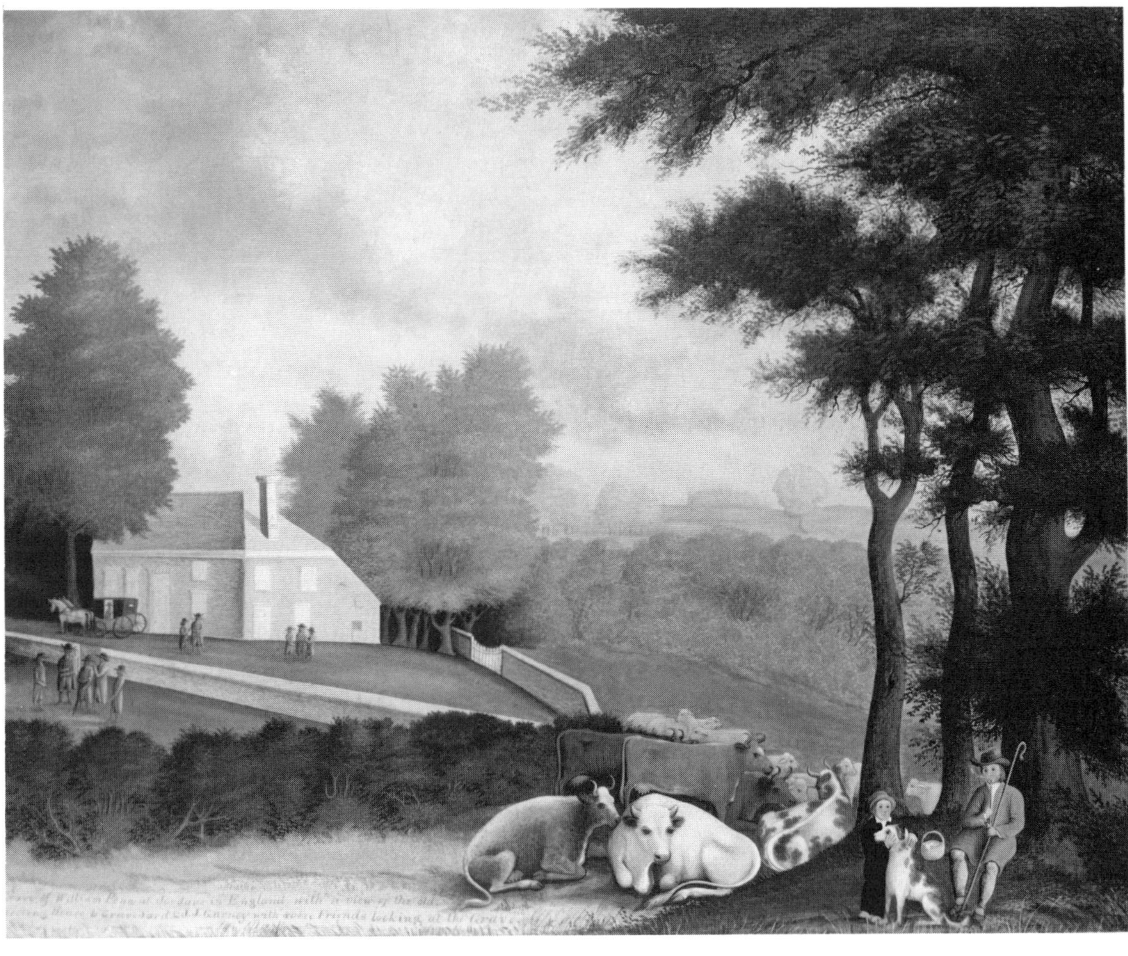

No. 100

THE GRAVE OF WILLIAM PENN, 1847–48. Oil on canvas, 24 × 30. Lettered on lower left margin of canvas: *"Grave of William Penn at Jordans in England with a view of the old/ Meeting House & Grave-Yard, & J. J. Gurney with some Friends looking at the Grave."* Contemporary nineteenth-century curly maple frame probably original. National Gallery of Art, Washington; gift of Edgar William and Bernice Chrysler Garbisch.

COMMENT: Bull, nursing ewe, and ram give place to three reclining cows, the spotted one of which appears in the artist's Cornell and Leedom farmscapes. The shepherd smokes his pipe, a small boy pets the sheep dog, while the basket—carried in the dog's mouth in the Newark version—rests between them on the grassy bank.

COLLECTIONS: Original provenance unknown. Acquired by Robert Carlen, Philadelphia; sold to Edith Gregor Halpert (Downtown Gallery), New York; to M. Knoedler & Co., to Joseph Katz Co., New York; to M. Knoedler & Co., New York; to Edgar William and Bernice Chrysler Garbisch; given by them to the National Gallery, Washington, D.C.

EXHIBITIONS: AARFAC, "Edward Hicks" (1960), no. 32, ill. p. 17.

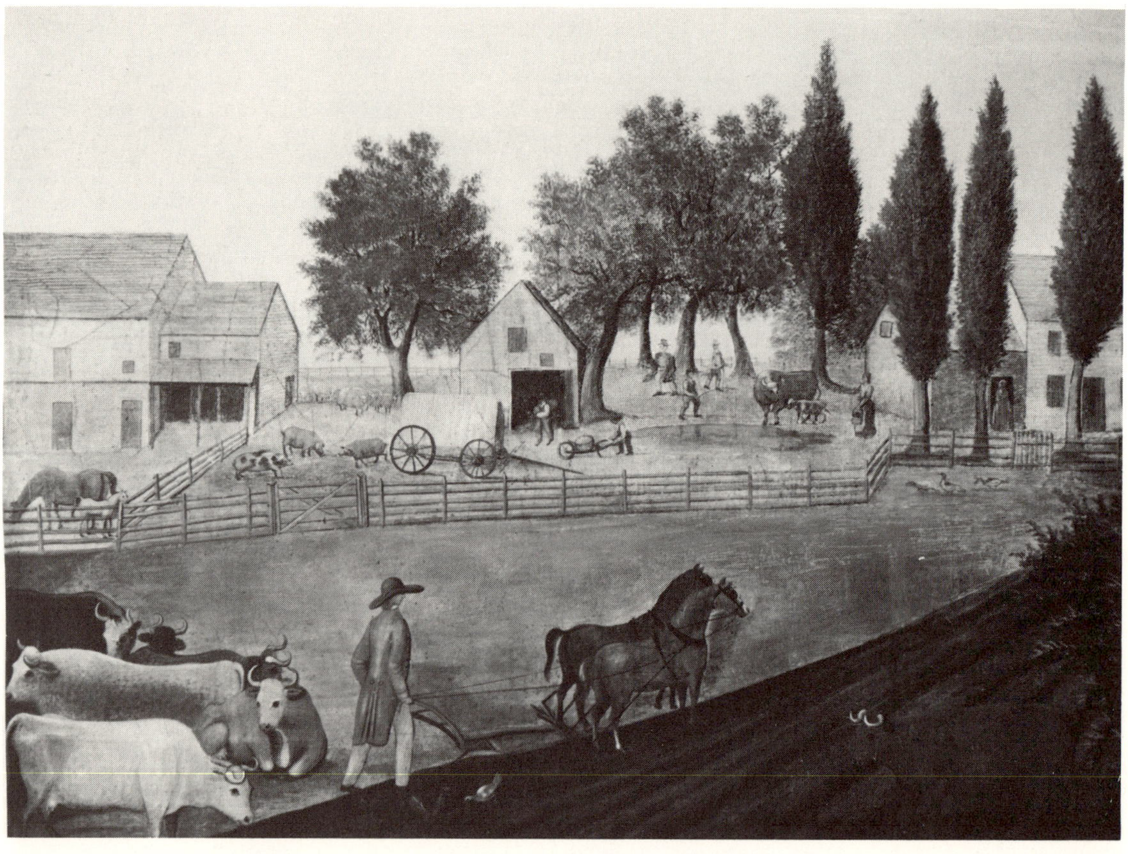

No. 101

THE RESIDENCE OF THOMAS HILLBORN, 1845. Oil on canvas, 23⅝ × 31⅞ inches. Lettered on top rail of stretcher: "Purchased by his son, Cyrus Hillborn, in 1845 when This Picture was painted, by Edward Hicks in his 66th year." Lettered on bottom rail: "The Residence of Thomas Hillborn in Newtown Township/Bucks County Pennsylvania, in the year 1821." Both inscriptions are upside down to the picture. Nineteenth-century pine frame, 4 inches wide, probably original.* Abby Aldrich Rockefeller Folk Art Center.

COMMENT: The first of the farmscapes, this sets the familial tone for later examples. A descendant, Harvey Hillborn Tomlinson, has identified Thomas Hillborn at the plow and his five sons—Thomas, Joseph, Mahlon, Cyrus, and Samuel—at various tasks in the background. Daughter Sarah carries a feed bucket and wife Martha stands in the doorway of the house.

COLLECTIONS: Cyrus Hillborn, Newtown, Pa.; his brother, Samuel Hillborn, Newtown, Pa.; to his son, Isaac Hillborn, Newtown, Pa.; to his daughter, Martha Hillborn Tomlinson, Newtown, Pa.; to her children: Ruth, Caroline, Ella, Anna, and Harvey Hillborn Tomlinson, who sold it to the Abby Aldrich Rockefeller Folk Art Center, Williamsburg, Va.

EXHIBITIONS: Carnegie/Corcoran, "Hicks, Kane, Pippin" (1966–67), p. 21; AARFAC, "Then and Now" (1970); AARFAC, "Arabella's Summer" (Williamsburg, Va., July 30–September 27, 1970); Allentown Art Museum, "Pennsylvania Folk Art" (Allentown, Pa., 1974, and William Penn Memorial Museum, Harrisburg, Pa., 1974–75), no. 94, p. 33.

---

*Wood for frame came from a mantlepiece in the house, says L. L. Beans, *The Life and Works of Edward Hicks* (Trenton, N.J., 1951), p. 19.

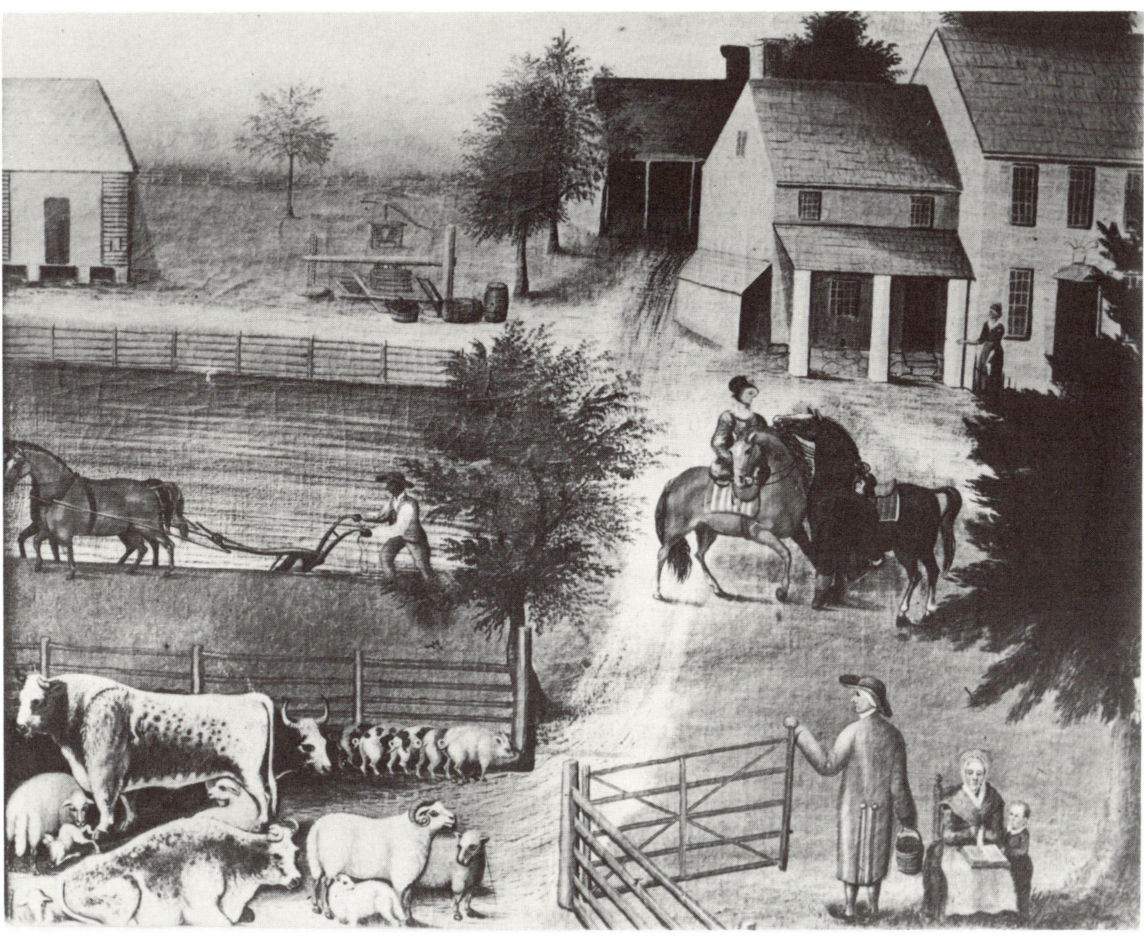

No. 102

THE RESIDENCE OF DAVID TWINING, 1845–46. Oil on canvas, 22¼ × 26⅛ inches. Original brown wood frame without lettering. Private collection.

COMMENT: Perhaps the earliest version of this popular subject. In the right foreground: David Twining, back to viewer, and his wife, Elizabeth, with a Bible on her lap and small Edward Hicks at her knee. The two horses are borrowed from Thomas Sully's *Washington*, but are here mounted by the Twinings' daughter, Mary, and her young husband, Jesse Leedom.

COLLECTIONS: Painted for Thomas and Sarah Twining Hutchinson (eldest of the four daughters of David and Elizabeth Twining), Newtown, Pa., who bought Twining farm in 1826 after the death of Beulah Twining Torbert; to their son, Dr. David Hutchinson, Newtown, Pa.; to his son, Edward Stanley Hutchinson; to his daughter, Rachel Hutchinson Lincoln, Elkhorn, W. Va.; to a private collector.

Photograph courtesy Mercer Museum, Bucks County Historical Society, Doylestown, Pa.

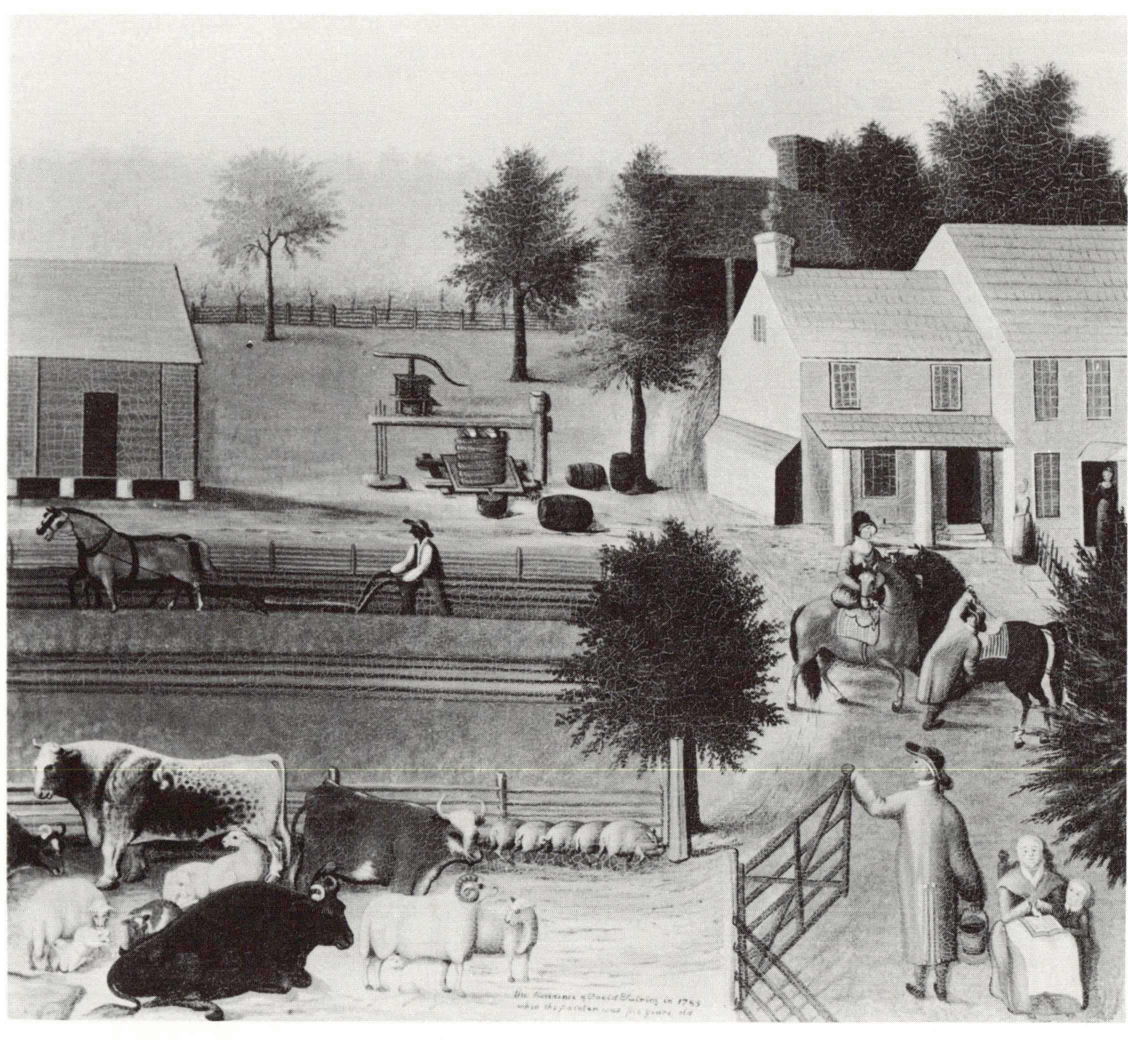

No. 103

THE RESIDENCE OF DAVID TWINING 1785, 1845–46. Oil on canvas, 26 × 29½ inches. Inscription at base of canvas, center: *"The Residence of David Twining in 1785/ when the painter was five years old."* Label on reverse, "Mr. Frank Carpenter." Four-inch double frame, with flat outer portion of dark stained wood and ¾ inch gold leaf inner frame, probably original. Museum of Art, Carnegie Institute, Pittsburgh, Howard N. Eavenson Americana Collection, 1962.

COMMENT: In the hooded doorway of the stone farmhouse stands Beulah (later Torbert), youngest of the Twining daughters. The massive bull in the group of livestock at lower left is similar in pose and color to that in *Landscape with Cattle* and in three examples of *The Grave of William Penn*, pictures on which the artist may have been working at about the same time that he painted this.

COLLECTIONS: Possibly painted for Sarah Hopkins Loines, New York City, only daughter of Elizabeth Twining Hopkins (1765–1832);* to Sarah's daughter, Elizabeth H., who married William Carpenter; to their son, Francis W. Carpenter; to his daughters, Mary, Evelyn, and Grace, North Greenwich, Conn.; to the North Greenwich Congregational Church, Conn.; through Dorothy C. Miller to M. Knoedler & Co, New York; to the Museum of Art, Carnegie Institute, Howard N. Eavenson Americana Collection, Pittsburgh, Pa.

---

*Of this second daughter of the Twinings, Edward Hicks wrote, "She married William Hopkins, a plain, exemplary young friend of Philadelphia and settled in that city. He died some years before his wife, in the house where they were married. Elizabeth died in New York" (*Memoirs*, p. 22). See also Thomas J. Twining, *The Twining Family* (Ft. Wayne, Ind.: Privately printed, 1905), p. 38, and Louise Celestia Mead Feltus, *Our Two Centuries in North Greenwich, Connecticut, 1728–1924* (Privately printed, 1945), p. 55.

EXHIBITIONS: Carnegie/Corcoran, "Hicks, Kane, Pippin" (1966–67), p. 31; M. Knoedler & Co., "What Is American in American Art?" (New York, 1971), no. 45, p. 55; Andrew Crispo Gallery, "Edward Hicks: A Gentle Spirit" (New York, 1975), no. 21, (col.); the Grand Rapids (Iowa) Art Museum, "Themes in American Painting" (Grand Rapids, Iowa, October 1–November 30, 1977), pl. 75, cat. J. Gray Sweney.

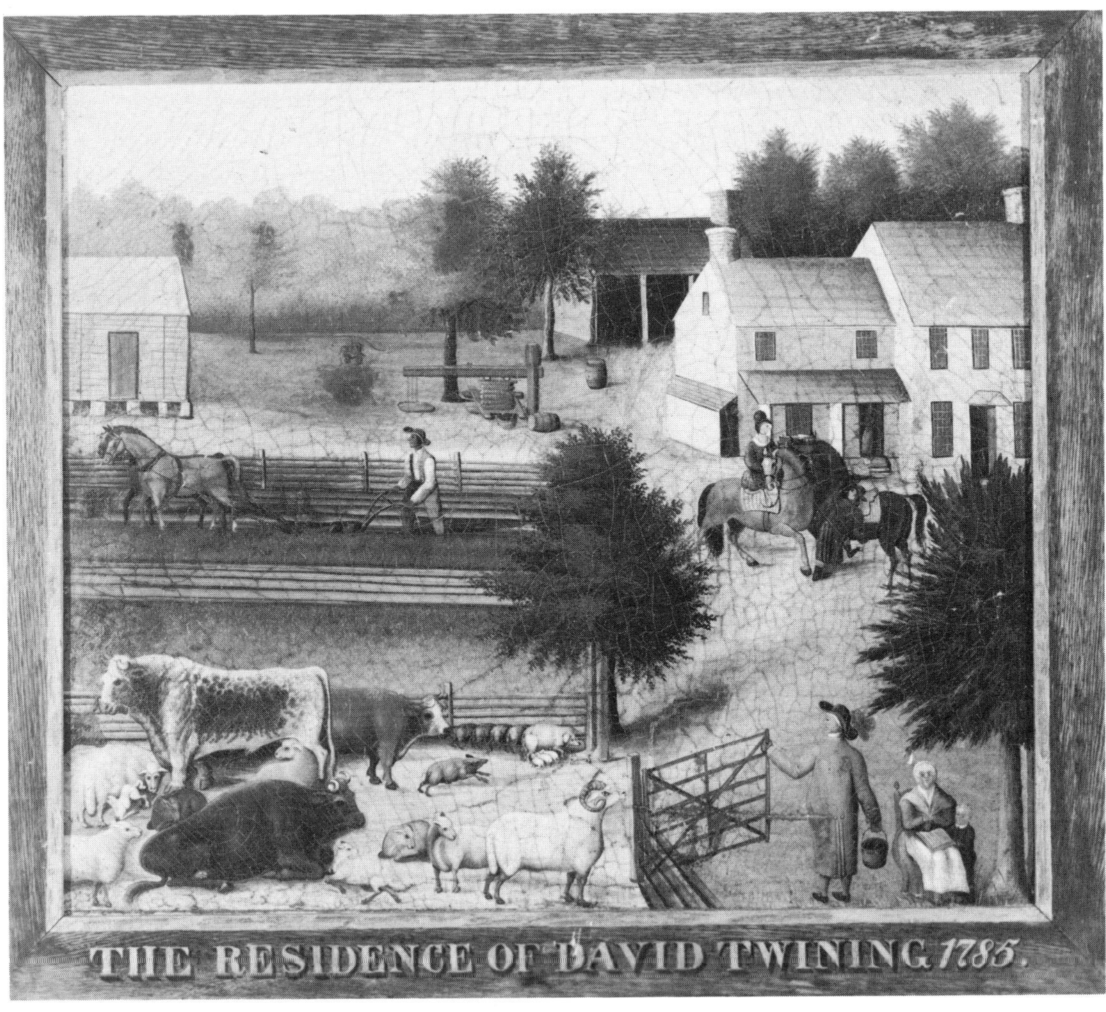

No. 104

THE RESIDENCE OF DAVID TWINING 1785, c. 1846. Oil on canvas, 26 × 29¾ inches. Original frame inscribed, "THE RESIDENCE OF DAVID TWINING *1785*," with gold band near inner edge. Andy Williams.

COMMENT: It is hard to determine whether this or the preceding canvas came first; both are part of a treatment that evolved gradually. In this version a tardy pig races to the trough, while a much smaller piglet hastens to the nursing sow. An impressive ram steps forth from his flock, raising his head as if in greeting.

COLLECTIONS: Provenance unknown, but Robert Carlen recalls examining this when it belonged to an owner in the Frankford area of Philadelphia, before it was acquired by Leonardo L. Beans of Trenton, N.J.; auctioned by Sotheby Parke Bernet, New York, to Andy Williams, Los Angeles, Calif.

EXHIBITIONS: AARFAC, "Edward Hicks" (1960), no. 35, p. 18 (not ill.).

Photograph copyright Sotheby Parke Bernet, Inc., New York.

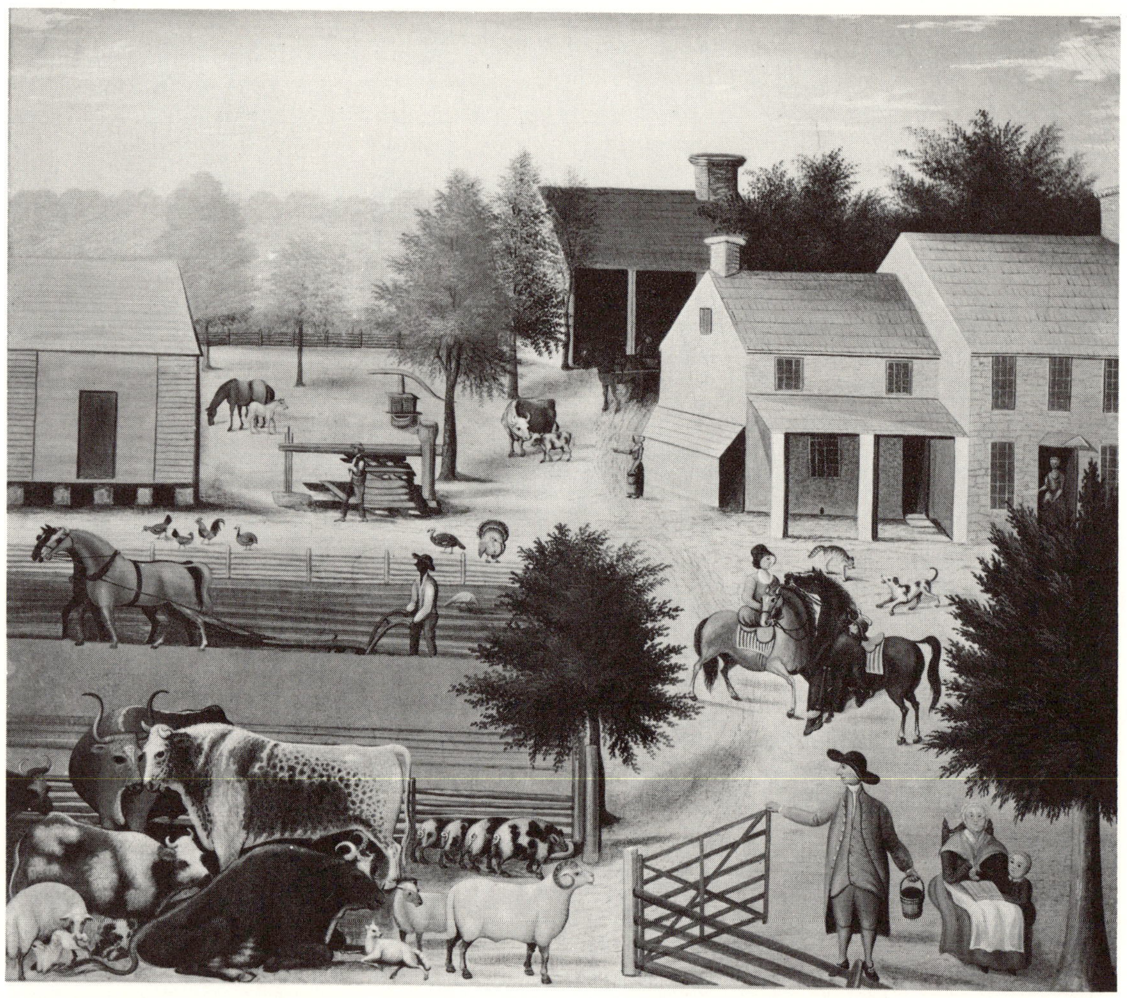

No. 105

THE RESIDENCE OF DAVID TWINING 1787, 1846–47. Oil on canvas, 26½ × 31½ inches. Original painted and stenciled frame, 2¼ inches wide, bordered in gold and with bottom member lettered in gold: "THE RESIDENCE OF DAVID TWINING 1787." Abby Aldrich Rockefeller Folk Art Center.

COMMENT: This work projects the viewer into a world still haunted by the medieval, with its sunless air and penchant for design. But it is a world alive with barking dog and spitting cat, with ewe and lamb, mare and foal, cow and calf, borrowed from woodcuts by Alexander Anderson (Mary C. Black and Jean Lipman, *American Folk Painting* [New York: Clarkson Potter, 1966] pp. 96–97). The figure of David Twining now faces the viewer.

COLLECTIONS: Probably commissioned by Charles Leedom (son of Mary Twining and Jesse Leedom), Newtown, Pa.; his granddaughter, Mrs. Lydia L. Knight, Newtown, Pa.; sold to the sculptor Carl Lindborg, Lansdowne, Pa.; to Mrs. John D. Rockefeller, Jr., New York City, given by her to the Museum of Modern Art, New York City, but subsequently transferred to the Metropolitan Museum. In 1955 it was purchased by her son, David Rockefeller, New York City, who gave it to Colonial Williamsburg, and after the establishment of the Abby Aldrich Rockefeller Folk Art Center at Williamsburg, Va., it became part of that collection.

EXHIBITIONS: Pennsylvania (now Philadelphia) Museum of Art, "The Art of the Common Man," traveling section (Philadelphia, 1933), no. 101.20*; Musée du Jeu de Paume with Museum of Modern Art. "Trois Siècles d'Art aux États Unis" (Paris, 1938); Museum of Modern Art, "Art in Our Time" (New York, 1939), no. 5; Department of Fine Arts, Carnegie Institute, "Survey of American Painting" (Pittsburgh, 1940), no. 24, pl. 32;

---

*This entry is open to question: Mrs. Rockefeller did not purchase the work till April 4, 1933, and in Philadelphia the exhibition ran only from February 4 to March 4, 1933 (AARFAC files).

Pennsylvania State University, "Pennsylvania Painters" (Mineral Industries, University Park, Pa., 1955), no. 19; AARFAC, "Edward Hicks" (1960), no. 36, p. 19 (not ill.); "American Folk Art from AARFAC" (traveling exhibition to Texas, 1962); Hunter Gallery, Chattanooga Art Association, "Old Masters from Southern and Southwestern Collections" (Chattanooga, Tenn., 1964); Museum of Early American Folk Art, *"Time-Life* Exhibition" (New York, 1966); Whitney Museum of American Art, "American Folk Painters of Three Centuries" (New York, 1980), p. 94 (col.).

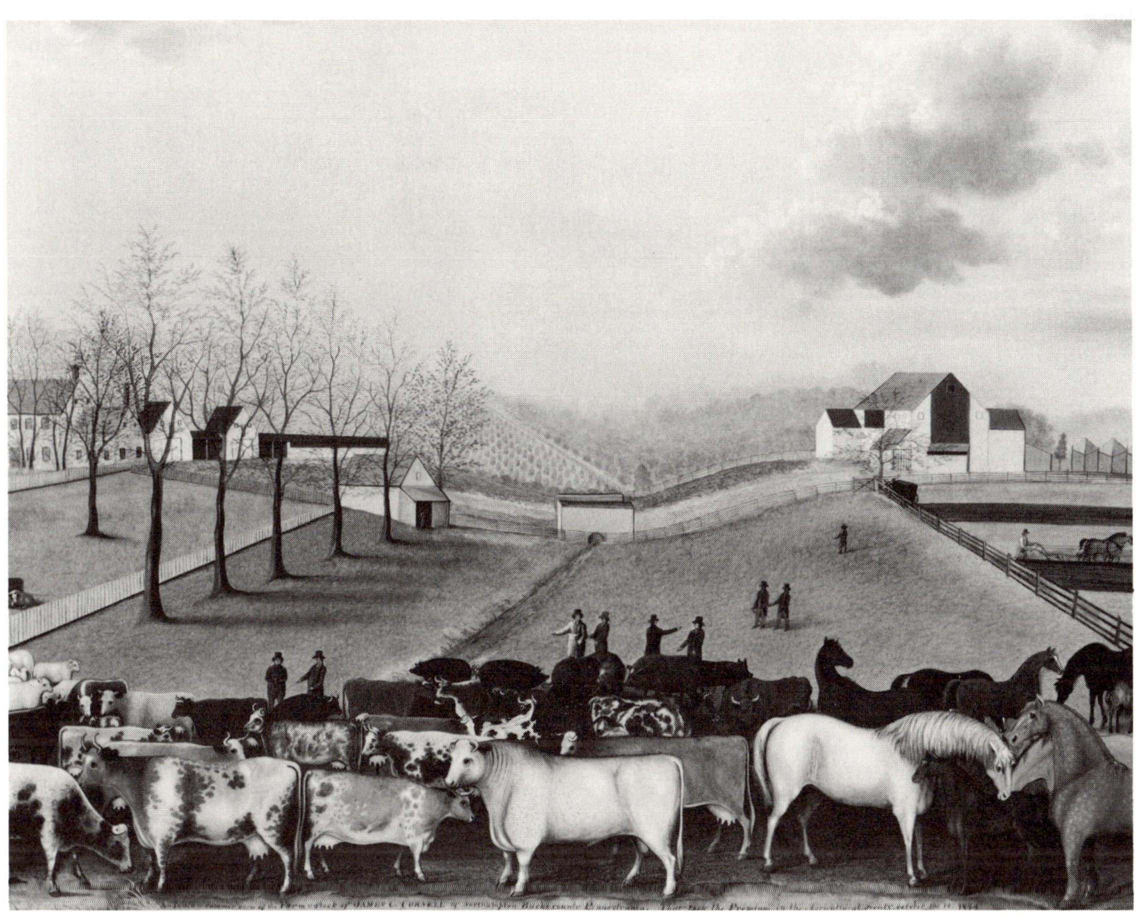

No. 106

CORNELL FARM, 1848: Oil on canvas, 36¾ × 49 inches. Inscribed at base of canvas: "*An Indian summer view of the Farm & Stock of JAMES C. CORNELL of Northampton, Bucks County, Pennsylvania, That took the Premium in the Agricultural Society: October the 12, 1848/ Painted by E. Hicks in the 69th year of his age.*" Original 5⅛-inch beveled oak veneer frame with raised outer edge. National Gallery of Art, Washington; gift of Edgar William and Bernice Chrysler Garbisch.

COMMENT: Master of his domain, James Cornell stands with his brothers, William and Adrian, against a golden landscape, surveying a foreground crowded with prize livestock. The great mottled bull of the artist's last years is here only faintly dappled.

COLLECTIONS: Painted for James C. Cornell, Northampton, Pa.; purchased from his descendants by Mr. and Mrs. J. Stanley Lee, Newtown, Pa.; to Edgar William and Bernice Chrysler Garbisch, New York City; presented by them to the National Gallery of Art, Washington, D.C.

EXHIBITIONS: Bucks County Bi-Centennial Celebration (Doylestown, Pa., 1882); National Gallery of Art, "American Primitive Painting"—Garbisch Collection (Washington, D.C., part 2, March 16–April 28, 1957), pl. 81; Town School Parents' Association, "Art Our Children Live With: a Loan Exhibition of American Art (Downtown Gallery, New York, December 9–21, 1957), no. 20; Brussels Universal and International Exhibition, "American Art" (Brussels, Belgium, April 17–October 18, 1958), no. 84 (ill.); AARFAC, "Edward Hicks" (1960), no. 37, p. 19 (not ill.); American Federation of Arts, "101 Masterpieces of American Primitive Painting," traveling exhibition through United States (1961–64), pl. 75; Carnegie/Corcoran, "Hicks, Kane, Pippin" (1966–67), no. 33 (col.); American Federation of Arts traveling exhibition, "American Naive Painting of the 18th and 19th Centuries" (Europe and U.S., 1968–70), pl. 73 (col.); Chrysler Museum of Art, "The New World, 1620–1970" (Provincetown, Mass., 1970), no. 15; M. Knoedler & Co., "What is American in American Art?" (New York, 1971), no. 46, p. 34 (col.); "Our Land, Our Sky, Our Water," American and Canadian Art organized for the International Exposition (Spokane, Wash., May 4–November 3, 1974), no. 15; National Gallery of Art, "American Naive Art"—Garbisch Collection (Washington, D.C., 1978–79); Whitney Museum of American Art, "American Folk Painters of Three Centuries" (February 26–May 13, 1980), p. 96 (col.); Terra Museum of American Art, "Life in 19th Century America" (Evanston, Ill., December 19, 1981–March 14, 1982).

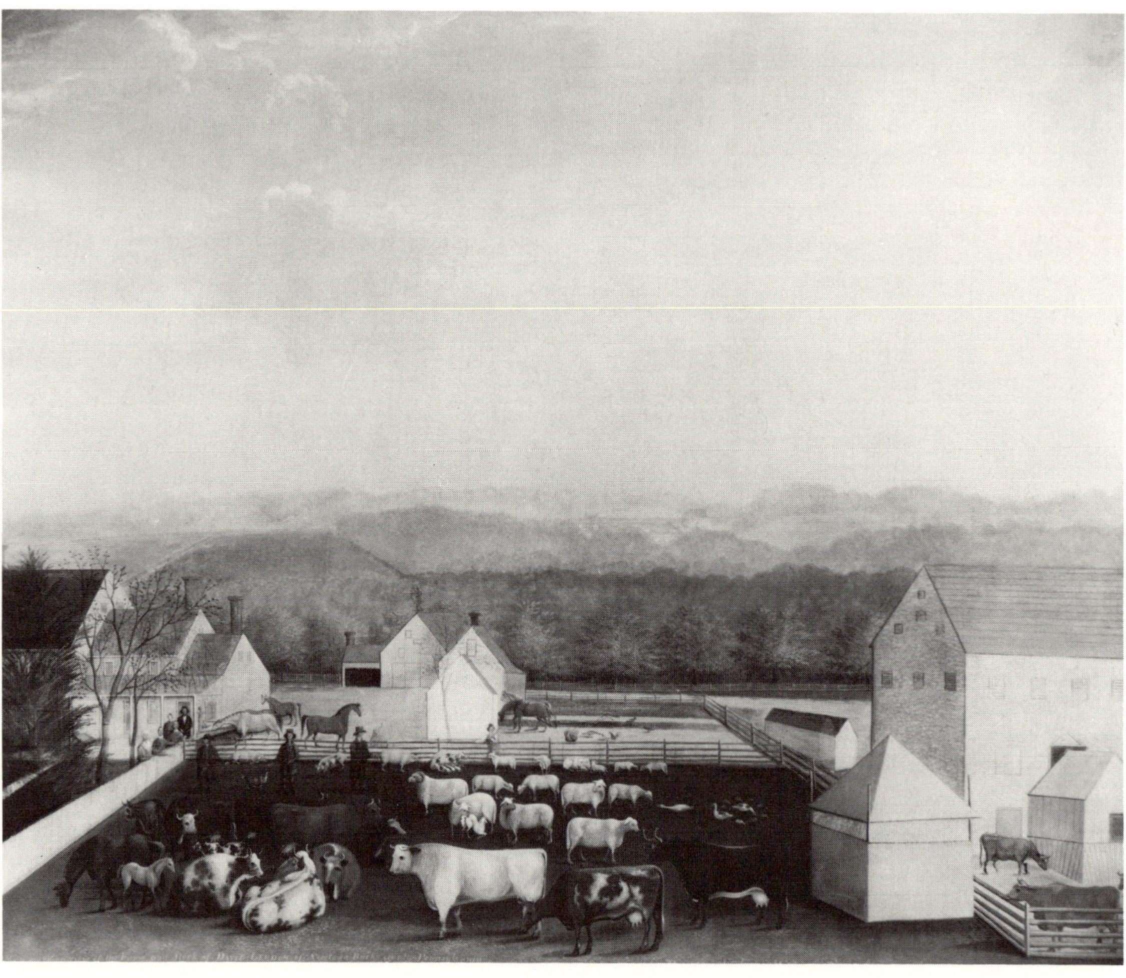

No. 107

LEEDOM FARM, 1849. Oil on canvas, 40 × 49 inches. Inscribed at base of canvas: "*A May morning view of the Farm and Stock of DAVID LEEDOM of Newtown, Bucks County—Pennsylvania/ with a representation of Himself. Wife. Father. Mother. Brothers. Sisters and Nephew.*" and "*Painted by Edw. Hicks in the 70th year of his age.*" Original mahogany veneered frame, 4½ inches wide and 2 inches deep. Abby Aldrich Rockefeller Folk Art Center.

COMMENT: Hicks's last farmscape is a summation of earlier examples. The plow, an active element in the Hillborn, Twining, and Cornell canvases, is here unharnessed, its driver has vanished, and the horses stand before the door of the red-roofed stable awaiting their reward for patient service. Of the surrounding farm buildings a British critic has written, "They have somehow been transformed into symbols of order and belief, as if they are places of worship" (Robert Melville, "American Museum in Britain," *Architectural Review* 29 [1961]:422).

COLLECTIONS: Painted for David Leedom, son of Jesse and Mary Twining Leedom. Sold by a descendant to Alfred Conrad, Newtown dealer, from whom it was purchased by Mr. and Mrs. John Law Robertson, Scranton, Pa.; from Mrs. Robertson, through M. Knoedler & Co., New York, to the Abby Aldrich Rockefeller Folk Art Center, Williamsburg, Va.

EXHIBITIONS: AARFAC, "Edward Hicks" (1960), no. 38 (col. cover); American Museum in Britain, "American Folk Art from the AARFAC" (Bath, Eng., 1961); Loan Exhibition from the AARFAC (Fort Worth, El Paso, and Austin, Texas, 1962); "American Folk Art from the AARFAC" (Santa Fe, N.M., Minneapolis, Minn., and Jacksonville, Fla., 1963–65); AARFAC Traveling Show (Hendrix College, Conway, Ark., 1965); Carnegie/Corcoran, "Hicks, Kane, Pippin" (1966–67), p. 35 (col.); High Museum of Art Antiques Show, Atlanta, "Folk Art in America: A Living Tradition: Selections from the AARFAC" (Atlanta, Ga., September 15–October 31, 1974), p. 43.

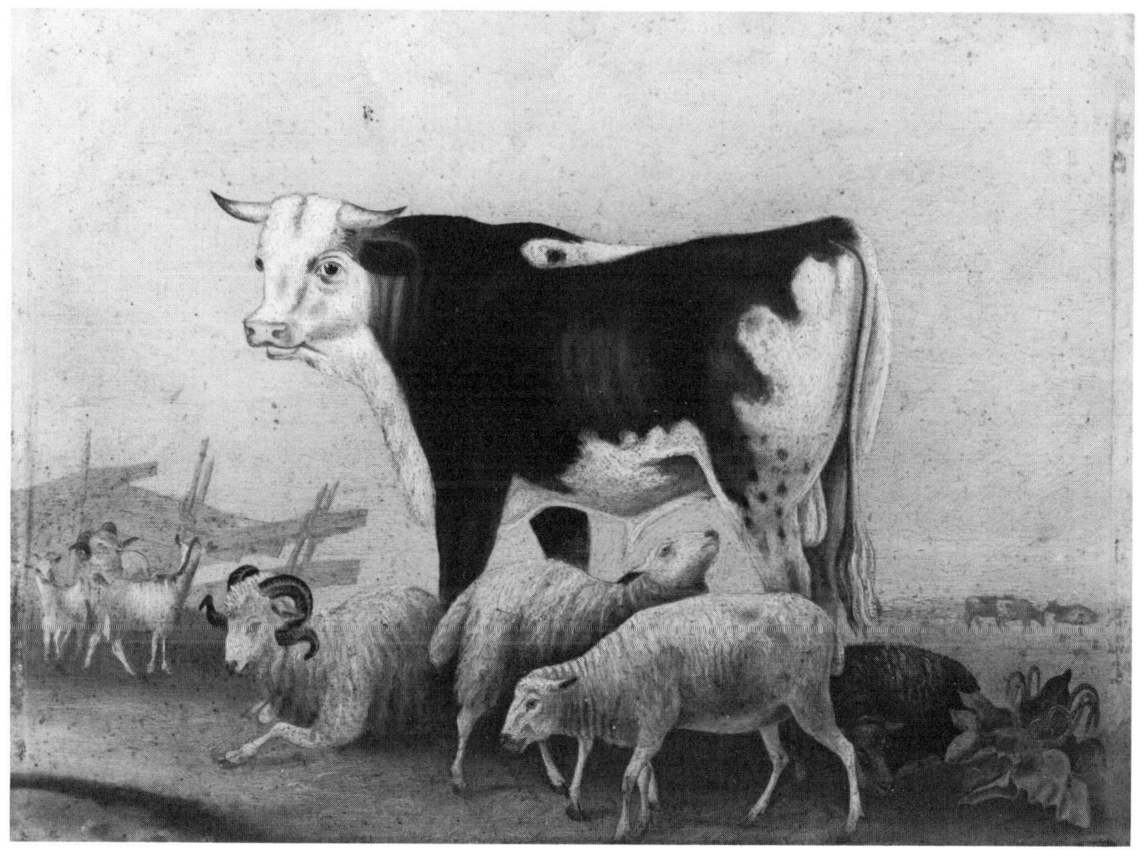

No. 108

JAMES CORNELL'S PRIZE BULL, 1846. Oil on poplar panel, 12 × 16⅛ inches. Signed on reverse, "Prize Bull/ Edw. Hicks/1846." Receipt removed from reverse reads, "James Cornell/To Edward Hicks De/To painting his prize bull, $15.00/Rec" 5th mo 16th 1846 the above in full/of all demands by me/Edward Hicks." Contemporary nineteenth-century molded wood frame, 1¼ inches wide, probably original. Abby Aldrich Rockefeller Folk Art Center.

COMMENT: This shows the influence of *The Young Bull* by Paul Potter (1625–54), Dutch landscape artist, apparently through the medium of instruction sheets by Gustav Canton offering models of farmyard animals. The prizewinner is surrounded by sheep and goats. "This goat," remarks Julius Held of the impressive old sire to the left, "is a stock-in-trade of almost all pastoral scenes derived from Dutch masters such as P. Potter and A.v.d. Velde" ("Edward Hicks and the Tradition," *Art Quarterly* 14 (1951):126).

COLLECTIONS: Painted for James C. Cornell, Northampton Township, Bucks County, Pa.; sold, presumably by a descendant, to Mrs. Lillian Harney, dealer in Trenton, N.J.; to the Abby Aldrich Rockefeller Folk Art Center, Williamsburg, Va.

EXHIBITIONS: AARFAC, "Edward Hicks" (1960), no. 31, p. 17 (not ill.); Carnegie/Corcoran, "Hicks, Kane, Pippin" (1966–67), p. 22; AARFAC, "Pets and Other Beasts" (Williamsburg, Va., 1969).

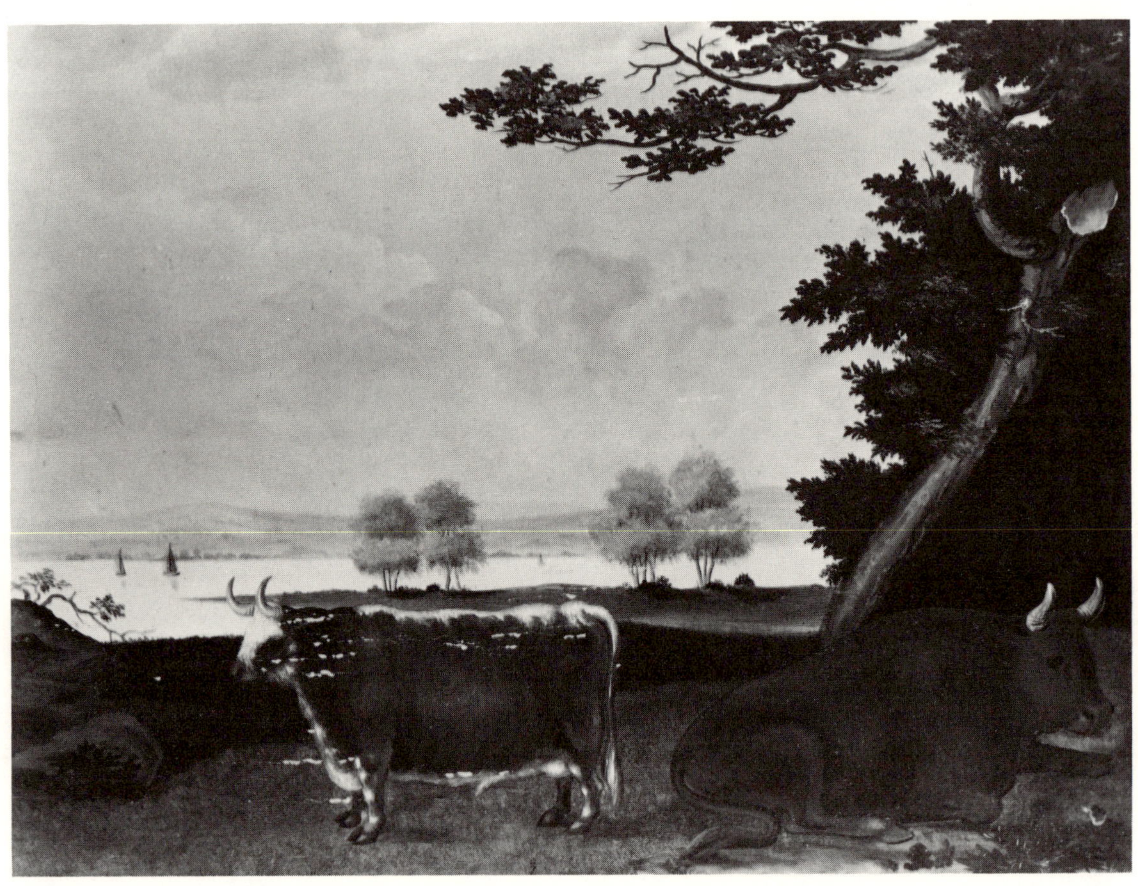

No. 109

PASTORAL LANDSCAPE, ca. 1846. Oil on wood panel, 16 × 21 inches. Block-cornered frame presumably original. Coe Kerr Gallery.

COMMENT: The crouching bovine, luminous clouds, and large weed in the right foreground are all characteristics of the Dutch landscape school. But the diagonal thrust of the tree is distinctively Hicks's own, appearing in several of his *Peaceable Kingdoms* of the late 1840s (Nos. 51, 52, and 57).

COLLECTIONS: Original provenance unknown. Private collection, Santa Fe, N.M., until 1978; to Hirschl & Adler Galleries, New York; to Coe Kerr Gallery, New York.

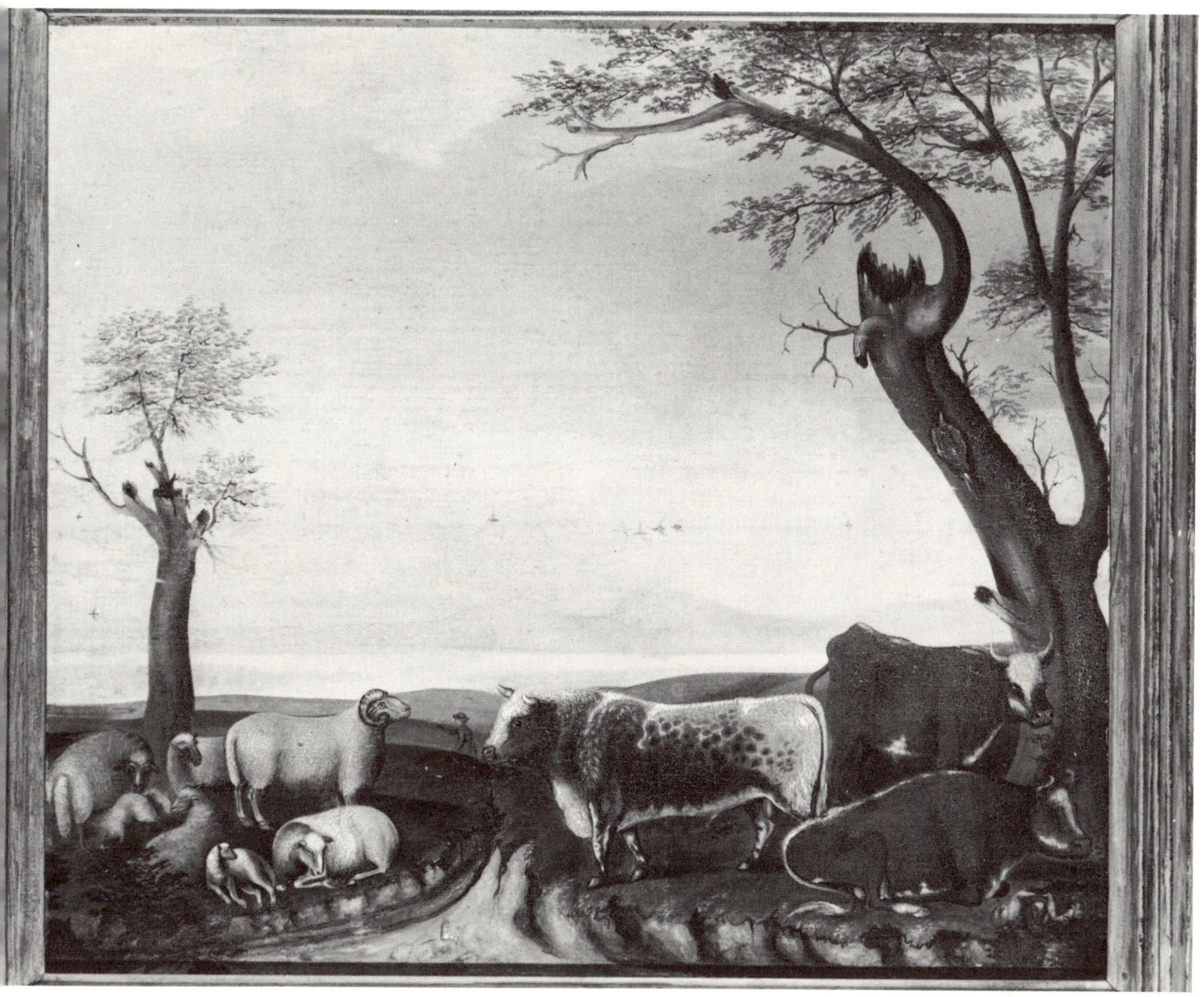

No. 110

LANDSCAPE WITH CATTLE, ca. 1846. Oil on wood panel, 17⅝ × 20⅝ inches.* Compound-molded frame, refinished to natural pinc, appears contemporary. Private collection.

COMMENT: A composition curiously divided between cattle to the right and sheep to the left, all seven of the latter appearing in the same poses as in the Beans' *Residence of David Twining* (No. 104). Human participation is minimal. But the pollarded trees suggest husbandry—though it is that of the Low Countries rather than Pennsylvania—while in the distance, between the heads of bull and ram, is a diminutive farmer, by tradition Squire Hart himself.

COLLECTIONS: Painted for Samuel Hart of Doylestown, Pa., a friend of the artist (see No. 42). Inherited by Natalie Hart, Villanova, Pa.; to her sister, Mrs. J. H. Ward Hinkson, Haverford, Pa.; sold to Robert Carlen Gallery, Philadelphia; to a private collector.

EXHIBITIONS: Bucks County Bi-Centennial Celebration (Doylestown, Pa., 1882); Carnegie/Corcoran, "Hicks, Kane, Pippin" (1966–67), p. 23 (ill.).

---

*Bottom width; top width 20¾ inches.

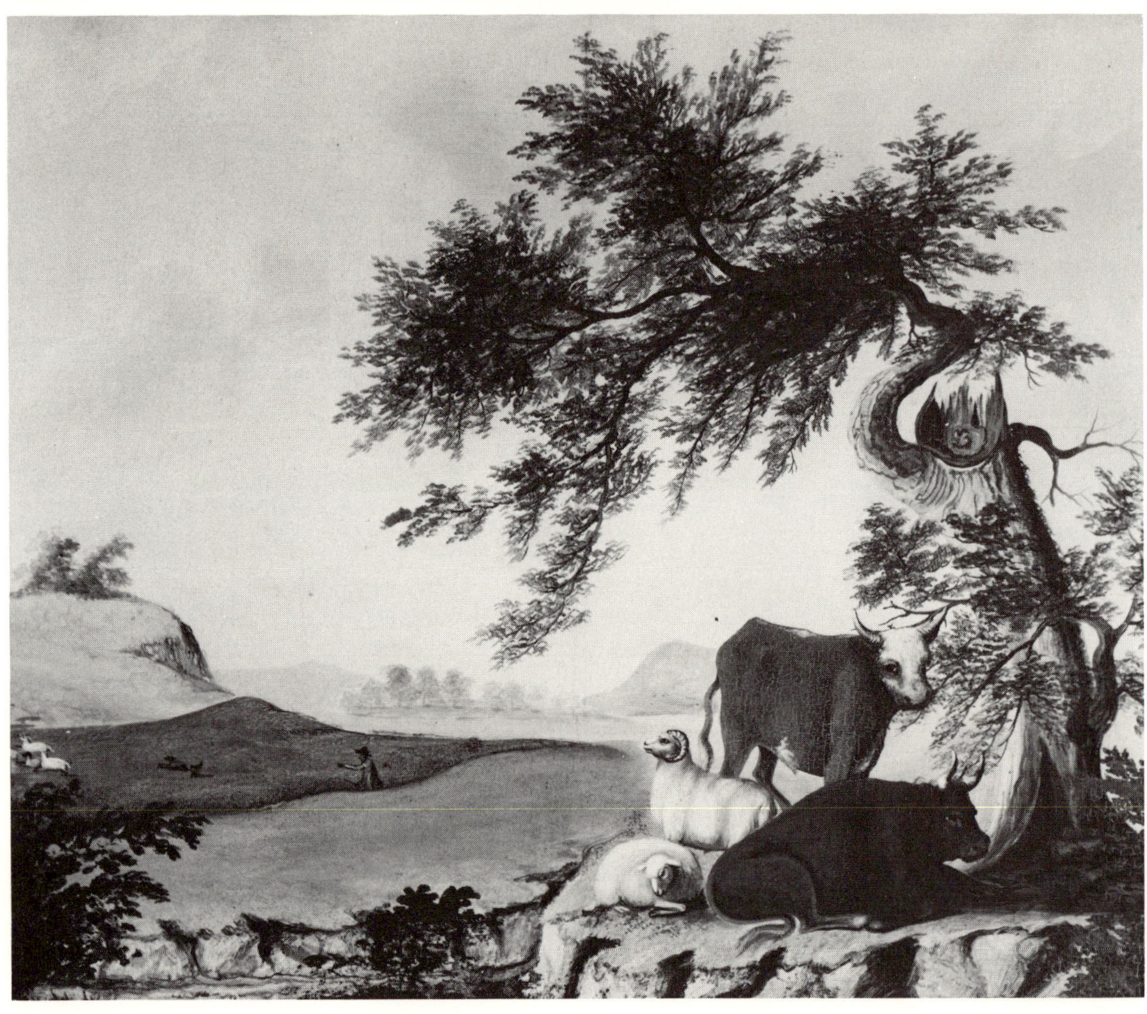

No. 111

PASTORAL LANDSCAPE, ca. 1846. Oil on poplar panel, 16¾ × 20 inches. Original frame was by Hicks, but has been replaced by contemporary nineteenth-century veneered frame 1⅞ inches wide. Abby Aldrich Rockefeller Folk Art Center.

COMMENT: A dramatic tree gives this work a vigor not present in Hicks's other pastorals. The panel appears to have been done in two half-sections joined vertically down the center. On the reverse are sketches similar to those on an early *Washington*. Charles Leedom, the original owner, told his granddaughter that prior to painting the panel Hicks had used it to experiment with color.

COLLECTIONS: Painted for Charles Leedom, Newtown, Pa., brother of David and son of Jesse and Mary Twining Leedom; to his granddaughter, Mrs. Lydia L. Knight, Newtown, Pa.; sold to Carl Lindborg, Lansdowne, Pa.; Down-town Gallery (Edith Gregor Halpert), New York; to John D. Rockefeller, Jr., New York, for Mrs. Abby Aldrich Rockefeller's Folk Art Collection, Williamsburg, Va.; loaned back to Mrs. Rockefeller to decorate cottage at Bassett Hall; purchased by John D. Rockefeller and later returned as a gift to the Abby Aldrich Rockefeller Folk Art Center and Colonial Williamsburg (1956).

EXHIBITIONS: Museum of Modern Art, "Masters of Popular Painting" (New York, 1938), no. 120, Courtesy Ludwell Paradise House; AARFAC, "Edward Hicks" (1960), no. 32, p. 17 (not ill.); Pine Manor Junior College, "Social and Cultural Aspects of American Life" (Wellesley, Mass., 1963); Arkansas Art Center Artmobile (Little Rock, Ark., 1966); Carnegie/Corcoran, "Hicks, Kane, Pippin" (1966–67), p. 24 (ill.).

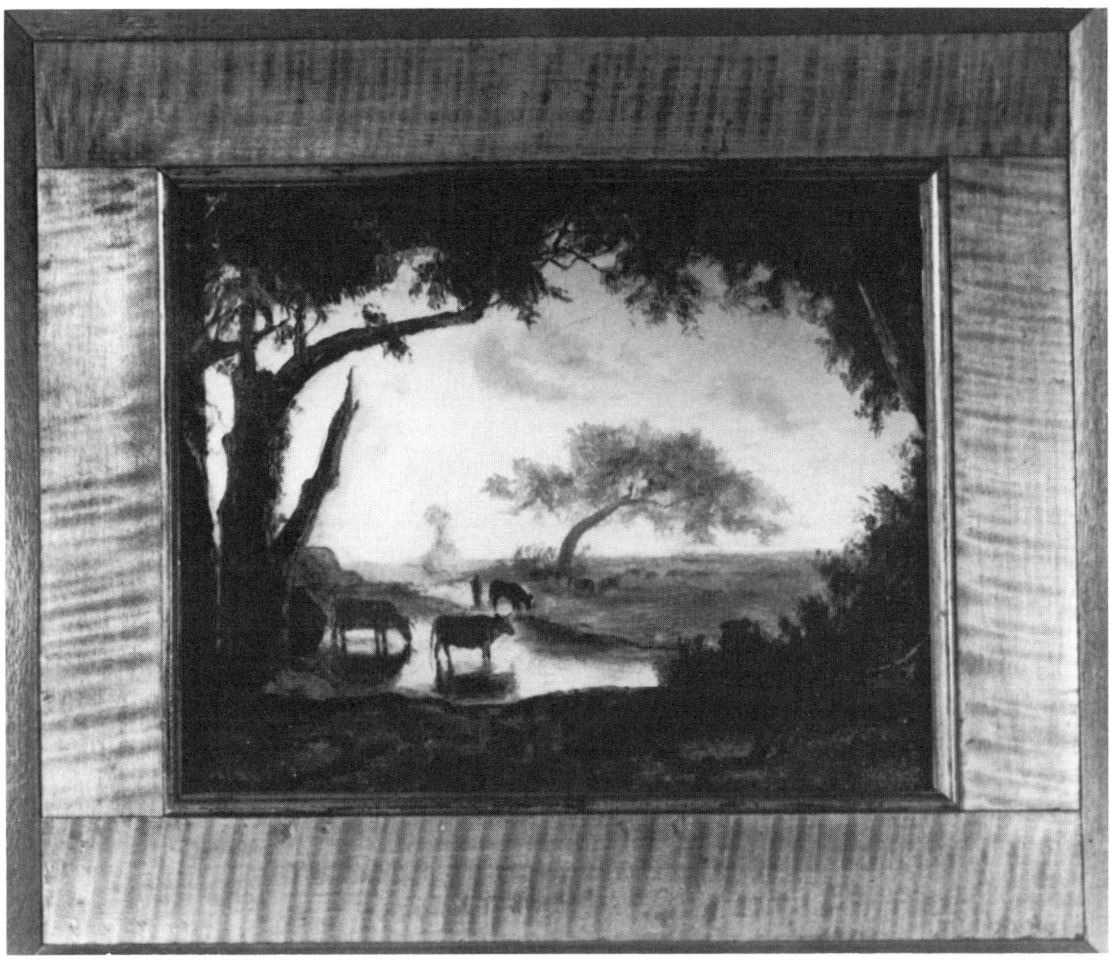

No. 112

LANDSCAPE WITH STREAM, ca. 1846. Oil on academy board, 7½ × 9½ inches. Paper label glued to reverse is inscribed in the painter's hand, "Edw. Hicks to his beloved / friend Mary Roberts sendeth / Greetings." Original 2-inch tiger maple frame with half-inch walnut molding. Mr. and Mrs. Malcolm Cade.

COMMENT: This small landscape shares elements with other works by Hicks: an orchard tree from *Hillborn Farm*, the arc of foliage at the right margin of the AARFAC *Grave of William Penn,* and the linear structure of *Indians Shooting Jaguar in a Tree*—all from the 1840s. The frame of tiger maple is an interesting variant on others of the period.

COLLECTIONS: According to family tradition this painting made for Mary Roberts shows the pasture of the Roberts, relatives of the Tomlinson brothers with whom Hicks served his apprenticeship as a coachmaker and painter. Sold in 1972 by a descendant, Bill Woolsey, an antique dealer of Lumberville, Bucks County, to Mrs. Malcolm Cade, Atlanta, Ga.

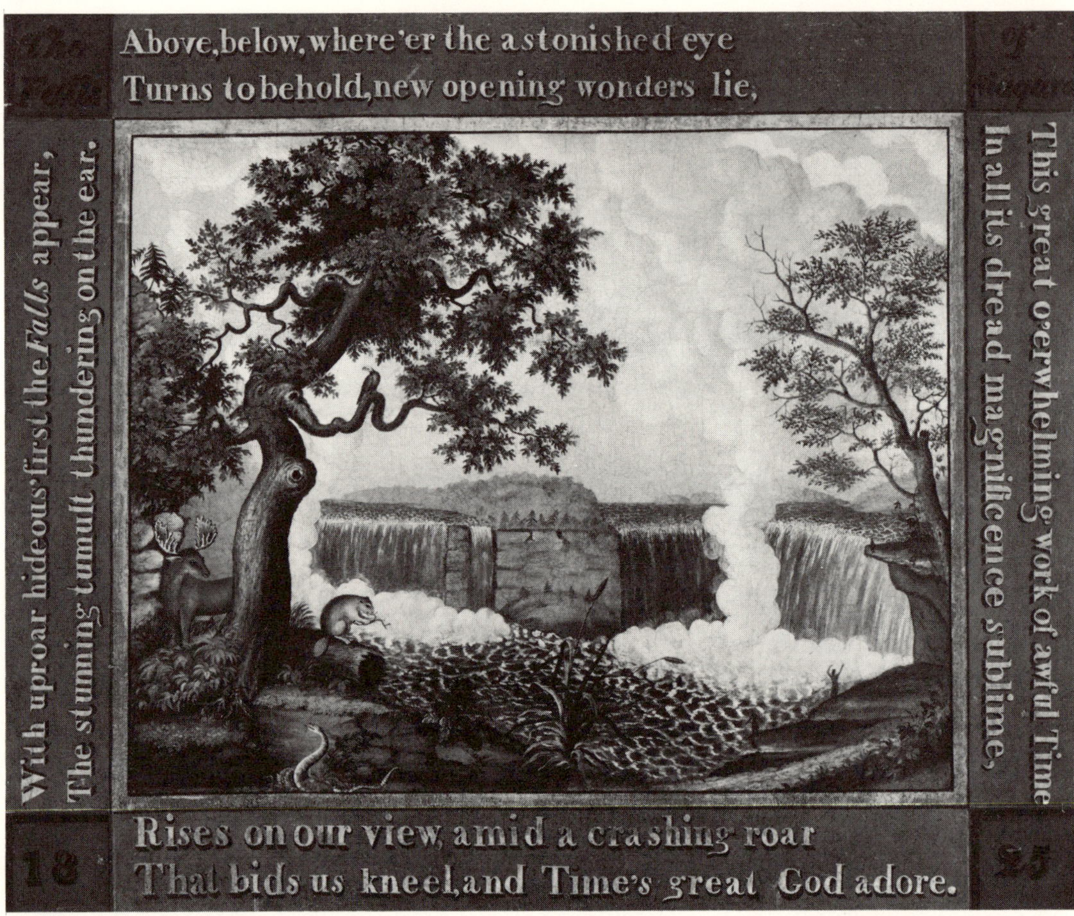

No. 113

THE FALLS OF NIAGARA, 1825. Oil on canvas, 31½ × 38 inches. Here the verses by Wilson (see below) read, "With uproar hideous' first the *Falls* appear,/ The stunning tumult thundering on the ear,/ Above, below, where'er the astonished eye/ Turns to behold, new opening wonders lie,/ This great o'erwhelming work of awful Time/ In all its dread magnificence sublime, / Rises on our view, amid a crashing roar/ That bids us kneel, and Time's great God adore." The four painted corner blocks are inscribed, from top left, *"The Falls"*/*"of Niagara"*/*"18"*/*"25,"* and are surrounded by a painted black border within the original black-etched frame. The Metropolitan Museum of Art; gift of Edgar William and Bernice Chrysler Garbisch, 1962.

COMMENT: Inspired by Alexander Wilson's "The Foresters," quoted above, the composition reflects a cartouche on an 1822 map by Henry S. Tanner that combines the Falls with the Natural Bridge of Virginia. Three small figures, also from Tanner's work, are often assumed to be Hicks and his friends Isaac Parry and Mathias Hutchinson, who journeyed to the Falls in 1819. In this version the border verses are ornamented with corner blocks that the artist later transposed to his *Peaceable Kingdom with Rhymed Borders.*

COLLECTIONS: Original provenance unknown. Discovered in Indiana; acquired by the Argosy Gallery, New York; to Edgar William and Bernice Chrysler Garbisch, New York, who gave it to the Metropolitan Museum of Art, New York.

EXHIBITIONS: Metropolitan Museum of Art and American Federation of Arts, "101 Masterpieces of American Primitive Painting from the Collection of Edgar William and Bernice Chrysler Garbisch" (New York, 1961–62), no. 47, ill. p. 73, listed 144; traveling exhibition (1962–64), no. 47, p. 146, ill. pl. 47; Lytton Gallery of Los Angeles County Museum of Art, Los Angeles, and the M. H. de Young Memorial Museum, San Francisco, "American Painting from the Metropolitan Museum of Art" (1966), no. 83, p. 95; American Federation of Arts, with Society of Four Arts, "Fifty Masterpieces of Primitive Painting" (Palm

Beach, Fla., 1967); American Federation of Arts, "American Naive Painting of the 18th and 19th Centuries" (Europe and United States, 1968–70), pl. 42; United States Pavilion, Japan World Exposition, "American Paintings" (Osaka, 1970), no. cat.; National Gallery of Art, Washington, D.C., City Art Museum of Saint Louis, and Seattle Art Museum, "Great American Paintings from the Boston and Metropolitan Museums" (1970–71), no. 16; Pushkin Museum, Moscow, and Hermitage, Leningrad, "One Hundred Paintings from the Metropolitan Museum, United States of America" (1975), pp. 235–236; Metropolitan Museum of Art, "A Bicentennial Treasury: American Masterpieces from the Metropolitan" (New York, 1976), listed in back; New York State Museum, "New York: The State of Art" (Albany, N.Y. 1977); Whitney Museum of American Art, "American Folk Painters of Three Centuries" (New York, 1980), p. 89 (col.).

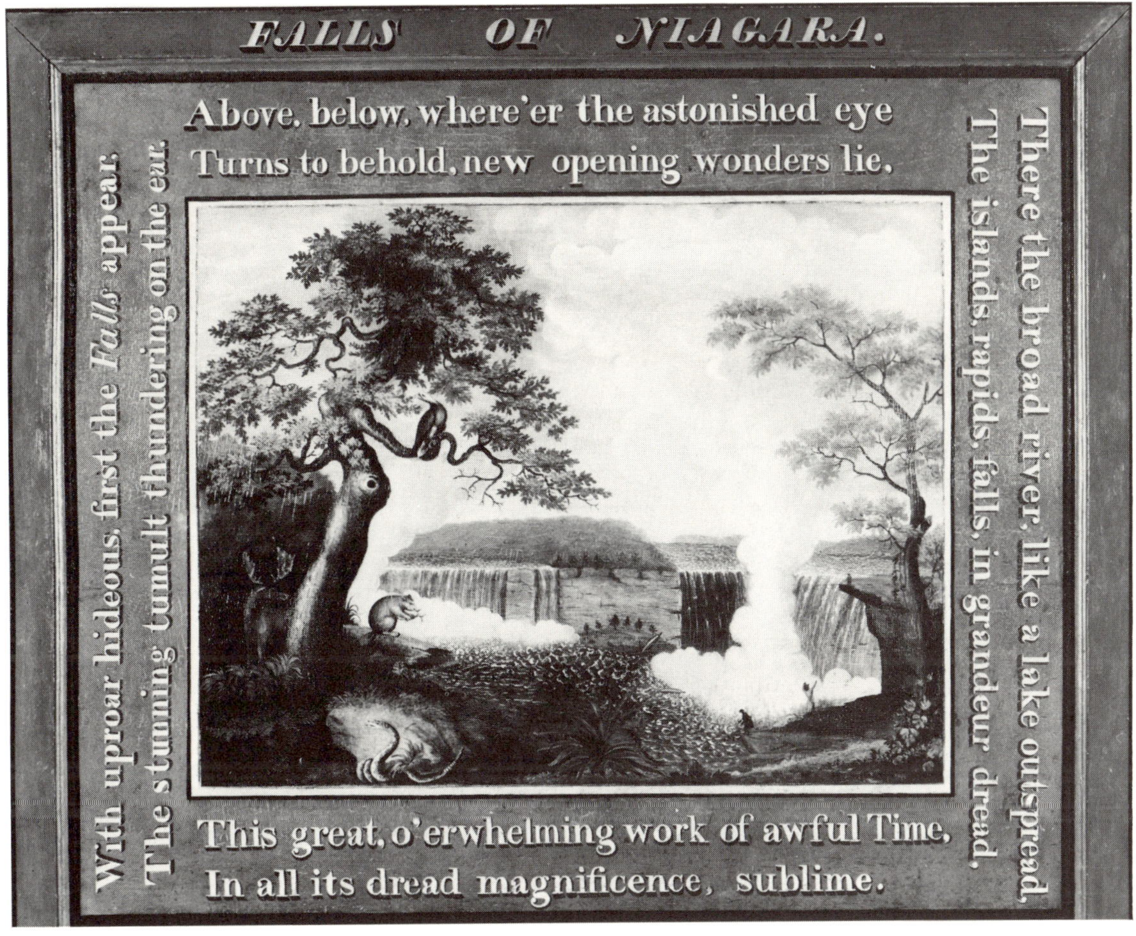

No. 114

THE FALLS OF NIAGARA, 1825–26. Oil on wood fireboard, 37¾ × 44½ inches, including frame, which is inscribed on top member, *"FALLS OF NIAGARA."* Landscape composition is surrounded by couplets: "With uproar hideous, first the *Falls* appear,/ The stunning tumult thundering on the ear./ Above, below, where'er the astonished eye/ Turns to behold, new opening wonders lie,/ There the broad river like a lake outspread,/ The islands, rapids, falls, in grandeur dread./ This great, o'erwhelming work of awful Time,/ In all its dread magnificence, sublime." Abby Aldrich Rockefeller Folk Art Center.

COMMENT: Much like the preceding, but the border varies in respect to one of Wilson's couplets. In general form this resembles the *Peaceable Kingdom* fireboard at Yale (No. 2), which has long been assigned to 1825. Both fireboards were owned by the Parrish family: conceivably they could have been a pair. Here the lower member of the frame has been replaced, possibly because the original was notched for andirons.

COLLECTIONS: Painted for Dr. Joseph Parrish, Philadelphia; to a descendant, Helen Parrish; sold to Dr. Arthur Edwin Bye, Holicong, Pa.; to Edward R. Barnsley, Newtown, Pa.;

purchased by the Abby Aldrich Rockefeller Folk Art Center, Williamsburg, Va.

EXHIBITIONS: Museum of Modern Art, "Masters of Popular Painting" (New York, 1938), no. 122B; AARFAC, "Edward Hicks" (1960), no. 17, p. 13, ill.;"American Folk Art from the AARFAC," American Museum in Britain (Bath, Eng., 1961); "Loan Exhibition from the AARFAC" (Fort Worth, El Paso, and Austin, Texas, 1962); "American Folk Art from the AARFAC" (Santa Fe, N.M. and Minneapolis, Minn. (1963–64); Albright Art Gallery, "Niagara Falls Exhibition" (Buffalo, N.Y., April 4–September 30, 1964); AARFAC Traveling Show (Hendrix College, Conway, Ark., 1965); Smithsonian Institution, "American Landscape: A Changing Frontier" (Washington, D.C., 1966); Carnegie/Corcoran, "Hicks, Kane, Pippin" (1966–67), p. 13, ill.; the Indiana University Art Museum, "The American Scene" (Bloomington, Ind., 1970).

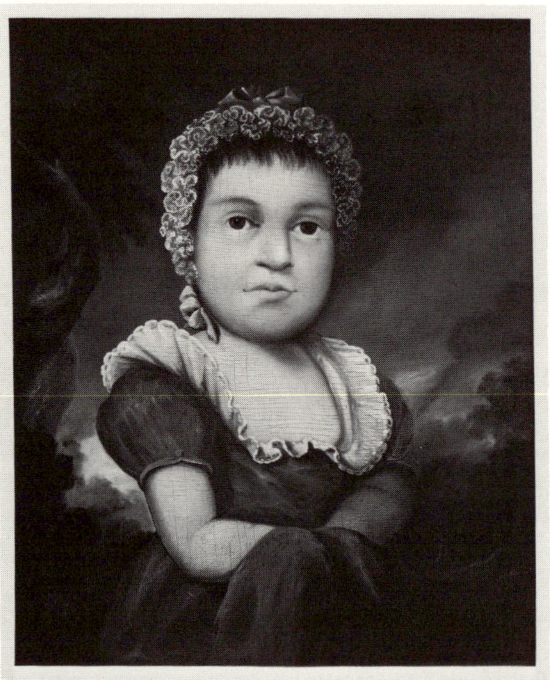

No. 115

PORTRAIT OF A CHILD, ca. 1835. Oil on wood panel, 17⅜ × 14⅜ inches. Flat, black-painted, 2½-inch frame possibly original. National Gallery of Art, Washington; gift of Edgar William and Bernice Chrysler Garbisch.

COMMENT: This little girl with brown eyes, green ribbons in her cap, and a bright red dress, is shown against a conventional landscape. There is nothing distinctive of Hicks in the work, but neither are there contraindications as to identification, and the provenance is that of an old Bucks County family.

COLLECTIONS: Robert Carlen recalls purchasing this from the Burton family near Bristol, Pa.; to Edith Gregor Halpert (American Folk Art Gallery), New York; to M. Knoedler & Co., New York; to Joseph Katz Co., New York; returned to M. Knoedler and Co., New York; to Edgar William and Bernice Chrysler Garbisch, New York, who bequeathed it to the National Gallery of Art, Washington, D.C.

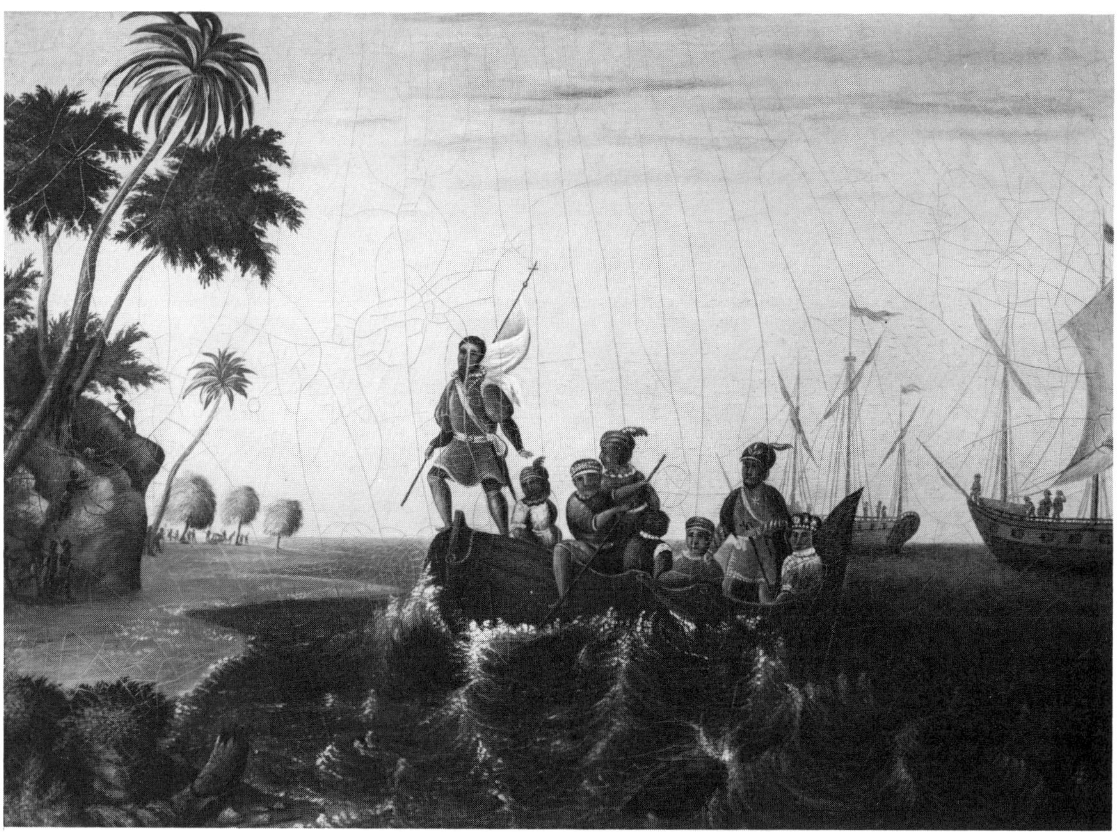

No. 116

THE LANDING OF COLUMBUS, ca. 1837. Oil on canvas, 17½ × 23½ inches. Original mahogany veneered frame with corner blocks, inscribed at bottom, "Columbus." National Gallery of Art, Washington; gift of Edgar William and Bernice Chrysler Garbisch.

COMMENT: As Alice Ford has pointed out, the subject was derived from an M. I. Danforth engraving after John G. Chapman's original, probably brought to Hicks's attention by a newsclipping from the *New York Mirror* (January 7, 1837) sent by his son-in-law, John J. Carle. The primitive painter added two palm trees to the background and exotic turbans to the Spaniards in the boat. "The painting is an exuberant copy," notes Mary C. Black, "with the composition moved closer to the viewer and Columbus made younger and swarthier than in the print" (*Edward Hicks 1780–1849*, AARFAC catalog, 1960, p. 14).

COLLECTIONS: Painted for the Janney family of Newtown, where the future painter was discovered in his infancy by Elizabeth Twining after the death of his own mother (Ford, xiv). Went south with Mary Janney after her marriage; given by a member of Goose Creek Meeting, Loudon County, Va., to a family in Silver Springs, Md.; sold to Robert Carlen Gallery, Philadelphia; to Edith Gregor Halpert, New York; to M. Knoedler and Co., New York; to Joseph Katz Co., New York; to M. Knoedler and Co., New York; to Edgar William and Bernice Chrysler Garbisch, New York; given by them to the National Gallery, Washington, D.C.

EXHIBITIONS: AARFAC, "Edward Hicks" (1960), no. 18, p. 13–14 (not ill.); National Gallery of Art, "American Primitive Painting"—Garbisch collection (Washington, D.C., Part 2, 1957), not in cat.

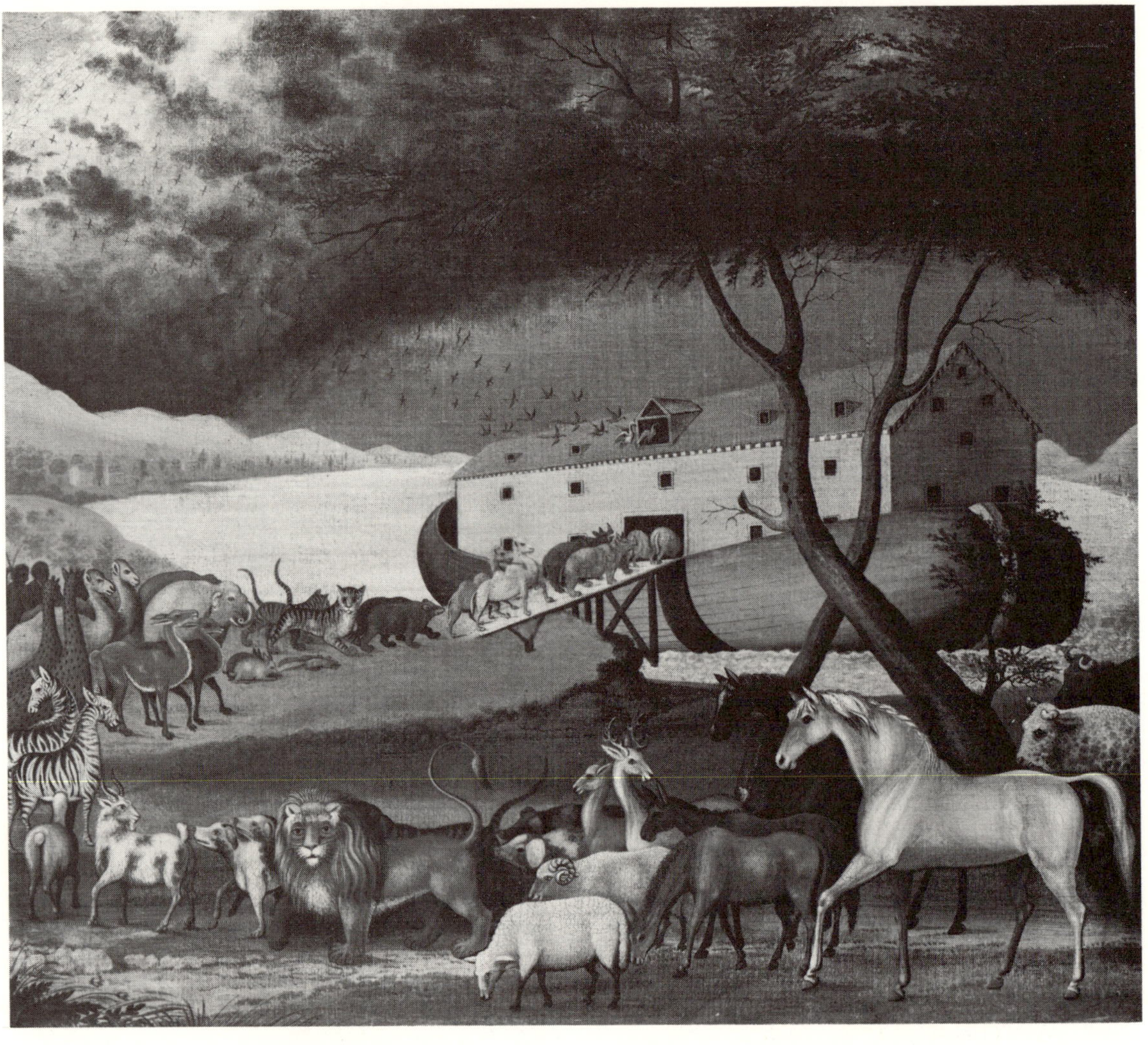

No. 117

NOAH'S ARK, 1846. Oil on canvas, 26½ × 30½ inches. On the reverse, across upper member of frame, is written, "Painted by E. Hicks in the 67th year of his age," and across the lower member, "And they went in unto Noah in the ark, two and two of all flesh, wherein is the breath of life Se. Gen.VII 15." Original molded wood frame. Philadelphia Museum of Art; bequest of Lisa Norris Elkins.

COMMENT: One of the most famous works of American folk art—and a vast improvement on the original 1844 lithograph by Nathaniel Currier from which it was taken. Hicks added the crossed tree trunks and cloud-hung firmament, and brought into the foreground the lovely white mare.

COLLECTIONS: Painted for Dr. Joseph Parrish, Burlington, N.J., son of the painter's friend and physician. Sold by a New Jersey family, presumably descendants, to Harry Shaw Newman, New York; to M. Knoedler & Co., New York; to Mr. and Mrs. William M. Elkins, Philadelphia; bequeathed by Mrs. Elkins to the Philadelphia Museum of Art.

EXHIBITIONS: Robert Carlen Gallery, "Hicks Centennial Exhibition" (Philadelphia, 1949); Philadelphia Museum of Art, "Masterpieces from Philadelphia Private Collections," part 2 (Philadelphia, 1950), no. 41 (not ill.); City Art Gallery, Manchester, Eng., and Smithsonian Institution, "American Primitive Art 1670–1954" (Whitechapel Art Gallery, London, 1955), no. 5; AARFAC, "Edward Hicks" (1960), no. 29, p. 16 (not ill.); Carnegie/Corcoran, "Hicks, Kane, Pippin" (1966–67), p. 25; University Art Museum, "The Hand and the Spirit" (Berkeley, Calif., 1972–73), no. 36, p. 87; Whitney Museum of American Art, "The Flowering of American Folk Art" (New York, 1974), no. 99, p. 75 (col.).

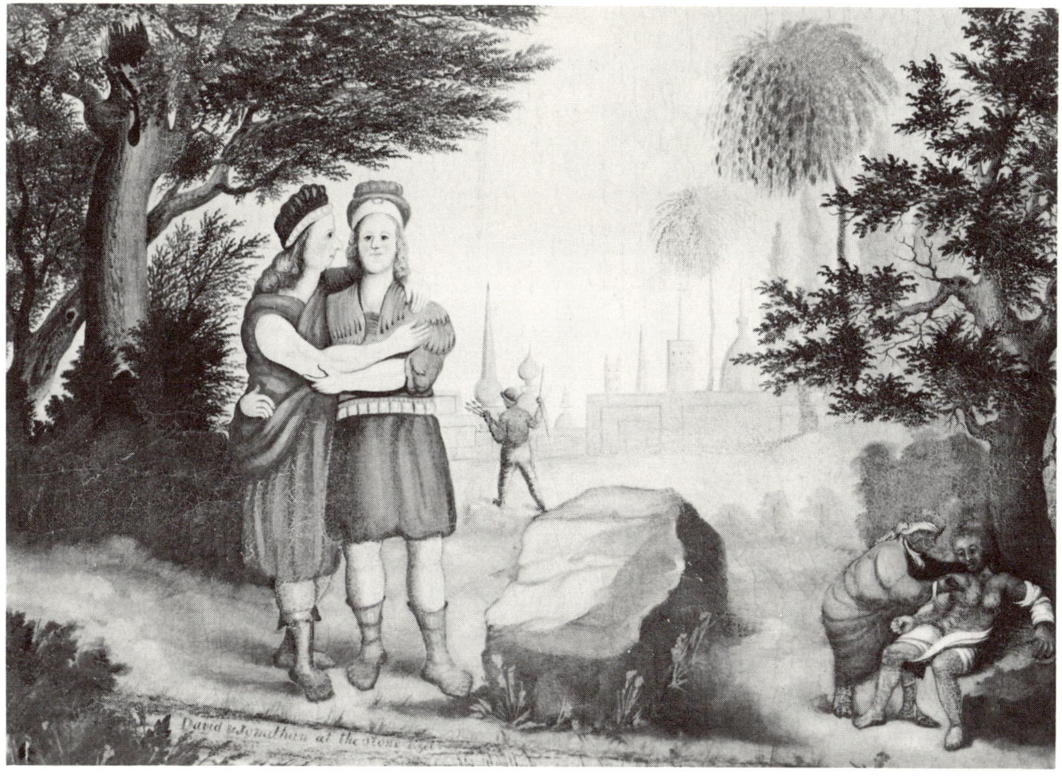

No. 118

DAVID AND JONATHAN AT THE STONE
EZEL, 1846. Oil on canvas, 24 × 32 inches.
Inscribed on canvas at lower left: *"David and
Jonathan at the stone Ezel."* written on re-
verse: "PAINTED BY EDW. HICKS IN HIS 67
Y^r." Contemporary nineteenth-century frame
of walnut and matching stained pine, 3½
inches wide, probably original. John Gordon
Gallery.

COMMENT: This is a curious composition,
unique among the artist's works, but the
monochrome treatment of distance is typical
of Hicks, and the trees are much like those of
his pastorals. The subject is the Bible story of
David's friendship with Jonathan, son of Saul,
king of Israel (I Samuel 20:18–42). Saul was
jealous of David, who feared for his life. The
two friends arranged that David would remain
hidden until notified of the king's mood by
Jonathan's shooting of an arrow near the stone
monument. The presence of Jonathan's young
attendant with arrows is self-explanatory, but
the two figures to the right are baffling; the
good Samaritan and the man, robbed and
beaten by thieves, whom he aided (Luke
10:30–37).* How does this New Testament
parable relate to the Old Testament story of

David and Jonathan? We can only assume the
Quaker minister is here preaching a sermon
on reconciliation: David and Jonathan remain
friends in the face of Saul's hostility, while
the kindly Samaritan shows mercy in spite of
traditional enmity between Samaria and
Judea.

COLLECTIONS: Early provenance unknown.
Leonardo L. Beans, Trenton, N.J.; auctioned
by Sotheby Parke Bernet, New York,; to John
Gordon Gallery, New York.

EXHIBITIONS: AARFAC, "Edward Hicks"
(1960), no. 28, p. 16 (not ill.).

Photograph copyright Sotheby Parke Bernet,
Inc., New York.

———
*Vignette from a 1772 engraving of Hogarth's
1736 painting in Saint Bartholomew's Hospital,
London, which was used by John Johnson in 1797
on a signboard for the Boston Dispensary. See Nina
Fletcher Little, "Sources of the Boston Dispensary's
Good Samaritan," *Antiques* 71(1957): 149. Hicks
also used this motif for a signboard. The *Newtown
Journal and Workingman's Advocate* for June 20,
1843, notes that on one side his sign for the Temperance House was the man who "fell among
thieves" (quoted by Edward R. Barnsley, *Historic
Newtown* [Newtown, Pa.: Privately printed, 1934],
p. 56).

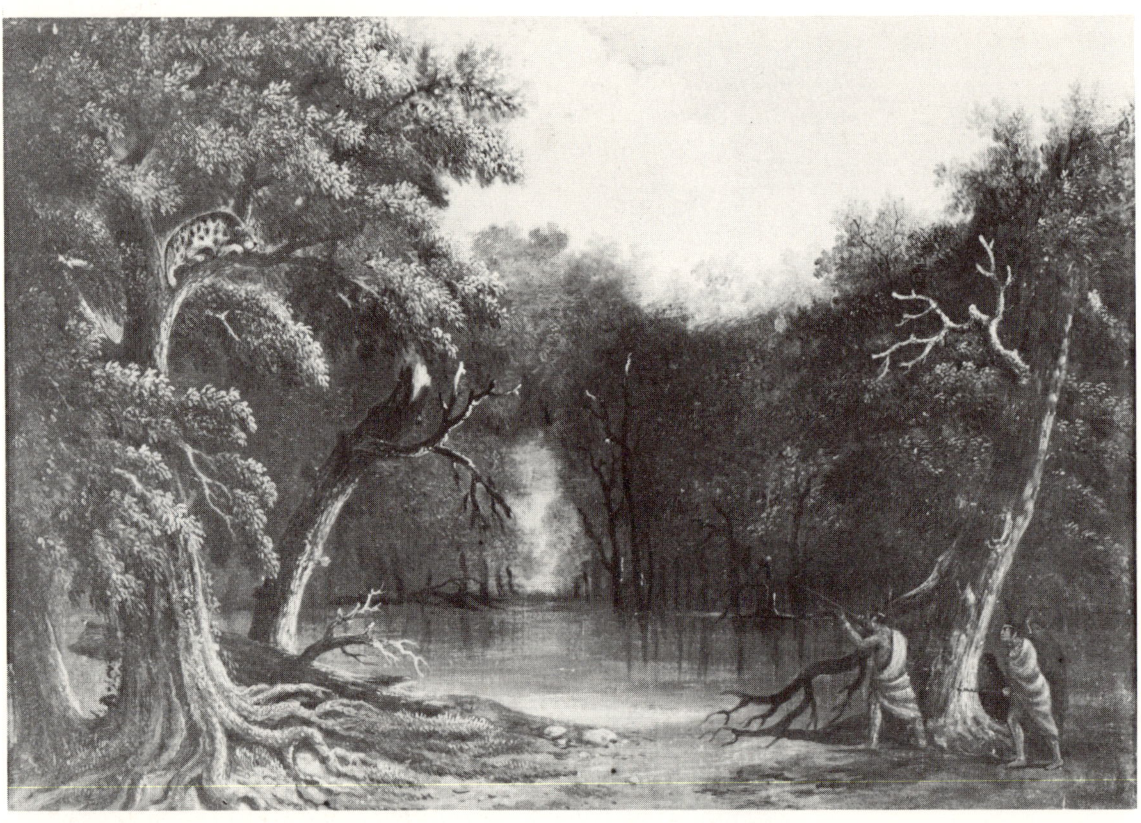

No. 119

INDIANS SHOOTING JAGUAR IN A TREE, 1846–47. Oil on canvas, mounted to masonite, 17 × 24½ inches. Inscribed on stretcher in red paint, "Painted by Edw. Hicks/in the 67 year of his age." Gilded soft wood frame possibly original. Shelburne Museum, Shelburne, Vermont; gift of Mrs. Brooks Shepard.

COMMENT: This is an unusual subject for Hicks, but it has certain elements of design typical of his work, such as the framing of the composition by a tree on either side, and the diagonal line of that on the right. Likewise the pose and alarmed expression of the belea-gured jaguar also suggest those of many leopards in the *Peaceable Kingdoms*. Because of the handwoven canvas the painting has been attributed to 1820–30, but if we accept the work as by Hicks we must certainly accept the inscription, which is substantially like those on his *David and Jonathan* and *Peaceable Kingdoms* 55, 56, and 57. We should note that the size of the canvas is unique for this late period. Lack of any vivid color is also puzzling.

COLLECTIONS: Provenance unknown; acquired in 1958 by Mrs. Brooks Shepard, Saxtons River, Vt., who presented it to the Shelburne Museum, Shelburne, Vt.

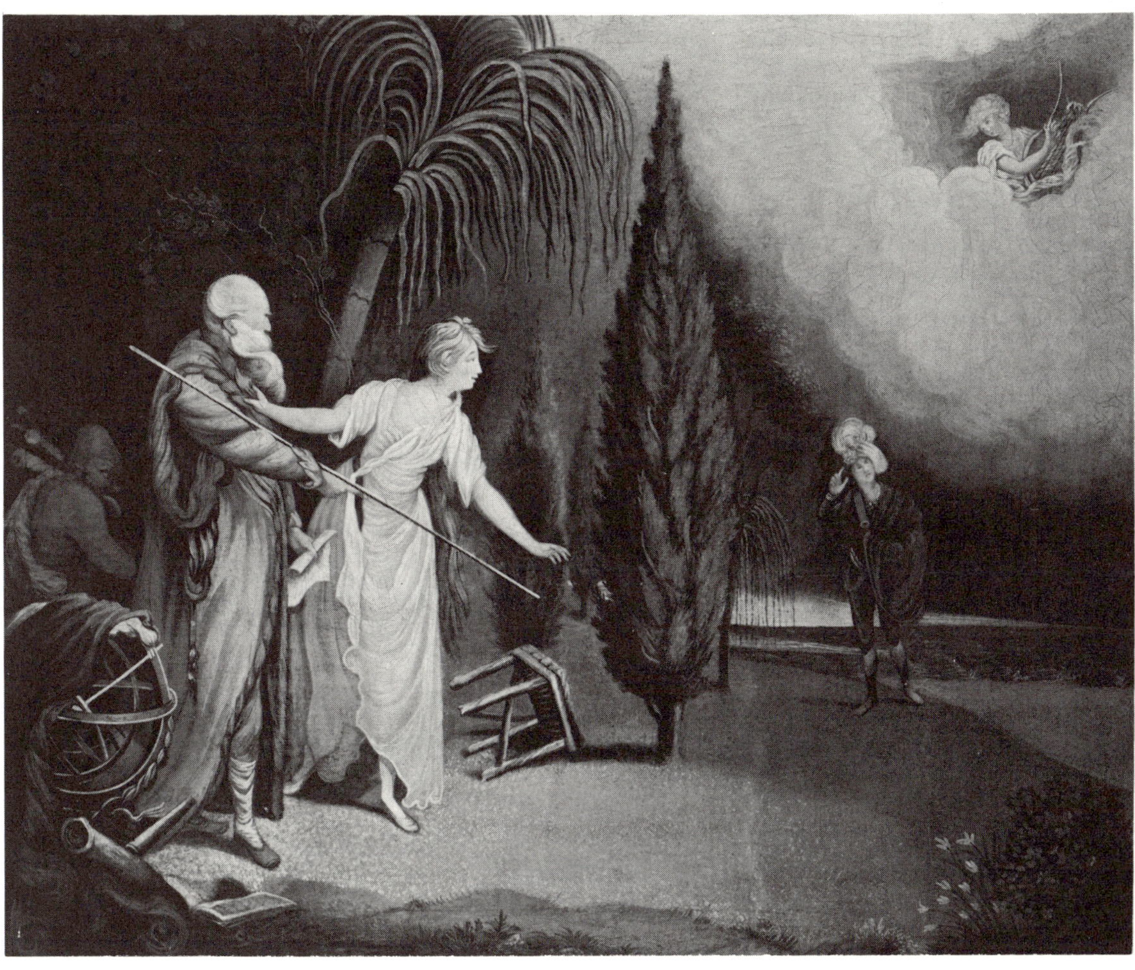

No. 120

THE TEMPEST, 1846–47. Oil on canvas, 25 × 30 inches. The Chrysler Museum, Norfolk, Virginia; gift of Edgar William and Bernice Chrysler Garbisch.

COMMENT: This scene from Shakespeare's last play, *The Tempest*, is an unlikely subject for the brush of a Quaker minister of the Gospel. Not only was the theater forbidden to Quakers of Hicks's time, but the specific episode (Act 4, sc. 1) shows Prospero with his magic wand summoning Juno and Ceres to bless the marriage of his daughter, Miranda, and her lover, Ferdinand. The lyre-player in the clouds is presumably his attendant spirit, Ariel, who serves as messenger to the pagan goddesses. At extreme left is Caliban, Prospero's deformed slave. Certain details suggest Hicks: the grapevine trailing over the massive

rock to the left (a combination used in his early *Peaceable Kingdoms*), the wind-blown flowers at extreme right, similar to those in *Noah's Ark*, and the spirelike trees that also occur in *Hillborn Farm* and *David and Jonathan*. But the theatrical figures are atypical of the artist, and together with the unlikely subject matter raise the question of authenticity.

COLLECTIONS: Provenance unknown. Edith Gregor Halpert, New York; to M. Knoedler & Co., New York; to Joseph Katz, New York; returned to Knoedler, who sold it to Edgar William and Bernice Chrysler Garbisch, who bequeathed it to the Chrysler Museum, Norfolk, Va.

EXHIBITIONS: American British Art Center, "Other Worlds" (New York, 1945).

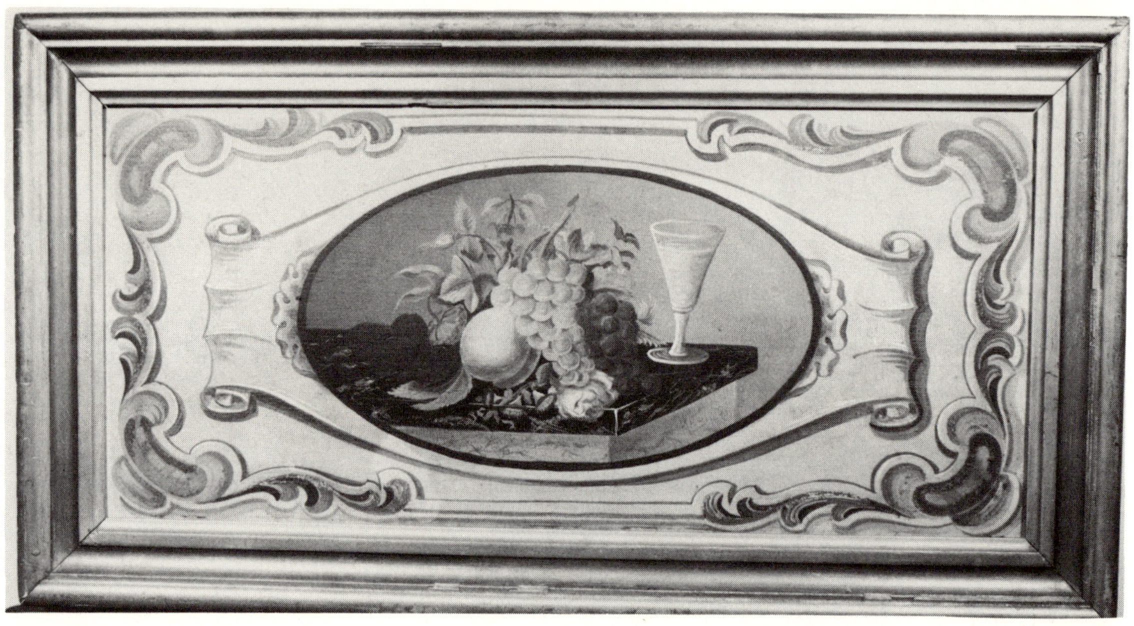

No. 121

FRUIT AND WINE STILL LIFE, ca. 1846. Oil on panel, 10 × 21 inches. Reverse inscribed, *"Painted by Edw. Hicks in the 67th year of his age."* Above this, and upside down to it, is a rough pencil sketch of glass and fruit, and above this, on the top member of the frame is incised, "This panel is from the dining room of the / P. Oliver Hough House on S. State St. Newtown." John Gordon Gallery.

COMMENT: It is difficult to evaluate this, as we have no similar work to compare it with. But the provenance is credible. Hicks painted many household objects for his livelihood, and it is reasonable to suppose that if Oliver Hough wanted any decorating done he would turn to Hicks to do it. For Hough was the son-in-law of the painter's good friend Joseph Briggs and it was Hough who prepared the artist/preacher's *Memoirs* for publication, which occurred in 1851, two years after

Hicks's death (Edna Pullinger, "Edward Hicks; Newtown Coach Painter, Among Friends," *Bucks County Historical Society Journal 2,* [1979]:209).

COLLECTIONS: P. Oliver Hough, Newtown, Pa., and presumably inherited by his descendants. The attractive façade of Hough House (built by William Linton in 1796 but occupied by the Hough sisters in the early years of the twentieth century), still fronts South State Street, but the interior was made into office accommodations in 1916, at which time this panel may well have been removed and put into its present frame. Acquired by C. B. Sloan & Co., Washington, D.C.; to Arthur R. Rupley, Alexandria, Va.; John Gordon Gallery, New York.

Photograph by Flynn Photography Ltd.

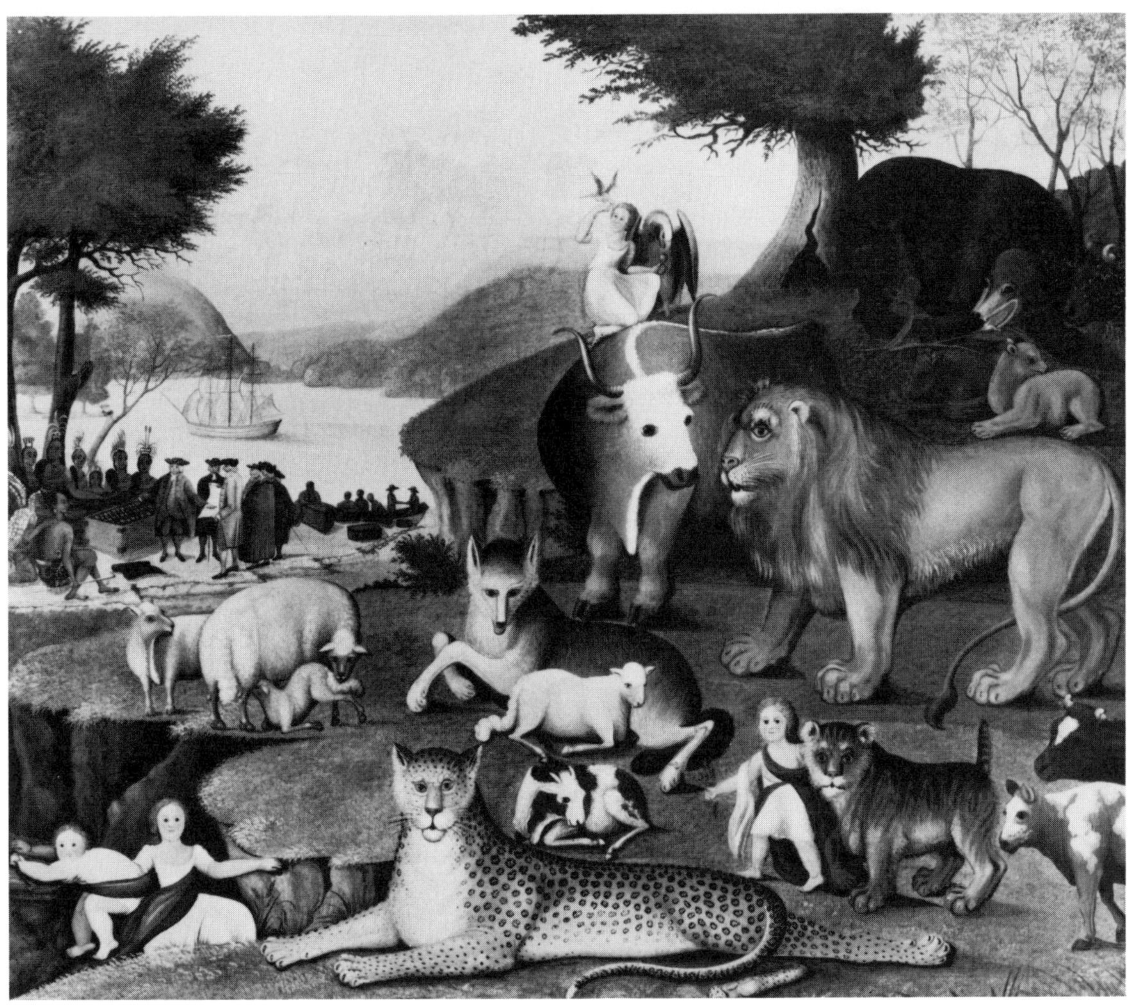

ADDENDUM

PEACEABLE KINGDOM WITH SERENE LEOPARD, ca. 1846. Oil on canvas, 26 × 29⅜ inches. Private collection.

COMMENT: This colorful canvas shares many characteristics with the Abendroth *Kingdom* (catalogue no. 54): an enlarged Penn's Treaty vignette, olive branch in the hand of the Divine Child, kneeling girl with eagle and dove perched on a slope of turf, and the ewe and sucking lamb seen also in Hicks's pastoral subjects. But here certain elements are positioned and proportioned differently. Note the prominence of the wolf, who has crept from his accustomed corner and now stretches above the leopard in the very center of the composition, as in the *Peaceable Kingdom* belonging to the Albright-Knox Art Gallery (catalogue no. 53).

COLLECTIONS: According to tradition this was presented by the artist in payment for a debt to a member of the Janney family—descendants of Thomas Janney, provincial councilor and friend of William Penn, who arrived in Bucks County, Pa., in 1683. By inheritance to Mrs. Beverly C. Compton of Baltimore; to Marguerite Riordan, dealer of Stonington, Conn.; to a private collector.

BIBLIOGRAPHY

BOOKS AND PAMPHLETS

Ashmead, Henry Graham. *History of Delaware County.* 1884. Reprint. Chester, Pa.: Concord Township Historical Society, 1968.

Bacon, Margaret Hope. *Valiant Friend: The Life of Lucretia Mott.* New York: Walker, 1980.

Barker, Virgil. *American Painting.* New York: Macmillan Co., 1950.

Barnsley, Edward R. *Historic Newtown.* Newtown, Pa: Privately printed, 1934.

Beans, Leonardo L. *The Life and Work of Edward Hicks.* Trenton, N.J.: Privately printed, 1951.

Binns, Henry Bryan. *A Life of Walt Whitman.* London: Methuen & Co., 1905.

Black, Mary C., and Lipman, Jean. *American Folk Painting.* New York: Clarkson N. Potter, 1966.

Boutell, Charles. *English Heraldry.* Rev. ed. London: Reeves & Turner, 1907.

Brey, Jane W. T. *A Quaker Saga.* Philadelphia: Dorrance & Co., 1967.

Brinton, Anna Cox. *Quaker Profiles: Pictorial and Biographical 1750–1850.* Wallingford, Pa.: Pendle Hill, 1964.

Brinton, Howard H. *Friends for Three Hundred Years.* New York: Harper & Bros., 1952.

Bryant, Jacob. *A New System or An Analysis of Ancient Mythology,* Vol. 3. London: For T. Payne, P. Elmsley, et al., 1774–76.

Burckhardt, Titus. *Alchemy: Science of the Cosmos, Science of the Soul.* Translated by William Stoddart. 1967. Reprint. New York: Penguin Books, 1971.

The Cabinet, or Works of Darkness Brought to Light. Philadelphia: Printed for the Compiler, 1824.

Campbell, Joseph. *Occidental Mythology.* New York: Viking Press, 1964.

Centennial of Newtown Friends Meeting, 1815–1915. Newtown, Pa.: Printed by the *Newtown Enterprise,* 1915.

A Chapter of Modern Chronicles, In Which Certain Events Which Lately Took Place in the City of Gotham Are Truly Set Forth. New York, 1826. Copy available at the Free Library of Philadelphia.

Cirlot, J. E. *A Dictionary of Symbols.* Translated by Jack Sage. New York: Philosophical Library, 1962.

Clarkson, Thomas. *Memoirs of the Private and Public Life of William Penn.* 2 vols. London: Longmans, Hurst, Rees, Orme, & Brown, 1813.

———. *A Portraiture of Quakerism.* 3 vols. London: Longmans, Hurst, Rees, Orme & Brown, 1806.

Cockburn, James. *A Review of the General and Particular Causes Which Have Produced the Late Disorders and Divisions in the Yearly Meeting of Friends, held in Philadelphia.* Philadelphia: Philip Price, 1829. Highly partisan, but clear, well organized, and valuable for reflecting the point of view of Edward Hicks and his fellow Hicksites.

Comly, John. *Journal of the Life and Religious Labors of John Comly, Late of Byeberry, Pennsylvania.* Philadelphia: Privately printed, 1853.

Davidson, Marshall, and Brill, Margot P. *The American Heritage History of Notable American Houses.* New York: American Heritage Publishing Co., 1971.

Davis, William W. H. *History of Bucks County.* Vol. 3. New York: The Lewis Publishing Co., 1905.

Davison, Robert A. *Isaac Hicks: New York Merchant and Quaker, 1767–1820.* Cambridge, Mass.: Harvard University Press, 1964.

Doherty, Robert W. *The Hicksite Separation: A Sociological Analysis of Religious Schism in Early-Nineteenth-Century America.* New Brunswick, N.J.: Rutgers University Press, 1967.

Drake, Thomas E. *Quakers and Slavery in America.* New Haven, Conn.: Yale University Press, 1950.

Drepperd, Carl W. *American Pioneer Arts and Artists.* Foreword by Rockwell Kent. Springfield, Mass.: The Pond-Eckberg Co., 1942.

Durand, John. *The Life and Times of A. B. Durand.* 1894. Reprint. New York: Kennedy Graphics, 1970.

Earle, Alice Morse. *Home Life in Colonial Days.* New York: Macmillan Co., 1898.

———. *Stage Coach and Tavern Days.* New York: Macmillan Co., 1900.

Earnest, Ernest. *John and William Bartram: Botanists and Explorers.* Philadelphia: University of Pennsylvania Press, 1940.

Eberlein, Harold Donaldson, and McClure, Abbott. *The Practical Book of Early American Arts and Crafts.* Philadelphia: Lippincott, 1916.

Emmott, Elizabeth Braithwaite. *The Story of Quakerism.* London: Friends Book Centre, 1929.

Evans, William Bacon. *Jonathan Evans and His Time, 1759–1839.* Boston: Christopher Publishing House, 1959.

Extracts Concerning the Divinity of our Lord and Saviour Jesus Christ. New York: Solomon W. Conrad for Philadelphia Yearly Meeting, 1823.

Feltus, Louise Celestia Mead. *Our Two Centuries in North Greenwich, Connecticut, 1728–1924.* Privately printed, 1945.

Ferguson, George. *Signs and Symbols in Christian Art.* New York: Oxford University Press, 1954.

Ferris, Benjamin. *The Letters of Paul and Amicus.* Wilmington, Del.: R. Porter, 1823.

Fisher, Jonathan. *Scripture Animals.* Foreword by Mary Ellen Chase. 1834. Reprint. Princeton, N.J.: Pyne Press, 1972.

The Flight Into Egypt. Arranged by Walter Kahoe from the Gospel of Pseudo Matthew. Illustrated by Gus Ullman. Moylan, Pa.: Rose Valley Press, 1972.

Forbush, Bliss. *Elias Hicks: Quaker Liberal.* New York: Columbia University Press, 1956.

Ford, Alice. *Edward Hicks: Painter of the Peaceable Kingdom.* Philadelphia: University of Pennsylvania Press, 1952. Reprinted by Kraus, 1973, with the same pagination.
The standard biography, based on free access to family papers and memorabilia.

———. *Pictorial Folk Art, New England to California.* New York: Studio Publications, 1949.

Foster, Jeremiah J. *An Authentic Report: Thomas Shotwell vs. Joseph Henrickson and Stacy DeCow.* 2 vols. Philadelphia: J. Harding, Printer, 1831.

Frost, J. William. *The Quaker Family in Colonial America: A Portrait of the Society of Friends.* New York: St. Martin's Press, 1973.

Goodrich, Charles A. *Lives of the Signers to the Declaration of Independence.* New York: William Reed & Co., 1829.

Grabar, André. *Christian Iconography: A Study of the Origins.* Bollingen Series vol. 10. Princeton, N.J.: Princeton University Press, 1968.

Groce, George, and Wallace, David H. *The New York Historical Society's Dictionary of Arts in America, 1564–1860.* New Haven, Conn.: Yale University Press, 1957.

Harris, Neil. *The Artist in American Society: The Formative Years 1790–1860.* New York: G. Braziller, 1966.

Haynes, George Emerson. *Edward Hicks, Friends Minister.* Doylestown, Pa.: Charles Ingerman at the Quixote Press, 1974.

Heal, Sir Ambrose. *London Tradesmen's Cards of the XVIII Century.* London: B. T. Batsford, 1925.

————. *The Signboards of Old London Shops.* London: B. T. Batsford, 1947.

Held, Julius. *P. P. Rubens: The Leopards.* Privately printed, 1970. Used as catalogue text for exhibition of the same name at the Art Museum, Princeton University, Princeton, N.J., 1973.

Hicks, Edward. *Sermons Delivered by Elias Hicks and Edward Hicks in Friends Meetings, New-York. In 5th Month, 1825.* Taken in shorthand by L. H. Clarke and M. T. C. Gould, New York: Sold by J. V. Seaman, 1825.

————. "Sermon by Edward Hicks, at Carpenters' Hall, Philadelphia, Sunday afternoon, August 19, 1827." In *The Quaker,* a series of sermons taken in shorthand by Marcus T. C. Gould, vol. 2. Philadelphia: Marcus T. C. Gould, 1827 (pp. 175–207).

————. *A Sermon by Edward Hicks Delivered at Friends Meeting, Green Street, Philadelphia on the evening of the 18th of 4th month, 1834, after the Conclusion of the Yearly Meeting.* Taken in shorthand, Darby: Printed by Y. S. Walter, 1834.

————. *A Word of Exhortation to Young Friends: Presented to them Without Money and Without Price by a Poor Illiterate Minister.* Philadelphia: J. Richards, 1845.

————. *A Little Present for Friends and Friendly People: In the Form of a Miscellaneous Discourse by a Poor Illiterate Mechanic.* Developed from a sermon at Goose Creek Meeting, Loudon County, Va., delivered on February 22, 1837, and taken in shorthand. Published with a reprint of *A Word of Exhortation.* Philadelphia: J. Richards, 1846.

————. *Memoirs of the Life and Religious Labours of Edward Hicks of Newtown, Bucks County, Pennsylvania.* Includes a diary, *A Little Present for Friends and Friendly People,* and *A Word of Exhortation.* Philadelphia: Merrihew & Thompson, 1851.

Hicks, Elias. *Letters of Elias Hicks.* New York: Isaac T. Hopper, 1834.

————. *Journal of the Life and Religious Labours of Elias Hicks.* New York: Isaac T. Hopper, 1832.

Hinshaw, William Wade. *Encyclopedia of American Quaker Genealogy.* Vols. 2 and 3. Ann Arbor, Mich.: Edwards Brothers, Inc., Printers, 1936–46.

Hole, Helen G. *Westtown Through the Years, 1799–1942.* Illustrated by Edward Shenton. Westtown, Pa.: Westtown Alumni Association, 1942.

The Hole in the Wall, or a Peep at the Creed Worshippers. Embellished with cuts by the Author, 1828.

James and Lucretia Mott: Life and Letters. Edited by Anna Davis Hallowell. Boston: Houghton, Mifflin & Co., 1884.

Janney, Samuel M. *An Examination of the Causes Which Led to the Separation of the Religious Society of Friends in America in 1827–28.* Philadelphia: T. Ellwood Zell, 1868.

————. *History of the Religious Society of Friends.* Vol. 4. Philadelphia: T. Ellwood Zell, 1867.

Johnson, Samuel. *Poems on Various Subjects.* Philadelphia: W. P. Gibbons, 1835. (Contains "To Edward Hicks on his proposition for painting an Historical piece commemorative of the progress of religious Liberty." This later appeared in *The Triple Wreath.* Edited by Ann Johnson Paxson (Philadelphia: 1844), pp. 80–82. The manuscript version, a typed copy of which is at Friends Historical Library, contains passages not in the printed version.)

————. *Letter from Samuel Johnson to Edward Hicks; with His Reply.* Philadelphia, 1845.

Jones, Mary Hoxie. *Quaker Poets Past and Present.* Wallingford, Pa.: Pendle Hill, 1975.

Jones, Rufus M. *Later Periods of Quakerism.* Vol. 2. London: Macmillan Co., 1921.

Jung, Carl. *The Portable Jung.* Edited by Joseph Campbell and translated by R. F. C. Hull. New York: Viking Press, 1971.

Larwood, Jacob [H. D. J. van Schevichaven], and Hotten, John Camden. *The History of Signboards.* Illustrated by J. Larwood. London: John Camden Hotten, 1866.

————. *English Inn Signs, being a Revised and Modernized Version of A History of Signboards.* Rev. ed. London: Chatto and Windus, 1951.

Larkin, Oliver W. *Art and Life in America.* New York: Rhinehart & Co., 1949.

Lindsay, Kenneth C. *The Works of John Vanderlyn, From Tammany to the Capitol.* A loan exhibition. Binghamton, N.Y.: University Art Gallery, State University of New York, 1970.

Mather, Eleanore Price. *Edward Hicks, Primitive Quaker: His Religion in Relation to His Art.* Wallingford, Pa.: Pendle Hill, 1970.

——. *A Peaceable Season.* Princeton, N.J.: Pyne Press, 1973.

Meadows, Cecil Austen. *Trade Signs and Their Origin.* London: Rutledge & Kegan Paul, 1957.

Mekeel, Arthur J. *Quakerism and a Creed.* Philadelphia: Friends Book Store, 1936.

Mosheim, Johan Lorenz. *An Ecclesiastical History.* London: A. Millar, 1765.

Newtown 275th Anniversary. Newtown, Pa.: Newtown Anniversary Commission, 1959.

Nicholson, Frederick. *Quakers and the Arts.* London: The Friends Home Service Committee, 1968.

Patterson, Mary S. *Martha Schofield: Servant of the Lord, 1839–1916.* Wallingford, Pa: Privately printed, 1944.

Price, Frederick Newlin. *Edward Hicks 1780–1949.* Swarthmore, Pa.: Benjamin West Society, Swarthmore College, 1945.

Pullinger, Edna S. *A Dream of Peace: Edward Hicks of Newtown.* Philadelphia: Dorrance and Co., 1973.

——. *Newtown's First Library Building.* Vol. 1. Newtown, Pa.: Bicentennial Publications of the Newtown Library Company, 1976.

Raine, Kathleen. *William Blake.* New York: Praeger, 1971.

Richardson, Edgar P. *American Romantic Painting.* Edited by Robert Freund. New York: E. Weyhe, 1944.

——. *Painting in America.* New York: Thomas Y. Crowell Co., 1956.

Ross, Isabel. *Margaret Fell: Mother of Quakerism.* London: Longmans, Green and Co., 1949.

Russell, Elbert. *The Separation After a Century.* Philadelphia: *The Friends Intelligencer,* 1928.

——. *The History of Quakerism.* New York: Macmillan Co., 1943.

Schiller, Gertrud. *Iconography of Christian Art.* Translated by Janet Seligman. 2 vols. Greenwich, Conn.: New York Graphic Society, 1971.

Singer, June K. *The Unholy Bible: A Psychological Interpretation of William Blake.* New York: Harper & Row, 1970.

Smedley, Robert C. *History of the Underground Railroad.* 1883. Reprint. New York: Arno, 1969.

Tolles, Frederick B. *Quakers and the Atlantic Culture.* New York: Macmillan Co., 1960.

Triggs, Oscar Lovell, ed. *The Complete Writings of Walt Whitman.* Vol. 3. New York: G. P. Putnam's Sons, 1902.

Twining, Thomas Jefferson. *The Twining Family: Descendants of William Twining, Sr., of Eastham, Mass.* Rev. ed. Fort Wayne, Ind.; Privately printed, 1905.

Wainwright, Nicholas B. *Paintings and Miniatures at the Historical Society of Pennsylvania.* Rev. ed. Philadelphia: Historical Society of Pennsylvania, 1974.

Watson, John Fanning. *Annals of Philadelphia and Pennsylvania.* 2 vols. Rev. ed. Philadelphia: Elijah Thomas, 1857.

Weems, Mason L. *Life of William Penn.* Philadelphia: H. C. Carey & I. Lea, 1822.

Wetherald, Thomas. *Sermons Delivered at Friends Meetings in Baltimore and Washington and at the State House in Annapolis.* Taken in shorthand by Marcus T. C. Gould. 1826. Reprint. Baltimore: J. Young, 1864.

Wilbur, Henry W. *The Life and Labors of Elias Hicks.* Philadelphia: Friends General Conference Advancement Committee, 1910.

PERIODICALS

Ayres, James. "Edward Hicks and his Sources." *Antiques* 109 (1976): 366–68.

Barker, Virgil. "Colloquial History Painting." *Art in America* 42 (1954): 118–124, and 156.

Black, Mary C. "& a Little Child Shall Lead Them." *Arts in Virginia* 1 (1960): 22–29.

———. "Three Folk Artists and Their Description of Pennsylvania." *1976 University Hospital Antiques Show* (catalogue). (1976): 34–38.

———. "Collectors: Edgar and Bernice Chrysler Garbisch." *Art in America* 62 (1969): 48–59.

Brinton, Ellen Starr. "Benjamin West's Painting of Penn's Treaty With the Indians." *Bulletin of the Friends Historical Association* 30 (1941): 99–189.

Buck, William J. "The Red Lion Inn, Bensalem Township." *Bucks County Historical Society Papers* 1 (1885): 485–88.

Bush, Lewis P. "Memoir of Benjamin Ferris." *Papers of the Historical Society of Delaware* 7 (1903): 5–36.

Bye, Arthur Edwin. "Edward Hicks, Painter Preacher." *Antiques* 29 (1936): 13–16. Reprinted in *Primitive Painters in America 1750–1950*, Jean Lipman and Alice Winchester, eds. (1950; reprint, Freeport, N.Y.: Books for Libraries Press, 1971), pp. 39–49.

———. "Edward Hicks, 1780–1849." *Bulletin of the Friends Historical Association* 32 (1943): 53–64.

Cahill, Holger. "Folk Art: Its Place in the American Tradition." *Parnassus* 4 (1932): 1–4.

———. "Early Folk Art in America." *Creative Art*, 11 (1932): 254–70.

———. "Artisan and Amateur." *Antiques* 59 (1951): 210–11.

Derfner, Phyllis. "Edward Hicks: Practical Primitivism and the 'Inner Light.'" *Art in America* 63 (1975): 76–79.

Doherty, Robert W. "The Growth of Orthodoxy." *Quaker History* 54 (1965): 24–34.

Doylestown Democrat, June 8, 1875, Bucks County Historical Society files.

Dresser, Louise. "The Peaceable Kingdom" *Worcester Museum Bulletin* 25 (1934): 25–30. Reprinted in *Design* 17 (1935): 39–49.

Ely, Warren. "Bogart's Inn: An Old Hostelry." *Bucks County Historical Society Papers* 3 (1901): 96–106.

"Extracts from the Correspondence of Charles Wilson [sic] Peale Relative to the Establishment of the Academy of the Fine Arts." *Pennsylvania Magazine of History and Biography* 9 (1885): 121–33.

Fackenthal, B. F. "Paintings and Other Works of Art in the Auditorium of the Bucks County Historical Society." *Bucks County Historical Society Papers* 7 (1935). Revised reprint, 1941, p. 8.

Fairbanks, Jonathan. "Benjamin L. Ferris: A Friend of Many Talents." *Catalogue of the Delaware Antiques Show* (Wilmington, 1966), pp. 77–87.

Feld, Stuart P. "The Tradition of the Primitive Imagination—Denied." *Antiques* 83 (1963): 99–101.

Ford, Alice. "The Publication of Edward Hicks's Memoirs." *Bulletin of the Friends Historical Association* 50 (1961): 4–11.

Guttenberg, John P. "Edward Hicks: A Journey to the Peaceable Kingdom." *American Art and Antiques* 2 (1979): 76–83.

Held, Julius. "Edward Hicks and the Tradition," *Art Quarterly* 14 (1951): 120–36.

"Hicks Called Greatest in America by Léger." *Art Digest* 6 (1931): 13.

Jackson, Joseph. "John A. Woodside, Philadelphia's Glorified Sign Painter," *Pennsylvania Magazine of History and Biography* 57 (1933): 58–65.

Jones, Louis C. "Liberty and considerable license." *Antiques* 74 (1958): 40–43.

Karlins, N. F. "Peaceable Kingdom Themes in American Folk Painting." *Antiques* 109 (1976): 738–41.

Kees, Ann. "The Peaceable Painter." *Antiques* 52 (1947): 254.

Leach, M. Atherton. "Guglielma Maria Springett, First Wife of William Penn." *Pennsylvania Magazine of History and Biography*, 57 (1933): 111–13.

Lipman, Jean. "Peaceable Kingdoms by Three Pennsylvania Primitives." *American Collector* 45 (1945): 6–7.

———. "The Composite Scene in Primitive Painting." *Gazette des Beaux Arts* 24 (1946): 119–28.

———. "Print to Primitive." *Antiques* 50 (1946): 41–43.

Little, Nina Fletcher. "Sources of the Boston Dispensary's Good Samaritan," *Antiques*, 71 (1957): 149.

Marsal, Sonia. "Edward Hicks: Quaker Painter," *Americas* 17 (1965): 5–14.

Mather, Eleanore Price. "In Detail: Edward Hicks's *Peaceable Kingdom*." *Portfolio* 2 (1980): 34–39.

———. "The Inward Kingdom of Edward Hicks." *Quaker History* 62 (1973): 3–13.

———. "A Quaker Icon." *Art Quarterly* 36 (1973): 84–99.

McCoubrey, John W. "Three Paintings by Edward Hicks." *Yale University Art Gallery Bulletin* 25 (1959): 16–21.

McNealy, Terry A. "The Red Lion Inn." *Bucks County Historical Society Journal* 1 (1974): 1–14.

Melville, Robert. "American Museum in Britain." *Architectural Review* 29 (1961): 422.

Miller, Dorothy C. "Discovery and Rediscovery." *Art in America* 33 (1945): 255–60.

Parry, Ellwood. "Edward Hicks and a Quaker Iconography." *Arts Magazine* 49 (1975): 92–94.

Paxson, Henry D., Jr. "Edward Hicks and His Paintings." *Bucks County Historical Society Papers* 6 (1932): 1–4.

The Phoenix, Swarthmore College 32 (1912–13) Academic Yr.: 1.

Pullinger, Edna S. "Edward Hicks and the Economic Crisis of 1837." *Bucks County Panorama* (1976): 18–22 and 32–33.

———. "Edward Hicks, Newtown Coach Painter, Among Friends." *Bucks County Historical Society Journal* 2 (1979): 202–24.

Ryan, Pat M., ed. "Mathias Hutchinson's Notes of a Journey (1819–20)." *Quaker History*, 68 (1979): 92–102, and 69 (1980): 36–57.

Salisbury, William. "American Old Masters." *The Antiquarian*, 12 (1929): 42.

Snow, Barbara. "Living with Antiques." *Antiques* 78 (1960): 239–42. Describes furniture and other heirlooms belonging to Hicks, now owned by his descendants.

Smith, Lettie A. "Edward Hicks." *Bucks County Historical Society Papers*, 1 (1906): 217–26. Read at a meeting of the Bucks County Historical Society in Solebury Meeting House, November 18, 1884, this is one of the earliest commentaries showing an appreciation of Hicks's painting.

Tatham, David. "Edward Hicks, Elias Hicks, and John Comly: Perspectives for the Peaceable Kingdom Theme." *The American Art Journal* 13 (1981): 37–50.

Tolles, Frederick B. "The Primitive Painter as Poet (with an attempted solution of an Iconographic Puzzle in Certain of Edward Hicks's *Peaceable Kingdoms*." *Bulletin of the Friends Historical Association* 50 (1961): 12–30.

———. "The Quaker Esthetic." *The American Quarterly* 2 (1959): 484–502.

Vlach, John Michael. "Quaker Tradition and the Paintings of Edward Hicks: A Strategy for the Study of Folk Art." *Journal of American Folklore* 94 (1981): 145–165.

Wilson, Alexander. "The Foresters." Serialized in *The Port Folio* 1 (1809)–3 (1810).

Winston, George P. "The Wolf Did With the Lambkin Dwell." *Pennsylvania History* 33 (1966): 261–73.

SELECTED CATALOGUES OF EXHIBITIONS

Selection of exhibition catalogues in which the paintings of Edward Hicks have appeared, arranged chronologically. For further examples see individual listings of Hicks's paintings:

[Cahill, Holger.] *American Primitives. An Exhibit of the Paintings of Nineteenth-Century Folk Artists.* Newark, N.J.: Newark Museum, 1930.

Halpert, Edith Gregor. *American Ancestors.* New York: Downtown Gallery, 1931.

Cahill, Holger. *American Folk Art: The Art of the Common Man in America, 1750–1900.* New York: Museum of Modern Art, 1932.

A Century of American Landscape Painting 1800–1900. Introduction by Lloyd Goodrich. New York: Whitney Museum of American Art, 1938.

Cahill, Holger, et al. *Masters of Popular Painting: Modern Primitives of Europe and America.* New York: Museum of Modern Art, 1938.

Art in Our Time. New York: Museum of Modern Art, 1939.

Survey of American Painting. Pittsburgh, Pa.: Department of Fine Arts, Carnegie Institute, 1940.

American Provincial Paintings from the Collection of J. Stuart Halladay and Herrel George Thomas. New York: Whitney Museum of American Art, 1942.

Halpert, Edith Gregor (compiler). *American Folk Art. A Collection of Painting and Sculpture Produced by Little Known and Anonymous Artists of the Eighteenth and Nineteenth Centuries.* Rev. ed. Exhibited at Ludwell Paradise House, Williamsburg, Va.: Colonial Williamsburg, 1947.

American Primitive Paintings from the Collection of Edgar William and Bernice Chrysler Garbisch. Washington, D.C.: National Gallery of Art, 1954 (part 1); 1957 (part 2).

American Folk Art from the Abby Aldrich Rockefeller Folk Art Collection. Introduction by Nina Fletcher Little. Traveling exhibition in cooperation with the American Federation of Art. Williamsburg, Va.: Colonial Williamsburg, 1959. (The first of AARFAC'S many traveling exhibitions.)

(Black, Mary C.). *Edward Hicks 1780–1849: A Special Exhibition Devoted to His Life and Work.* Introduction and chronology by Alice Ford. Williamsburg, Va.: Colonial Williamsburg, 1960.

Three Centuries of American Folk Painting. New York: Metropolitan Museum of Art, 1965.

Arkus, Leon Anthony. "Edward Hicks 1780–1849." In *Three Self-Taught Pennsylvania Artists: Hicks, Kane, Pippin.* Pittsburgh, Pa.: Museum of Art, Carnegie Institute, 1966.

American Naive Painting of the Eighteenth and Nineteenth Centuries: One Hundred Eleven Masterpieces from the Collection of Edgar William and Bernice Chrysler Garbisch. Exhibited in Europe and the United States. New York: American Federation of Arts, 1969.

Goodrich, Lloyd, and Black, Mary. *What Is American in American Art?* New York: M. Knoedler, 1971.

Dillenberger, Jane, and Taylor, Joshua C. *The Hand and the Spirit: Religious Art in America 1700–1900.* Berkeley, Calif.: University Art Museum, Berkeley, 1972.

Folk Art in America, A Living Tradition: Selections from the Abby Aldrich Rockefeller Collection, Williamsburg, Virginia. Atlanta: High Museum of Art, 1974.

Pennsylvania Folk Art. Allentown, Pa.: Allentown Art Museum, 1974.

Lipman, Jean, and Winchester, Alice. *The Flowering of American Folk Art 1776–1876.* New York: Viking Press with Whitney Museum of American Art, 1974.

Anderson, Dennis R. *Three Hundred Years of American Art in the Chrysler Museum.* Norfolk, Va.: Chrysler Museum at Norfolk, 1975.

Edward Hicks: A Gentle Spirit. Text by Eleanore Price Mather, reprinted from "A Quaker Icon" in *The Art Quarterly* (1973). New York: Andrew Crispo Gallery, 1975.

Symbols of Peace: William Penn's Treaty with the Indians. Essays by Charles Coleman Sellers and Anthony N. B. Garvan. Philadelphia: Pennsylvania Academy of the Fine Arts with Dickinson College, 1976.

Ames, Kenneth L. *Beyond Necessity: Art and the Folk Tradition.* From the collections of the Winterthur Museum, at the Brandywine River Museum, Chadds Ford, Pa. Winterthur, Del.: Henry Francis du Pont Winterthur Museum, 1977.

The Animal Kingdom in American Art. Syracuse, N.Y.: Everson Museum of Art, 1978. In celebration of the purchase of a *Peaceable Kingdom* for the museum by popular subscription.

Jean Lipman and Tom Armstrong, eds., *American Folk Painters of Three Centuries,* "Edward Hicks, 1780–1849" by Eleanore Price Mather. New York: Hudson Hill Press with Whitney Museum of American Art, 1980.

Kallir, Jane. *The Folk Art Tradition: Naive Painting in Europe and the United States.* Foreword by Robert Bishop. New York: Galerie St. Etienne and Viking Press, 1981.

MANUSCRIPTS

Friends Historical Library, Swarthmore College, Swarthmore, Pa.

Comly, John. Letters to Isaac Hicks, 1817–19.

Ferris, Benjamin. "An Account of the Separation in the Society of Friends in 1827."

Genealogical MSS on Quaker families.

Hicks, Edward. Letters.

———. Manuscript of *Memoirs*, 1843–49.

Jackson, Halliday. "A History of the Separation," c. 1832

Johnson, Samuel. Typescript of poem, "To Edward Hicks on his proposition . . .," transcribed by Alice Ford.

Meeting Records

Bucks Quarterly Meeting Minutes, 1827–28.

Makefield Monthly Meeting Minutes, 1820–51.

Middletown Monthly Meeting Minutes, 1803–14.

Newtown Preparative Meeting Minutes, 1817–49.

Philadelphia Yearly Meeting Minutes, Hicksite, 1827–30.

Wrightstown Monthly Meeting Minutes, 1814–20.

Speers, Nancy. "Hicks Family."

Wetherald, Thomas. Letters to wife, children, and cousins," 1823–26.

Quaker Collection, Haverford College, Haverford, Pa.

"Dictionary of Quaker Biography" in typescript, compiled by William Bacon Evans.

Evans, Thomas. "At a Yearly Meeting held in Philad[a] in the 4th mo. 1827."

Miscellaneous letters.

Historical Society of Pennsylvania, Philadelphia

Genealogical data on Quaker families, including "A Genealogy of the Descendants of John Linton . . ." by Morris Linton.

The Spruance Library of the Bucks County Historical Society, Doylestown, Pa.

Correspondence of Edward R. Barnsley, Arthur E. Bye, Robert W. Carle, Henry Chapman Mercer, and Henry D. Paxson concerning Hicks's paintings.

Hicks, Edward. Letters.

———. Shop Ledger.